The Spirit Catches You and You Fall Down

"Fadiman describes with extraordinary skill the colliding worlds of Western medicine and Hmong culture." —*The New Yorker*

"This fine book recounts a poignant tragedy . . . It has no heroes or villains, but it has an abundance of innocent suffering, and it most certainly does have a moral . . . [A] sad, excellent book."
—Melvin Konner, *The New York Times Book Review*

"An intriguing, spirit-lifting, extraordinary exploration of two cultures in uneasy coexistence . . . A wonderful aspect of Fadiman's book is her even-handed, detailed presentation of these disparate cultures and divergent views—not with cool, dispassionate fairness but rather with a warm, involved interest that sees and embraces both sides of each issue . . . Superb, informal cultural anthropology—eye-opening, readable, utterly engaging." —Carole Horn, *The Washington Post Book World*

"This is a book that should be deeply disturbing to anyone who has given so much as a moment's thought to the state of American medicine. But it is much more . . . People are presented as [Fadiman] saw them, in their humility and their frailty—and their nobility."
—Sherwin B. Nuland, *The New Republic*

"Anne Fadiman's phenomenal first book, *The Spirit Catches You and You Fall Down*, brings to life the enduring power of parental love in an impoverished refugee family struggling to protect their seriously ill infant daughter and ancient spiritual traditions from the tyranny of welfare bureaucrats and intolerant medical technocrats."
—Al Santoli, *The Washington Times*

"A unique anthropological study of American society."
—Louise Steinman, *Los Angeles Times*

"Some writers . . . have done exceedingly well at taking in one or another human scene, then conveying it to others—James Agee, for instance . . . and George Orwell . . . It is in such company that Anne Fadiman's writing belongs." —Robert Coles, *Commonweal*

"When the Lees hedged their bets in 1982 in Merced by taking Lia to the hospital after one of her seizures, everybody lost. Fadiman's account of why Lia failed to benefit over the years from Western medicine is a compelling story told in achingly beautiful prose."
—Steve Weinberg, *Chicago Tribune*

"A deeply humane anthropological document written with the grace of a lyric and the suspense of a thriller." —Abby Frucht, *Newsday*

"Fadiman's meticulously researched nonfiction book exudes passion and humanity without casting a disparaging eye at either the immigrant parents, who don't speak English, or the frustrated doctors who can't decipher the baby's symptoms . . . *The Spirit Catches You and You Fall Down* conveys one family's story in a balanced, compelling way."
—Jae-Ha Kim, *The Cleveland Plain Dealer*

"Fadiman's sensitive reporting explores a vast cultural gap."
—*People* Magazine

"Compellingly written, from the heart and from the trenches. I couldn't wait to finish it, then reread it and ponder it again. It is a powerful case study of a medical tragedy."
—David H. Mark, *Journal of the American Medical Association*

"*The Spirit Catches You and You Fall Down* is Fadiman's haunting account, written over a nine-year period, of one very sick girl in Merced, California . . . What happens to Lia Lee is both enlightening and deeply disturbing." —Kristin Van Ogtrop, *Vogue*

"Fadiman gives us a narrative as compelling as any thriller, a work populated by the large cast of characters who fall in love with Lia. This is a work of passionate advocacy, urging our medical establishment to consider how their immigrant patients conceptualize health and disease. This astonishing book helps us better understand our own culture even as we learn about another—and changes our deepest beliefs about the mysterious relationship between body and soul." —*Elle*

"The other day, I picked up a book I had no intention of buying. Eight hours later, having lifted my head only long enough to pay for the book and drive home, I closed Anne Fadiman's *The Spirit Catches You and You Fall Down* and started calling friends . . . This is an important book."
—Wanda A. Adams, *The Honolulu Advertiser*

The Spirit Catches You
and You Fall Down

The Spirit Catches You
and You Fall Down

———

A Hmong Child,

Her American Doctors,

and the Collision of Two Cultures

———

Anne Fadiman

Farrar, Straus and Giroux / New York

Farrar, Straus and Giroux
18 West 18th Street, New York 10011

Copyright © 1997 by Anne Fadiman
All rights reserved
Distributed in Canada by Douglas & McIntyre Ltd.
Printed in the United States of America
Published in 1997 by Farrar, Straus and Giroux
First paperback edition, 1998

The Library of Congress has cataloged the hardcover edition as follows:
Fadiman, Anne, 1953–
    The spirit catches you and you fall down : a Hmong child, her American
doctors, and the collision of two cultures / Anne Fadiman.
        p.   cm.
    Includes bibliographical references and index.
    ISBN 0-374-26781-2 (cloth : alk. paper)
    1. Transcultural medical care—California—Case studies.   2. Hmong
American children—Medical care—California.   3. Hmong Americans—
Medicine.   4. Intercultural communication.   5. Epilepsy in children.
I. Title.
RA418.5.T73F33   1997
306.4′61—dc21   97-5175

Paperback ISBN-13: 978-0-374-52564-4
Paperback ISBN-10: 0-374-52564-1

Designed by Abby Kagan

www.fsgbooks.com

31   32

Contents

Preface

Under my desk I keep a large carton of cassette tapes. Even though they have all been transcribed, I still like to listen to them from time to time.

Some of them are quiet and easily understood. They are filled with the voices of American doctors, interrupted only occasionally by the clink of a coffee cup or the beep of a pager. The rest of the tapes— more than half of them—are very noisy. They are filled with the voices of the Lees, a family of Hmong refugees from Laos who came to the United States in 1980. Against a background of babies crying, children playing, doors slamming, dishes clattering, a television yammering, and an air conditioner wheezing, I can hear the mother's voice, by turns breathy, nasal, gargly, or humlike as it slides up and down the Hmong language's eight tones; the father's voice, louder and slower and more vehement; and my interpreter's voice, mediating in Hmong and English, low and deferential in each language. The hubbub summons a whoosh of sense-memories: the coolness of the red metal folding chair, reserved for guests, that was always set up as soon as I arrived in the apartment; the shadows cast by the amulet that hung from the ceiling and swung in the breeze on its length of

grocer's twine; the tastes of Hmong food, from the best (*quav ntsuas*,*
a sweet stalk similar to sugarcane) to the worst (*ntshav ciaj*,* congealed
raw pig's blood).

I sat on the Lees' red folding chair for the first time on May 19,
1988. Earlier that spring I had come to Merced, California, where
they lived, because I had heard that there were some strange misunderstandings going on at the county hospital between its Hmong patients and its medical staff. One doctor called them "collisions," which
made it sound as if two different kinds of people had rammed into
each other, head on, to the accompaniment of squealing brakes and
breaking glass. As it turned out, the encounters were messy but rarely
frontal. Both sides were wounded, but neither side seemed to know
what had hit it or how to avoid another crash.

I have always felt that the action most worth watching is not at
the center of things but where edges meet. I like shorelines, weather
fronts, international borders. There are interesting frictions and incongruities in these places, and often, if you stand at the point of
tangency, you can see both sides better than if you were in the middle
of either one. This is especially true, I think, when the apposition is
cultural. When I first came to Merced, I hoped that the culture of
American medicine, about which I knew a little, and the culture of
the Hmong, about which I knew nothing, would in some way illu-
minate each other if I could position myself between the two and
manage not to get caught in the cross fire.

Nine years ago, that was all theory. After I heard about the Lees'
daughter Lia, whose case had occasioned some of the worst strife the
Merced hospital had ever seen, and after I got to know her family and
her doctors, and after I realized how much I liked both sides and how
hard it was to lay the blame at anyone's door (though God knows I
tried), I stopped parsing the situation in such linear terms, which
meant that without intending to, I had started to think a little less like
an American and a little more like a Hmong. By chance, during the
years I worked on this book, my husband, my father, my daughter,

---

* These phrases are pronounced, roughly, "kwa ntshwa" and "ntsha tya." For an
explanation, and a basic guide to pronouncing the other Hmong words and
phrases in this book, see "Note on Hmong Orthography, Pronunciation, and
Quotations," on page 291.

and I all experienced serious illnesses, and, like the Lees, I found my-self spending a lot of time in hospitals. I passed many hours in waiting rooms gnawing on the question, What is a good doctor? During the same period, my two children were born, and I found myself often asking a second question that is also germane to the Lees' story: What is a good parent?

I have now known the people in this book for much of my adult life. I am sure that if I had never met Lia's doctors, I would be a different kind of patient. I am sure that if I had never met her family, I would be a different kind of mother. When I pull a few cassettes from the carton beneath my desk and listen to random snatches, I am plunged into a pungent wash of remembrance, and at the same time I am reminded of the lessons I am still learning from both of the cultures I have written about. Now and then, when I play the tapes late at night, I imagine what they would sound like if I could somehow splice them together, so the voices of the Hmong and the voices of the American doctors could be heard on a single tape, speaking a common language.

A.F.

The Spirit Catches You
and You Fall Down

1

Birth

If Lia Lee had been born in the highlands of northwest Laos, where her parents and twelve of her brothers and sisters were born, her mother would have squatted on the floor of the house that her father had built from ax-hewn planks thatched with bamboo and grass. The floor was dirt, but it was clean. Her mother, Foua, sprinkled it regularly with water to keep the dust down and swept it every morning and evening with a broom she had made of grass and bark. She used a bamboo dustpan, which she had also made herself, to collect the feces of the children who were too young to defecate outside, and emptied its contents in the forest. Even if Foua had been a less fastidious housekeeper, her newborn babies wouldn't have gotten dirty, since she never let them actually touch the floor. She remains proud to this day that she delivered each of them into her own hands, reaching between her legs to ease out the head and then letting the rest of the body slip out onto her bent forearms. No birth attendant was present, though if her throat became dry during labor, her husband, Nao Kao, was permitted to bring her a cup of hot water, as long as he averted his eyes from her body. Because Foua believed that moaning or screaming would thwart the birth, she labored in silence, with the exception of an occasional prayer to her ancestors. She was so quiet that although most of her babies were born at night, her older children slept undisturbed on a communal bamboo pallet a few feet away, and woke only when they heard the cry of their new brother or sister. After each birth, Nao Kao cut the umbilical cord with heated scissors and tied it with string. Then Foua washed the baby with water she had carried from the stream, usually in the early phases of labor, in a wooden and bamboo pack-barrel strapped to her back.

Foua conceived, carried, and bore all her children with ease, but had there been any problems, she would have had recourse to a variety of remedies that were commonly used by the Hmong, the hilltribe to which her family belonged. If a Hmong couple failed to produce children, they could call in a *txiv neeb*, a shaman who was believed to have the ability to enter a trance, summon a posse of helpful familiars, ride a winged horse over the twelve mountains between the earth and the sky, cross an ocean inhabited by dragons, and (starting with bribes of food and money and, if necessary, working up to a necromantic sword) negotiate for his patients' health with the spirits who lived in the realm of the unseen. A *txiv neeb* might be able to cure infertility by asking the couple to sacrifice a dog, a cat, a chicken, or a sheep. After the animal's throat was cut, the *txiv neeb* would string a rope bridge from the doorpost to the marriage bed, over which the soul of the couple's future baby, which had been detained by a malevolent spirit called a *dab*, could now freely travel to earth. One could also take certain precautions to avoid becoming infertile in the first place. For example, no Hmong woman of childbearing age would ever think of setting foot inside a cave, because a particularly unpleasant kind of *dab* sometimes lived there who liked to eat flesh and drink blood and could make his victim sterile by having sexual intercourse with her.

Once a Hmong woman became pregnant, she could ensure the health of her child by paying close attention to her food cravings. If she craved ginger and failed to eat it, her child would be born with an extra finger or toe. If she craved chicken flesh and did not eat it, her child would have a blemish near its ear. If she craved eggs and did not eat them, her child would have a lumpy head. When a Hmong woman felt the first pangs of labor, she would hurry home from the rice or opium fields, where she had continued to work throughout her pregnancy. It was important to reach her own house, or at least the house of one of her husband's cousins, because if she gave birth anywhere else a *dab* might injure her. A long or arduous labor could be eased by drinking the water in which a key had been boiled, in order to unlock the birth canal; by having her family array bowls of sacred water around the room and chant prayers over them; or, if the difficulty stemmed from having treated an elder member of the family with insufficient respect, by washing the offended relative's fingertips and apologizing like crazy until the relative finally said, "I forgive you."

Soon after the birth, while the mother and baby were still lying together next to the fire pit, the father dug a hole at least two feet deep in the dirt floor and buried the placenta. If it was a girl, her placenta was buried under her parents' bed; if it was a boy, his placenta was buried in a place of greater honor, near the base of the house's central wooden pillar, in which a male spirit, a domestic guardian who held up the roof of the house and watched over its residents, made his home. The placenta was always buried with the smooth side, the side that had faced the fetus inside the womb, turned upward, since if it was upside down, the baby might vomit after nursing. If the baby's face erupted in spots, that meant the placenta was being attacked by ants underground, and boiling water was poured into the burial hole as an insecticide. In the Hmong language, the word for placenta means "jacket." It is considered one's first and finest garment. When a Hmong dies, his or her soul must travel back from place to place, retracing the path of its life geography, until it reaches the burial place of its placental jacket, and puts it on. Only after the soul is properly dressed in the clothing in which it was born can it continue its dangerous journey, past murderous *dabs* and giant poisonous caterpillars, around man-eating rocks and impassable oceans, to the place beyond the sky where it is reunited with its ancestors and from which it will someday be sent to be reborn as the soul of a new baby. If the soul cannot find its jacket, it is condemned to an eternity of wandering, naked and alone.

Because the Lees are among the 150,000 Hmong who have fled Laos since their country fell to communist forces in 1975, they do not know if their house is still standing, or if the five male and seven female placentas that Nao Kao buried under the dirt floor are still there. They believe that half of the placentas have already been put to their final use, since four of their sons and two of their daughters died of various causes before the Lees came to the United States. The

Lees believe that someday the souls of most of the rest of their family will have a long way to travel, since they will have to retrace their steps from Merced, California, where the family has spent fifteen of its seventeen years in this country; to Portland, Oregon, where they lived before Merced; to Honolulu, Hawaii, where their airplane from Thailand first landed; to two Thai refugee camps; and finally back to their home village in Laos.

The Lees' thirteenth child, Mai, was born in a refugee camp in Thailand. Her placenta was buried under their hut. Their fourteenth child, Lia, was born in the Merced Community Medical Center, a modern public hospital that serves an agricultural county in California's Central Valley, where many Hmong refugees have resettled. Lia's placenta was incinerated. Some Hmong women have asked the doctors at MCMC, as the hospital is commonly called, if they could take their babies' placentas home. Several of the doctors have acquiesced, packing the placentas in plastic bags or take-out containers from the hospital cafeteria; most have refused, in some cases because they have assumed that the women planned to eat the placentas, and have found that idea disgusting, and in some cases because they have feared the possible spread of hepatitis B, which is carried by at least fifteen percent of the Hmong refugees in the United States. Foua never thought to ask, since she speaks no English, and when she delivered Lia, no one present spoke Hmong. In any case, the Lees' apartment had a wooden floor covered with wall-to-wall carpeting, so burying the placenta would have been a difficult proposition.

When Lia was born, at 7:09 p.m. on July 19, 1982, Foua was lying on her back on a steel table, her body covered with sterile drapes, her genital area painted with a brown Betadine solution, with a high-wattage lamp trained on her perineum. There were no family members in the room. Gary Thueson, a family practice resident who did the delivery, noted in the chart that in order to speed the labor, he had artificially ruptured Foua's amniotic sac by poking it with a foot-long plastic "amni-hook"; that no anesthesia was used; that no episiotomy, an incision to enlarge the vaginal opening, was necessary; and that after the birth, Foua received a standard intravenous dose of Pitocin to constrict her uterus. Dr. Thueson also noted that Lia was a "healthy infant" whose weight, 8 pounds 7 ounces, and condition were "appropriate for gestational age" (an estimate he based on observation alone, since Foua had received no prenatal care, was not certain how long she had been pregnant, and could not have told Dr. Thueson even if she had known). Foua thinks that Lia was her largest baby, although she isn't sure, since none of her thirteen elder children were weighed at birth. Lia's Apgar scores, an assessment of a newborn infant's heart rate, respiration, muscle tone, color, and reflexes, were good: one minute after her birth she scored 7 on a scale of 10, and four minutes later she scored 9. When she was six minutes old, her color was described as "pink" and her activity as "crying." Lia was shown briefly to her mother. Then she was placed in a steel and Plexiglas warmer, where a nurse fastened a plastic identification band around her wrist and recorded her footprints by inking the soles of her feet with a stamp pad and pressing them against a Newborn Identification form. After that, Lia was removed to the central nursery, where she received an injection of Vitamin K in one of her thighs to prevent hemorrhagic disease; was treated with two drops of silver nitrate solution in each eye, to prevent an infection from gonococcal bacteria; and was bathed with Safeguard soap.

Foua's own date of birth was recorded on Lia's Delivery Room Record as October 6, 1944. In fact, she has no idea when she was born, and on various other occasions during the next several years she would inform MCMC personnel, through English-speaking relatives such as the nephew's wife who had helped her check into the hospital for Lia's delivery, that her date of birth was October 6, 1942, or, more frequently, October 6, 1926. Not a single admitting clerk ever appears to have questioned the latter date, though it would imply that Foua gave birth to Lia at the age of 55. Foua is quite sure, however, that October is correct, since she was told by her parents that she was born during the season in which the opium fields are weeded for the second time and the harvested rice stalks are stacked. She invented the precise day of the month, like the year, in order to satisfy the many Americans who have evinced an abhorrence of unfilled blanks on the innumerable forms the Lees have encountered since their admission to the United States in 1980. Most Hmong refugees are familiar with this American trait and have accommodated it in the same way. Nao Kao Lee has a first cousin who told the immigration officials that all nine of his children were born on July 15, in nine consecutive years, and this information was duly recorded on their resident alien documents.

When Lia Lee was released from MCMC, at the age of three days, her mother was asked to sign a piece of paper that read:

> I CERTIFY that during the discharge procedure I received my baby, examined it and determined that it was mine. I checked the Ident-A-Band® parts sealed on the baby and on me and found that they were identically numbered 5043 and contained correct identifying information.

Since Foua cannot read and has never learned to recognize Arabic numerals, it is unlikely that she followed these instructions. However, she had been asked for her signature so often in the United States that she had mastered the capital forms of the seven different letters contained in her name, Foua Yang. (The Yangs and the Lees are among the largest of the Hmong clans; the other major ones are the Chas, the Chengs, the Hangs, the Hers, the Kues, the Los, the Mouas, the Thaos, the Vues, the Xiongs, and the Vangs. In Laos, the clan name came first, but most Hmong refugees in the United States use it as a surname. Children belong to their father's clan; women traditionally retain their clan name after marriage. Marrying a member of one's own clan is strictly taboo.) Foua's signature is no less legible than the signatures of most of MCMC's resident physicians-in-training, which, particularly if they are written toward the end of a twenty-four-hour shift, tend to resemble EEGs. However, it has the unique distinction of looking different each time it appears on a hospital document. On this occasion, FOUAYANG was written as a single word. One A is canted to the left and one to the right, the Y looks like an X, and the legs of the N undulate gracefully, like a child's drawing of a wave.

It is a credit to Foua's general equanimity, as well as her characteristic desire not to think ill of anyone, that although she found Lia's birth a peculiar experience, she has few criticisms of the way the hospital handled it. Her doubts about MCMC in particular, and American medicine in general, would not begin to gather force until Lia had visited the hospital many times. On this occasion, she thought the doctor was gentle and kind, she was impressed that so many people were there to help her, and although she felt that the nurses who bathed Lia with Safeguard did not get her quite as clean as she had gotten her newborns with Laotian stream water, her only major complaint concerned the hospital food. She was surprised to be offered ice water after the birth, since many Hmong believe that cold foods during the postpartum period make the blood congeal in the womb instead of cleansing it by flowing freely, and that a woman who does not observe the taboo against them will develop itchy skin or diarrhea in her old age. Foua did accept several cups of what she remembers as hot black water. This was probably either tea or beef broth; Foua is sure it wasn't coffee, which she had seen before and would have recognized. The black water was the only MCMC-provided food that passed her lips during her stay in the maternity ward. Each day, Nao Kao cooked and brought her the diet that is strictly prescribed for Hmong women during the thirty days following childbirth: steamed rice, and chicken boiled in water with five special postpartum herbs (which the Lees had grown for this purpose on the edge of the parking lot behind their apartment building). This diet was familiar to the doctors on the Labor and Delivery floor at MCMC, whose assessments of it were fairly accurate gauges of their general opinion of the Hmong. One obstetrician, Raquel Arias, recalled, "The Hmong men carried these nice little silver cans to the hospital that always had some kind of chicken soup in them and always smelled great." Another obstetrician, Robert Small, said, "They always brought some horrible stinking concoction that smelled like the chicken had been dead for a week." Foua never shared her meals with anyone, because there is a postpartum taboo against spilling grains of rice accidentally into the chicken pot. If that occurs, the newborn is likely to break out across the nose and cheeks with little white pimples whose name in the Hmong language is the same as the word for "rice."

Some Hmong parents in Merced have given their children American names. In addition to many standard ones, these have included Kennedy, Nixon, Pajama, Guitar, Main (after Merced's Main Street), and, until a nurse counseled otherwise, Baby Boy, which one mother, seeing it written on her son's hospital papers, assumed was the name the doctor had already chosen for him. The Lees chose to give their daughter a Hmong name, Lia. Her name was officially conferred in a ceremony called a *hu plig*, or soul-calling, which in Laos always took place on the third day after birth. Until this ceremony was performed, a baby was not considered to be fully a member of the human race, and if it died during its first three days it was not accorded the customary funerary rites. (This may have been a cultural adaptation to the fifty-percent infant mortality rate, a way of steeling Hmong mothers against the frequent loss of their babies during or shortly after childbirth by encouraging them to postpone their attachment.) In the United States, the naming is usually celebrated at a later time, since on its third day a baby may still be hospitalized, especially if the birth was complicated. It took the Lee family about a month to save enough money from their welfare checks, and from gifts from their relatives' welfare checks, to finance a soul-calling party for Lia.

Although the Hmong believe that illness can be caused by a variety of sources—including eating the wrong food, drinking contaminated water, being affected by a change in the weather, failing to ejaculate completely during sexual intercourse, neglecting to make offerings to one's ancestors, being punished for one's ancestors' transgressions, being cursed, being hit by a whirlwind, having a stone implanted in one's body by an evil spirit master, having one's blood sucked by a *dab*, bumping into a *dab* who lives in a tree or a stream, digging a well in a *dab*'s living place, catching sight of a dwarf female *dab* who eats earthworms, having a *dab* sit on one's chest while one is sleeping, doing one's laundry in a lake inhabited by a dragon, pointing one's finger at the full moon, touching a newborn mouse, killing a large snake, urinating on a rock that looks like a tiger, urinating on or kicking a benevolent house spirit, or having bird droppings fall on one's head—by far the most common cause of illness is soul loss. Although the Hmong do not agree on just how many souls people have (estimates range from one to thirty-two; the Lees believe there is only one), there is a general consensus that whatever the number, it is the life-soul, whose presence is necessary for health and happiness, that tends to get lost. A life-soul can become separated from its body through anger, grief, fear, curiosity, or wanderlust. The life-souls of newborn babies are especially prone to disappearance, since they are so small, so vulnerable, and so precariously poised between the realm of the unseen, from which they have just traveled, and the realm of the living. Babies' souls may wander away, drawn by bright colors, sweet sounds, or fragrant smells; they may leave if a baby is sad, lonely, or insufficiently loved by its parents; they may be frightened away by a sudden loud noise; or they may be stolen by a *dab*. Some Hmong are careful never to say aloud that a baby is pretty, lest a *dab* be listening. Hmong babies are often dressed in intricately embroidered hats (Foua made several for Lia) which, when seen from a heavenly perspective, might fool a predatory *dab* into thinking the child was a flower. They spend much of their time swaddled against their mothers' backs in cloth carriers called *nyias* (Foua made Lia several of these too) that have been embroidered with soul-retaining motifs, such as the pigpen, which symbolizes enclosure. They may wear silver necklaces fastened with soul-shackling locks. When babies or small children go on an outing, their parents may call loudly to their souls before the family returns home, to make sure that none remain behind. Hmong families in Merced can sometimes be heard doing this when they leave local parks after a picnic. None of these ploys can work, however, unless the soul-calling ritual has already been properly observed.

Lia's *hu plig* took place in the living room of her family's apartment. There were so many guests, all of them Hmong and most of them members of the Lee and Yang clans, that it was nearly impossible to turn around. Foua and Nao Kao were proud that so many people had come to celebrate their good fortune in being favored with such a healthy and beautiful daughter. That morning Nao Kao had sacrificed a pig in order to invite the soul of one of Lia's ancestors, which was probably hungry and would appreciate an offering of food, to be reborn in her body. After the guests arrived, an elder of the Yang clan stood at the apartment's open front door, facing East 12th Street, with two live chickens in a bag on the floor next to him, and chanted a greeting to Lia's soul. The two chickens were then killed, plucked, eviscerated, partially boiled, retrieved from the cooking pot, and examined to see if their skulls were translucent and their tongues curled upward, both signs that Lia's new soul was pleased to take up residence in her body and that her name was a good one. (If the signs had been inauspicious, the soul-caller would have recommended that another name be chosen.) After the reading of the auguries, the chickens were put back in the cooking pot. The guests would later eat them and the pig for dinner. Before the meal, the soul-caller brushed Lia's hands with a bundle of short white strings and said, "I am sweeping away the ways of sickness." Then Lia's parents and all of the elders present in the room each tied a string around one of Lia's wrists in order to bind her soul securely to her body. Foua and Nao Kao promised to love her; the elders blessed her and prayed that she would have a long life and that she would never become sick.

_____

2

Fish Soup

In an intermediate French class at Merced College a few years ago, the students were assigned a five-minute oral report, to be delivered in French. The second student to stand up in front of the class was a young Hmong man. His chosen topic was a recipe for *la soupe de poisson*: Fish Soup. To prepare Fish Soup, he said, you must have a fish, and in order to have a fish, you have to go fishing. In order to go fishing, you need a hook, and in order to choose the right hook, you need to know whether the fish you are fishing for lives in fresh or salt water, how big it is, and what shape its mouth is. Continuing in this vein for forty-five minutes, the student filled the blackboard with a complexly branching tree of factors and options, a sort of piscatory flowchart, written in French with an overlay of Hmong. He also told several anecdotes about his own fishing experiences. He concluded with a description of how to clean various kinds of fish, how to cut them up, and, finally, how to cook them in broths flavored with various herbs. When the class period ended, he told the other students that he hoped he had provided enough information, and he wished them good luck in preparing Fish Soup in the Hmong manner.

The professor of French who told me this story said, "Fish Soup. That's the essence of the Hmong." The Hmong have a phrase, *hais cuaj txub kaum txub*, which means "to speak of all kinds of things." It is often used at the beginning of an oral narrative as a way of reminding the listeners that the world is full of things that may not seem to be connected but actually are; that no event occurs in isolation; that you can miss a lot by sticking to the point; and that the storyteller is likely to be rather long-winded. I once heard Nao Kao Lee begin a description of his village in Laos by saying, "It was where I was born and where my father was born and died and was buried and where my father's father died and was buried, but my father's father was born in China and to tell you about that would take all night." If a Hmong tells a fable, for example, about Why Animals Cannot Talk or Why Doodle Bugs Roll Balls of Dung, he is likely to begin with the beginning of the world. (Actually, according to *Dab Neeg Hmoob: Myths, Legends and Folk Tales from the Hmong of Laos*, a bilingual collection edited by Charles Johnson, those two fables go back only to the *second* beginning of the world, the time after the universe turned upside down and the earth was flooded with water and everyone drowned except a brother and sister who married each other and had a child who looked like an egg, whom they hacked into small pieces.) If I were Hmong, I might feel that what happened when Lia Lee and her family encountered the American medical system could be understood fully only by beginning with the *first* beginning of the world. But since I am not Hmong, I will go back only a few hundred generations, to the time when the Hmong were living in the river plains of north-central China.

For as long as it has been recorded, the history of the Hmong has been a marathon series of bloody scrimmages, punctuated by occasional periods of peace, though hardly any of plenty. Over and over again, the Hmong have responded to persecution and to pressures to assimilate by either fighting or migrating—a pattern that has been repeated so many times, in so many different eras and places, that it begins to seem almost a genetic trait, as inevitable in its recurrence as their straight hair or their short, sturdy stature. Most of the conflicts took place in China, to which the prehistoric ancestors of the Hmong are thought to have migrated from Eurasia, with a stopover of a few millennia in Siberia. These northerly roots would explain the references in Hmong rituals, including some that are still practiced during the New Year celebrations and at funerals, to a Hmong homeland called *Ntuj Khaib Huab*, which (according to a 1924 account by François Marie Savina, a French apostolic missionary who served in Laos and Tonkin) "was perpetually covered with snow and ice; where the days and the nights each lasted for six months; the trees were scarce and very small; and the people were also very small, and dressed entirely in furs." European ancestry would also explain why the Hmong have fairer skin than other Asian peoples, no epicanthic folds beneath their eyelids, and sometimes big noses. It would not explain why Ssuma Ch'ien, a Chinese scholar of the Han dynasty in the second century B.C., described the Hmong as a race "whose face, eyes, feet, and hands resembled those of other people, but under their armpits they had wings, with which, however, they were unable to fly." It would also fail to explain why, as late as the nineteenth century, many Chinese claimed that the Hmong had small tails.

The Chinese called the Hmong the Miao or Meo, which means, depending on which linguistic historian you read, "barbarians," "bumpkins," "people who sound like cats," or "wild uncultivated grasses." In any case, it was an insult. ("Hmong," the name they prefer themselves, is usually said to mean "free men," but some scholars say that, like "Inuit," "Dine," and many other tribal names the world over, it simply means "the people.") The Hmong called the Chinese sons of dogs. The Chinese viewed the Hmong as fearless, uncouth, and recalcitrant. It was a continuing slap in the face that they never evinced any interest in adopting the civilized customs of Chinese culture, preferring to keep to themselves, marry each other, speak their own language, wear their own tribal dress, play their own musical instruments, and practice their own religion. They never even ate with chopsticks. The Hmong viewed the Chinese as meddlesome and oppressive, and rebelled against their sovereignty in hundreds of small and large revolts. Though both sides were equally violent, it was not a symmetrical relationship. The Hmong never had any interest in ruling over the Chinese or anyone else; they wanted merely to be left alone, which, as their later history was also to illustrate, may be the most difficult request any minority can make of a majority culture.

The earliest account of Hmong-Chinese relations concerns a probably mythical, but emotionally resonant, emperor named Hoang-ti, who was said to have lived around 2700 B.C. Hoang-ti decided that the Hmong were too barbaric to be governed by the same laws as everyone else, and that they would henceforth be subject to a special criminal code. Instead of being imprisoned like other offenders, the Hmong who were not executed outright were to have their noses, ears, or testicles sliced off. The Hmong rebelled; the Chinese cracked down; the Hmong rebelled again; the Chinese cracked down again; and after a few centuries of this the Hmong gradually retreated from their rice fields in the valleys of the Yangtze and Yellow rivers, moving to more and more southerly latitudes and higher and higher altitudes. "That is how the Miao* became mountain people," wrote Father Savina. "That is also how they were able to preserve their independence in the midst of other peoples, maintaining intact, along with their language and their customs, the ethnic spirit of their race."

Around A.D. 400, the Hmong succeeded in establishing an independent kingdom in the Honan, Hupeh, and Hunan provinces. Since even among themselves they were (as Father Jean Mottin, a modern French missionary in Thailand, has put it) "allergic to all kind of authority," the power of their kings was limited by a complex system of village and district assemblies. Though the crown was hereditary, each new king was chosen from among the former king's sons by an electorate of all the arms-bearing men in the kingdom. Since the Hmong practiced polygyny, and kings had an especially large number of wives, the pool of candidates was usually ample enough to afford an almost democratically wide choice. The Hmong kingdom lasted for five hundred years before the Chinese managed to crush it. Most of the Hmong migrated again, this time toward the west, to the mountains of Kweichow and Szechuan. More insurrections followed. Some Hmong warriors were known for using poisoned arrows; others went into battle dressed in copper and buffalo-hide armor, carrying knives clenched between their teeth in addition to the usual spears and shields. Some Hmong crossbows were so big it took three men to draw them. In the sixteenth century, in order to keep the Hmong from venturing outside Kweichow, the Ming dynasty constructed the Hmong Wall, a smaller version of the Great Wall of China that was one hundred miles long, ten feet tall, and manned by armed guards.

---

* Savina was not intentionally insulting the Hmong when he called them by the offensive term "Miao." "Meo" and "Miao" were widely used until the early 1970s, when the scholar Yang Dao successfully campaigned for the general acceptance of "Hmong."

For a time the Hmong were contained, but not controlled. Gabriel de Magaillans, a Jesuit missionary who traveled through China in the seventeenth century, wrote that they "pay no tribute to the emperor, nor yield him any obedience. . . . The Chinese stand in fear of them; so that after several trials which they have made of their prowess, they have been forced to let them live at their own liberty."

The Chinese tried to "pacify" and "sinicize" the Hmong by telling them that they had to surrender their arms, that they had to wear Chinese clothes, that the men had to cut their hair short, and that they were forbidden to sacrifice buffalos. Those who submitted were called the "Cooked Miao"; those who refused were the "Raw Miao." There were a lot more Raw Miao than cooked ones. In 1730 or thereabouts, hundreds of Hmong warriors killed their wives and children, believing they would fight more fiercely if they had nothing to lose. (It worked for a while. Thus unencumbered, they seized several passes, severing Chinese supply lines, before they themselves were all killed or captured.) In 1772, a small army of Hmong squashed a large army of Chinese in eastern Kweichow by rolling boulders on their heads while they were marching through a narrow gorge. The Manchu emperor, Ch'ien-lung, decided he would be satisfied with nothing less than the extermination of the entire Hmong tribe, a goal whose unsuccessful pursuit ultimately cost him twice what he had spent conquering the entire kingdom of Turkestan. Ch'ien-lung dispatched another general to the Hmong regions. After many months of sieges and battles, the general told Sonom, the Hmong king of greater Kintchuen, that if he surrendered, his family would be spared. Sonom swallowed this story. When he and his family were brought before the emperor, they were chopped into bits, and their heads were placed in cages for public exhibition.

It is, perhaps, no surprise that by the beginning of the nineteenth century, a large number of Hmong decided that they had had enough of China. Not only were they fed up with being persecuted, but their soil was also getting depleted, there was a rash of epidemics, and taxes were rising. Although the majority of the Hmong stayed behind— today there are about five million Hmong in China, more than in any other country—about a half million migrated to Indochina, walking the ridgelines, driving their horses and cattle ahead of them, carrying everything they owned. As was their custom, they went to the highlands, settling first in what are now Vietnam and Laos, and later in Thailand. For the most part, they built their villages in places where no one else wanted to live. But if the local tribes objected or demanded tribute, the Hmong fought back with flintlock blunderbusses, or with their fists, and usually won. Father Mottin quotes an official who said, "I saw a Meo take my son by the feet and break his spine against the posts of my hut." After the French established control over Indochina in the 1890s, the Hmong rebelled against their extortionate tax system in a series of revolts. One of them, called the Madman's War, which lasted from 1919 to 1921, was led by a messianic figure named Pa Chay, who had a habit of climbing trees so that he could receive his military orders directly from heaven. His followers blew away large numbers of colonial soldiers with ten-foot-long cannons made from tree trunks. Only after the French granted them special administrative status in 1920, acknowledging that the best way to avoid being driven crazy by them was to leave them alone, did the Hmong of Laos, who constituted the largest group outside China, settle down peaceably to several unbroken decades of farming mountain rice, growing opium, and having as little contact as possible with the French, the lowland Lao, or any of the other ethnic groups who lived at lower elevations.

The history of the Hmong yields several lessons that anyone who deals with them might do well to remember. Among the most obvious of these are that the Hmong do not like to take orders; that they do not like to lose; that they would rather flee, fight, or die than surrender; that they are not intimidated by being outnumbered; that they are rarely persuaded that the customs of other cultures, even those more powerful than their own, are superior; and that they are capable of getting very angry. Whether you find these traits infuriating or admirable depends largely on whether or not you are trying to make a Hmong do something he or she would prefer not to do. Those who have tried to defeat, deceive, govern, regulate, constrain, assimilate, intimidate, or patronize the Hmong have, as a rule, disliked them intensely.

On the other hand, many historians, anthropologists, and missionaries (to whom the Hmong have usually been polite, if not always receptive, as long as the proselytizing has not been coercive) have developed a great fondness for them. Father Savina wrote that the Hmong possessed "a bravery and courage inferior to that of no other

people," because of which "they have never had a homeland, but neither have they ever known servitude and slavery." William Robert
Geddes, an Australian anthropologist, spent most of 1958 and 1959
in Pasamliem, a Hmong village in northern Thailand. (Though more
Hmong lived in Laos and Vietnam, most Western observers in the
last half century or so have worked in Thailand because of its stabler
political situation.) Geddes did not find his fieldwork easy. The villagers were too proud to sell him food, so he had to transport his
supplies by packhorse, nor would they allow themselves to be hired
to build him a house, so he had to employ opium addicts from a Thai
village lower down the mountain. However, the Hmong eventually
won his deep respect. In his book *Migrants of the Mountains*, Geddes
wrote:

> The preservation by the Miao of their ethnic identity for such a long
> time despite their being split into many small groups surrounded by dif-
> ferent alien peoples and scattered over a vast geographic area is an out-
> standing record paralleling in some ways that of the Jews but more
> remarkable because they lacked the unifying forces of literacy and a doc-
> trinal religion and because the features they preserved seem to be more
> numerous.

Robert Cooper, a British anthropologist who spent two years studying
resource scarcity in four Hmong communities in northern Thailand,
described his research subjects as

> polite without fawning, proud but not arrogant. Hospitable without
> being pushy; discreet respecters of personal liberty who demand only that
> their liberty be respected in return. People who do not steal or lie. Self-
> sufficient people who showed no trace of jealousy of an outsider who said
> he wanted to live like a Hmong yet owned an expensive motorcycle, a
> tape-recorder, cameras, and who never had to work for a living.

From his post in the Hmong village of Khek Noi, also in northern
Thailand, Father Mottin wrote in his *History of the Hmong* (a wonderful book, exuberantly translated from the French by an Irish nun
who had once been the tutor to the future king of Thailand, and
printed, rather faintly, in Bangkok):

Though they are but a small people, the Hmong still prove to be great men. What particularly strikes me is to see how this small race has always manged [sic] to survive though they often had to face more powerful nations. Let us consider, for example, that the Chinese were 250 times more numerous than they, and yet never found their way to swallow them. The Hmong . . . have never possessed a country of their own, they have never got a king worthy of this name, and yet they have passed through the ages remaining what they have always wished to be, that is to say: free men with a right to live in this world as Hmong. Who would not admire them for that?

One of the recurring characters in Hmong folktales is the Orphan, a young man whose parents have died, leaving him alone to live by his wits. In one story, collected by Charles Johnson, the Orphan offers the hospitality of his humble home to two sisters, one good and one snotty. The snotty one says:

What, with a filthy orphan boy like you? Ha! You're so ragged you're almost naked! Your penis is dirty with ashes! You must eat on the ground, and sleep in the mud, like a buffalo! I don't think you even have any drink or tobacco to offer us!

The Orphan may not have a clean penis, but he is clever, energetic, brave, persistent, and a virtuoso player of the *qeej*, a musical instrument, highly esteemed by the Hmong, that is made from six curving bamboo pipes attached to a wooden wind chamber. Though he lives by himself on the margins of society, reviled by almost everyone, he knows in his heart that he is actually superior to all his detractors. Charles Johnson points out that the Orphan is, of course, a symbol of the Hmong people. In this story, the Orphan marries the good sister, who is able to perceive his true value, and they prosper and have children. The snotty sister ends up married to the kind of *dab* who lives in a cave, drinks blood, and makes women sterile.

3

The Spirit Catches You and You Fall Down

"gaug dab peg" The spirit catches you and you fall down.

When Lia was about three months old, her older sister Yer slammed the front door of the Lees' apartment. A few moments later, Lia's eyes rolled up, her arms jerked over her head, and she fainted. The Lees had little doubt what had happened. Despite the careful installation of Lia's soul during the *hu plig* ceremony, the noise of the door had been so profoundly frightening that her soul had fled her body and become lost. They recognized the resulting symptoms as *qaug dab peg*, which means "the spirit catches you and you fall down." The spirit referred to in this phrase is a soul-stealing *dab*; *peg* means to catch or hit; and *qaug* means to fall over with one's roots still in the ground, as grain might be beaten down by wind or rain.

In Hmong-English dictionaries, *qaug dab peg* is generally translated as epilepsy. It is an illness well known to the Hmong, who regard it with ambivalence. On the one hand, it is acknowledged to be a serious and potentially dangerous condition. Tony Coelho, who was Merced's congressman from 1979 to 1989, is an epileptic. Coelho is a popular figure among the Hmong, and a few years ago, some local Hmong men were sufficiently concerned when they learned he suffered from *qaug dab peg* that they volunteered the services of a shaman, a *txiv neeb*, to perform a ceremony that would retrieve Coelho's errant soul. The

Hmong leader to whom they made this proposition politely discouraged them, suspecting that Coelho, who is a Catholic of Portuguese descent, might not appreciate having chickens, and maybe a pig as well, sacrificed on his behalf.

On the other hand, the Hmong consider *qaug dab peg* to be an illness of some distinction. This fact might have surprised Tony Coelho no less than the dead chickens would have. Before he entered politics, Coelho planned to become a Jesuit priest, but was barred by a canon forbidding the ordination of epileptics. What was considered a disqualifying impairment by Coelho's church might have been seen by the Hmong as a sign that he was particularly fit for divine office. Hmong epileptics often become shamans. Their seizures are thought to be evidence that they have the power to perceive things other people cannot see, as well as facilitating their entry into trances, a prerequisite for their journeys into the realm of the unseen. The fact that they have been ill themselves gives them an intuitive sympathy for the suffering of others and lends them emotional credibility as healers. Becoming a *txiv neeb* is not a choice; it is a vocation. The calling is revealed when a person falls sick, either with *qaug dab peg* or with some other illness whose symptoms similarly include shivering and pain. An established *txiv neeb*, summoned to diagnose the problem, may conclude from these symptoms that the person (who is usually but not always male) has been chosen to be the host of a healing spirit, a *neeb*. (*Txiv neeb* means "person with a healing spirit.") It is an offer that the sick person cannot refuse, since if he rejects his vocation, he will die. In any case, few Hmong would choose to decline. Although shamanism is an arduous calling that requires years of training with a master in order to learn the ritual techniques and chants, it confers an enormous amount of social status in the community and publicly marks the *txiv neeb* as a person of high moral character, since a healing spirit would never choose a no-account host. Even if an epileptic turns out not to be elected to host a *neeb*, his illness, with its thrilling aura of the supramundane, singles him out as a person of consequence.

In their attitude toward Lia's seizures, the Lees reflected this mixture of concern and pride. The Hmong are known for the gentleness with which they treat their children. Hugo Adolf Bernatzik, a German ethnographer who lived with the Hmong of Thailand for several years during the 1930s, wrote that the Hmong he had studied regarded a

Txiv neeb - person with a healing spirit

child as "the most treasured possession a person can have." In Laos, a baby was never apart from its mother, sleeping in her arms all night and riding on her back all day. Small children were rarely abused; it was believed that a *dab* who witnessed mistreatment might take the child, assuming it was not wanted. The Hmong who live in the United States have continued to be unusually attentive parents. A study conducted at the University of Minnesota found Hmong infants in the first month of life to be less irritable and more securely attached to their mothers than Caucasian infants, a difference the researcher attributed to the fact that the Hmong mothers were, without exception, more sensitive, more accepting, and more responsive, as well as "exquisitely attuned" to their children's signals. Another study, conducted in Portland, Oregon, found that Hmong mothers held and touched their babies far more frequently than Caucasian mothers. In a third study, conducted at the Hennepin County Medical Center in Minnesota, a group of Hmong mothers of toddlers surpassed a group of Caucasian mothers of similar socioeconomic status in every one of fourteen categories selected from the Egeland Mother-Child Rating Scale, ranging from "Speed of Responsiveness to Fussing and Crying" to "Delight."

Foua and Nao Kao had nurtured Lia in typical Hmong fashion (on the Egeland Scale, they would have scored especially high in Delight), and they were naturally distressed to think that anything might compromise her health and happiness. They therefore hoped, at least most of the time, that the *qaug dab peg* could be healed. Yet they also considered the illness an honor. Jeanine Hilt, a social worker who knew the Lees well, told me, "They felt Lia was kind of an anointed one, like a member of royalty. She was a very special person in their culture because she had these spirits in her and she might grow up to be a shaman, and so sometimes their thinking was that this was not so much a medical problem as it was a blessing." (Of the forty or so American doctors, nurses, and Merced County agency employees I spoke with who had dealt with Lia and her family, several had a vague idea that "spirits" were somehow involved, but Jeanine Hilt was the only one who had actually asked the Lees what they thought was the cause of their daughter's illness.)

Within the Lee family, in one of those unconscious processes of selection that are as mysterious as any other form of falling in love, it was obvious that Lia was her parents' favorite, the child they considered the most beautiful, the one who was most extravagantly hugged and kissed, the one who was dressed in the most exquisite garments (embroidered by Foua, wearing dime-store glasses to work her almost microscopic stitches). Whether Lia occupied this position from the moment of her birth, whether it was a result of her spiritually distinguished illness, or whether it came from the special tenderness any parent feels for a sick child, is not a matter Foua and Nao Kao wish, or are able, to analyze. One thing that is clear is that for many years the cost of that extra love was partially borne by her sister Yer. "They blamed Yer for slamming the door," said Jeanine Hilt. "I tried many times to explain that the door had nothing to do with it, but they didn't believe me. Lia's illness made them so sad that I think for a long time they treated Yer differently from their other children."

During the next few months of her life, Lia had at least twenty more seizures. On two occasions, Foua and Nao Kao were worried enough to carry her in their arms to the emergency room at Merced Community Medical Center, which was three blocks from their apartment. Like most Hmong refugees, they had their doubts about the efficacy of Western medical techniques. However, when they were living in the Mae Jarim refugee camp in Thailand, their only surviving son, Cheng, and three of their six surviving daughters, Ge, May, and True, had been seriously ill. Ge died. They took Cheng, May, and True to the camp hospital; Cheng and May recovered rapidly, and True was sent to another, larger hospital, where she eventually recovered as well. (The Lees also concurrently addressed the possible spiritual origins of their children's illnesses by moving to a new hut. A dead person had been buried beneath their old one, and his soul might have wished to harm the new residents.) This experience did nothing to shake their faith in traditional Hmong beliefs about the causes and cures of illness, but it did convince them that on some occasions Western doctors could be of additional help, and that it would do no harm to hedge their bets.

County hospitals have a reputation for being crowded, dilapidated, and dingy. Merced's county hospital, with which the Lees would become all too familiar over the next few years, is none of these. The

MCMC complex includes a modern, 42,000-square-foot wing—it looks sort of like an art moderne ocean liner—that houses coronary care, intensive care, and transitional care units; 154 medical and surgical beds; medical and radiology laboratories outfitted with state-of-the-art diagnostic equipment; and a blood bank. The waiting rooms in the hospital and its attached clinic have unshredded magazines, unsmelly bathrooms, and floors that have been scrubbed to an aseptic gloss. MCMC is a teaching hospital, staffed in part by the faculty and residents of the Family Practice Residency, which is affiliated with the University of California at Davis. The residency program is nationally known, and receives at least 150 applications annually for its six first-year positions.

Like many other rural county hospitals, which were likely to feel the health care crunch before it reached urban hospitals, MCMC has been plagued with financial problems throughout the last twenty years. It accepts all patients, whether or not they can pay; only twenty percent are privately insured, with most of the rest receiving aid from California's Medi-Cal, Medicare, or Medically Indigent Adult programs, and a small (but to the hospital, costly) percentage neither insured nor covered by any federal or state program. The hospital receives reimbursements from the public programs, but many of those reimbursements have been lowered or restricted in recent years. Although the private patients are far more profitable, MCMC's efforts to attract what its administrator has called "an improved payer mix" have not been very successful. (Merced's wealthier residents often choose either a private Catholic hospital three miles north of MCMC or a larger hospital in a nearby city such as Fresno.) MCMC went through a particularly rough period during the late eighties, hitting bottom in 1988, when it had a $3.1 million deficit.

During this same period, MCMC also experienced an expensive change in its patient population. Starting in the late seventies, Southeast Asian refugees began to move to Merced in large numbers. The city of Merced, which has a population of about 61,000, now has just over 12,000 Hmong. That is to say, one in five residents of Merced is Hmong. Because many Hmong fear and shun the hospital, MCMC's patient rolls reflect a somewhat lower ratio, but on any given day there are still Hmong patients in almost every unit. Not only do the Hmong fail resoundingly to improve the payer mix—more than eighty percent are on Medi-Cal—but they have proved even more costly than other indigent patients, because they generally require more time and attention, and because there are so many of them that MCMC has had to hire bilingual staff members to mediate between patients and providers.

There are no funds in the hospital budget specifically earmarked for interpreters, so the administration has detoured around that technicality by hiring Hmong lab assistants, nurse's aides, and transporters, who are called upon to translate in the scarce interstices between analyzing blood, emptying bedpans, and rolling postoperative patients around on gurneys. In 1991, a short-term federal grant enabled MCMC to put skilled interpreters on call around the clock, but the program expired the following year. Except during that brief hiatus, there have often been no Hmong-speaking employees of any kind present in the hospital at night. Obstetricians have had to obtain consent for cesarean sections or episiotomies using embarrassed teenaged sons, who have learned English in school, as translators. Ten-year-old girls have had to translate discussions of whether or not a dying family member should be resuscitated. Sometimes not even a child is available. Doctors on the late shift in the emergency room have often had no way of taking a patient's medical history, or of asking such questions as Where do you hurt? How long have you been hurting? What does it feel like? Have you had an accident? Have you vomited? Have you had a fever? Have you lost consciousness? Are you pregnant? Have you taken any medications? Are you allergic to any medications? Have you recently eaten? (The last question is of great importance if emergency surgery is being contemplated, since anesthetized patients with full stomachs can aspirate the partially digested food into their lungs, and may die if they choke or if their bronchial linings are badly burned by stomach acid.) I asked one doctor what he did in such cases. He said, "Practice veterinary medicine."

On October 24, 1982, the first time that Foua and Nao Kao carried Lia to the emergency room, MCMC had not yet hired any interpreters, de jure or de facto, for any shift. At that time, the only hospital employee who sometimes translated for Hmong patients was a janitor, a Laotian immigrant fluent in his own language, Lao, which few

Hmong understand; halting in Hmong; and even more halting in English. On that day either the janitor was unavailable or the emergency room staff didn't think of calling him. The resident on duty practiced veterinary medicine. Foua and Nao Kao had no way of explaining what had happened, since Lia's seizures had stopped by the time they reached the hospital. Her only obvious symptoms were a cough and a congested chest. The resident ordered an X ray, which led the radiologist to conclude that Lia had "early bronchiopneumonia or tracheobronchitis." As he had no way of knowing that the bronchial congestion was probably caused by aspiration of saliva or vomit during her seizure (a common problem for epileptics), she was routinely dismissed with a prescription for ampicillin, an antibiotic. Her emergency room Registration Record lists her father's last name as Yang, her mother's maiden name as Foua, and her "primary spoken language" as "Mong." When Lia was discharged, Nao Kao (who knows the alphabet but does not speak or read English) signed a piece of paper that said, "I hereby acknowledge receipt of the instructions indicated above," to wit: "Take ampicillin as directed. Vaporizer at cribside. Clinic reached as needed 383-7007 ten days." The "ten days" meant that Nao Kao was supposed to call the Family Practice Center in ten days for a follow-up appointment. Not surprisingly, since he had no idea what he had agreed to, he didn't. But when Lia had another bad seizure on November 11, he and Foua carried her to the emergency room again, where the same scene was repeated, and the same misdiagnosis made.

On March 3, 1983, Foua and Nao Kao carried Lia to the emergency room a third time. On this occasion, three circumstances were different: Lia was still seizing when they arrived, they were accompanied by a cousin who spoke some English, and one of the doctors on duty was a family practice resident named Dan Murphy. Of all the doctors who have worked at MCMC, Dan Murphy is generally acknowledged to be the one most interested in and knowledgeable about the Hmong. At that time, he had been living in Merced for only seven months, so his interest still exceeded his knowledge. When he and his wife, Cindy, moved to Merced, they had never heard the word "Hmong." Several years later, Cindy was teaching English to Hmong adults and Dan was inviting Hmong leaders to the hospital to tell the residents about their experiences as refugees. Most important, the Murphys counted a Hmong family, the Xiongs, among their closest friends. When one of the Xiong daughters wanted to spend the summer working in Yosemite National Park, Chaly Xiong, her father, initially refused because he was afraid she might get eaten by a lion. Dan personally escorted Chaly to Yosemite to verify the absence of lions, and persuaded him the job would do his daughter good. Four months later, Chaly was killed in an automobile accident. Cindy Murphy arranged the funeral, calling around until she found a funeral parlor that was willing to accommodate three days of incense burning, drum beating, and *qeej* playing. She also bought several live chickens, which were sacrificed in the parking lot of the funeral parlor, as well as a calf and a pig, which were sacrificed elsewhere. When Dan first saw the Lees, he instantly registered that they were Hmong, and he thought to himself: "This won't be boring."

Many years later, Dan, who is a short, genial man with an Amish-style beard and an incandescent smile, recalled the encounter. "I have this memory of Lia's parents standing just inside the door to the ER, holding a chubby little round-faced baby. She was having a generalized seizure. Her eyes were rolled back, she was unconscious, her arms and legs were kind of jerking back and forth, and she didn't breathe much—every once in a while, there would be no movement of the chest wall and you couldn't hear any breath sounds. That was definitely anxiety-producing. She was the youngest patient I had ever dealt with who was seizing. The parents seemed frightened, not terribly frightened though, not as frightened as I would have been if it was my kid. I thought it might be meningitis, so Lia had to have a spinal tap, and the parents were real resistant to that. I don't remember how I convinced them. I remember feeling very anxious because they had a real sick kid and I felt a big need to explain to these people, through their relative who was a not-very-good translator, what was going on, but I felt like I had no time, because we had to put an IV in her scalp with Valium to stop the seizures, but then Lia started seizing again and the IV went into the skin instead of the vein, and I had a hard time getting another one started. Later on, when I figured out what had happened, or not happened, on the earlier visits to the ER, I felt good. It's kind of a thrill to find something someone else has missed, especially when you're a resident and you are looking for excuses to make yourself feel smarter than the other physicians."

Among Dan's notes in Lia's History and Physical Examination record were:

HISTORY OF PRESENT ILLNESS: The patient is an 8 month, Hmong female, whose family brought her to the emergency room after they had noticed her shaking and not breathing very well for a 20-minute period of time. According to the family the patient has had multiple like episodes in the past, but have never been able to communicate this to emergency room doctors on previous visits secondary to a language barrier. An english speaking relative available tonight, stated that the patient had had intermittent fever and cough for 2–3 days prior to being admitted.

FAMILY & SOCIAL HISTORY: Unobtainable secondary to language difficulties.

NEUROLOGICAL: The child was unresponsive to pain or sound. The head was held to the left with intermittent tonic-clonic [first rigid, then jerking] movements of the upper extremities. Respirations were suppressed during these periods of clonic movement. Grunting respirations persisted until the patient was given 3 mg. of Valium I.V.

Dan had no way of knowing that Foua and Nao Kao had already diagnosed their daughter's problem as the illness where the spirit catches you and you fall down. Foua and Nao Kao had no way of knowing that Dan had diagnosed it as epilepsy, the most common of all neurological disorders. Each had accurately noted the same symptoms, but Dan would have been surprised to hear that they were caused by soul loss, and Lia's parents would have been surprised to hear that they were caused by an electrochemical storm inside their daughter's head that had been stirred up by the misfiring of aberrant brain cells.

Dan had learned in medical school that epilepsy is a sporadic malfunction of the brain, sometimes mild and sometimes severe, sometimes progressive and sometimes self-limiting, which can be traced to oxygen deprivation during gestation, labor, or birth; a head injury; a tumor; an infection; a high fever; a stroke; a metabolic disturbance; a drug allergy; a toxic reaction to a poison. Sometimes the source is obvious—the patient had a brain tumor or swallowed strychnine or crashed through a windshield—but in about seven out of ten cases, the cause is never determined. During an epileptic episode, instead of following their usual orderly protocol, the damaged cells in the cerebral cortex transmit neural impulses simultaneously and chaotically. When only a small area of the brain is involved—in a "focal" seizure—an epileptic may hallucinate or twitch or tingle but retain consciousness. When the electrical disturbance extends to a wide area—in a "generalized" seizure—consciousness is lost, either for the brief episodes called petit mal or "absence" seizures, or for the full-blown attacks known as grand mal. Except through surgery, whose risks consign it to the category of last resort, epilepsy cannot be cured, but it can be completely or partially controlled in most cases by anticonvulsant drugs.

The Hmong are not the only people who might have good reason to feel ambivalent about suppressing the symptoms. The Greeks called epilepsy "the sacred disease." Dan Murphy's diagnosis added Lia Lee to a distinguished line of epileptics that has included Søren Kierkegaard, Vincent van Gogh, Gustave Flaubert, Lewis Carroll, and Fyodor Dostoyevsky, all of whom, like many Hmong shamans, experienced powerful senses of grandeur and spiritual passion during their seizures, and powerful creative urges in their wake. As Dostoyevsky's Prince Myshkin asked, "What if it is a disease? What does it matter that it is an abnormal tension, if the result, if the moment of sensation, remembered and analysed in a state of health, turns out to be harmony and beauty brought to their highest point of perfection, and gives a feeling, undivined and undreamt of till then, of completeness, proportion, reconciliation, and an ecstatic and prayerful fusion in the highest synthesis of life?"

Although the inklings Dan had gathered of the transcendental Hmong worldview seemed to him to possess both power and beauty, his own view of medicine in general, and of epilepsy in particular, was, like that of his colleagues at MCMC, essentially rationalist. Hippocrates' skeptical commentary on the nature of epilepsy, made around 400 B.C., pretty much sums up Dan's own frame of reference: "It seems to me that the disease is no more divine than any other. It has a natural cause just as other diseases have. Men think it is divine merely because they don't understand it. But if they called everything divine which they do not understand, why, there would be no end of divine things."*

Lia's seizure was a grand mal episode, and Dan had no desire to do anything but stop it. He admitted her to MCMC as an inpatient. Among the tests she had during the three days she spent there were a spinal tap, a CT scan, an EEG, a chest X ray, and extensive blood work. Foua and Nao Kao signed "Authorization for and Consent to Surgery or Special Diagnostic or Therapeutic Procedures" forms, each several hundred words long, for the first two of these. It is not known whether anyone attempted to translate them, or, if so, how "Your physician has requested a brain scan utilizing computerized tomography" was rendered in Hmong. None of the tests revealed any apparent cause for the seizures. The doctors classified Lia's epilepsy as "idiopathic": cause unknown. Lia was found to have consolidation in her right lung, which this time was correctly diagnosed as aspiration pneumonia resulting from the seizure. Foua and Nao Kao alternated nights at the hospital, sleeping in a cot next to Lia's bed. Among the Nurse's Notes for Lia's last night at the hospital were: "0001. Skin cool and dry to touch, color good & pink. Mom is with babe at this time & is breastfeeding. Mom informed to keep babe covered with a blanket for the babe is a little cool." "0400. Babe resting quietly

---

* Despite this early attempt by Hippocrates (or perhaps by one of the anonymous physicians whose writings are attributed to Hippocrates) to remove the "divine" label, epilepsy continued, more than any other disease, to be ascribed to supernatural causes. The medical historian Owsei Temkin has noted that epilepsy has held a key position historically in "the struggle between magic and the scientific conception." Many treatments for epilepsy have had occult associations. Greek magicians forbade epileptics to eat mint, garlic, and onion, as well as the flesh of goats, pigs, deer, dogs, cocks, turtledoves, bustards, mullets, and eels; to wear black garments and goatskins; and to cross their hands and feet: taboos that were all connected, in various ways, with chthonic deities. Roman epileptics were advised to swallow morsels cut from the livers of stabbed gladiators. During the Middle Ages, when epilepsy was attributed to demonic possession, treatments included prayer, fasting, wearing amulets, lighting candles, visiting the graves of saints, and writing the names of the Three Wise Men with blood taken from the patient's little finger. These spiritual remedies were far safer than the "medical" therapies of the time—still practiced as late as the seventeenth century—which included cauterizing the head with a hot iron and boring a hole in the skull to release peccant vapors.

with no acute distress noted. Mom breast feeds off & on." "0600. Sleeping." "0730. Awake, color good. Mother fed." "1200. Held by mother."

Lia was discharged on March 11, 1983. Her parents were instructed, via an English-speaking relative, to give her 250 milligrams of ampicillin twice a day, to clear up her aspiration pneumonia, and twenty milligrams of Dilantin elixir, an anticonvulsant, twice a day, to suppress any further grand mal seizures.

4

4

Do Doctors Eat Brains?

In 1982, Mao Thao, a Hmong woman from Laos who had resettled in St. Paul, Minnesota, visited Ban Vinai, the refugee camp in Thailand where she had lived for a year after her escape from Laos in 1975. She was the first Hmong-American ever to return there, and when an officer of the United Nations High Commissioner for Refugees, which administered the camp, asked her to speak about life in the United States, 15,000 Hmong, more than a third of the population of Ban Vinai, assembled in a soccer field and questioned her for nearly four hours. Some of the questions they asked her were: Is it forbidden to use a *txiv neeb* to heal an illness in the United States? Why do American doctors take so much blood from their patients? After you die, why do American doctors try to open up your head and take out your brains? Do American doctors eat the livers, kidneys, and brains of Hmong patients? When Hmong people die in the United States, is it true that they are cut into pieces and put in tin cans and sold as food?

The general drift of these questions suggests that the accounts of the American health care system that had filtered back to Asia were not exactly enthusiastic. The limited contact the Hmong had already had with Western medicine in the camp hospitals and clinics had done little to instill confidence, especially when compared to the experiences with shamanistic healing to which they were accustomed. A *txiv neeb* might spend as much as eight hours in a sick person's home; doctors forced their patients, no matter how weak they were, to come to the hospital, and then might spend only twenty minutes at their bedsides. *Txiv neebs* were polite and never needed to ask questions; doctors asked many rude and intimate questions about patients' lives, right down to their sexual and excretory habits. *Txiv neebs* could render an immediate diagnosis; doctors often demanded samples of blood (or even urine or feces, which they liked to keep in little bottles), took X rays, and waited for days for the results to come back from the laboratory—and then, after all that, sometimes they were unable to identify the cause of the problem. *Txiv neebs* never undressed their patients; doctors asked patients to take off all their clothes, and sometimes dared to put their fingers inside women's vaginas. *Txiv neebs* knew that to treat the body without treating the soul was an act of patent folly; doctors never even mentioned the soul. *Txiv neebs* could preserve unblemished reputations even if their patients didn't get well, since the blame was laid on the intransigence of the spirits rather than the competence of the negotiators, whose stock might even rise if they had had to do battle with particularly dangerous opponents; when doctors failed to heal, it was their own fault.

To add injury to insult, some of the doctors' procedures actually seemed more likely to threaten their patients' health than to restore it. Most Hmong believe that the body contains a finite amount of blood that it is unable to replenish, so repeated blood sampling, especially from small children, may be fatal. When people are unconscious, their souls are at large, so anesthesia may lead to illness or death. If the body is cut or disfigured, or if it loses any of its parts, it will remain in a condition of perpetual imbalance, and the damaged person not only will become frequently ill but may be physically incomplete during the next incarnation; so surgery is taboo. If people lose their vital organs after death, their souls cannot be reborn into new bodies and may take revenge on living relatives; so autopsies and embalming are also taboo. (Some of the questions on the Ban Vinai soccer field were obviously inspired by reports of the widespread practice of autopsy and embalming in the United States. To make the leap from hearing that doctors removed organs to believing that they ate them was probably no crazier than to assume, as did American doctors, that the Hmong ate human placentas—but it was certainly scarier.)

The only form of medical treatment that was gratefully accepted by at least some of the Hmong in the Thai camps was antibiotic therapy, either oral or by injection. Most Hmong have little fear of needles, perhaps because some of their own healers (not *txiv neebs*, who never touch their patients) attempt to release fevers and toxicity through acupuncture and other forms of dermal treatment, such as massage; pinching; scraping the skin with coins, spoons, silver jewelry, or pieces of bamboo; applying a heated cup to the skin; or burning the skin with a sheaf of grass or a wad of cotton wool. An antibiotic shot that could heal an infection almost overnight was welcomed. A shot to immunize someone against a disease he did not yet have was something else again. In his book *Les naufragés de la liberté*, the French physician Jean-Pierre Willem, who worked as a volunteer in the hospital at the Nam Yao camp, related how during a typhoid epidemic, the Hmong refugees refused to be vaccinated until they were told that only those who got shots would receive their usual allotments of rice —whereupon 14,000 people showed up at the hospital, including at least a thousand who came twice in order to get seconds.

When Foua Yang and Nao Kao Lee brought their three sick children to the hospital at Mae Jarim, they were engaging in behavior that many of the other camp inhabitants would have considered positively aberrant. Hospitals were regarded not as places of healing but as charnel houses. They were populated by the spirits of people who had died there, a lonesome and rapacious crew who were eager to swell their own ranks. Catherine Pake, a public health nurse who spent six months working at Phanat Nikhom (a camp where refugees from Laos, Vietnam, and Cambodia came for their final "processing" before they were sent to a country of permanent asylum), concluded from a study of the hospital log that "in comparison to refugees of other ethnic groups, the Hmong have the lowest per capita rate of visits." (Pake also discovered, not coincidentally, that the Hmong had an extremely "high utilization rate" of indigenous healing arts: shamanism, dermal treatments, herbalism. She published an article in the *Journal of Ethnobiology* identifying twenty medicinal plants she had collected under the tutelage of Hmong herbalists, which, in various forms— chopped, crushed, dried, shredded, powdered, decocted, infused with hot water, infused with cold water, mixed with ashes, mixed with sulphur, mixed with egg, mixed with chicken—were indicated for burns, fever, weakness, poor vision, broken bones, stomachaches, painful urination, prolapsed uterus, insufficient breast milk, arthritis, anemia, tuberculosis, rabies, scabies, gonorrhea, dysentery, constipation, impotence, and attacks by a *dab ntxaug*, a spirit who lives in the jungle and causes epidemics when he is disturbed. In this last case, the plant, *Jatropha curcas*, is crushed and its oil left in a cup, to be consumed not by the patient but by the *dab*.)

Wendy Walker-Moffat, an educational consultant who spent three years teaching and working on nutritional and agricultural projects in Phanat Nikhom and Ban Vinai, suggests that one reason the Hmong avoided the camp hospitals is that so many of the medical staff members were excessively zealous volunteers from Christian charitable organizations. "They were there to provide medical aid, but they were also there—though not overtly—to convert people," Walker-Moffat told me. "And part of becoming converted was believing in Western medicine. I'll never forget one conversation I overheard when I was working in the hospital area at Ban Vinai. A group of doctors and nurses were talking to a Hmong man whom they had converted and ordained as a Protestant minister. They had decided that in order to get the Hmong to come into the hospital they were going to allow a traditional healer, a shaman, to practice there. I knew they all thought shamanism was witch-doctoring. So I heard them tell this Hmong minister that if they let a shaman work in the medical center he could only give out herbs, and not perform any actual work with the spirits. At this point they asked the poor Hmong minister, 'Now *you* never go to a shaman, do you?' He was a Christian convert, he knew you cannot tell a lie, so he said, 'Well, yes, I do.' But then their reaction was so shocked that he said, 'No, no, no, I've never been. I've just heard that *other* people go.' What they didn't realize was that—to my knowledge, at least—no Hmong is ever fully converted."

In 1985, the International Rescue Committee assigned Dwight Conquergood, a young ethnographer with a special interest in shamanism and performance art, to design an environmental health program for Ban Vinai. He later wrote:

> I heard horror story after horror story from the refugees about people who went to the hospital for treatment, but before being admitted had

their spirit-strings cut from their wrists by a nurse because "the strings were unsanitary and carried germs." Doctors confidently cut off neck-rings that held the life-souls of babies intact. Instead of working in co-operation with the shamans, they did everything to disconfirm them and undermine their authority. . . . Is it any wonder that the Hmong community regarded the camp hospital as the last choice of available health care options? In the local hierarchy of values, consulting a shaman or herbalist, or purchasing medicine available in the Thai market just outside the entrance to the camp, was much preferred and more prestigious than going to the camp hospital. The refugees told me that only the very poorest people who had no relatives or resources whatsoever would sub-ject themselves to the camp hospital treatment. To say that the camp hospital was underutilized would be an understatement.

Unlike the other camp volunteers, who commuted from an expa-triate enclave an hour away, Conquergood insisted on living in Ban Vinai, sharing the corner of a thatched hut with seven chickens and a pig. His first day in the camp, Conquergood noticed a Hmong woman sitting on a bench, singing folk songs. Her face was decorated with little blue moons and golden suns, which he recognized as stickers the camp clinic placed on medication bottles to inform illiterate patients whether the pills should be taken morning or night. The fact that Conquergood considered this a delightful example of creative costume design rather than an act of medical noncompliance suggests some of the reasons why the program he designed turned out to be the most (indeed, possibly the only) completely successful attempt at health care delivery Ban Vinai had ever seen.

Conquergood's first challenge came after an outbreak of rabies among the camp dogs prompted a mass dog-vaccination campaign by the medical staff, during which the Ban Vinai inhabitants failed to bring in a single dog to be inoculated. Conquergood was asked to come up with a new campaign. He decided on a Rabies Parade, a procession led by three important characters from Hmong folktales—a tiger, a chicken, and a *dab*—dressed in homemade costumes. The cast, like its audience, was one hundred percent Hmong. As the parade snaked through the camp, the tiger danced and played the *qeej*, the *dab* sang and banged a drum, and the chicken (chosen for this crucial role because of its traditional powers of augury) explained the etiology of rabies through a bullhorn. The next morning, the vaccination stations were so besieged by dogs—dogs carried in their owners' arms, dogs dragged on rope leashes, dogs rolled in on two-wheeled pushcarts—that the health workers could hardly inoculate them fast enough. Conquergood's next production, a sanitation campaign in which a parade of children led by Mother Clean (a huge, insanely grinning figure on a bamboo frame) and the Garbage Troll (dressed in ragged clothes plastered with trash) sang songs about latrine use and refuse disposal, was equally well received.

During Conquergood's five months in Ban Vinai, he himself was successfully treated with Hmong herbs for diarrhea and a gashed toe. When he contracted dengue fever (for which he also sought conventional medical treatment), a *txiv neeb* informed him that his homesick soul had wandered back to Chicago, and two chickens were sacrificed to expedite its return. Conquergood considered his relationship with the Hmong to be a form of barter, "a productive and mutually invigorating dialog, with neither side dominating or winning out." In his opinion, the physicians and nurses at Ban Vinai failed to win the cooperation of the camp inhabitants because they considered the relationship one-sided, with the Westerners holding all the knowledge. As long as they persisted in this view, Conquergood believed that what the medical establishment was offering would continue to be rejected, since the Hmong would view it not as a gift but as a form of coercion.

_____

5

Take as Directed

Between the ages of eight months and four and a half years, Lia Lee was admitted to MCMC seventeen times and made more than a hundred outpatient visits to the emergency room and to the pediatric clinic at the Family Practice Center. "Hmong ♀," read the admission notes. Then, "Hmong ♀ well known to this facility." Then, "Hmong ♀ very well known to this facility." Sometimes instead of "Hmong" the notes say "H'mond" or "Mong" or, in one note transcribed from a tape dictated by a resident, "Mongoloid"—an attempt by a tired typist to make sense of a strange syllable not to be found in any medical dictionary. Under "How Arrived," the notes always say "Via mo's arms"; under "Initial Diagnostic Impression," always "seizure disorder of unknown etiology," and sometimes fever and pneumonia and infections of the middle ear; under "Insurance Coverage," always Medi-Cal; under amount paid by patient, always zero. Almost all the admission notes contain the phrase "language barrier." On one assessment form, a nurse's aide with a Hispanic surname has written, "unable to obtain parient speak no english." On another form, in the space marked "Communication Problems," another nurse has summed up the situation with a single word: "Hmong."

Foua and Nao Kao always knew exactly when a seizure was coming, because Lia knew. The aura, a sense of premonition common to epileptics and sufferers of migraine and angina, can take many forms, from mildly peculiar sensations—sudden tastes or smells, tingling, flushing, *déjà vu*, *jamais vu* (the feeling that an experience is utterly unfamiliar)—to mortal terror. Physicians in the eighteenth century called the frightening auras *angor animi*, "soul anguish," a concept any Hmong might recognize. Before Lia fell, she would run to her parents to be hugged. She also demanded plenty of hugs from them when she was feeling fine, but they recognized these occasions as different because she had a strange, scared expression, and they would gently pick her up and lay her on the mattress they kept for this purpose on the floor of their living room (which was otherwise unfurnished). Sometimes there was twitching on one side of her body, usually the right. Sometimes she had staring spells. Sometimes she seemed to hallucinate, rapidly scanning the air and reaching for invisible objects. As Lia got older, the abnormal electrical activity spread to larger and larger areas of her brain and triggered more frequent grand mal episodes. As she lay face up, her back would arch so violently that only her heels and the back of her head would touch the mattress, and then, after a minute or so of rigid muscle contractions, her arms and legs would start to thrash. During the first phase, her respiratory muscles contracted along with the rest of her body, and she would often stop breathing. Her lips and nail beds turned blue. Sometimes she gave high-pitched gasps, foamed at the mouth, vomited, urinated, or defecated. Sometimes she had several seizures in a row; between them, she would tense, point her toes, and cry a strange deep cry.

In the most serious episodes, Lia would continue seizing and seizing without regaining consciousness. This condition, called "status epilepticus" when it lasts for twenty minutes or longer, is what the doctors in the MCMC emergency room feared most. Lia usually remained in "status" until massive doses of anticonvulsant medication could be administered intravenously. Inserting a needle into the vein of a baby who is having convulsions is like shooting, or trying to shoot, a very small moving target. While the hapless young resident who happened to be on call maneuvered the needle, he or she was always acutely aware that as each second ticked away during the phases of respiratory arrest, Lia's brain was being deprived of oxygen. When I asked one nurse whether this caused brain damage, he said, "If you want to know what a five-minute seizure is like, go stick your head in a bucket of water for five minutes and take some deep breaths." Over the course of several years, Lia was treated at least once, and sometimes many times, by each of MCMC's residents. Frightening as it was to be on duty when Lia was brought in at 3:00 a.m., there was probably no other group of family practice residents in the United States who by the end of their three-year program were so familiar with the management of pediatric grand mal seizures.

The residents were merely the first line of defense. Every time Lia came to the emergency room, either Neil Ernst or Peggy Philp, the two supervising pediatricians who served on the faculty of the family practice residency program, was paged and, no matter how late it was, drove to the hospital (a trip that could be accomplished, at just under the speed limit, in seven minutes). Peggy Philp was the physician Dan Murphy consulted during Lia's first admission to MCMC. The note she wrote six days after Lia's discharge read, in part:

> This is a very interesting young infant who presents with a history of right focal seizures. One leading to a grand mal seizure. I feel that probably the grand mal seizure caused an aspiration pneumonia and hence apnea, causing her extreme distress when she showed up in the Emergency Room on the day of admission. The child has apparently done well on her Dilantin, although she has continued to have some right focal seizures. . . . My feeling is that this child probably has some form of benign focal seizures of infancy. These are not especially common, but can often be quite benign in nature. Since there is apparently some chance that these will generalize, it is probably worth while to keep the child on Dilantin therapy to suppress a grand mal seizure. I would check the Dilantin level to make sure that it remains therapeutic. . . . I think that the prognosis for this child's intellectual development remains good.

Looking back on this optimistic document several years later, Peggy explained, "Most epileptics are controlled relatively easily by seizure medications. Lia's disorder turned out to be much more severe than what you usually see in classic epilepsy." Lia's chart eventually grew to five volumes, longer than the chart of any other child who has ever been admitted to MCMC, and weighed thirteen pounds eleven ounces, considerably more than Lia weighed when she was born there. Neil and Peggy once went through a photocopy of it with me. Over a period of several evenings, the two doctors worked with the same briskness and efficiency they would have brought to a patient's diagnostic examination, arranging the thousands of pages in neat stacks, rapidly discarding any they deemed irrelevant, never skipping over—in fact, often specifically pointing out—details that failed to put them in the best possible light, and stopping every once in a while to laugh ruefully at the chart's many errors. (The errors were invariably made by transcribers, nurses, or other physicians; their own contributions were flawless and usually even legible.) " 'She was seen to have lice coming out of her nose.' Lice. That can't be right. Ice? Mice? Rice! Shoot, that's what it is, rice!" Sometimes Neil would stop and stare at a page, often one that seemed anesthetically dull to me, and shake his head and sigh and say, "Oh God, Lia." When we looked through the records of Lia's first visits to the emergency room, he started to flip the pages back and forth with angry little slapping motions. He had forgotten that she had had epileptic seizures for five months before they were diagnosed and medicated, and was wondering in retrospect whether the course of her life might have been different if his hospital had offered her optimal medical care from the beginning.

Neil Ernst and Peggy Philp are married to each other. They alternate call nights, and each prayed that when a Lia Lee call came, it would be the other one's turn to roll out of bed. Neil and Peggy are both the children of physicians, both high school valedictorians, both Phi Beta Kappa graduates of Berkeley. They met when they were nineteen and eighteen, two tall, good-looking, athletic premed students who recognized in each other the combination of idealism and workaholism that had simultaneously contributed to their successes and set them apart from most of their peers. By the time their lives intersected with Lia's, they shared a practice and a half, as well as an office, a beeper, and a byline on the articles they had published in medical journals. Neil's curriculum vitae, which was flush with academic and professional honors, was the only one I have ever seen that noted Marital Status and Children first. Their schedules were arranged in such a way that one of them was always home in the afternoon when their two sons got out of school. Every morning, the alarm buzzed at 5:45. If it was Monday, Wednesday, or Friday, Neil got up and ran eight miles. If it was Tuesday, Thursday, or Sunday, Peggy got up and ran eight miles. They alternated Saturdays. Their runs were the only time either of them was entirely alone for more than a few minutes, and they never skipped or traded a morning, even if they had been up most of the night on call at MCMC. "I am a fairly driven and compulsive kind of person," Neil told me one night in the living room of their extremely neat ranch-style house, the care of which was evenly split between them. Peggy was on call at the hospital. "Peggy is very similar to me. We get along real well. *Real, real* well. Medically, we complement each other. My strengths are infections, asthma, and allergies. Peggy is strong in hematology and she's better than I am in child development. When you're confronted with a difficult decision, it's nice to talk to someone whose judgment you respect. Am I thinking okay? Would you offer anything else? Can I do anything else? If I feel like a dumbshit I can be a dumbshit with her. We don't have to impress each other. If she was not in my life it would . . . well, take a while for me to be able to function."

I once asked Teresa Callahan and Benny Douglas—a pair of married family physicians who trained as residents under Neil Ernst and Peggy Philp and who, like their mentors, now share a practice—what they thought of them. Teresa said, "It's hard to perceive them separately." Benny said, "I mean, like, Neil apostrophe n apostrophe Peggy is the way we think of them. Neil 'n' Peggy know everything and they never make mistakes. They are perfect. If we ever had problems all we had to do was call Neil 'n' Peggy and they would figure it out." Teresa said, "Neil 'n' Peggy are controlled, Neil especially, almost to a fault. I have even heard him say, about getting angry or crying, that he just doesn't feel comfortable doing things like that. But that doesn't mean he isn't compassionate. He prides himself on establishing a good rapport with his clinic patients, including some very difficult ones, some Spanish speaking, and most patients accept what he and Peggy say as gospel and do whatever they say. Few other people I know would have gone to the lengths they did to provide good medical care to Lia. They were always thinking about her. Whenever they had to go away, they'd tell all the residents, 'Now if this little fat Hmong girl comes in seizing. . . .' "

Lia was indeed fat. Her Physical Growth chart shows that although her height usually hovered around the fifth percentile for her age (not unusual for a Hmong child), her weight climbed as high as the seventy-fifth percentile. Her thick subcutaneous padding compounded the challenges that awaited the doctors in the emergency room. Neil Ernst wrote in a pediatric clinic note that in addition to her seizure disorder, "Lia's other problem, which is of considerable concern, is the fact that she is quite overweight, which makes intravenous access during the time of seizures quite difficult. Considerable effort has gone into weight control in this child. The father apparently likes Lia the way she is and is somewhat resistant to this problem." (In Laos, where food was often scarce, a plump Hmong child was perceived as healthy and especially well cared for.)

A vein hidden under fat is hard to palpate. Like a drug user who loses veins after repeated needle sticks, Lia eventually lost the antecubital veins in both forearms and the saphenous vein above her left ankle after doctors frantically searching for needle placement cut them open and tied them off. During most of her hospitalizations, the arm or leg with the IV line was bandaged to a board, and sometimes she was secured to her crib as well. "Lia's IVs were precious," explained Neil. "The less she moved, the longer the IVs would last." One Nurse's Note reads: "2400. IV infusing R antecubital space with signs of infiltration @ 30cc/hr via pump. Father here. Soft restraint to L arm. 0015. Father had untied restraint & placed child on cot on floor. Returned child to bed, soft restraint to R arm. Tried to explain to father reason but difficult due to communication barrier."

Nao Kao did not understand why the nurses had tied up his daughter. His confidence in their ability to care for Lia was further strained the morning after this note was written, when he left the hospital at 4:00 a.m. to catch two or three hours of sleep at home and returned at 7:30 to find that Lia had a bump on her forehead the size of a goose egg, the result of having fallen out of her crib during his brief absence. Not only had Lia gotten hurt while under the supervision of people who claimed to know more than the Lees about how to keep her healthy, but those people had then responded to the accident in a manner that, from the Lees' point of view, was inexplicably sadistic. Foua and Nao Kao believed the best way to keep Lia safe and content, especially when she was ill or in pain, was to have her sleep next to them, as she always did at home, so they could immediately comfort her whenever she cried. The nurses, however, decided to guard against future falls by rigging a net over Lia's crib and caging her inside, out of reach of her parents' arms.

"A hospital is a scary place for any parent," Vonda Crouse, a physician at Valley Children's Hospital in Fresno who is on the faculty of the Merced family practice residency program, told me. "You see people wake up your sleeping child to take their blood pressure, take their temperature, check their pulse rate, and count respirations. You see them put a bag on your kid to measure the output of urine and stool. When your child is in the hospital, suddenly somebody else is feeding them, somebody else is changing their pants, somebody else is deciding how and when they will be bathed. It takes all the autonomy of being a parent away, even for folks who have had a lot of medical experience. It would be that much harder if you were from another culture and didn't understand the purpose of all these things."

Aside from the time Lia fell on her head, one or another of her parents was almost always present around the clock during her hospital stays. Some typical Nurse's Notes: "Does not like to be separated from mo; relaxes when held by mo." "Is quiet as long as mom holds her, otherwise screams most of the time." "Child is happy & babbling, plays with toys. Mom here. Babe content." "Being carried papoose style by fa." "Mother here & breast feeds eagerly. Cruises sides of crib. Makes baby sounds." "Awake, walking around to the hallway with the father then returned to the room. Father trying to put her back to sleep." "Baby was in wagon sitting up and had generalized seizure lasting 1 min. Father grabbed her right away no injuries." "Mother holding. No seizures this shift. Up in mom's arms, waves 'Bye Bye.'"

The MCMC nursing staff came to know Lia well—better, in fact, than most of them would have wished. After she was old enough to walk, whenever she was well enough to get out of bed she ran up and down the corridor in the pediatric unit, banging on doors, barging into the rooms of other sick children, yanking open the drawers in the nursing station, snatching pencils and hospital forms and prescription pads and throwing them on the floor. "You'd hear that Lia was in the ER," recalled Sharon Yates, a nurse's aide. "Lia, Lia. Oh please, you'd say, don't let her up! But up she'd come." Evelyn Marciel, a nurse, said, "Lia was a pretty girl, soft and cute and fast. Her mother wouldn't wean her and she was real dependent on the breast. She was a little Houdini. She could get out of anything, and she'd hurt herself even if she had her wrists bound up, so you could never let her alone." "Her attention span was real short," said Gloria Rodriguez, a nurse. "We taught her to say bye, play patty-cake, smile, and clap hands. But she always wanted to be held, she always put her hands up to be carried because that's what her parents did. With other Hmong families the sons are the ones who are loved. Hmong fathers say, Girl okay if die, want many boy. But this family, they wanted so much for her to live, they just adored her." Many of the doctors remember Lia with affection because, unlike most of their pediatric patients, she was always physically demonstrative. "She liked skin," recalled Kris Hartwig, one of the residents who took care of Lia. "Even when I was trying to start an intravenous line, she'd be going pick, pick, pick at my arm. When you asked for a hug you could always get one from Lia." Peggy Philp said, "A lot of little kids, after being through all that, would just cry and hide in a corner or something, but Lia was very bold and she wasn't afraid of you. So you kind of liked her because she was a character, even though you hated her because she was so frustrating and she caused you so much grief."

Lia hated swallowing her medications. Some Nurse's Notes: "Meds given but did not like." "Tries to spit out Phenobarb when given. Lips pursed tightly to prevent this med given." "Fought taking medicine even crushed Phenobarb tablets in applesauce. Spits well." "Pt. very good at spitting out meds, given slowly with arms held & mouth puckered open." "Spit out popsicle with medicine crushed in, had to repeat dose with strawberry ice cream this time taken well." The Lees had an even harder time persuading Lia to take her medications than the nurses did, since they were reluctant to restrain her arms or force anything down her throat. And even when Lia was cooperative, Foua and Nao Kao were often uncertain about exactly what they were supposed to give her. Over time, her drug regimen became so complicated and underwent so many revisions that keeping track of it would have been a monumental task even for a family that could read English. For the Lees, it proved to be utterly confounding.

The anticonvulsant medication originally prescribed by Peggy Philp was Dilantin, which is commonly used to control grand mal seizures. Three weeks after her first MCMC admission, after Lia had a seizure in the hospital waiting room that appeared to be triggered by a fever, Peggy changed the prescription to phenobarbital, which controls febrile seizures better than Dilantin. Lia seized several times during the next two weeks, so since neither drug appeared to work adequately alone, Peggy then prescribed them both simultaneously. Consulting neurologists later prescribed two other anticonvulsants, Tegretol (which was originally to be used along with both Dilantin and phenobarbital, and then just with phenobarbital) and Depakene (which was to be used in place of all the previous anticonvulsants). Because lung and ear infections frequently accompanied Lia's seizures, antibiotics, antihistamines, and bronchodilating drugs were also prescribed from time to time.

By the time she was four and a half, Lia's parents had been told to give her, at various times, Tylenol, ampicillin, amoxicillin, Dilantin, phenobarbital, erythromycin, Ceclor, Tegretol, Benadryl, Pediazole, Vi-Daylin Multivitamins with Iron, Alupent, Depakene, and Valium. Because these medications were prescribed in varying combinations, varying amounts, and varying numbers of times a day, the prescriptions changed twenty-three times in less than four years. Some of the drugs, such as vitamins and anticonvulsants, were supposed to be given every day no matter how Lia was feeling, and when they ran out, her parents were supposed to renew the prescriptions; some, such as antibiotics, were supposed to be given for a specific period of time, and though they were prescribed only when Lia displayed certain symptoms, the prescriptions were to be finished (but not renewed) even if those symptoms disappeared; antifebrile medications, prescribed in the hope of warding off fever-triggered seizures before they happened, were supposed to be administered only if Lia had a temperature, a plan that might have worked better if her parents had been able to read a thermometer. Several of the medications were available in different forms, and were sometimes prescribed as elixirs (all of which were pink or red and came in round bottles) and sometimes as tablets (almost all of which were white and came in round bottles). Foua and Nao Kao, of course, had no idea what the labels said. Even if a relative or the hospital janitor was on hand to translate when a bottle was handed to the Lees, they had no way of writing down the instructions, since they are illiterate in Hmong as well as English; and because the prescriptions changed so frequently, they often forgot what the doctors told them. Measuring the correct doses posed additional problems. Liquids were difficult because the Lees could not read the markings on medicine droppers or measuring spoons. Pills were often no easier. At one point, when Lia was two, she was supposed to be taking four different medications in tablet form twice a day, but because each of the pills contained an adult dose, her parents were supposed to cut each of the tablets into fractions; and because Lia disliked swallowing the pills, each of those fractions had to be pulverized with a spoon and mixed with food. If she then ate less than a full helping of the adulterated food, there was no way to know how much medicine she had actually consumed.

At first, it did not occur to Lia's doctors that the Lees would fail to administer her medications correctly. The first few prescriptions simply read "Take as directed." In May of 1983, two months after Lia's first hospital admission, when a blood test showed a subtherapeutic level of phenobarbital in Lia's system, Peggy Philp assumed that the prescribed amount was being given, and raised the dosage. The next month, when the levels tested low again, she began to suspect that when Lia's mother said she was giving the medicines as prescribed, she was either confused or lying. This was a dismaying realization. The only way to determine the optimal type and amount of anticonvulsant medications for Lia was to observe the level of her seizure activity and repeatedly test the medication level in her blood, but the test results were inconclusive unless the doctors knew exactly what was going into her system.

"Lia continued to have seizures," said Peggy. "But was she having those seizures because she didn't have enough phenobarbital in her blood or was she having seizures in spite of having enough phenobarbital in her blood? And if the parents weren't giving what we told them to give, was it because they hadn't understood or because they didn't want to? We just couldn't tell." The absence of good interpreters was only part of the communication problem. Neil felt that Nao Kao put up a "stone wall" and was sometimes deliberately deceitful. Peggy felt that Foua was "either very stupid or a loonybird" because her answers, even on those occasions when they were accurately translated, often didn't make sense. Neither doctor could tell how much of their inability to get through was caused by what they perceived as defects of intelligence or moral character, and how much was caused by cultural barriers. Neil recalled later, "It felt as if there was this layer of Saran Wrap or something between us, and they were on one side of it and we were on the other side of it. And we were reaching and reaching and we could kind of get into their area, but we couldn't touch them. So we couldn't really accomplish what we were trying to do, which was to take care of Lia."

On June 28, 1983, MCMC asked the Merced County Health Department to send a nurse to the Lee home, accompanied by a Hmong interpreter, to try to improve the family's compliance with Lia's medication regimen. She was the first of a succession of public health nurses who were to visit the Lees over the next four years. One of the longest-lasting of them, Effie Bunch, told me, "The referrals were always the same. Febrile seizures, noncompliant mother, noncompliant mother, noncompliant mother, noncompliant mother, noncompliant mother. And the nurse's notes were always the same too. They always started out, 'The plan is. . . .' We all had a go at Lia and we all burned out." The visiting nurses tried putting stickers on the bottles, blue for the morning medications, red for the noon medications, yellow for the night medications. When Lia was taking elixirs, they tried drawing lines on the plastic syringes or medicine droppers to mark the correct doses. When she was taking pills, they tried posting charts on which they had drawn the appropriate pie-shaped fractions. They tried taping samples of each pill on calendars on which they had drawn suns and sunsets and moons. They tried putting the pills in plastic boxes with compartments for each day. Effie Bunch said, "I remember going over there and asking the mom to show me the meds. There they would be, a little stack of bottles in the kitchen next to the tomatoes and onions, sort of like a decoration in the corner. It wasn't hard to tell that the parents were really unhappy with the medical care. Because Lia was on such high doses, she had an appointment with Dr. Philp or Dr. Ernst almost every week and had a blood level drawn two or three days before and maybe another blood level two or three days afterwards, and there were so many changes that it was just totally mind-boggling. I don't think the mom and dad ever truly understood the connection between a seizure and what it did to the brain. And I don't know how else you get through to them that they have to give the meds. My general impression was that they really felt we were all an intrusion and that if they could just do what they thought best for their child, that child would be fine. They were courteous and they were obstinate. They told us what we wanted to hear. What we really knew about them wouldn't fill the bottom of a cup."

When Lia was between the ages of one and two, some of the notes the visiting nurses wrote on Merced County Health Department Encounter Forms were:

Home visit made with interpreter. Parents state infant is doing the same. Were unaware of appt. @ Peds clinic for today. Were confused about proper dosage of medicine and which to give. . . . Several meds in refrigerator that are outdated included Amoxil and Ampicillin. Also one bottle of medication with illegible label. Dr. Ernst contacted concerning correct dosage of Phenobarb and Dilantin. Correct administration demonstrated. Outdated medication discarded.

Mother states she went to MCMC as scheduled for blood test, but without interpreter was unable to explain reason for being there and could not locate the lab. Is willing to have another appt. rescheduled. States infant has not had any seizures. Have finished antibiotic. Are no longer giving Phenobarb because parents insist it causes diarrhea shortly after administration. Mother states she feels intimidated by MCMC complex but is willing to continue treatment there.

Reluctant to give meds but has been giving Phenobarb & Tegretol but refuses to give Dilantin. State it changes child's "spirit" & makes face look different. . . . Each drug is in small compartment with appropriate day & time but medications gone from wrong day.

Home visit again with interpreter who explained to the mother the importance of giving all 3 medications daily at correct times (mother has wall plaque which visually demonstrates type of med, amt & time to give medication) & possible results of return of seizures if meds not given. Mother seems to understand & states she'll continue to give Phenobarb & Tegretol but only 25 mg. of Dilantin AM & PM instead of 25 mg. at AM & 50 mg. PM. Agree to have continued care at Peds clinic.

Home visit made with interpreter. Didn't have Medi-Cal card for child so didn't go to clinic. Doesn't know where Medi-Cal cards are. Mother has now decided to give 200 mg. Tegretol AM, 25 Dilantin in AM and 60 mg. Phenobarb at night. Mother seems very agitated.

Father out of house for rest of day—shopping. Mother still seems very unhappy with medical staff making decisions for daughter. Interpreter states mother *is* unhappy and Public Health nurse observed same by mothers tone of voice & body movements. Assured mother that child can be seen in Peds clinic Monday even without the Medi-Cal card.

Home visit by interpreter to discuss childs care with father. Interpreter states father also mistrusts medical system & wants another opinion but didn't state who or where.

Mother states they just returned from hospital that AM. . . . Diagnosis for hospitalization unknown to mother but antibiotic prescribed. Mother says she gave client Tegretol & Phenobarb this AM but that she feels there is no reason to give them as they don't do anything and that the Dilantin (previously prescribed) caused the child to be wild.

It did not take long for the public health nurses to answer Peggy Philp's question about whether the Lees were being noncompliant because they hadn't understood the instructions or because they didn't want to give the drugs. (Both.) Their faith in medicines had not been strengthened by two routine immunizations Lia had received against diphtheria, pertussis, and tetanus, to which, like many children, she had reacted with a fever and temporary discomfort. All of Lia's anti-convulsant drugs had far more serious and longer-lasting side effects. In some cases phenobarbital can cause hyperactivity—it may have been responsible for the riotous energy the nurses always noticed when Lia was hospitalized—and, in several recent studies, it has been associated with lowered I.Q. scores. Dilantin can cause hair to grow abnormally all over the body, and gum tissue to bleed and puff out over the teeth. Too much phenobarbital, Dilantin, or Tegretol can cause unsteadiness or unconsciousness. Although Foua and Nao Kao erroneously attributed Lia's "wildness" to the Dilantin instead of the phenobarbital, they were correct in perceiving that the medicines were far from innocuous. From that point, it was not an enormous leap to the conclusion they had reached by April 3, 1984, when a public health nurse noted, "Father had become more and more reluctant to give medications at all because he feels that the medicines are causing the seizures and also the fever."

The idea that the drugs prescribed to cure, or at least attempt to treat, an illness are in fact *causing* it is not one that most doctors ever encounter. Doctors are used to hearing patients say that drugs make them feel bad, and indeed the unpleasant side effects of many medications are one of the main reasons that patients so often stop taking them. But most patients accept the doctor's explanation of why they got sick in the first place, and even if they resist the recommended treatment, they at least believe their doctor has prescribed it in good faith and that it is not designed to hurt them. Doctors who deal with the Hmong cannot take this attitude for granted. What's more, if they continue to press their patients to comply with a regimen that, from the Hmong vantage, is potentially harmful, they may find themselves, to their horror, running up against that stubborn strain in the Hmong character which for thousands of years has preferred death to surrender.

John Aleman, a family physician in Merced, once hospitalized a Hmong infant with severe jaundice. In order to determine whether therapy with special fluorescent lights would be sufficient or whether it would be necessary to perform a partial exchange transfusion, he had to take repeated blood samples to measure the baby's bilirubin level. After two or three samples, the parents said their baby might die if any more blood was removed. The doctor explained through an interpreter that the body is capable of manufacturing new blood, and he poured one cc of water into a teaspoon to demonstrate what an insignificant amount was being taken. To his amazement, his logical arguments only strengthened the parents' opposition. They said if the doctor drew any more blood against their will, they would both commit suicide. Fortunately, at this point Dr. Aleman asked his Hmong interpreter what he should do (a strategy not open to Lia's doctors during her early years, since no competent interpreter was available). The interpreter volunteered to call a Western-educated Hmong leader who was likely to understand the doctor's treatment plan; the leader called the head of the family's clan; the head of the clan called the father's father; the father's father called the father; the father talked to the mother; and, having thus received the request through a familiar and acceptable hierarchy, the parents were able to back down without loss of face. The baby had the blood tests and was successfully treated with phototherapy.

In 1987, Arnie Vang, a two-year-old Hmong boy who lived in

Fresno, was diagnosed at Valley Children's Hospital with testicular cancer. (Arnie's real name, the one conferred in his *hu plig* ceremony, was Tong, but his father preferred to call him Arnie because it sounded more American.) His parents, both teenagers who had attended American high schools and spoke and read English fairly well, consented, though reluctantly, to the surgical removal of the affected testis. After the surgery, Arnie's doctor, an Indian-born oncologist who had never had a Hmong patient before, explained that the next step was a course of chemotherapy. She handed the parents a piece of paper on which she had typed the names of the drugs he would receive and their possible side effects. Her predictions turned out to be accurate. Arnie, who had appeared perfectly healthy after his surgery, lost all his shiny black hair within three weeks after his first cycle of chemotherapy, and every time the drugs were administered, he vomited. Arnie's parents concluded that the chemotherapy was making him sick and refused to bring him in for further treatment. After giving the Vangs three days' warning, his doctor called Child Protective Services, the state agency that deals with child abuse, which dispatched two social workers and two police officers to their house.

Arnie's mother, Dia Xiong, explained to me later, "When they come, my husband isn't there. I say, Wait for my husband. But they say they can't wait. I say, Please that you go away. I hold my son. I hold him so tight. I say, Give my son back. Two police, they hold my hand behind my back. I can't move. I am scared. My two daughters are crying. The police hold my hand, they take my son away! I scream and cry. Then I take my husband's guns from the bedroom closet. They were two long guns. We bought them to shoot squirrels and deer, not to shoot people. I say I will kill myself and the little girls if they don't bring him back. I just yell, Please bring my son back to me. I say, Just bring! I want to hold my son!" A SWAT team was summoned, and for three hours the Vangs' immediate neighborhood was closed to traffic. Finally some police officers brought Arnie back from the hospital, and when Dia Xiong saw him, she dropped the guns and was driven, in handcuffs, to the psychiatric unit of a local hospital. She was released the next day, and no criminal charges were filed against her. Arnie's doctor administered one of the three remaining cycles of chemotherapy, but agreed, although it was against standard protocol, to forgo the last two. Arnie is still in remission today. His doctor was haunted for years by the thought that three lives were nearly lost in order to save one—"and for that one life," she told me, her voice shaking and her eyes filling with tears, "the cure wasn't even a hundred percent certain."

One night, while Lia Lee was in the emergency room at MCMC for the umpteenth time and a translator was present, Dan Murphy, who happened to be on call, brought up the subject of her anticonvulsant medications. Her mother informed him that she didn't think you should ever have to give a medicine forever. (It is likely that the only Western drugs Foua and Nao Kao had encountered in Asia were fast-acting antibiotics.) Dan recalled, "I remember that I was just watching them and they looked very resolute, like, you know, we are doing what we think is right. They weren't about to take any garbage. I felt they really cared for Lia, and they were doing the best, the absolute best they knew how as parents, to take care of the kid. That is what I felt about them. I don't remember having a feeling of anger, but I remember having a little bit of a feeling of awe at how differently we looked at the world. It was very foreign to me that they had the ability to stand firm in the face of expert opinion. Neil and Peggy are easily the best pediatricians in the county, yet Lia's parents didn't hesitate to say no to them or modify the drug dosage or do things however they saw fit. And the other thing that was different between them and me was that they seemed to accept things that to me were major catastrophes as part of the normal flow of life. For them, the crisis was the *treatment*, not the epilepsy. I felt a tremendous responsibility to stop the seizures and to make sure another one never happened again, and they felt more like these things happen, you know, not everything is in our control, and not everything is in your control."

Soon after this encounter, in the late afternoon of January 20, 1984, Dan Murphy was on call again when Lia came to the emergency room in the throes of a grand mal seizure. Among the notes he dictated were: "The patient is an 18-month-old Hmong child with a long history of seizures. The parents report that they had discontinued the medications about 3 months ago because the patient was doing so well." Dan did not have much time to reflect on this alarming news, because shortly after he started Lia's phenobarbital IV and admitted her to the hospital, he was called to assist at another emergency room crisis in which the patient died, and, immediately thereafter, he was summoned to the obstetrical unit to deliver a baby. At 11:20 p.m., in the thirteenth hour of a thirty-three-hour shift, Dan was paged because Lia had started seizing again, this time violently. Since Lia had responded well to the phenobarbital, Dan had not summoned Neil Ernst or Peggy Philp to the hospital. He therefore had to deal on his own with the most severe episode of status epilepticus Lia had yet suffered. He administered two more massive doses of phenobarbital. "Sometimes you have to give so much medicine to stop the seizure that they stop breathing," said Dan. "That happened." Lia turned blue. First Dan gave her mouth-to-mouth resuscitation, and when she failed to resume breathing on her own, he decided that a breathing tube had to be placed down her trachea. "Lia was only the second child I had ever intubated under crash circumstances, and I didn't feel all that confident. You have this instrument that looks sort of like a flashlight, with a blade that snaps down, and you have to get the tongue out of the way, and the problem is that if you don't know exactly what you are doing, instead of putting the tube down the trachea you put it down the esophagus, and you start to ventilate but the patient is not getting any oxygen. So it's literally a do-or-die situation, either you get it in and they do okay or you don't and they might die. This time I saw what I needed to see and the tube went right in and it worked perfectly and I felt really good. I thought, well, I guess I am becoming a doctor."

Lia's parents were standing outside the ward while Dan intubated Lia. "By the time they came back in, she was unconscious and she had this tube taped to her mouth. I remember that they were very upset about that. I remember that the mother just had a very displeased look on her face." Because MCMC was not equipped with a respirator for babies, Dan decided that Lia, who was being given oxygen on a temporary basis through a manually operated bag, should be transferred by ambulance to their pediatric backup facility, Valley Children's Hospital in Fresno, sixty-five miles south of Merced. She regained consciousness there, and was able to breathe on her own after twenty-four hours on a respirator. Lia spent nine days in Fresno, spiking high temperatures from aspiration pneumonia and gastroenteritis, but did not seize again. On her History and Physical Examination form, her name is listed as Lai Lee; on her discharge summary, she is Lee Lei.

Through an English-speaking cousin who accompanied Foua and Nao Kao to Fresno, the admitting resident was told that Lia had been off medications for one week (rather than the three months recorded by Dan Murphy) because the prescription had run out and the family had not refilled it. The resident wrote, without irony, "I am not entirely sure if all the history is reliable."

Two months later, Peggy Philp noted in an Ambulatory Care Physician's Report that Lia, who was then twenty months old, had "no words (altho used to say sev. words)." In her diagnosis, she wrote "?Dev. delay"—a conclusion she had dreaded reaching for some time. It is not surprising that a child who had seized as frequently and severely as Lia was beginning to show the first signs of retardation, but Neil and Peggy found the situation particularly tragic because they considered it preventable. Looking into Lia's future, they foresaw a steady decrease in intellectual capacity unless the Lees started giving Lia her anticonvulsants regularly—and even that might not halt the decline, since the brain damage resulting from her erratic medication regimen had already made her seizure disorder far less tractable than it would have been if compliance had been perfect from the start. Neil and Peggy perceived Lia as being more retarded (though still only mildly so) than the visiting public health nurses did. Effie Bunch said, "The doctors only saw her when she was sick and never in her home environment. When we saw her, sometimes she was a windup toy because of the phenobarbital and sometimes she was post-seizure and looked like a little ball of dough in the corner, but sometimes she was just bright and cute and actively playing, happy, gay, climbing, crawling, on her mother's back, laughing and chattering and what have you." Testing Lia's intelligence was difficult because her hyperactivity made it hard for her to focus on assigned tasks, and both the doctors' instructions and Lia's verbal responses were always filtered through interpreters of dubious competence. When Neil and Peggy administered a Denver Developmental Screening Test at fourteen months, the results were normal, but at twenty-two months, although Lia passed "Plays ball with examiner," "Plays pat-a-cake," "Imitates speech sounds," and "Neat pincer grasp of raisin," she failed "Uses spoon, spilling little," "Washes and dries hands," "Points to 1 named body part," "3 words other than Mama, Dada," and "Tower of 8 cubes."

When Lia was two, a consulting neurologist recommended that she be started on Tegretol, continued on Dilantin, and gradually weaned off phenobarbital because it was contributing to, or even entirely causing, her hyperactivity. Unfortunately, the Lees had now decided that they liked phenobarbital, disliked Dilantin, and were ambivalent about Tegretol. A visiting nurse once found Lia dazed and staggering after receiving an overdose of phenobarbital (which, though it can raise some patients' energy levels when taken in normal doses, has the opposite effect when taken to excess). The next day, when Lia was brought to the pediatric clinic, the resident on duty—who happened to be Gary Thueson, the doctor who had delivered her—noted, "Apparently parents felt if phenobarb was good 2x is better so double dosed yesterday." On July 20, 1984, Neil Ernst wrote in a Pediatric Clinic Note (a copy of which he sent to the Health Department):

> The mother states that she will not give the Dilantin at home. In addition, she also states that she has increased the child's Phenobarbital to 60 mg. b.i.d. Finally the mother states that she ran out of Tegretol and the child has received no Tegretol in the last 4 days. The mother brought a large sack full of medication bottles and on closer examination by myself there were 3 half empty bottles of Tegretol. The mother stated that she was unaware that these bottles were Tegretol. In addition, the mother also was unable to identify the Dilantin bottle and gave that bottle to me and said that she did not want it at home.

On rereading this note many years later, Neil said he could still remember the rage he had felt when he wrote it. He and Peggy, who are both aware, and even proud, of their joint reputation for glacial unflappability, couldn't remember another case that had made them feel this way. "I remember wanting to shake the parents so that they would understand," said Peggy. A handful of times, Neil gave Foua a hug while Lia was seizing, but most of the time, while Lia was between the ages of eighteen months and three and a half years, he was too angry to feel much sympathy toward either of her parents. "The best thing I could have given Lia's mother was compassion, and I wasn't giving her any and I knew that I wasn't giving her any," he said. "There was just too much aggravation. It was like banging your head against a wall constantly and not making any headway. There was the frustration of the nighttime calls and the length of time it took and the amount of energy and sorrow and lack of control. I mean, every time I saw Lia I would just, you know, it was like—ohhhhh, you would just get so frustrated! When she came to the emergency room in status there would be sort of like a very precipitous peak of anger, but it was quickly followed by the fear of having to take care of a horribly sick child who it was very difficult to put an IV in." Peggy added, "Some of the anger came from that. From our own fear."

It was hard to work so hard and not receive a single word of thanks—in fact, to have their efforts invariably greeted with resentment. Neil and Peggy never dwelled on the financial aspects of the case, since one of the reasons they chose to work in Merced was, in Neil's words, "to serve underserved people regardless of their form of payment." But it was an undeniable fact that Lia's family had never paid a penny for the hundreds of hours of care she had received—and yet failed utterly to appreciate the generosity of Medi-Cal and of Neil and Peggy's services, which, because of the low level of reimbursements, were, in effect, partially voluntary. (No other pediatricians practicing in Merced at that time were willing to accept Medi-Cal patients.) The Lees also never showed their doctors the kind of deference reflexively displayed by even their most uncooperative American patients. It was as if Neil and Peggy's four years of medical school, their three years of residency, their awards, their publications, their telephone consultations with neurologists, even the hours they spent in the Merced Public Library reading old *National Geographic* articles about the Hmong, all counted for nothing. The worst aspect of the case was that as conscientious physicians and dedicated parents, they found it agonizing to watch Lia, as it would have been for them to watch any child, fail to receive the treatment they believed might help her lead a normal life. And it seemed as if the situation would never end. However frustrated they were, they never considered abandoning the case. Unless Lia died, they could see themselves driving to the emergency room in the middle of the night until she was grown up and had graduated to the care of an internist, with whom they already felt an anticipatory bond of sympathy.

In June of 1984, Neil and Peggy found out that Foua was pregnant again. They were appalled. This baby would be number fifteen; eight had survived. Foua's age was unknown—it was listed on her maternity registration form as fifty-eight, a number no one at MCMC seems to have questioned—but Neil and Peggy had assumed that she had already gone through menopause. "When we found out she was having another, we said, how could this happen?" Neil recalled. "This must have been the last egg that was possibly fertilizable, and it got fertilized. We were just dreading how this baby might turn out, that it might have Down syndrome and heart problems and that we were going to have to deal with *two* sick kids in this family. *Just* what we needed. Lia's mom refused to have an amnio. Not that she would have aborted anyway." Foua also vehemently refused a tubal ligation, a sterilizing procedure urged by a nurse who knew Lia and feared another Lee child might be born with epilepsy. She continued to breast-feed Lia throughout her pregnancy. On November 17, 1984, when Lia was two and a half, Pang Lee—a healthy, vigorous, completely normal baby girl—was born. After the birth, Foua breast-fed both Lia and Pang. She was exhausted and, according to a Child Welfare report, "overwhelmed."

On April 30, 1985, four days after Lia's eleventh hospitalization at MCMC, a visiting public health nurse found that the Lees were giving Lia a double dose of Tegretol pills, which they had stored in an old phenobarbital bottle. On May 1, the nurse noted that Lia's father "now refuses to give any Tegretol whatsoever." That same day, Neil noted that when Lia came to the pediatric clinic, "the family stated to me through the interpreter that they have stopped the Phenobarbital 5 days ago and the child apparently has received no Phenobarbital since hospital discharge. Mother stated that the combination of Tegretol and Phenobarbital was 'too strong' for the child and she decided to stop the medication."

Neil sent a copy of this note to the Health Department and to Child Protective Services. In it, he also wrote that

because of poor parental compliance regarding the medication this case obviously would come under the realm of child abuse, specifically child neglect. . . . Unless there could be some form of compliance with the medication regimen and control of the child's seizure disorder, this child is at risk for status epilepticus which could result in irreversible brain damage and also possibly death. It is my opinion that this child should be placed in foster home placement so that compliance with medication could be assured.

The Superior Court of the State of California immediately acted on Neil's request, declaring Lia Lee to be a Dependent Child of the Juvenile Court who was to be removed from the custody of her parents.

6

High-Velocity Transcortical Lead Therapy

It was said in the refugee camps in Thailand that the Hmong in America could not find work, were forbidden to practice their religion, and were robbed and beaten by gangs. It was also said that Hmong women were forced into slavery, forced to have sex with American men, and forced to have sex with animals. Dinosaurs lived in America, as well as ghosts, ogres, and giants. With all this to worry about, why did the 15,000 Hmong who gathered on the Ban Vinai soccer field to voice their deepest fears about life in the United States choose to fixate on _doctors_?

A year after I first read the account of that gathering, as I was attempting to deal out a teetering pile of notes, clippings, and photocopied pages from books and dissertations into several drawerfuls of file folders, I had a glimmering of insight. There were hundreds of pages whose proper home I was at a loss to determine. Should they go in the Medicine folder? The Mental Health folder? The Animism folder? The Shamanism folder? The Social Structure folder? The Body/Mind/Soul Continuum folder? I hovered uncertainly, pages in hand, and realized that I was suspended in a large bowl of Fish Soup. Medicine _was_ religion. Religion was society. Society was medicine. Even economics were mixed up in there somewhere (you had to have or borrow enough money to buy a pig, or even a cow, in case someone got sick and a sacrifice was required), and so was music (if you didn't have a *qeej* player at your funeral, your soul wouldn't be guided on its posthumous travels, and it couldn't be reborn, and it might make your relatives sick). In fact, the Hmong view of health care seemed to me to be precisely the opposite of the prevailing American one, in which the practice of medicine has fissioned into smaller and smaller subspecialties, with less and less truck between bailiwicks. The Hmong carried holism to its ultima Thule. As my web of cross-references grew more and more thickly interlaced, I concluded that the Hmong preoccupation with medical issues was nothing less than a preoccupation with life. (And death. And life after death.)

Not realizing that when a man named Xiong or Lee or Moua walked into the Family Practice Center with a stomachache he was actually complaining that the entire universe was out of balance, the young doctors of Merced frequently failed to satisfy their Hmong patients. How could they succeed? They could hardly be expected, as Dwight Conquergood had done at Ban Vinai, to launch a parade of tigers and *dabs* through the corridors of MCMC. They could hardly be expected to "respect" their patients' system of health beliefs (if indeed they ever had the time and the interpreters to find out what it was), since the medical schools they had attended had never informed them that diseases are caused by fugitive souls and cured by jugulated chickens. All of them had spent hundreds of hours dissecting cadavers, and could distinguish at a glance between the ligament of Hesselbach and the ligament of Treitz, but none of them had had a single hour of instruction in cross-cultural medicine. To most of them, the Hmong taboos against blood tests, spinal taps, surgery, anesthesia, and autopsies—the basic tools of modern medicine—seemed like self-defeating ignorance. They had no way of knowing that a Hmong might regard these taboos as the sacred guardians of his identity, indeed, quite literally, of his very soul. What the doctors viewed as clinical efficiency the Hmong viewed as frosty arrogance. And no matter what the doctors did, even if it never trespassed on taboo territory, the Hmong, freighted as they were with negative expectations accumulated before they came to America, inevitably interpreted it in the worst possible light.

Whenever I talked to Hmong people in Merced, I asked them what they thought of the medical care they and their friends had received.

"The doctor at MCMC are young and new. They do what they want to do. Doctor want to look inside the woman body. The woman very pain, very hurt, but the doctor just want to practice on her."

"One lady, she is cry, cry, cry. She do not want doctor to see her body. But this country there is the rule. If you want to stay here you must let doctor examine the body."

"Most old people prefer not to go to doctor. They feel, maybe doctor just want to study me, not help my problems. They scary this. If they go one time, if they not follow appointment and do like doctor want, doctor get mad. Doctor is like earth and sky. He think, you are refugee, you know nothing."

"It took us an hour to see the doctor. Other people who are rich, they treat them really well and they do not wait."

"This lady she had some blisters inside the mouth and the doctor he say, you need surgical treatment. She say, no, I just need medication for pain only. And he say, I know more than you do. He completely ignore what she ask."

"My half brother his body was swollen and itchy, and the doctors say, hey, you got a cancer and we need to operate. He agreed to sign the operation but then he didn't want to do it. But he say to me, I already sign everything and the doctor going to send me to jail if I change my mind."

"Hmong should never sign anything at MCMC. The student doctors just want to experiment on the poor people and they kill the poor people."

"The doctor is very busy. He takes people that are sick, he produces people that are healthy. If he do not produce, his economic will be deficit. But the Hmong, he will want the doctor to calmly explain and comfort him. That does not happen. I do not blame the doctor. It is the system in America."

All of the people quoted here speak English, and thus belong to the most educated and most Americanized segment of Hmong society in Merced—the segment most likely to understand and value Western medical care. Nonetheless, their version of reality fails to match that of their doctors pretty much across the board. From the doctors' point of view, the facts are as follows: MCMC is indeed a teaching hospital, but this works to its patients' advantage, since it has attracted skilled faculty members who must constantly update their knowledge and techniques. The young residents are all M.D.s, not students. The Hmong spend a long time in the waiting area, but so does everyone else. Patients who change their minds about surgery do not go to jail. The doctors do not experiment on their patients. Neither do they kill them, though their patients do sometimes die, and are more likely to do so if, like the Hmong, they view the hospital as a dreaded last resort to be hazarded only when all else fails.

Although the doctors at MCMC are not aware of most of the Hmong's specific criticisms—they would be unlikely to ask, and the Hmong would be unlikely to answer—they certainly know the Hmong do not like them, and that rankles. The residents may be exhausted (since their shifts are up to twenty-four hours long, and until recent years were up to thirty-three hours long); they may be rushed (since many clinic appointments are only fifteen minutes long); but they are not—and they *know* they are not—greedy or spiteful. Most of them have chosen the field of family practice, which is the lowest-paying of all medical specialties, for altruistic reasons. "Of course, some of the subspecialists would say we went into family medicine because we weren't smart enough to be urologists or ophthalmologists," Bill Selvidge, MCMC's former chief resident, told me. "If we *were* urologists, we'd be making a lot more money and we wouldn't have to get up so often in the middle of the night."

Bill is an old college friend of mine. It was he who first told me about the Hmong of Merced, whom he described as being such challenging patients that some of his fellow doctors suggested the preferred method of treatment for them was high-velocity transcortical lead therapy. (When I asked Bill what that meant, he explained, "The patient should be shot in the head.") Bill himself did not seem to find the Hmong quite as exasperating as some of his colleagues did, perhaps because of the lessons in cultural relativism he had learned during the two years he had spent with the Peace Corps in Micronesia, and perhaps because, as he pointed out to me, the Hmong acted no stranger than his next-door neighbors in Merced, a family of white fundamentalist Christians who had smashed their television set and then danced a jig around it. (The neighbors' children had then offered to smash Bill's set as well. He had politely declined.) Bill was the sort of person I'd always wanted to have as a doctor myself, and before I came to Merced, I found it hard to believe that his Hmong patients weren't prostrate with gratitude.

When refugees from Laos started settling in Merced County in the early 1980s, none of the doctors at MCMC had ever heard the word "Hmong," and they had no idea what to make of their new patients. They wore strange clothes—often children's clothes, which were approximately the right size—acquired at the local Goodwill. When they undressed for an examination, the women were sometimes wearing Jockey shorts and the men were sometimes wearing bikini underpants with little pink butterflies. They wore amulets around their necks and cotton strings around their wrists (the sicker the patient, the more numerous the strings). They smelled of camphor, mentholatum, Tiger Balm, and herbs. When they were admitted to the hospital, they brought their own food and medicines. The parents of one of Neil Ernst's patients, a small boy with a gastrointestinal disorder, once emptied his intravenous bottle and replaced its contents with what Neil described as green slime, an herbal home brew whose ingredients the doctors never determined. Hmong patients made a lot of noise. Sometimes they wanted to slaughter live animals in the hospital. Tom Sult, a former MCMC resident, recalled, "They'd bang the crap out of some kind of musical instrument, and the American patients would complain. Finally we had to talk to them. No gongs. And no dead chickens."

Neil Ernst and Peggy Philp were shocked to discover quarter-sized round lesions, some reddish and some hypopigmented, on the abdomens and arms of some of their pediatric patients. They looked like burns. Some of the lesions had healed and others were still crusty, suggesting that the skin had been traumatized on more than one occasion. Neil and Peggy immediately called the Child Protective Services office to report that they had identified several cases of child abuse. Before the cases were prosecuted, they learned from a San Francisco doctor that the lesions were the result of dermal treatments—rubbing the skin with coins or igniting alcohol-soaked cotton under a tiny cup to create a vacuum—that were common among several Asian ethnic groups, and that they were a "traditional healing art," not a form of abuse. (I once attended a conference on Southeast

Asian health care issues at which a prominent doctor showed some slides of coin-rubbing lesions and told the audience, "It doesn't hurt." The young Lao woman sitting next to me whispered, "Yes it does.") Dan Murphy remembers that when he was a resident, he heard a story about a Hmong father in Fresno who was sent to jail after black marks were discovered on his child's chest by an elementary school teacher. The father hanged himself in his cell. The story is probably apocryphal (though it is still in wide circulation), but Dan and the other doctors believed it, and they were shaken to realize how high the stakes could be if they made a tactical error in dealing with the Hmong.

And there were so many ways to err! When doctors conferred with a Hmong family, it was tempting to address the reassuringly Americanized teenaged girl who wore lipstick and spoke English rather than the old man who squatted silently in the corner. Yet failing to work within the traditional Hmong hierarchy, in which males ranked higher than females and old people higher than young ones, not only insulted the entire family but also yielded confused results, since the crucial questions had not been directed toward those who had the power to make the decisions. Doctors could also appear disrespectful if they tried to maintain friendly eye contact (which was considered invasive), touched the head of an adult without permission (grossly insulting), or beckoned with a crooked finger (appropriate only for animals). And doctors could lose the respect of their patients if they didn't act like authority figures. The young residents at MCMC did not enhance their status by their propensities for introducing themselves by their first names, wearing blue jeans under their white coats, carrying their medical charts in little backpacks, and drinking their coffee from Tommee Tippee cups. Doctors could get into trouble if they failed to take the Hmong's religious beliefs into account. For example, it was important never to compliment a baby's beauty out loud, lest a *dab* overhear and be unable to resist snatching its soul. Similarly, when a seventeen-year-old Hmong patient once asked if her failure to get pregnant might be attributable to the *dab* who frequently visited her in her dreams, sometimes sitting on the edge of her bed and sometimes having sexual intercourse with her, it was fortunate that the resident on duty in OB-GYN Clinic listened with calm attention instead of diagnosing an acute psychosis and dispatching her to a locked ward. On the other hand, bending over backwards to be culturally sensitive did not always work. Bill Selvidge once examined a depressed middle-aged Hmong woman with severe headaches. Surmising that some of her problems stemmed from cultural dislocation and that her spirits might be buoyed by traditional treatment, he recommended that she see a *txiv neeb*. However, as he reported in his clinic note, "She is reluctant to go to a shaman, partly because she is now Catholic and partly because it takes too many chickens and/or pig that have to be killed in her home for her to satisfy shamans and traditional healers. She may have tried this in the past because she indicates a previous landlord told her to leave home after police were called when some members of her family were just about to sacrifice a pig." Disappointed, Bill prescribed aspirin.

Compared to the other patients that frequented Merced Community Medical Center, the Hmong were not only trickier but sicker. They had a high incidence of high blood pressure, anemia, diabetes, hepatitis B, tuberculosis, intestinal parasites, respiratory infections, and tooth decay. Some of them had injuries or illnesses they had acquired during the war in Laos or its aftermath: gunshot wounds, chronic shoulder pain from carrying M-16 rifles, deafness from exploding artillery shells. "And how long have you had these headaches?" asked one bored doctor. His Hmong patient replied matter-of-factly, "Ever since I got shot in the head." Another doctor, wondering if a Hmong patient's unusual neuropathies might have been caused by nutritional deficiencies, learned that while fleeing to Thailand the man had spent several months living in the jungle, subsisting largely on insects.

Before receiving clearance to be admitted to the United States, all Hmong, like other refugees, undergo medical screenings by physicians employed by the International Organization for Migration. The physicians must sign forms indicating that they have specifically examined the visa applicants for, and found them free of, eight contagious diseases (leprosy, tuberculosis, five venereal diseases, and, since 1987, positive antibodies for HIV) and eight mental conditions, including "Sexual Deviation," "Psychopathic Personality," and "Previous Occurrence of One or More Attacks of Insanity." Paul DeLay, the former director of the Refugee Clinic at San Francisco General Hospital, explained to me, "You get the impression that these problems are being carefully screened for back in Thailand. In fact, the exam takes approximately ten seconds. All you get is a blood test for syphilis and HIV, a quick skin check for leprosy, and a chest X ray for TB. Early on, you could buy a clear X ray on the black market. In '81 it got a little harder because the immigration officials started stapling a photo of the person to the X ray, but it was still possible. And despite what it says on the form, there's absolutely no screening for 'mental conditions.' In the early days, some medical person would walk down the aisle of the airplane and if somebody looked psychotic they'd be thrown off. So if a family was worried about their crazy relative they'd just load him up with opium so he'd fall asleep." DeLay pointed out that although few refugees are rejected for medical reasons, it is a terrible crisis for the ill person's family when this does happen, especially because once an applicant is "medically excluded" by one potential country of asylum, he is unlikely to be accepted anywhere else. "All of this means that the refugees have one more reason to be afraid of doctors," said DeLay.

Once a refugee arrives in the United States, post-immigration screening is not legally required, so although most states have refugee health programs, many Hmong choose not to be screened and thus encounter the medical system for the first time during an emergency. In Merced, new arrivals are voluntarily processed through the county's public health department, which checks primarily for tuberculosis and intestinal parasites. Though funding is too meager to allow more than a cursory examination during which the patient undresses only from the waist up, refugees who are pregnant or have glaringly evident medical problems are referred to the hospital or clinic.

Merced's health department is also responsible, according to its former director, Richard Welch, for "dealing with the problems no one else in the community wants to get their hands dirty dealing with." For example, when a rumor circulated in Merced that a Hmong family was raising rats to eat, a public health worker paid a call. "One of the children in the family had diarrhea, so the question was, did the rats have salmonella or shigella?" recalled Karen Olmos, a nurse in the health department's communicable disease program. "I told the worker, For God's sake, don't just barge in and tell them you want to see the rats! So she went over there on some other pretext, and there were the rat cages. She could see the rats were from the pet store, not the gutter—they were *big* whoppers. Instead of making the family feel bad about the rats, she simply suggested that they raise rabbits instead. Low start-up cost, high yield, high protein." On another occasion, the health department launched an investigation after sixty Hmong with diarrhea arrived at the MCMC emergency room. It turned out that for a major feast on a hot summer day, a pig infected with salmonella had been butchered, ripened in the sun for six hours, and served in various forms, including ground raw pork mixed with raw blood.

Although by the mid-eighties the regular staffs of the health department and the hospital had become inured, if not resigned, to dealing with the Hmong, each year brought a fresh crop of family practice residents who had to start from scratch. Avid for exotic medical experiences and hoping that, with its large refugee population, Merced might be sort of like the Peace Corps (but with good hamburgers), these new arrivals were deeply disappointed to find that their Hmong patients spent most of the time staring at the floor and speaking in monosyllables, of which the most frequent was "yes." After a while, they began to realize that "yes" simply meant that the patients were politely listening, not that they agreed with or even had any idea what the doctor was talking about. It was typically Hmong for patients to appear passively obedient—thus protecting their own dignity by concealing their ignorance and their doctor's dignity by acting deferential—and then, as soon as they left the hospital, to ignore everything to which they had supposedly assented.

When no interpreter was present, the doctor and the patient stumbled around together in a dense fog of misunderstanding whose hazards only increased if the patient spoke a little English, enough to lull the doctor into mistakenly believing some useful information had been transferred. When an interpreter *was* present, the duration of every diagnostic interview automatically doubled. (Or tripled. Or centupled. Because most medical terms had no Hmong equivalents, laborious paraphrases were often necessary. In a recently published Hmong-English medical glossary, the recommended Hmong translation for "parasite" is twenty-four words long; for "hormone," thirty-one words; and for "X chromosome," forty-six words.) The prospect of those tortoise-paced interviews struck fear into the heart of every chronically harried resident. And even on the rare occasions when there was a perfect verbatim translation, there was no guarantee that either side actually understood the other. According to Dave Schneider, who served his residency in Merced in the late eighties, "The language barrier was the most obvious problem, but not the most important. The biggest problem was the cultural barrier. There is a tremendous difference between dealing with the Hmong and dealing with anyone else. An *infinite* difference." Dan Murphy said, "The Hmong simply didn't have the same concepts that I did. For instance, you can't tell them that somebody is diabetic because their pancreas doesn't work. They don't have a word for pancreas. They don't have an *idea* for pancreas. Most of them had no concept that the organs they saw in animals were the same as in humans, because they didn't open people up when they died, they buried them intact. They knew there was a heart, because they could feel the heartbeat, but beyond that—well, even lungs were kind of a difficult thing to get into. How would you intuit the existence of lungs if you had never seen them?"

Hmong patients might not understand the doctors' diagnoses, but if they had summoned the courage to visit the clinic, they wanted to be told that *something* was wrong and to be given something, preferably a fast-acting antibiotic, to fix it. The doctors had a hard time meeting these expectations when the Hmong complained, as they frequently did, of vague, chronic pain. "I have a particular series of diagnostic questions I usually ask when a patient complains of pain," said Dave Schneider. "I ask what makes it better and what makes it worse? Is it sharp? Dull? Piercing? Tearing? Stinging? Aching? Does it radiate from one place to another? Can you rate its severity on a scale from one to ten? Is it sudden? Is it intermittent? When did it start? How long does it last? I would try to get an interpreter to ask a Hmong patient these questions, and the interpreter would shrug and say, 'He just says it hurts.' "

It has been well known since the aftermath of the Second World War that because of the enormous psychological traumas they have suffered, refugees of all nationalities have an unusually high incidence of somatization, in which emotional problems express themselves as physical problems. After dozens of gastrointestinal series, electromyograms, blood tests, and CT scans, the Merced doctors began to realize that many Hmong complaints had no organic basis, though the pain was perfectly real. Because so little could be done for them and because they were so depressing to be around, Hmong with "total body pain" were among the clinic's least popular patients. I once heard a resident try to persuade a physician's assistant to take over one of his cases. "No, Steve," said the assistant. "No, I do *not* want to see an elderly Hmong woman with multiple complaints and depression. I will take your coughs and your back problems, but don't give me one of those!" In order to show they were taking the complaints seriously, some doctors prescribed what they called "the Hmong cocktail"— Motrin (an anti-inflammatory), Elavil (an antidepressant), and vitamin B_{12}. But the patients did not usually get better. "For the underlying problems," explained Bill Selvidge, "there was no treatment that it was in my power to offer."

If Hmong patients left the Family Practice Clinic without a prescription (for example, if they had a cold or flu), they sometimes felt cheated and wondered if they were being discriminated against. But if they *were* given a prescription, no one knew if it would be followed. "You'd say, take a tablespoon of that," said Mari Mockus, a nurse at the clinic. "They'd say, 'What's a tablespoon?' " One patient refused to swallow a pill because it was an inauspicious color. Long-term therapy—for example, the doses of isoniazid that must be taken every day for a year to treat tuberculosis—was always problematic, especially if the illness was asymptomatic. Whatever the prescription, the instructions on pill bottles were interpreted not as orders but as malleable suggestions. Afraid that medicines designed for large Americans were too strong for them, some Hmong cut the dosage in half; others double-dosed so they would get well faster. It was always frightening for the doctors to prescribe potentially dangerous medications, lest they be misused. In one notorious case, the parents of a large Hmong family en route from Thailand to Hawaii were given a bottle of motion sickness pills before they boarded the plane. They unintentionally overdosed all their children. The older ones merely slept, but by the time the plane landed, the infant was dead. The medical examiner elected to withhold the cause of death from the parents, fearing they would be saddled with an impossible burden of guilt if they learned the truth.

When a Hmong patient required hospitalization, MCMC nurses administered the medications, and the doctors could stop wondering whether the dose was going to be too high or too low. There was plenty else to worry about. When they walked into a hospital room, they often had to run a gantlet of a dozen or more relatives.

Decisions—especially about procedures, such as surgery, that violated Hmong taboos—often took hours. Wives had to ask their husbands, husbands had to ask their elder brothers, elder brothers had to ask their clan leaders, and sometimes the clan leaders had to telephone even more important leaders in other states. In emergency situations, the doctors sometimes feared their patients would die before permission could be obtained for life-saving procedures. All too often, permission was refused. "They won't do something just because somebody more powerful says do it," said Dan Murphy. "They will sit back and watch and sort of mentally chew it over, and then they may or may not do it. That attitude has been very culturally adaptive for the Hmong for thousands of years, and I think that it is still culturally adaptive, but when it hit the medical community, it was awful."

Teresa Callahan once saw a patient in the emergency room who had an ectopic pregnancy that required the immediate removal of a Fallopian tube. "I told her over and over again that if the tube ruptured at home she might die before she could get to the hospital. I called her husband and her mother and her father and her grandparents, and they all said nope. All that mattered to them was that she would have one less tube and she might not be able to have kids after that, and when they heard that, it was no, no, no. She'd rather die. I had to watch her walk out the door knowing she had something that could kill her." (Several days later, the woman consented to the surgery after consulting a Thai doctor in Fresno. Teresa does not know how he persuaded her.) Another Hmong woman, examined shortly before she went into labor, was told that because her baby was in a breech position, a cesarean section was indicated. Although breech births in Laos often meant death to both mother and child, the woman attempted to give birth at home rather than submit to the surgery. The attempt failed. Dave Schneider was on call when an ambulance brought her to the hospital. "I got paged at 3:00 or 4:00 a.m.," he recalled. " 'Dr. Schneider, *stat* to the emergency room, there's a lady coming in with a breech baby that won't come out.' The paramedics came in wheeling this Hmong woman on a gurney. She was making no noise, just moving her head around in panic. There was a blanket partly over her. I have a very clear visual memory of lifting the covers to reveal a pair of little blue legs, not moving, hanging out of her vagina." Dave delivered the baby vaginally by manually stretching the cervix over its head. The mother recovered, but the baby died of oxygen deprivation.

Most Hmong women did go to the hospital to give birth, erroneously believing that babies born at home would not become U.S. citizens. Doctors were more likely to encounter them on the Labor and Delivery floor than in any other medical context because they had so many children. In the mid-eighties, the fertility rate of Hmong women in America was 9.5 children, which, according to one study, was "at the upper limits of human reproductive capacity," second only to the Hutterites. (The fertility rate of white Americans is 1.9 children, and of black Americans, 2.2.) This rate has undoubtedly decreased—though it has not been recently quantified—as young Hmong have become more Americanized, but it is still extraordinarily high. The large size of Hmong families is the inevitable result of two circumstances: Hmong women usually marry during their teens, sometimes as early as thirteen or fourteen, thus allowing their reproductive years to extend nearly from menarche to menopause; and, as a rule, they are highly suspicious of contraception. In 1987, when Donald Ranard, a researcher on refugee issues at the Center for Applied Linguistics in Washington, D.C., visited Ban Vinai, he learned that in an effort to curb the exploding birthrate of the camp's inhabitants, the administrators had promised free cassette recorders to women who volunteered to take contraceptive pills. Many women accepted both the tape recorders and the pills, but they soon discovered a marvelous paradox: the contraceptives, which they had probably never intended to swallow in the first place, were a superior fertilizer. So the pills ended up being ground up and sprinkled on Hmong vegetable plots, while the gardeners continued to get pregnant.

The Hmong have many reasons for prizing fecundity. The most important is that they love children. In addition, they traditionally value large families because many children were needed to till the fields in Laos and to perform certain religious rites, especially funerals; because the childhood mortality rate in Laos was so high; because so many Hmong died during the war and its aftermath; and because many Hmong still hope that their people will someday return to Laos and defeat the communist regime. In the refugee camps, Hmong newborns were often referred to as "soldiers" and "nurses." The frequent ap-

pearance at MCMC of Hmong women on the Merced public assistance rolls who were about to give birth to their eighth, tenth, or
fourteenth child did not endear them to those staff members who have
strong ideas about family planning. "I am totally disgusted by the
breeding rate," said Robert Small, an obstetrician who is well known
for his clinical proficiency, his unapologetic contempt for the Hmong,
and his propensity for mixed metaphors. "The Hmong breed like flies
as if the golden goose of welfare will continue to lay eggs forever."

According to Dr. Small, the Hmong are highly uncooperative obstetrical patients. "They don't do a damn thing you tell them," he
said. "They just come in late and drop it out. In fact, they wouldn't
come at all if they didn't need to get the birth certificate so they could
get more welfare. You or I, we can't conceive of the degree of ignorance. They're almost a Stone Age people. Hell, they never went to
a doctor before. They just had a baby in the camp or the mountains
or wherever the hell they came from." Because they were approximately as fond of most doctors as Robert Small was of them, Hmong
women who arrived in Merced in the refugee influx of the early and
mid-eighties tended to avoid prenatal care.* They were particularly
frightened of pelvic exams performed by male doctors. (In the Hmong
healing system, *txiv neebs* and herbalists, who do not touch their
patients, may treat people of the opposite sex, but in the more intimate sphere of dermal therapy—massage, acupuncture, pinching, coin
rubbing—men usually treat men, and women women.) Once they
were in labor, the women preferred to wait until the last minute to
arrive at the hospital. They often gave birth in the parking lot, the

---

* Most Hmong women, though more Americanized now, still avoid prenatal care
until at least the second trimester of their pregnancies. Several studies suggest
that their pregnancies usually have good outcomes nonetheless, with babies delivered at term, at normal weight, and without complications. Several cultural
factors—low rates of drinking and smoking, nutritious diets—work in their favor.
In addition, as obstetrician Raquel Arias explained to me, "Hmong women have
proven pelves. If you had an inadequate pelvis back in Laos, it was lost to evo-
lution. There was no one available to do a C-section for disproportion, so those
women died, and their pelves died with them. Also, Hmong don't marry Swedes.
They marry people who are genetically similar to them, so they are likely to have
babies that are the right size for their bodies."

emergency room, or the elevator. Wheelchairs at MCMC were called "Hmong birthing chairs" because so many Hmong babies were born in them en route to the Labor and Delivery floor.

Even if they got to the hospital on time, the women made so little noise during labor that the hospital staff, not realizing birth was imminent, often failed to transfer them from labor beds to delivery tables. A few doctors found this forbearance admirable. "We were told in medical school that childbearing is one of the three or four most painful things that can happen to a person," said Dave Schneider. "Most women scream. Hmong women don't make any sound at all. They are just remarkably, unbelievably stoic."

The obstetric nurses were less impressed by the silence of their Hmong patients. Dan Murphy explained, "The nurses' attitude was more, 'Why didn't they tell us they were about to deliver? What are they, stupid?' I think it was kind of a displaced anxiety. I don't think that they were angry at the Hmong so much as they were anxious because the Hmong didn't fit the pattern they had been trained to deal with." Some other ways in which Hmong women failed to fit the pattern included squatting during delivery and refusing permission for episiotomy incisions to enlarge the vaginal opening. Although Lia's mother, when she lived in Laos, had preferred to go through labor alone, many Hmong women were used to being held from behind by their husbands, who massaged their bellies with saliva and hummed loudly just before the baby emerged. The husbands made it very clear what they expected from the doctors. "One father slapped my hand when I was controlling the progress of the baby's head," recalled Kris Hartwig. "The nurses got very upset because he violated the sterile field. Then, as I was clamping the umbilical cord, he reached down and touched the cord and said, 'This is how long it has to be.'"

Because neither of the father's demands endangered the health of the mother or the child, Kris Hartwig complied. But what if a patient (or her husband or father or brother, who was more likely to make the decision) refused an episiotomy that her doctors believed would prevent an imminent fourth-degree laceration—a laceration that the husband or father or brother might then forbid the doctor to stitch up? Or, worse still, what if the fetal monitor indicated that the baby's heartbeat had dangerously decelerated, and the family refused to sign a consent form for an emergency cesarean section?

I asked Raquel Arias—by common consent, the MCMC obstetrician with the most dazzling combination of skill and empathy—what she did when the wishes of her Hmong patients conflicted with the standard of medical care she was accustomed to providing. "I have the same standard of care for the Hmong as I have for everyone else," she said. "My hands are just tied to provide it. So I give them suboptimal care. Sometimes you can find middle ground and try to understand where they are coming from, which is hard, but not impossible. Sometimes you can persuade them to do what you want. You keep telling them stuff and if you want it bad enough then maybe it'll work. It is when the well-being of the fetus is in jeopardy—a fetus that in our perspective is a full person who should have the rights and privileges that all citizens of this country have—and the beliefs and customs of the family seem to be going against what you believe is in the fetus's best interest, that you have the worst conflict. When that happens, it is an unbelievably terrible situation to be in. It is awful. It is not the kind of tension you feel when you get mad at someone from your own background who is doing something they know is bad, like smoking or drinking while they are pregnant. This is a different kind of tension because they don't know that they are doing something bad. According to their beliefs and principles, they are trying to protect the mother and the baby and their way of life. And what you think is necessary happens to be exactly the opposite of what they think is appropriate."

Listening to Raquel, I was struck, as I often was, by the staggering toll of stress that the Hmong exacted from the people who took care of them, particularly the ones who were young, idealistic, and meticulous. During Hmong labors that were going badly, Raquel bit her fingernails (which were impeccably polished with Purple Passion enamel) to the quick. Sukey Waller, a psychologist at Merced Community Outreach Services who was highly regarded in local Hmong circles, went through a period of throwing up before going to work each morning. Benny Douglas, a resident who was known for his imperturbable calm, was so upset by one problematic case (an elderly Hmong woman had gastric cancer, and Benny hadn't been able to persuade her sons to consent to her surgery) that he developed severe insomnia. I remember seeing Benny slumped forlornly in a chair, alone in the residents' call room at dusk, dictating his notes about Mrs. Thao into a little tape recorder while he drank cup after Tommee Tippee cup of coffee and reflexively picked at his eyelashes.

When I asked Dan Murphy why he thought caring for the Hmong caused so much stress, he said, "People in the early years of their medical careers have invested an incredible amount of time and energy and pain in their training, and they have been taught that what they've learned in medical school is the only legitimate way to approach health problems. I think that is why some young doctors go through the roof when Hmong patients reject what we have to offer them, because it intimates that what Western medicine has to offer is not much."

The only doctor I met in Merced who seemed untroubled either by his encounters with the Hmong, or by the question of whether he was providing optimal care, was Roger Fife, a family physician who served his residency at MCMC in the early eighties and then joined the staff of a local private hospital. Dr. Fife estimated that seventy percent of his clientele was Hmong, a fraction unequaled in any other practice in town. When I asked him why he was so popular, he was able to offer no explanation other than "Maybe I talk slower than the other doctors." His patients have no problem explaining. Every Hmong I asked said exactly the same thing: "Dr. Fife doesn't cut." On the whole, that was true. Dr. Fife generally did not perform epi-siotomies on Hmong women, though he did not know why they didn't want them, never having asked. He avoided cesarean sections when-ever possible, and he had particularly endeared himself to his Hmong patients by handing them their babies' placentas in plastic bags when-ever they requested them, though he had no idea what they did with them and said he had never been curious. Roger Fife is not held in high esteem at MCMC. "He's a little thick," one resident told me. "He's not the most intelligent graduate our program has ever had," said another. "He's an adequate physician," said a third, choosing his words carefully. Though I doubt that even the most ecumenical of Merced's doctors would wish to have *more* Hmong patients, still it must have been galling for these residents to realize that the Hmong community overwhelmingly preferred a doctor whose standard of care they believed to be inferior to their own. Roger Fife happened to espouse a philosophy that carried more weight with the Hmong than any degree of knowledge, intelligence, or technical skill. When I asked him why he didn't usually force his Hmong patients to comply with conventional American medical practices, he shrugged and said, "It's their body."

7

Government Property

Neil Ernst was a doctor of a different breed. It would have gone completely against his grain to apply two different standards of care to his patients: a higher one for the Americans, a lower one for the Hmong. But might Lia Lee have been better off if her family had brought her to Roger Fife? Might Neil actually have compromised Lia's health by being so uncompromising? That latter question still bothers him. For example, if Lia's prescriptions hadn't been changed so often, her parents might have been more likely to give her her medications, since they would have been less confused and more confident that the doctors knew what they were doing. Neil was pretty sure, however, that because Lia's condition was progressive and unpredictable, he could treat it best by constantly fine-tuning her drug regimen. If he had chosen a single pretty-good anticonvulsant and stuck with it, he would have had to decide that Lia wasn't going to get the same care he would have given the daughter of a middle-class American family who would have been willing and able to comply with a complex course of treatment. Which would have been more discriminatory, to deprive Lia of the optimal care that another child would have received, or to fail to tailor her treatment in such a way that her family would be most likely to comply with it?

A decade ago, that is not the way Neil looked at the situation. He never seriously considered lowering his standard of care. His job, as he saw it, was to practice good medicine; the Lees' job was to comply. Lack of compliance constituted child endangerment, which is a form of child abuse. He postponed calling Child Protective Services for as long as he could, giving Lia's parents every possible chance to reform, talking the case over with his wife nearly every night, worrying that "what happened in Fresno" might happen in Merced. (He and Peggy had both heard, and believed, the rumor about the Hmong father in Fresno who hanged himself in his prison cell after being unjustly arrested for child abuse.) Neil finally decided that he had no choice but to request that Lia be placed in foster care. Other options he has considered in retrospect, such as arranging for a nurse to visit the Lee house three times every day to give Lia her medicine or enlisting the help of Hmong community leaders to increase parental compliance, either seemed at the time to have insuperable bureaucratic obstacles or simply didn't occur to him. When I asked Neil whether, once he had made up his mind, he continued to brood about the effect his decision would have on the Lee family, he said, "Yeah, sure. I mean, you always do. But you get so single-minded about the child's welfare that you can pretty effectively suppress any kind of bad feelings you have about what you do to the parents. And there was another part—and here I am speaking for myself, not for Peggy—which is that I felt that there was a lesson that needed to be learned. I don't know if this is a bigoted statement, but I am going to say it anyway. I felt it was important for these Hmongs to understand that there were certain elements of medicine that we understood better than they did and that there were certain rules they had to follow with their kids' lives. I wanted the word to get out in the community that if they deviated from that, it was not acceptable behavior."

Once he had determined that Lia's parents were endangering her health, it was fully within Neil's legal rights to file a report with Child Protective Services. In fact, he might have committed a crime if he *hadn't* filed a report. Failure to report child abuse is a prosecutable offense in forty-four states, including California. Because physicians —along with other health care workers, teachers, day-care employees, and police officers—are especially likely to come across evidence of abuse, all fifty states have immunity clauses in their child welfare laws that protect these groups from civil or criminal charges after they file abuse reports, even if they are found to be wrong.

The fact that Lia's parents refused to give her the medications at least in part because of cultural or religious reasons (of which Neil was only hazily aware) would probably have cut little ice in court, even if the Lees had been savvy enough to try to defend their actions. If a child had not been involved, things would have been different. In cases involving competent adults, the principle of autonomy almost always takes legal precedence over the principle of beneficence, which means, for example, that a Jehovah's Witness has a right to refuse a blood transfusion, or a Christian Scientist a course of chemotherapy, even if he or she dies as a result. But with a minor, the state has the right—indeed, the obligation—to force the patient to comply with a life-saving treatment, even if it is forbidden by the family's religion. "Parents may be free to become martyrs themselves," wrote Justice Robert Jackson in a 1943 Supreme Court decision. "But it does not follow that they are free, in identical circumstances, to make martyrs of their children." Several parents who belong to fundamentalist sects have been jailed after the deaths of children whom they had attempted to cure with faith healing; no Christian Scientist has yet been imprisoned, though several have been convicted of involuntary manslaughter or child endangerment and sentenced to a combination of fines, probation, and community service.* If parents who practice these relatively mainstream religions have so consistently failed to sway the courts, it is doubtful that a judge would have been favorably impressed

---

* In 1996, the Supreme Court declined to review the civil case of *McKown v. Lundman*, in which an eleven-year-old diabetic named Ian Lundman slipped into a fatal coma after his mother, his stepfather, and two Christian Science practitioners prayed for him instead of administering insulin. The boy's father, who was not a Christian Scientist, had won a damages award of $1.5 million, the first ever obtained against Christian Scientists after a child's death. By refusing to overturn this award, the Supreme Court signaled its lack of sympathy for faith healing. Although popular opinion favored the Supreme Court and condemned the Christian Science Church, an interesting dissent was expressed in a *New York Times* editorial by Stephen L. Carter, a Yale law professor. Carter pointed out that according to a recent Gallup poll, four out of five Americans believe that prayer can cure disease, and nearly half say they have been healed by prayer themselves. He concluded sardonically, "By refusing to intervene in *McKown v. Lundman*, the Supreme Court has reinforced a societal message that has grown depressingly common: It is perfectly O.K. to believe in the power of prayer, so long as one does not believe in it so sincerely that one actually expects it to work."

had the Lees informed him that they were shamanistic animists who believed their daughter's illness was caused by the loss of her soul and could be treated most effectively by animal sacrifice.

Neil never had any desire to have Lia's parents prosecuted, and no legal action was ever taken against them. All he wanted was to get Lia out of their hands and into the stewardship of someone who would administer her medications exactly as he prescribed them. On May 2, 1985, she was placed temporarily in a foster home run by two Mennonite sisters who, whenever she became hyperactive, strapped her into an infant car-seat on the living room floor. After two weeks, she was returned home and her parents were given one last chance. Blood tests continued to show that they were giving her less than the prescribed dose of Tegretol. At this point, the Merced Department of Child Protective Services filed Petition #15270 with the Superior Court of the State of California, "In the Matter of LIA LEE, a Person coming within the Provisions of the Juvenile Court Law." The petition began:

> Your petitioner is informed, believes and therefore alleges,
> (1) That the above named minor resides at: 37 East 12th St., Apt. A, Merced, California.
> (2) That said minor is two years 11 months of age, having been born on the 19th day of July, 1982.
> (3) That said minor comes within the provisions of section 300 Subdivision A of the Juvenile Court Law of the State of California, as follows: Said minor is in need of proper and effective parental care and has no parent willing to or capable of exercising such care and control. Said minor is an epileptic with a complex seizure disorder, and the parents are administering sub-therapeutic medication levels. As a result of the parents' failure to comply with medication instructions, said minor has had multiple hospitalizations and severe seizures which have been life-threatening. The doctor states that said minor needs to be removed from the parental home at this time to preserve the life of said minor. There is a substantial danger to the physical health of said minor and there are no reasonable means by which said minor's physical health can be protected without removing the minor from her parents' physical custody.

It concluded:

WHEREFORE, your petitioner prays that this Court declare said minor to be a Dependent Child of the Juvenile Court.

On June 26, Lia was removed from her home again, this time for a placement of at least six months. Her parents were not notified in advance that she was going to be taken. When the CPS workers arrived, Foua was out of the house, visiting relatives. Several years later, Nao Kao told me, through an interpreter, what had happened. (He was under the impression that the social workers, who were accompanied by a Hmong interpreter named Sue Xiong, were police officers.) "The police came to take Lia away. Sue told the doctor that we didn't give Lia any medicine and that is why the doctors got mad and they came to take Lia away. I was very angry. I almost killed the translator. I said, This is my child and I love her. The police said for six months Lia is government property."

Foua told me, "When I came home my husband told me that they took the baby and he said that they didn't tell them where they took the baby. I didn't know any English so I didn't know what to think or what to say. I told my elder relatives, but they said, Well, if those people came to take her, then you can't do anything. I cried so much that I thought my eyes would go blind."

It was interesting to me that almost none of the MCMC residents—even those who had taken care of Lia many times in the emergency room and, years later, could recall the medical aspects of her case in minute detail—were aware, until I told them, that Neil had arranged to have Lia removed from her family. When they heard about it, every one of them disagreed with his decision, though none of them could suggest a better alternative. Neil had not deliberately concealed what had happened. It was simply not his habit to discuss emotionally charged topics, especially ones about which he felt apprehensive or ambivalent, with anyone but his wife. When I told Dan Murphy about Lia's placement in foster care, he was astounded. "Neil must have been just desperate to do something like that," he said. "That's the first time I've ever heard of a child being taken away from good caretakers. You know, it's usually somebody who is willfully harming their child, either through extreme neglect or through actually doing them damage, but Lia's parents really loved their kid. If *I* was in another country and somebody took my kid for reasons that

I couldn't understand, I would at least start considering violent alternatives, I really would."

In Merced's Hmong community, especially among the Lee and Yang clans, everyone knew about what had happened. The news of Lia's disappearance confirmed what many people had already suspected, that doctors were not to be trusted and that they were in league with other coercive authorities—a lesson of sorts, but not the one Neil had in mind. Long after the event, I asked Kia Lee and Koua Her, two Hmong interpreters who worked for the public health department, what they had thought of the matter. (Kia is a woman and Koua a man.) They both remembered it well. "Maybe they should not take Lia away," said Kia diplomatically. "Maybe this was not right. The parents not want to hurt the child. They try very hard to be good parents. They lost many child in Laos and they love this child very very much. In Laos, the parent have one hundred percent responsibility over the child. How can you say you can take it away unless it is orphan?" Koua said more sharply, "It was *not* necessary for CPS to take the kid. If they don't care about the kid, okay, but parents love the kid more than others in the house. The mother was crying and crying all the time. The father he was not crying, he was very angry. Hmong men do not cry even if you feel sad. In Laos, I never heard of this happening in my life."

In a master's thesis in anthropology called "Analysis of Cultural Beliefs and Power Dynamics in Disagreements About Health Care of Hmong Children," a Minnesota physician named Kathleen Ann Culhane-Pera summarized the Hmong attitude toward responsibility in pediatric medical cases:

> Hmong parents believe parents are responsible for the child's welfare and for deciding the child's medical treatment. Since parents gave birth to the child, provide for the child's physical needs, and love the child, they are the ones who decide the treatment approach for the child. Because family members love the child and are part of the family, they can assist the parents in making decisions about the optimal actions. Respected family lineage leaders also assist parents in making difficult decisions about serious conditions. But as physicians are not family members, they cannot make decisions for the child. . . . If doctors take over the parents' responsibility, and decide to treat without parental permission, then doctors are responsible for the consequences. If the child dies, it is their fault;

and how will they repay the parents? Indeed, how will they pay for the life?

As long as doctors and parents continue to negotiate, even if they disagree, the conflict is confined to differences in belief systems. "Once the police are called and court orders are obtained, however, the difficulties escalate to another level," wrote Culhane-Pera. "The differences are no longer about beliefs. The differences are about power. Doctors have power to call the police and to access state power which Hmong parents do not have." Because the Hmong have historically been so resistant to authority, they are especially confused and enraged when they are stripped of their power in a country to which they have fled because of its reputation for freedom. As one parent, whose sick child was forced to have a spinal tap after the doctor obtained a court order, told Culhane-Pera, "The way we feel, the United States is more communist than our country is." Another angry parent who had had a similar experience told her, "No matter how much we don't know about technology, about human health, physical, but we have seen a lot in experience too. I don't want any doctor to treat any human being like an animal. Animals, they don't understand, but human beings do, we do know how to talk. We do understand like anyone who is a human being. We are just refugees but we are human beings like any doctor too."

Once a child is removed from parental custody, Child Protective Services must file an explanatory petition within two days, and a detention hearing is usually scheduled for the day after the petition is filed. Nao Kao Lee appeared in court on June 28, 1985, accompanied by a public defender. No one remembers whether an interpreter was there as well. The judge approved CPS's petition to detain Lia; Nao Kao, who was unaware that it was permissible to object, is recorded as assenting. The plan detailed in the Disposition of Case #15270 called for Lia to remain in foster care for six months, the minimum time that Neil estimated would be needed to stabilize her seizure disorder. Her parents would be permitted weekly visits, though these did not start until she had been away from home for more than a month. In fact, following a policy, common at the time, that was intended to prevent distraught parents from immediately retrieving their children, CPS did not inform Foua and Nao Kao of their daughter's whereabouts for several weeks. According to Nao Kao, "After one month, I went to my cousin who speaks English and asked him to call the police and ask where Lia is because my wife was missing Lia too much and she was going crazy." Lia was to be reunited with her family after six months only if the court was persuaded that her parents would comply with her medication regimen. Child Protective Services was to work with them to increase that likelihood. If the court did not decide within a year that Lia could safely return to her family, the Lees would permanently lose custody.

It was the responsibility of CPS to find Lia an appropriate foster home. Her caseworker filled out a form for "Specialized Foster Care"—that is, care for a child with unusual medical or behavioral problems. Among the "Behavior Problems of Child" that she circled were: "Has had one or more violent episodes, causing minor physical injury within the last year." "Has caused minor [property] damage on six or more occasions within the past year." "Displays self-injurious behavior (biting, scratching) at least once a month." "Becomes aggressive or hostile when frustrated." "Does not participate in social activities." "Does not participate in group projects." "Is hyperactive in all environments." "Is resistive in all situations." "Has temper tantrums daily." The caseworker was to add up the points and rank the cumulative severity of the problem behavior on a scale from 40 (the best) to 70 (the worst). At 81, Lia's score was off the scale. The only categories in which she received favorable—indeed, perfect—scores were "No evidence of depressive behavior," "Responds to affection appropriately," and "Gives affection appropriately."

A day or two before Lia was removed from her home, Dee and Tom Korda, a couple living twenty-five miles northwest of Merced who had recently been certified as foster parents, received a call from CPS. "We've got a two-year-old Hmong girl with epilepsy," said the social worker. "Can you handle it?" At the time, Dee Korda had never heard the word "Hmong," had four children of her own, was pregnant with her fifth, and was taking care of another foster child, her first. "Sure," she said. Dee told me several years later, "I was so eager I would have taken anything they offered."

I was curious to meet the Kordas, because when I called Dee, the first thing she had said was, "How are Foua and Nao Kao? Don't you just love them?" Since at that point I had never heard an American say a good word about the Lees, and since I subscribed to the conventional wisdom that biological parents and foster parents are natural enemies, her question threw me somewhat off balance. When I arrived at the Kordas' rambling one-story house, which was in a dairy community dotted with peach and almond orchards, I was greeted by several large dogs that Dee and Tom, with the help of the five biological and six foster children, most of them retarded or emotionally disturbed, who were living with them at the time, were raising as canine guides for the blind. As we sat in the living room, Dee simultaneously showed me a small scrapbook full of pictures of Lia (she keeps one for every child she has cared for) and dispensed hugs to children of various sizes and races who wandered in and out.

After Lia arrived in the Korda house, she cried continuously for ten days. "Lia was the only child I've ever heard who could cry while inhaling and exhaling," said Dee. "In and out, loud and abrasive, on and on and on. I know she was crying for them, for her mom and dad, even though she didn't know the words to tell me. I'd find her curled in the bathtub, her face real worried and troubled and confused and sad. Sometimes she would pound at the door like a caged animal and shout, 'Na! Na! Na! Na!' Now I know that means daddy in Hmong." (In fact, Lia was probably saying *niam*—pronounced "nya"—which means mother; the word for father is *txiv*.) Because the Kordas spoke no Hmong, they had no way of comforting Lia verbally. The only thing that seemed to help was constant physical contact. During the day, Dee simultaneously carried Lia in a backpack and her own youngest child, who was nine months old when Lia arrived, in a frontpack. At night, Lia usually slept in the Kordas' bed, which was ten and a half feet wide, large enough to accommodate a substantial fraction of the household. When Lia was inconsolable, Dee, guessing correctly that she had never been weaned, breastfed her alongside her own baby. "If there was ever going to be a way, it was Lia's way," she told me. "That's what she was used to. Her family let her rule the roost at home because she was the special child, the princess. Oh, Lia could be ornery and strong-willed, but she was a sweetie too. She'd crawl on your lap. She was so beautiful. We didn't mean nothing to her at first, but she learned to love us. She knew how to love and how to let people love her. We were blessed to have Lia."

Jeanine Hilt, the CPS caseworker, frequently visited the Kordas during this period and kept a Welfare Services Contact Record that gives some idea of what the Kordas' less blessed days with Lia were like. Some of the entries:

> Lia's problems are very behavioral. Cries constantly. Real disruptive, real anger. Will cry non-stop 2-5 a.m.—kicking. Won't give in. Family is on edge.

> Tantruming. Withholds food. Looks at Dee, takes off her panties and pees.

> Pooping on floor now.

> Bit herself on lip.

> Lia crying 4 days straight. Smearing feces.

> Intense crying again. Stripped herself, peed on the floor, went on a wave of destruction. Had to sedate her.

Noting that Lia had "inflicted numerous injuries on other children ranging from bruises to cuts requiring stitches"; that she required constant supervision to keep her from "activities that she has previously experienced as harmful or dangerous, i.e., hot water, bathtubs, high places, swimming pool, etc."; and that the Kordas were providing an "extremely high level of care," Jeanine Hilt successfully petitioned the Department of Human Resources to pay Dee and Tom the unusually high fee of $1,000 a month for taking care of Lia. (The Lees had supported themselves and the seven of their nine surviving children who were living at home, including Lia, on $790 a month in welfare payments plus $84 that Lia, whose epilepsy had qualified her for disability funding, received as Supplemental Security Income.)

In her letter to the Department of Human Resources, Jeanine Hilt also noted that Dee Korda was taking Lia to between two and five doctors' appointments a week. Despite the fact that Dee followed the anticonvulsant prescriptions to the letter (a task that sometimes required holding Lia down and repeating the doses after she spat them all over Dee's clothes), Lia was still seizing. In fact, she seized more frequently at the Kordas' than she had when she was living with her own family. She was hospitalized four times at Emanuel Medical Center in Turlock, the town nearest the Kordas' home, and on one occasion was transferred from Emanuel to MCMC, which did not make a favorable impression on Dee. "The MCMC nurses wouldn't talk to her nice and soft," she told me. "When she soiled her bed, it wasn't Oh honey, it was My god what a mess. They'd tie both arms and both legs with cloth, like nursing homes use on old people. It was degrading." Lia's new doctors in Turlock changed her prescription several times, eliminating first the phenobarbital and then the Tegretol and substituting various combinations of Dilantin, Depakene, and Ritalin. According to Dee, the new regimens had fewer side effects. "Tegretol and phenobarbital were the worst combination for Lia," she said. "The *worst*. When she took them she was drunk, she couldn't navigate or walk. I think that's why her parents wouldn't give them to her. Then she'd have a seizure and everyone would get mad at them." Lia's coordination improved, but her seizures continued.

After they found out where their daughter had been taken, Lia's family visited her whenever their nephew, who owned a car, could give them a ride. The first time they visited, Dee showed them how she carried Lia on her back, just the way Foua did, and how Lia slept in the family bed. The Korda children lent the Lee children bathing suits, and they all swam together in the backyard pool. Pang crawled on the lawn with Dee's baby. Eventually, the Lees' twelve-year-old daughter May became friends with the Kordas' ten-year-old daughter Wendy, and once spent a whole week at their house. Foua embroidered a *nyias*, a Hmong baby carrier, for Dee. After a few months went by, Dee started leaving her own baby with Foua when she took Lia to medical appointments—perhaps the first instance in the history of Child Protective Services that a foster mother has asked a legally abusive parent to baby-sit for her. It did not take the Kordas long to decide that CPS had made a mistake in taking Lia away from her family (though CPS, when Dee told them so, did not agree). "I was attached to Lia, but she really needed to be at home," said Dee. "Foua and Nao Kao were so warm, so caring, and they loved that child so much. I'm bitter. They never should have been in the system." By the time I met Dee, she had taken care of a total of thirty-five foster children, most of whom had been severely battered or sexually abused by their parents. Lia was the only one for whom she had ever recommended reunification.

At the end of each of the Lees' visits to the Kordas' house, Lia tried to get in the car with them and screamed with panic when they drove away without her. Nao Kao told me, "The family really took care of Lia and really cared for her too, but maybe she missed us too much and that is why she got sicker. We missed her too. I do not know how to describe how we missed her." Foua said, "Our bed was empty without her. I loved her a lot and I had always held her during the night and didn't let her sleep by herself. I cried every night when I got in the bed and she was not there." Two months after Lia had been taken from her family, Nao Kao told the caseworker that he wanted to commit suicide if Lia did not come home. Four months after that, Nao Kao came home to find Foua pointing a knife at herself. He took the knife away. A month later, Jeanine Hilt's case log noted that Foua was hysterical and threatening suicide again. Child Protective Services considered placing the entire family in a psychiatric hospital, but decided against it.

Lia did not return home after six months, as the Lees had expected her to. On December 18, 1985, at the Six-Month Reunification Hearing, the court ruled that Foua and Nao Kao had failed to demonstrate their ability to comply with their daughter's medical regimen. First, they had refused to sign a Social Services Plan that had been presented to them in August, which stated, among other things, that in order for reunification eventually to take place, the Lees must agree to "make and meet medical appointments for our child, including appointments for routine care and illness, and learn how to properly administer her medication." A CPS worker wrote on the Plan, "Their feeling is that Lia should be returned to their care at once; consequently they declined to sign the agreement." Second, when Lia had been permitted a week-long home visit in September as a test of her parents' compliance, they had failed miserably. The CPS petition against reunification noted:

> The parents were again instructed, via interpreter, on the proper method of administering the medications. Color coded graphics were also utilized to reinforce the instructions. The parents stated they understood and

indicated that they would follow through immediately. During this visit the parents were allowed to have the minor treated by a Shamin [sic] from the Hmong culture. Home calls by social workers were completed during the time the minor was at home and the medications were checked and it appeared as though the medications were being administered. The parents report no seizures. Lia was returned to the foster home on September 9, 1985 and was hospitalized later that day. Blood level checks revealed that no traces of any medications were found in the minor's blood. Dr. Goel [Lia's pediatrician at Emanuel Medical Center] stated that the parents did not give Lia any medicine as the medication remains in the body for at least ten days. The medication vials were returned empty by the parents.

Jeanine Hilt wrote in her case log that when Lia returned to the Kordas, her chest was covered with coin-rubbing lesions. Foua and Nao Kao had obviously opted for traditional healing techniques and, as Jeanine noted, "trashed the meds." Four days after this home visit, Lia had three grand mal seizures and six petit mal seizures, after which her developmental deficits became far more pronounced. The petition stated that

language delays were noted, her motor skills regressed, she would not eat or maintain eye contact, and she engaged in repeated head-banging behavior. Lia also became encopretic [fecally incontinent], engaged in a variety of self-abusive behaviors such as scratching and biting, could not sleep, was abusive to other children, and lost all ability to recognize safe situations. These regressions were all related to the parents' failure to administer the medication while Lia was in their care. These regressive behaviors have continued.

Despite these setbacks, Jeanine Hilt was determined to try to continue to educate the Lees about Lia's medications so that they could regain custody before twelve months elapsed and they legally lost her for good. Jeanine spent dozens of hours working with Foua. Her task was aided by the fact that Lia's drug regimen was radically simplified in February of 1986. Dee had taken Lia to Valley Children's Hospital in Fresno for extensive neurological testing, where Terry Hutchison, a pediatric neurologist, reached a tentative diagnosis of Lennox-Gastaut Syndrome, a rare form of epilepsy characterized by mental retardation and several forms of hard-to-control seizures. Dr. Hutchison decided that Depakene, used alone, was the drug of choice. (Neil and Peggy had considered Depakene but had decided against it because it can cause liver failure; once Lia was started on it, they wished they had prescribed it themselves.) Pediatric Depakene is a liquid that tastes pleasantly of cherries, and it was far easier to administer than the complicated combinations of bitter ground-up pills Lia had previously been taking. Jeanine showed Foua how to use a plastic syringe to squirt the liquid into Lia's mouth, placing a piece of masking tape at the 8-cc mark because Foua couldn't read numbers. Foua practiced with water until she was proficient, then graduated to Depakene.

Jeanine felt that Foua was slowly learning to trust her and was making good progress. She did not develop a similarly intimate relationship with Nao Kao, who continued to fear that Lia would never come home. He was wary of Jeanine, but he was not angry at her. His rage was reserved for Sue Xiong, the interpreter who had accompanied the CPS workers on the day of Lia's original detention. Sue Xiong, a sophisticated, well-educated Hmong woman who had married an American, was not a popular figure in Merced's traditional Hmong community. Intermarriage is rare among the Hmong. According to Jeanine Hilt, "Culturally Sue was pretty white, and she dressed real cute and was not at home having babies and sustaining the Hmong culture very well, so a lot of Hmong really saw her as selling out." Sue Xiong once told Nao Kao that she had informed CPS she did not think he should get his daughter back. In February of 1986, when Lia was at Valley Children's Hospital in Fresno, Nao Kao says Sue Xiong scolded him, and he became convinced that she was not accurately translating his statements to the doctors. The next day, back in Merced, Jeanine Hilt, Sue Xiong, and a CPS supervisor came to the Lee house. Nao Kao told me, "I was outside and Sue came inside and she called me and said, Come in here, you come in here. At that time, I was ready to hit Sue, and I got a baseball bat right there. My son-in-law was with me, and he grabbed me and told me not to do it. The supervisor and Jenny [Jeanine] asked what's the matter, and my son-in-law translated what I was saying, and I said I did not like Sue and I was going to beat Sue to death right there that day. And then Sue said that she had a lot of work to do, so she left. I told the supervisor, This person is not good. Do not bring her here anymore. If you bring her here again, I'm going to get a gun and shoot her." (When I called

Sue Xiong to ask her about this incident, at first she told me—in the most elegant English I had ever heard a Hmong speak—that she could not recall either the argument or the Lee family, which I found surprising, since I knew that before she married her American husband she had been married to Nao Kao's nephew. Finally she said, "The family didn't appreciate my services, so I didn't want to be involved anymore.")

It is a credit to Jeanine Hilt's faith in the Lees that Sue Xiong's near encounter with Nao Kao's baseball bat did not permanently disqualify them from regaining custody of their daughter. The way Jeanine saw it, Nao Kao had plenty of reasons to be angry, and as long as he didn't take out his anger in the form of medical noncompliance, it should not interfere with the reunification of his family. Starting on February 18, 1986, the Lees were permitted to keep Lia for a series of overnight visits under Jeanine's supervision. Blood tests showed they had administered adequate levels of Depakene. In the petition CPS filed at Lia's Twelve-Month Reunification Hearing, Jeanine Hilt wrote:

As the Lees' skill increased, the visits were extended. The undersigned provided extensive supervision three times daily while the minor was in the home. Supervision decreased as the Lees demonstrated their willingness to maintain the medication regime. . . . The undersigned has worked with the Lees on maintaining a daily schedule including proper diet, naps, and discipline. . . . Mr. and Mrs. Lee are to be commended for their cooperation and positive efforts in working with the undersigned in spite of their divergent cultural beliefs. As a result of their hard work, trust in the physician [neurologist Terry Hutchison], and the undersigned, we have made incredible headway in resolving Lia's serious medical problem.

Lia returned home on April 30, 1986.

8

Foua and Nao Kao

In 1988, during my first few weeks in Merced, seven doctors at the Merced Community Medical Center separately mentioned the case of Lia Lee to me, but each of them told me it was not worth investigating, because her parents mistrusted Americans and would almost certainly refuse to let me see Lia's medical and legal records, or to talk with me themselves. Even if they agreed to meet me, I was assured that I would find them silent, obtuse, and almost pathologically lacking in affect.

I was ready to be discouraged. Before I came to Merced, I had never met a Hmong, but I had received plenty of advice from anthropologists I'd read or consulted on what to do when I did: Don't raise your voice. Take off your shoes. Don't offer to shake hands with a man or people will think you're a whore. If a man offers to shake hands with *you*, indicate your lower status by placing your left hand under your right wrist in order to support the weight of his honored and important hand. If you walk with a Hmong leader, stay behind him and to his left. Use an older male interpreter to compensate for your lack of status as a younger woman. Don't ever say no to an offer of food, even if it's chicken feet.

It did not seem a promising sign that my friend Bill Selvidge, the doctor who had invited me to Merced to meet his Hmong patients, had bookshelves jammed with ethnographic monographs on the Ik, the !Kung, and the Palauans, but during his two years in Merced had never had an extended conversation with a Hmong over the age of fourteen, had never been invited inside a Hmong home, and had learned only one word of Hmong: *mob* ("it hurts"). If an anthropologically inclined Peace Corps veteran had made so little headway, how could I expect to get anywhere myself? Indeed, my first few Hmong encounters proved disastrous. It probably did not help that, mortally afraid of committing a faux pas, I was as jumpy as the legendary Hmong princess who, hiding inside a large funeral drum after an eagle as big as eleven houses had eaten everyone else in her village, mistook her handsome young rescuer for the eagle and told him, "If you have come to eat me, do it quickly, please!" Then she fainted. (Later, however, she married him.)

My first meetings with Hmong families were set up by a Hmong-speaking lowland Lao woman who worked as a nurse's aide at MCMC. It did not immediately occur to me that I had found the best possible way to guarantee myself a chilly reception, since almost all Hmong mistrusted the hospital and, concluding that I was associated with the nurse's aide and therefore with MCMC, automatically mistrusted me too. I also had bad luck with my first two interpreters. Carefully following my advisers' instructions, I asked two middle-aged men in turn, each an important figure in his clan, to translate for me. My experiences with them were identical. I would ask a question. The interpreter would translate. The Hmong I was questioning would talk animatedly to the interpreter for four or five minutes. Then the interpreter would turn to me and say, "He says no."

I was beginning to fear that the Hmong community was impenetrable when I met Sukey Waller, the psychologist at Merced Community Outreach Services whom one doctor at MCMC had described as "a sort of hippie-ish revolutionary" and Bill had described as the American most locally respected by the Hmong. I had talked with Sukey by phone from New York City before I came to Merced. She had told me, "Here's my home number. If you get my answering machine, you will find I speak so slowly it sounds as if I'm in the middle of a terrible depression or on drugs. Please don't be alarmed. It's just that I get a lot of calls from clients who can't understand fast English." Sukey's business card read, in Hmong and Lao, "Fixer of

Hearts." She explained to me, "Psychological problems do not exist for the Hmong, because they do not distinguish between mental and physical illness. Everything is a spiritual problem. It's not really possible to translate what I do into Hmong—a shaman is the closest person to a psychotherapist—but fixing hearts was the best metaphor I could find. The only danger is that they might think I do open-heart surgery. *That* would certainly make them run in the other direction." Sukey introduced me to five Hmong leaders, representing four of the most influential of Merced's fourteen clans, and, because I arrived at their homes and offices in her company, I was warmly received by each one. Two of them became irreplaceable sources and, over time, valued friends. When I asked Sukey why the Hmong community accepted her so readily, she said, "The Hmong and I have a lot in common. I have an anarchist sub-personality. I don't like coercion. I also believe that the long way around is often the shortest way from point A to point B. And I'm not very interested in what is generally called the truth. In my opinion, consensual reality is better than facts."

Sukey quickly disabused me of two notions. One was that it was necessary to walk a razor's edge of proper etiquette on either side of which lay catastrophe. She said matter-of-factly, "I've made a million errors. When I came here everyone said you can't touch people on the head, you can't talk to a man, you can't do this, you can't do that, and I finally said, this is crazy! I can't be restricted like that! So I just threw it all out. Now I have only one rule. Before I do anything I ask, Is it okay? Because I'm an American woman and they don't expect me to act like a Hmong anyway, they usually give me plenty of leeway." She also punctured my burgeoning longing for an American interpreter. For one thing, she informed me that even though there were thousands of Hmong living in Merced, not a single American in town spoke Hmong. For another, in her opinion, someone who merely converted Hmong words into English, however accurately, would be of no help to me whatsoever. "I don't call my staff interpreters," she told me. "I call them cultural brokers. They teach me. When I don't know what to do, I ask them. You should go find yourself a cultural broker."

So I found May Ying Xiong. May Ying was a twenty-year-old clerk-typist at the Merced County Office of Refugee Services. Her name means Opium Poppy. She was the girl whose father, Chaly

Xiong, afraid that she would be eaten by lions if she took a summer job with the Youth Conservation Corps, had occasioned Dan Murphy's lion-scouting trip to Yosemite. Chaly, who died in 1983, was a first lieutenant in the Royal Lao Army, one of the few Hmong military officers who had been trained in the United States by the CIA. He was also a famous *txiv neeb* who, while riding his wooden shaman's bench, an embodiment of the winged horse that carried him in search of wandering souls, was renowned for shaking so hard during his ritual trance that it took two assistants to hold him. To complete May Ying's distinguished résumé, she had at age eighteen been Second Runner-Up in the national Miss Hmong pageant, held annually in the Fresno Civic Auditorium, in which she had worn three formal costumes (one Hmong, one Lao, one American) and been judged on her poise, grace, beauty, and speaking ability. When asked, "If you were chosen to be Miss Hmong, what would you do to set an example for future young Hmong ladies?" May Ying had answered, "I would encourage children to go to school and young ladies not to get married too young." One month later, she married an engineering student named Pheng Ly in a Hmong-American ceremony that involved the sacrifice of a chicken and the consumption of many bottles of Löwenbräu. May Ying took great pride in the fact that Pheng had paid her family the unusually high brideprice of $1,800; she in turn had contributed a dowry that consisted of a trust fund left by her father, a silver necklace, a silver belt, gold earrings, three embroidered skirts, two formal Hmong costumes, two pieces of embroidery embellished with antique French colonial coins, and a '73 Ford Granada.

Despite the admonitions of the seven doctors, I decided to try to meet Lia's parents, bringing May Ying as my cultural broker. I figured that if she was the third-most-poised Hmong woman in the United States, she had as good a chance as anyone of being able to deal with the Lees. Despite May Ying's impressive qualifications, she and I, by virtue of our gender and ages, constituted a decidedly low-status team. That turned out to be an advantage. I didn't need more status in the Lee home. If anything, I needed *less* status. Ever since they had arrived in the United States, the Lees had been meeting Americans who, whether because of their education, their knowledge of English, or their positions of relative authority, had made them feel as if their family didn't count for much. Being belittled is the one thing no

Hmong can bear. When Laos was under French colonial rule, the Hmong were required literally to crawl whenever they were in the presence of a Lao official, forbidden to raise their heads until they were acknowledged. It is no accident that in one popular Hmong folktale, an arrogant official is turned into a mouse, upon which the tale's hero, a Hmong archetype in the guise of a cat, takes delight in pouncing. With May Ying at my side, I was not an official, not a threat, not a critic, not a person who was trying to persuade the Lees to do anything they did not wish to do, not even someone to be taken very seriously. My insignificance was my saving grace.

Meeting a Hmong is like getting into a speakeasy: everything depends on who sent you. My appointment with the Lees had been arranged by Blia Yao Moua, one of the Hmong leaders to whom Sukey had introduced me, a man fortuitously unconnected to the hospital or any other American institution. What's more, May Ying's husband, Pheng, belonged to the same clan as the Lees (Lee and Ly are differently spelled Americanizations of the Hmong surname *Lis*), which led Foua and Nao Kao to treat my cultural broker like a long-lost niece. Within thirty seconds, I could see I was dealing with a family that bore little resemblance to the one the doctors had described. The Lees struck me as smart, humorous, talkative, and energetic. I wish I could say that it was my skill as an interviewer that brought out these excellent qualities. In truth, I repeatedly embarrassed May Ying by asking her to translate questions of such surpassing ignorance that after I got to know the Lees I began to feel my primary role in their household was as a source of mirth. May Ying referred to these questions ("Did you bury your children's placentas?" "In Laos, were there a lot of *dabs* who lived in the rivers, lakes, and trees?" "Do you sacrifice pigs?") as my "Is the Pope Catholic?" questions because any fool would know the answers were yes. Once, when I asked in which part of their house in Laos the family had relieved themselves, Foua laughed so hard she almost fell off her bamboo stool. "In the forest, of course!" she finally gasped, tears running down her cheeks.

The Lees were a good-looking couple. Foua looked about forty-five and Nao Kao about ten years older; they had never learned their birth dates. They were both short, and although neither was fat, they looked well-rooted, as if it would take a gale force wind, or maybe even an earthquake, to knock them over. Foua had glossy black hair that she usually wore in a bun, but sometimes she loosened it absent-mindedly while she was talking, and it unfurled to her waist. Nao Kao wore glasses with thick black frames that made him look intellectual and a little nerdy, like a teacher of an obscure branch of mathematics at a minor college. Except on special occasions, when they wore Hmong clothes, they both wore loosely fitting American outfits of pastel polyester. Sometimes Foua wore a long gray cotton skirt and a pink T-shirt, decorated with palm trees, that said CALIFORNIA, a word she of course could not read.

When I first met Foua and Nao Kao, they had seven children still at home. The nine of them lived in a three-room apartment in a two-story stucco building south of the train tracks and west of the Kmart, in a down-at-heel neighborhood that twenty years ago was mostly Hispanic and now is mostly Hmong. Like most Hmong apartments, it contained hardly any furniture aside from a television set, which was usually on. There were no books. Hung close to the ceiling, to show respect, was a heterogeneous collection of family photographs and posters, including an outdated calendar from a Thai rice company, a Time-Life illustrated chart of Combat Jets of the World, and a picture of several dozen Smurfs gathered around a campfire. The bedroom shared by the older children was plastered with posters of U2, Bon Jovi, Whitesnake, and Mötley Crüe. The family's most prized possession, a three-foot-long bamboo *qeej* that only Nao Kao knew how to play, was carefully mounted over the toilet. The most important part of the Lee home was the parking lot. It was there, in an overflowing collection of dozens of old five-gallon plastic buckets and discarded motor-oil cans, that Foua cultivated her personal pharmacopoeia of medicinal plants, which, boiled or ground in her mortar and pestle, were used to cure sore throats, stomachaches, sprained limbs, and postpartum pain, among other ailments.

I was to spend hundreds of hours in this apartment, usually in the evenings, after May Ying got off work. Because Foua and Nao Kao could not read or write in any language, they were excessively interested in and therefore inhibited by note-taking, but they were entirely comfortable with a tape recorder. (Most Hmong in Merced communicated with relatives in Thai refugee camps via audiocassette. I could never decide whether this was incongruously high-tech or whether it was an organic extension of their preliterate oral tradition.) When addressing Foua, May Ying prefaced each question with the word *pog*, a title connoting both respect and intimacy that means, literally, "paternal grandmother." After a few months, Foua started to address May Ying as *mi May*, dear little May, and me as *mi Anne*. At about the same time, at their request, I started calling Foua *tais* (maternal grandmother) and Nao Kao *yawm txiv* (maternal grandfather).

The Lees unhesitatingly granted me access to all of Lia's records at MCMC, Valley Children's Hospital in Fresno, the Merced County Health Department, and Child Protective Services. After I read them, however, I quickly learned that it was not helpful to ask May Ying to relay such questions as "Can you tell me about the time Dr. Selvidge admitted Lia to MCMC with right upper lobe pneumonia on June 28, 1986, at 10:50 p.m.?" The doctors' diagnoses were untranslatable, and in any case they would have meant little to the Lees. Furthermore, Foua and Nao Kao lumped the dozens of health care providers they had encountered at MCMC under the generic heading of "Lia's doctors." Even Neil Ernst and Peggy Philp, who had met Lia's family innumerable times, were relegated by their unshakably high status (and also perhaps, from a Hmong point of view, by their unpronounceability) to a category too distant to allow such intimacies as being called by name. The difficulty of establishing a parallel chronology between Lia's medical chart and her family's experience of her illness was compounded by the fact that the Lees did not tell time in the same way the hospital record-keepers did. Years were identified not by number but by salient event. For instance, 1982 was "the year the spirit first caught Lia and she fell down"; 1985 was "the year Lia became government property." When they had lived in Laos, the Lees, like other Hmong, had subdivided the year not by the months of the Gregorian calendar but by lunar cycles designated by their primary agricultural activities. The first cycle, for example, which followed the Hmong New Year celebration in late November or early December, was the one during which rice and corn were hauled home and the opium harvest was begun. The fifth cycle was the one during which corn was planted. The twelfth cycle was the one during which rice was harvested and opium was weeded. Because the Lees were now unemployed welfare recipients rather than farmers, and each month's activities (or their lack) were nearly identical to every other month's, they no longer oriented themselves by the Hmong calendar and consequently often had trouble remembering when—even in what season—an event had occurred. But when they referred to times of the day, they continued to use the Hmong phrases ("first cock crow," "second cock crow," "time that the sun inclines," "time that shadows cover the valley," "pig-feeding time," "full darkness"), even though no cocks or pigs had lived on East 12th Street within living memory of any resident of Merced.

The Lees politely submitted to my questions about Lia, often answering at length, but they also had their own agenda, which, as Nao Kao once put it, was "to tell you about Hmong culture so you can understand our way and explain it to the doctors." Their favorite time for these cultural lessons was about 10:30 p.m., after they'd gathered conversational steam for at least four hours. One night, just as May Ying and I were getting ready to leave, Foua decided to explain soul loss to me. "Your soul is like your shadow," she said. "Sometimes it just wanders off like a butterfly and that is when you are sad and that's when you get sick, and if it comes back to you, that is when you are happy and you are well again." Nao Kao added, "Sometimes the soul goes away but the doctors don't believe it. I would like you to tell the doctors to believe in our *neeb*." (The word *neeb*, or healing spirit, is often used as shorthand for *ua neeb kho*, the shamanic ritual, performed by a *txiv neeb*, in which an animal is sacrificed and its soul bartered for the vagrant soul of a sick person.) "The doctors can fix some sicknesses that involve the body and blood, but for us Hmong, some people get sick because of their soul, so they need spiritual things. With Lia it was good to do a little medicine and a little *neeb*, but not too much medicine because the medicine cuts the *neeb*'s effect. If we did a little of each she didn't get sick as much, but the doctors wouldn't let us give just a little medicine because they didn't understand about the soul."

On another late-night occasion Nao Kao explained that the Hmong often got sick because of their encounters with malevolent *dabs*, but that the doctors didn't understand this either and therefore failed to treat these patients effectively. "I will give you an example," he said. "There is a man named Mr. Xiong, and he has a son who went to swim at Bear Creek." Bear Creek is a small, muddy river that flows through Applegate Park, north of downtown Merced. "And while Mr. Xiong's son was sleeping, the *dab* that lives in Bear Creek came up to him and talked to him and made him sick and restless and crazy. The doctors and nurses in Merced gave this young man shots and medicines, and the young man hated the doctors and nurses, because the only way to cure that kind of sickness is to sacrifice a dog, and this country won't allow you to kill dogs." Foua told me that a *dab* had caught her just the previous week at the county reservoir. She knew this had happened because after she returned home, she felt afraid, and when she closed her eyes, she could sense that a *dab* was near. She left all the lights on that night to frighten the *dab* away, and she did not become sick. (Several months later, I was to learn that Merced's *dabs* were not confined to natural surroundings. Chong Moua, a Hmong woman who cleaned Bill Selvidge's house once a week, told me that every Hmong in town knew about the *dab* who lived at the intersection of Highway 99 and G Street. This *dab* liked to cause accidents by making Hmong drivers fall asleep or making the cars of approaching Americans invisible.)

The longer I spent with the Lees, the more firmly Foua took me in hand. She improved my manners by teaching me, via May Ying, how to say please and thank you in Hmong. When she learned that I occasionally got headaches, she gave me detailed instructions on how to treat them by rubbing an egg-covered coin up and down my body. I think she was disappointed that I never actually contracted a headache on her premises so that she could heal it then and there. "But you remember," she said. "Next time, you do it the way I said."

When Foua had known me for almost a year, she decided to get me married. The Hmong have a phrase, "a flower full of honey and ready for the bee," which is used to describe a marriageable girl of fifteen or sixteen. I was thirty-five, and had thus been ready for the bee for two decades. When my boyfriend visited me in Merced, Foua realized that she finally had an opportunity to do something about this appalling situation. Her plan, of which she did not inform me in advance, was to dress me as a Hmong bride, a transformation she was certain would render me irresistible.

My makeover took place on a sweltering summer day. The temperature in the Lees' bedroom must have been well over 100°. Out of a battered suitcase that she kept in the back of her closet, Foua extracted piece after piece of exquisite *paj ntaub*. (*Paj ntaub*, which means "flower cloth," is a traditional Hmong textile art in which geometric or organic designs—spiderwebs, ram's heads, tiger's eyebrows, ele-phant's feet—are worked in embroidery, batik, appliqué, and reverse appliqué. In Laos, a Hmong man was said to value two qualities most highly in a wife: her ability to sing poetry and her skill at *paj ntaub*.) Foua had made these clothes for her daughters. They constituted the lion's share of the family's wealth.

Assisted by her fourteen-year-old daughter May, the oldest Lee girl still living at home, and by May Ying Xiong, Foua dressed me like a doll. I was completely at their mercy, since I had no idea which garment was coming next and, when it came, what part of my body it was supposed to adorn. First Foua picked up a *phuam*, a pink-and-black sash at least twenty feet long, and wound it around me like a ribbon around a maypole. Its function was the precise opposite of a girdle's: it was supposed to fatten me up, to transform me into a healthy Hmong farm wife who looked capable of carrying heavy loads of rice. Then came the *tiab*, a pink, green, and yellow skirt with about five hundred accordion pleats, which, if it had been spread out, would have been wider than I was tall. Its cross-stitching was so fine it looked like beading. May Ying told me later that it had probably taken Foua the better part of two years to make, and that it would take her several hours to restitch threads through each of its pleats to prepare it again for storage. Over that went a pink brocade *sev*, a kind of apron, whose *paj ntaub* work was protected by an American refinement, a layer of plastic wrap. On my upper half I wore a blue-and-black jacket called a *tsho* (the same word as the Hmong term for "placenta," one's first garment) and four *hnab tshos*, pocketlike bags decorated with dangling silver coins, which were hung bandolier-style across my chest and weighed a ton. Around my neck went a five-tier necklace of hollow silver. Around my calves May Ying wrapped a pair of black puttees called *nrhoob*. And on my head Foua balanced the *pièce de résistance*, a *kausmom*, a pink, green, and yellow hat, bedizened with its own set of silver coins, that was shaped like a pagoda and jingled whenever I moved. Although I nearly died of heat prostration during the forty-five minutes it took Foua, May, and May Ying to wrestle all this stuff onto me, I felt for the first time in my not very fashionable adulthood that I understood the ritual pleasure of women gussying each other up and giggling like crazy in rooms to which men were forbidden entrance.

While all this was taking place, my friend George w
the air-conditioned living room, watching a boxing matc.
sion with Nao Kao and wondering what I was doing. Neither he no.
Nao Kao spoke a word of each other's language, but they communicated in the universal language of male bonding by throwing punches
in the air and making appreciative grunts. When I emerged from the
bedroom, George was, in a word, stunned. He didn't think I looked
good, exactly. He told me later that I resembled Tom Kitten in "The
Roly-Poly Pudding," after Mrs. Whiskers ties him up and covers him
with pie dough. However, Foua's work must in some way have had
the intended effect, because a week later George asked me to marry
him. When we told Foua that we were engaged, she didn't act in the
least surprised.

Later, when I complimented Foua on her beautiful needlework,
she said matter-of-factly, "Yes, my friends are proud of me because
of my *paj ntaub*. The Hmong are proud of me." That is the only time
I ever heard her say anything kind about herself. She was otherwise
the most self-deprecating woman I had ever met. One night, when
Nao Kao was out for the evening, she remarked, out of the blue, "I
am very stupid." When I asked her why, she said, "Because I don't
know anything here. I don't know your language. American is so hard,
you can watch TV all day and you still don't know it. I can't dial the
telephone because I can't read the numbers. If I want to call a friend,
my children will tell me and I will forget and the children will tell me
again and I will forget again. My children go to the store to buy food
because I don't know what is in the packages. One time when I went
to the hospital I went to the bathroom, and the hall went that way
and that way and that way and that way, and I didn't know which way
to go, and I couldn't get back to where I was because too many sad
things have happened to me and my brain is not good anymore."

When I suggested that I would have had at least as much trouble
finding my way around her village in Laos as she had finding her way
around MCMC, Foua said, "Maybe, but in Laos it was easy. I didn't
know how to do anything but farm." Venturing that it couldn't have
been quite so easy as she claimed, I asked her to describe a typical day
in Houaysouy, the village in the northwestern province of Sayaboury
where the Lee family had lived. She tilted her head to one side for a
moment, thinking. Then she said, "In the season when you have to

tend to the rice fields, you get up at first cock crow. In the other seasons, you can wake up at second or third cock crow. Even at third cock crow it is before dawn, and it is dark, so the first thing you do is light a lamp. The lamp was like this." Foua walked into the kitchen and came back holding the bottom three-quarters of a Mountain Dew can, which was filled with oil and had a homemade cloth wick. "In Merced, when the electricity goes out, we still use one like this," she said.

"First you cook the rice for your children," she continued. "Then you clean the house with the broom you tied together yourself. After you are finished sweeping you go and cut wild grasses to give to the pigs, and you cut more for the cows, and you feed the pigs and the cows and the chickens. Then you walk to the fields. You carry the baby on your back, and if you have two children your husband carries one on his back too, and if you have a lot of children you can leave some of the smaller ones home with the big ones. Our parents grew opium, but we just grew rice, and also peppers, corn, and cucumbers. When it is planting time, first you make a hole in the ground like this." She walked back to the kitchen and, after rummaging around for something with which to demonstrate to me the use of a dibble stick, returned with a cardboard tube that had once held a roll of paper towels, which she proceeded to stab at one-foot intervals into her living room's brown wall-to-wall carpeting. "Like this. Then you put the seeds in the holes. You and your husband do it together. In other seasons you clear the fields and harvest the rice and thresh and winnow the rice and grind the corn."

At this point in her narrative, her daughter May walked in, wearing shorts, a T-shirt that said TIME FOR THE BEACH, and pink plastic earrings. May was three and a half when her family left Laos. She sat on the carpet at her mother's feet and listened. "The farm place was far from where we lived," said Foua, "farther than from here to Bear Creek. If you leave the farm when it is still light, it is dark by the time you get home. When you get home you go to the stream and carry the water for cooking and bathing in a barrel on your back." Foua showed me how she had made the pack-barrel, gesturing with her fingers to illustrate how the bamboo was wrapped around the wooden staves. "You bathe the babies by boiling the water and then you pour it with a smaller bowl. The older children can bathe themselves. You bring corn for the chickens and you feed the pigs, and then you cook for your family. We usually just ate leftover rice from our first meal, with a little vegetables, because we ate meat only about once a month. You cook on the hot coals of the fire and you use the fat from the last pig you killed to fry with. The smoke just goes through spaces in the roof. After dinner you sew by the light of that lamp. In the fields you wear clothes that are old and dirty and ripped up, but the children have to have good clothes for New Year's, so you sew for them at night."

I asked Foua to describe their house. "It is made of wood from the forest," she said, "some wood as big as telephone poles. The thatching is bamboo. I helped build it. Our relatives helped us too, and then we help our relatives when they need a house. Our house is all one room but it is very nice. The floor is earth. If you want to sleep, you take some bamboo, you cut it open and split it into small pieces that are springy and make it into a bed. We sleep next to the fireplace where it is warm because we don't have any blankets. My husband sleeps on one side holding a baby, I sleep on the other side holding another baby, and the older children keep each other warm."

While Foua was telling me about the dozens of tasks that constituted her "easy" work in Laos, I was thinking that when she said she was stupid, what she really meant was that none of her former skills were transferable to the United States—none, that is, except for being an excellent mother to her nine surviving children. It then occurred to me that this last skill had been officially contradicted by the American government, which had legally declared her a child abuser.

I asked Foua if she missed Laos. She was silent for a few seconds, rocking back and forth on her low bamboo stool while her daughter looked at her, waiting curiously for her answer. Then she said, "When you think about Laos and about not having enough food and those dirty and torn-up clothes, you don't want to think. Here it is a great country. You are comfortable. You have something to eat. But you don't speak the language. You depend on other people for welfare. If they don't give you money you can't eat, and you would die of hunger. What I miss in Laos is that free spirit, doing what you want to do. You own your own fields, your own rice, your own plants, your own fruit trees. I miss that feeling of freeness. I miss having something that really belongs to me."

9

A Little Medicine and a Little Neeb

W hen Lia came back," recalled Nao Kao, "the car came up here and when the door opened, she just jumped up and ran into her home. Her sisters and brother were too happy to even do anything. Everyone just went out and hugged her. That night she was in our bed and we were so happy to have her sleeping by our side."

Looking over Lia's sparse medical records from the spring and summer of 1986, around the time of her fourth birthday, Peggy Philp summed up the first few months after her return from foster care in three words: "Nothing interesting here." The Lees would disagree. Neil and Peggy had previously spent hours recounting the details of medically complex periods in Lia's history that Foua and Nao Kao had summarized for me in a few minutes; now the tables were turned, and a period that seemed uneventful from the doctors' perspective was revealed, from the Lees' perspective, to be one of the richest in her life.

The first thing Foua and Nao Kao did after Lia returned was to celebrate her homecoming and bolster her health by sacrificing a cow. In Laos, most of the chickens, pigs, cows, and buffalos kept by Hmong families were reserved for sacrifices to propitiate ancestors or cure illnesses by offering the souls of the slaughtered animals as ransom for fugitive souls. Even families too poor to keep animals of their own were guaranteed occasional meat in their diets by being invited to *neeb* ceremonies performed by wealthier villagers. According to Dwight Conquergood, sacrifice is a sacred act performed with "respect and reverence." He has written, "The souls of sacrificed animals are precious and vitally connected to human souls. Animals are not considered to be as far removed from the human species as they are in our world view. . . . Since the bonding between the life-souls of the patient and sacrificed animal is so intimate, it is likened to souls being wedded together." Eric Crystal, the coordinator of the Center for Southeast Asia Studies at U.C. Berkeley, takes an equally approbatory, if not quite so high-minded, view. "So what if some Hmong feel that they have to slaughter animals to make the proper kinds of sacrifices?" he once asked me rhetorically. "Why not? It happens because people usually mark religious events that are important to them by getting together with relatives, and it is very difficult in this world to get a whole bunch of relatives together, whether you are living in some village in Laos or in Manhattan, without giving them something to eat. So you sacralize the event. The whole animal is offered, and the whole animal is eaten. I mean the *whole* animal, ninety-eight percent of it, intestines and everything, in a very ecologically sound way. Americans toss away a huge amount of meat. We also kind of slip it under the rug that people actually have to kill animals to eat them. Indeed, it may be shocking to many Americans to find out that their $1.99-a-pound chicken breast actually had to get its throat cut in a processing plant. So Americans are *real* shocked if they find out that the Hmong are doing it right in their own houses."

During the last decade, shocked Americans have responded to the ritual killings performed by devotees of other religions by invoking legal sanctions. In Hialeah, Florida, animal rights activists and community leaders passed an anti-sacrifice ordinance in 1987 to prevent priests of the Afro-Cuban Santería faith from slaughtering animals, a practice one local resident said "blights the image of South Florida." (The ban was overturned, but it took four years and a Supreme Court decision.) In Los Angeles, where followers of Santería and several other Hispanic sects were suspected of nailing cows' tongues to trees and leaving entrails on sidewalks, an ordinance was passed in 1990 that made animal sacrifice punishable by a six-month prison term and a fine of up to $1,000. It is still on the books, though it is not currently being enforced. In Merced, almost every Hmong family I met sacrificed animals on a regular basis. In fact, a fourteen-year-old boy I knew, a member of the Moua clan, once complained that he hardly ever had enough free time on weekends because his parents made him attend so many of his relatives' *neeb* ceremonies. Until the mid-nineties, however, most American residents of Merced had little idea what was going on, and no one seemed concerned that it might blight the image of Central California. "Well, *I* haven't run into any sacrificial chickens," Pat Lunney, the chief of police, told me with some amusement several years ago. "Sacrifices?" said Steve Nord, the city attorney. "Do they really do that?"

The Hmong have a phrase, *yuav paim quav*, which means that the truth will eventually come to light. Literally, it means "feces will be excreted." I knew it was only a matter of time before feces would be excreted on the subject of Hmong animal sacrifices, and indeed, in 1996, tipped off by local newspaper coverage of a dog sacrifice in Fresno, the residents of Merced began to realize that similar things might be taking place in *their* town. That the animals were killed quickly and cleanly—and, unlike the products of a meat-packing plant, were actually thanked for their services—failed to extenuate what seemed like aberrant behavior. The result was an ordinance banning the slaughter of livestock and poultry within city limits. For most Hmong, the need to heal sick family members far outweighed the claim of a mere law, so they paid no attention, and few neighbors were nosy enough to report them. However, rumors about the sparsity of dogs and cats on Merced's south side, which had circulated *sotto voce* for several years, upped their volume.

The rumors were false, but that did nothing to stop them. Dan Murphy told me where they had originated. "There was a small stove fire in a Hmong house here a few years back," he said, "and one of the firemen opened the refrigerator. There was a roast pig in there. The fireman thought it was a dog, and he told his friends, and they told theirs, and instantly people were saying that the reason there aren't so many strays around here anymore is that the Hmong are eating them all, and you'd better lock up your dog at night. Well, Dang Moua heard this." Dang Moua is a local Hmong leader. "And he went and got the fire chief and brought him over to the house and opened the refrigerator and said, 'This is a pig. Can't your men tell the difference between a pig and a dog?' And that should have settled it. But you know, it's not as much fun to tell about the resolution of a story as it is to tell about the genesis, so that part didn't get spread around very far."

The Hmong of Merced do not sacrifice dogs, which they know are protected by American law and custom—though some of them, like the victim of the *dab* of Bear Creek that Nao Kao told me about, may have wished that they could. They do, however, frequently sacrifice pigs and chickens, which they buy live from Hmong or American farmers. To sacrifice a cow, as the Lees did, is a rare and important event. It was the first time they had done so during their six years in the United States. Lia's cow cost $300, a monumental sum for a family of nine who were living on $9,480 a year, plus food stamps. When I asked Nao Kao where the money had come from, he said, "Lia had her own money from the government." It took me a moment to understand: he had bought the sacrificial cow with three and a half months' worth of Lia's Supplemental Security Income, a use to which federal disability assistance had probably never before been put.

Because Nao Kao had no way of transporting a live cow to East 12th Street, he bought one from an American rancher who lived near Merced, had it slaughtered, and, with the help of some of his clansmen, cut it in pieces small enough to stuff into plastic garbage bags that fit on the floor and in the trunk of his cousin's subcompact car. After they returned home, a *txiv neeb* performed the ritual chant that accompanied his journey to the realm of the unseen. During the chant, the cow's severed head was sitting on the Lees' front stoop, welcoming Lia's soul. When I asked the Lees whether any American passersby might have been surprised by this sight, Foua said, "No, I don't think they would be surprised, because it wasn't the whole cow on the doorstep, only the head." Nao Kao added, "Also, Americans would think it was okay because we had the receipt for the cow."

After the ceremonial portion of the *neeb* was complete, the Lees and their many invited relatives sat down and ate a large, festive meal of fried beef, boiled beef, a spicy ground-beef dish called *laab*, and a stew called *kua quav*. When I asked May Ying what *kua quav* was, she said, "It's made out of cow's intestines and the heart and the liver and the lungs, and you chop it up really fine, and there is a part that is what is inside the intestines, and you chop that up too. Then you boil it all up together and you put lemon grass and herbs in it. It has a really bad name when you translate it. I guess you could call it, oh, doo-doo soup." (The literal translation of *kua quav* is liquid excrement.) "It's a classic."

The celebratory mood of Lia's first few days home began to dissipate as the Lees came to feel, more strongly with each passing week, that the child who had been taken from them had been returned in a damaged condition. According to May Lee, Lia had once been able to count in English and Hmong and knew all the tunes and lyrics of the traditional Hmong New Year's songs. "Before the Americans took her away, Lia was really smart," said Nao Kao. "If you came in the door, she would say hello and bring a chair for you. But after those months that she was government property, I don't know what they did to her. Maybe they gave her too much medicine, or maybe she got sick because she missed us too much, because after that, when people come, it seems she does not know them, and she could only speak a little." The Lees were under the impression that the court had returned Lia to them because foster care had made her sicker, clear evidence that her family's care was superior. When I told Neil and Peggy this, they were surprised. They had also noted Lia's worsening developmental deficits, but in their view her downward intellectual slide had begun before she was removed from parental custody, had been temporarily arrested by her regular drug regimen during foster care, and had then been seriously aggravated by the seizures she had had after her catastrophic week-long visit home in September 1985, during which her parents had failed to administer any medications. Neil and Peggy were even more surprised—and grieved—to learn that the Lees believed Lia had been taken from them in the first place not to safeguard her health but "because the doctors were angry at us" for being noncompliant, and wished to inflict punishment. And when I told them that Foua and Nao Kao, in their willingness to travel the middle road of "a little medicine and a little *neeb*," viewed themselves as eminently reasonable and their doctors as incapable of compromise, Neil and Peggy shook their heads in puzzlement and consternation.

In order to keep Lia's condition from deteriorating further, the Lees stepped up their program of traditional medicine. I had often heard doctors at MCMC complain that the Hmong seemed to care less than Americans did whether their sick children got better, since they spurned the hospital's free medical care. Unbeknownst to their doctors, the Hmong actually took their children's health so seriously that they frequently budgeted large fractions of their public assistance stipends or indebted themselves to relatives in order to pay for expensive services not covered by Medi-Cal. For example, the Lees spent $1,000 on amulets filled with sacred healing herbs from Thailand, which Lia wore constantly around her neck. They also tried a host of less costly but time-consuming therapies. Foua inserted a silver coin that said "1936 Indochine Française" into the yolk of a boiled egg, wrapped the egg in a cloth, and rubbed Lia's body with it; when the egg turned black, that meant the sickness had been absorbed. She massaged Lia with the bowl of a spoon. She sucked the "pressure" out of Lia's body by pressing a small cup heated with ashes against her skin, creating a temporary vacuum as the oxygen-depleted air inside the cup cooled. She pinched Lia to draw out noxious winds. She dosed Lia with tisanes infused from the gleanings of her parking-lot herb garden. Finally, she and Nao Kao tried changing Lia's name to Kou, a last-ditch Hmong remedy based on the premise that if a patient is called by a new name, the *dab* who stole her soul will be tricked into thinking that she is someone else, and the soul can return. According to Foua, this plan was foiled because Lia's doctors persisted in calling her Lia, thus ruining the subterfuge.

The Lees' most ambitious act of healing was taking Lia to visit a famous *txiv neeb* in Minnesota. "We had heard this *txiv neeb* was very special because he can fix people and he gives good medicines," explained Nao Kao, in the deferential tones of someone describing a distinguished specialist he has gone to great trouble and expense to consult at the Mayo Clinic. "When this *txiv neeb* was younger he had gotten sick himself with the same thing as Lia, where the spirit catches you and you fall down. For the Hmong people, they usually get that kind of sickness before they become a *txiv neeb*, and maybe when Lia was grown up, that would have happened to her too, and she would be a *txiv neeb*. This *txiv neeb* was also a member of the Lee clan, so that is why we took Lia to Minnesota."

Nao Kao, one of his brothers, one of his grown daughters, his son-in-law, and Lia spent three days driving to Minnesota. "We rested one night in Salt Lake City and one night in Wyoming," said Nao Kao, "and then we took another day to get to Nebraska and then we took the whole night from Nebraska to get to Minnesota. We just stopped to get gas. I only drove for three hours in Wyoming because Lia kept trying to hug me, so I couldn't drive, so someone else drove and I just held her." He did not remember where the *txiv neeb* had lived, but recalled that it was several hours beyond St. Paul. "The *txiv neeb* tied spirit-strings around Lia's wrist and gave her some green medicine from roots and things like that. Some of it was boiled and you drink the juice and some of it you boil until it crystallizes and it gets really sticky, and after it dries you eat it." The three family members who had accompanied them stayed in Minnesota with relatives, and Nao Kao, again using SSI money, flew home with Lia, filled with optimism about her future well-being.

Once I asked Bill Selvidge why Merced's doctors never seemed to ask their Hmong patients how *they* treated their illnesses, and he replied that because the Hmong dressed at least approximately in American clothes, had driver's licenses, and shopped in supermarkets, it never occurred to his colleagues—and only rarely to him—that they might practice esoteric healing arts. "If you went down to the rain forest and talked to the Yanomamo," he said, "you'd be surprised if they *didn't* come up with all sorts of fantastic spirit stories. You'd be surprised if they sat there and started saying, you know, 'Where is the penicillin for my impetigo?' But if you took them to this setting, the way the Hmong have come here, and you dressed them up and they drove a car and came to MCMC, you wouldn't expect to hear those spirit stories anymore."

Neil and Peggy had no idea what the Lees were doing to heal Lia because they never thought to ask. The only American who did ask, and who therefore learned of the $1,000 amulets and at least some of the animal sacrifices, was Jeanine Hilt. I would have expected the Lees to focus the most burning rays of their resentment on Jeanine, an official representative of the very agency that had confiscated their daughter. On the contrary, the Lees chose to categorize her not as Lia's abductor but as her patron, "the person who gave Lia her disability money." Aside from Dee Korda, Jeanine was the only American I talked to who didn't describe the Lees as closemouthed and dim; not coincidentally, she was also the only American I ever heard Foua or Nao Kao refer to by name. They called her Jenny. She responded by learning the names of all eight of Lia's siblings: Chong, Zoua, Cheng, May, Yer, True, Mai, and Pang. Compared to the Olympian Drs. Ernst and Philp, who never volunteered their first names, Jeanine seemed warm and unpretentious. Even her size—five feet one and comfortably rounded—was closer to the Hmong scale. Neil and Peggy were respectively six two and five nine, and seemed even taller because they had such perfect posture. Jeanine also had more success keeping the lines of communication snarl-free, partly because, as a social worker, she was able to make house calls. (In all their years of dealing with the Lees, Neil never visited their home and Peggy visited only once.) She took the sensible step of using May, the Lees' most Americanized daughter, as her interpreter. Not only was May's English excellent—like my interpreter, May Ying Xiong, she had learned it in an American high school, so her grammar and vocabulary were superior to those of almost any Hmong adult—but after Jeanine left, Foua and Nao Kao were able to ask May, as often as was necessary, "Explain what Jenny said again."

Jeanine's empathy for the Lees may have been deepened by two factors: she understood what it was like to live with a chronic illness, because she had severe asthma herself; and she admired the closeness of Hmong families, because her relations with her own family, who were fundamentalist Christians, had been strained for many years, ever since they had learned she lived with a lesbian partner. She had no children of her own. Unlike the MCMC nurses who considered Lia a burden and a pest, Jeanine thought she was a delightful child. "I just totally fell in love with her," Jeanine recalled. "Lia wasn't your typical kid that would play appropriately with toys and, you know, do all the right things. She was like a little blowfly flitting about, just totally out of control and wild and unsocialized but—well, absolutely adorable. Physically, I found her a very attractive child. She was real cute and real huggable. I mean, this kid could give you a hug like no other kid could. She would climb into your arms and sit in your lap and just give you a terrific bear hug and grab your glasses and pinch your cheeks until they hurt."

Jeanine's involvement in Lia's case rapidly escalated from a pro-

fessional assignment to an obsession. A typical Hilt letter, written with
cheerful officiousness to Judith Eppley, a counselor at a regional
agency for the developmentally disabled:

RE: Lia Lee

Dear Judy,
Please forward, to me, copies of all psychologicals, neurologicals, assessments, evaluations, reports, work-ups, impressions, studies, reviews, ru-
minations, appraisals, opinions, etc. on the above named minor. I hope
that covers it. Thanks for your help!

Sincerely,

Jeanine Hilt
Social Worker

In Neil's opinion, Jeanine was "a large pain in the ass." He remembered innumerable times when she had nagged him for information
about Lia or for prescriptions for medical equipment he considered
unnecessary, such as an electronic digital thermometer that she hoped
to teach Foua to use, with May's help in reading the numbers.
Whatever she requested was always needed "*immediately*" and at no
cost to the Lees. "Jeanine took on the Lees like a crusade," said
Neil. "She always wanted to be notified about any change in Lia's
condition, and, my God, it wasn't like we didn't have six billion other
things that we had to think of. If you forgot to call her she'd read
you the riot act. I think she had trouble understanding that Lia
was just one of hundreds or thousands of patients that we took care
of and we couldn't drop everything and do exactly what she wanted.
But it was a double-edged sword. She was good, too. Jeanine was an
incredible patient advocate. There was nothing she wouldn't do for
this kid."

One of the things Jeanine arranged was to have Lia bused three
days a week to the Schelby Center for Special Education, the county
school for retarded and disabled children. She hoped that Schelby
would help socialize Lia as well as giving Foua an occasional respite.
Lia's teacher, Sunny Lippert, recalled, "Lia was very spoiled. Jeanine
Hilt told us the family felt that she talked to the gods during her
seizures and that they had this euphoric idea that she was a princess.

They fixed her special things to eat, and whatever she wanted, they did. If she raised her arms her mother would carry her through the house. She got rather chubby, and the more she sat around and let people do things for her, the heavier she got. She was a beautiful child. Her mother just groomed her until she was immaculate. Lia could charm the hair right off a dog. She was the type you'd just want to pick up, but I had a rule in my room: *No one could pick up Lia.* Of course, as soon as she went home, her family kept right on catering to her."

Believing that Lia's behavioral problems stemmed partly from a lack of daily structure, Jeanine posted the following on the Lees' wall:

LIA'S SCHEDULE

7 - Wake-up
   Breakfast
   Bath

8 - Meds
   Leave for school

1 - Home from school

2 - Meds
   Nap

4 - Playtime

6 - Dinner

7 - Bath
   Pyjamas

8 - Meds
   Bed

Despite May's help in reading it, this schedule never fully took hold, partly because of Foua's and Nao Kao's orientation to the cock-crow system rather than to the clock. Another fruitless effort was a list of instructions about how to administer Tylenol and Valium to prevent febrile seizures when Lia spiked a temperature. Jeanine went to great trouble to have it translated into swirly Lao script, failing to realize that no one in the Lee family spoke or read Lao. But in her most important goal—persuading the Lees to administer Lia's medicine—

Jeanine achieved a stunning success. Blood tests showed that Lia was regularly maintaining a therapeutic level of Depakene. During her first four months at home, she had only one seizure, her best record since infancy. Jeanine attributed this period of unusual health to the Depakene; the Lees attributed it to the successful intervention of the *txiv neeb* in Minnesota.

In September of 1986, Lia fell off a swing at the Schelby Center, hit her head, and went into status epilepticus, the condition, dreaded by all her doctors, in which her seizures, instead of spontaneously resolving after a few minutes, continued one after another with no intervals of consciousness. It was unclear whether Lia fell because she seized or whether she seized because she fell, but in any case, when she was taken to the hospital, she was found to have adequate levels of Depakene in her bloodstream. Parental noncompliance, for once, was manifestly not a factor. Nao Kao's diagnosis was that "the teacher made her drop from the swing and when she fell she was scared and her soul went away too, so she got sick again." In Lia's MCMC admission summary, her medical history was noted to be "complicated" and her social history to be "very complicated."

Neil remembers this admission, Lia's fourteenth stay at MCMC, to be the most harrowing she had ever had. "She'd been doing real well—*real, real* well—and then came this unbelievable set of problems. She had a bad seizure, all of this food crap started coming out of her mouth and she aspirated a lot of it into her lungs, she went into respiratory failure, she couldn't breathe for herself so we had to intubate her, then the breathing tube caused some local irritation of the trachea, so after we pulled it out she started breathing with a lot of difficulty and we had to reintubate her, and then she got this very unusual infection of the airway from the irritation. The parents had to go along with a lot of stuff, an oxygen mask, lots of IVs, blood work, an arterial line to measure the oxygen and carbon dioxide in her blood, real invasive stuff." Nao Kao remembered this as the time when Lia "had a lot of plastic all over her." He or Foua slept by Lia's side every one of the fourteen nights she spent in the hospital. He recalled, "The doctors made Lia stay so long in the hospital, and it just made her sicker and sicker."

Neil and Peggy co-authored an article in the *Pediatric Infectious Disease Journal*, called "Bacterial Tracheitis Caused by *Branhamella catarrhalis*," about Lia's tracheal infection. "Lia got published!" is how Neil put it when he showed me the article several years later. In it, they wrote:

> Our case clearly demonstrates that this agent [*B. catarrhalis*] has the potential for being an opportunistic infection in the compromised respiratory tract of a pediatric patient. Our patient's hospital-acquired infection was most probably the result of a local injury to the trachea from a cuffed endotracheal tube and from alteration of oral bacterial flora with intravenously administered penicillin.

Not every doctor would choose to publicize a nosocomial, or hospital-acquired, infection, especially if, as was the case here, it was he rather than an inexperienced resident who had been responsible for inflicting the "local injury." When I read the article, I was struck, as I had often been before, by how much more interested Neil and Peggy were in the truth than in making themselves look good. I was also struck by the fact that Nao Kao was absolutely right: the hospital *had* made Lia sicker.

Only three weeks after Lia was discharged, she was admitted again, despite adequate levels of medication, with severe seizures and fever. Neil and Peggy were horrified. "I had been really impressed that she was having such good control with the Depakene," recalled Neil, "and then she had two seizures within a month and I said, Oh God, here we go again. The Depakene is not working! I couldn't think of any good way to keep her seizures from getting worse. I remember we thought about putting her under anesthesia to stop her shaking the next time she came in, so we could at least get an IV in. And I remember Dan Murphy and I had a few conversations about whether we should try surgery, to try to cauterize part of Lia's brain. I really didn't know what to do. I was just grabbing at straws."

Peggy said, "The seizures were getting very, very long. Before, sometimes they used to stop on their own, but these didn't. It seemed like it took more medication to stop them, and we were afraid that one day we were going to try to get in an IV and just not be able to do it, because Lia was so fat and because we'd already cut down so many of her veins. If she seized long enough she was going to gork her brain out. Early that fall we started to get this feeling of doom.

We talked about it a lot. It was hard to imagine that the Lia era would ever be over, but I remember thinking it was going to be. We were just waiting for the big one."

Neil said, "I felt like there was this giant snowball that was coming down the mountain and we were trying to hold it up there and it just kept pushing us. I remember talking to the parents and telling them that Lia's seizures were getting worse and more frequent and that someday she might have one we couldn't stop. It was so haunting. I started to have nightmares that it was going to happen, and I would be the one on call, and I couldn't stop it and she was going to die right before my eyes. It was inevitable. It was just a matter of when."

_____

10

War

A folktale collected in 1924 by François Marie Savina, the French missionary, reports that when the Hmong lived in the primordial northern homeland where the days and nights were six months long, they were once involved in a land dispute with some neighboring tribes. Their king resolved it as follows. Each tribe would select an envoy who would walk as far as he could during the six months between sunset to sunrise, returning to the king's golden palace at the end of his journey. All the territory he covered would belong to his tribe. If one of the envoys failed to reach the palace, his tribe would be commanded to live wherever he stood at the moment the sun rose. At daybreak, the Hmong envoy was standing on a high pinnacle, and this is why, ever since then, the Hmong have always lived in the mountains, where they are the first to see the sun rise and the last to see it set.

If that footsore walker had ended up standing on the plains instead, the fate of the Hmong would have been entirely different. Almost every aspect of the tribe's history and character proceeds from the essential fact that they are montagnards. As a Hmong proverb puts it, "Fish swim in the water; birds fly in the air; the Hmong live in the mountains." The Hmong language has dozens of terms for mountains of different shapes, different slopes, different elevations. "Ask a Miao

[Hmong] the name of his country of origin," wrote Savina, "and he will answer with the name of a mountain. Such-and-such is the mountain where I was born, he will say. Ask him where that mountain happened to be, and he will indicate whether it was to the north, the south, the east, or the west, instead of telling you whether it was in China, in Tonkin, or in Laos." When a Hmong was obliged to descend to the lowlands, Savina observed, he could easily be identified by his peculiar gait. "Accustomed to frequenting steep, rocky paths . . . he would forget he was walking on a smooth, flat road, and he would raise his foot too high with each step, as if he were climbing a staircase or feared he were going to trip. On the plain, a Miao was as much out of his element as a sailor on dry land."

In prewar Laos, the various ethnic groups were as stratified as a pousse-café. The Lao lived in the plains. The Karen and the Khmu lived above the altitude of 50 meters. The Mien lived above 400 meters. "And finally," wrote Father Jean Mottin, "at the highest altitudes for the people of these regions, between 1,000 and 2,000 meters if it is possible, live the Hmong. Seek among the highest and most inaccessible mountains and there you will find them, for it is there they find themselves at home!" The lowland Lao may have been richer, more numerous, and politically more powerful, but the Hmong, peering down at their putative masters like eagles looking at mice, always managed to maintain an unbudgeable sense of superiority. As it had in China, their ethnic identity remained pure. Assimilation was easy to resist because their contacts with the dominant culture were so few. They rarely visited the plains, which they called "the land of leeches," believing—with some justification, given the greater incidence of tropical diseases at low elevations—that doing so would make them sick. No one passed through their territory en route to anywhere else. And although they were occasionally visited by Yunnanese traders bringing silver, cloth, thread, shoes, and cooking pots, they were able to keep trade to a minimum because they were so self-sufficient. They produced all their own food as well as all the fodder for their livestock. Using homemade flintlock rifles, or crossbows made of wood, bamboo, and hemp, they hunted birds, rats, monkeys, gibbons, deer, wild pigs, and tigers. They fished the mountain streams. They gathered fruits, greens, wild mushrooms, tubers, and bamboo shoots. They picked slow-moving grasshoppers from the undersides of leaves in the early morning cold, and roasted them. They tied chicken feathers around the thoraxes of bees, followed them back to their hives, smoked out the bees, removed the honey, picked out the bee larvae, and steamed them. When they got thirsty in the forest, they plucked large upturned leaves shaped like dishes and drank the dew.

In the Hmong language, there are hundreds of lyrical two-word expressions—not the stuff of poetry but of everyday speech—that onomatopoeically describe various sounds. These alliterative expressions, collected by the linguist Martha Ratcliff, give some inkling of the intimate relationship the Hmong of Laos had with the natural world. Some samples: *zuj ziag*, a cicada singing; *lis loos*, bees buzzing; *nplhuj nplhoos*, a boar grunting; *mig mog*, tigers playing; *ig awg*, wild pigs fighting in close combat; *txij txej*, a rat or mouse crying out in a snake's mouth; *xuj xuav*, a snake undulating; *txiv txev*, birds chirping; *rhuj rhuav*, birds shuffling through leaves looking for insects; *plig plawg*, a bird rising from its nest on the ground; *zig zuag*, monkeys swishing through the treetops with a continuous noise; *tsig tsuag*, monkeys leaping through the treetops with separate noises; *nruj nreev*, a tree popping fast before it falls; *nrhuj nrhawv*, a tree popping slowly before it falls; *vig vag*, a tree brushing through other trees and underbrush while it falls; *nqaj nqug*, many trees falling one right after another; *pij pauj*, fruit falling on the ground; *pliv ploov*, fruit falling in water; *xuj xuav*, a long, easy, all-day rain.

Like most people who live close to the land, the Hmong were farmers. Foua Yang once told me that everyone in her village did the same work, so no one was more important than anyone else. There was no class system. Since no one knew how to read, no one felt deprived or inconvenienced by the lack of literacy. Everything the next generation needed to know was passed on orally and by example: how to venerate the ancestors, how to play the *qeej*, how to conduct a funeral, how to court a lover, how to track a deer, how to build a house, how to embroider a skirt, how to butcher a pig, how to flail a load of rice.

Although they harvested enough rice, corn, and vegetables for their own needs, the only crop the Hmong could indisputably grow better than the lowland Lao, because it was specifically suited to the cool temperatures and alkaline soils of the highlands, was the opium poppy. There is, of course, a legend about it. Once, long ago, there was a wanton Hmong beauty whose libertinage led to her early death. From her grave grew a flower. Its pod exuded a sap whose fragrance enabled anyone who inhaled it to reexperience the ecstasy her lovers had once enjoyed. Through the medium of dreams, she initiated her posthumous acolytes into the mysteries of opium cultivation and preparation. The dreams must have been highly instructive, for ever since the end of the eighteenth century, when the British East India Company introduced the opium poppy to China, the Hmong have been master opium growers, drawn willy-nilly into an international trade they neither created nor controlled. In Laos, the French colonial government encouraged them to pay their taxes in raw opium in order to supply the official lowland network of government-licensed opium dens. The Hmong complied with ease. They knew how to choose the best soil for growing opium by tasting it for its lime content. They knew how to broadcast the poppy seeds in cornfields so the young plants would be protected by the corn stalks. They knew how to incise the pods with triple-bladed knives (cutting neither so deep that the sap dripped to the ground nor so lightly that it was trapped inside the pods), wait until the extruded sap coagulated and turned brown, scrape it, wrap it in poppy petals or banana leaves, knead it, and form it into bricks. My Hmong dictionary lists twenty-nine terms related to opium cultivation and smoking, from *riam yeeb* (the knife used to score the pods) to *yeeb tseeb* (the needlelike tool used to hold the wad of opium while preparing it for smoking). Surprisingly few Hmong aside from the chronically ill and the elderly were addicts. Opium was reserved mainly to facilitate the ceremonial trances of *txiv neebs*; to dull the pain of headaches, toothaches, snakebites, and fever; to stanch diarrhea; and to ease the discomforts of old age. Young addicts, most of whom were men, shouldered a heavy burden of shame. Stigmatized by their diminished ability to work, they not only had trouble finding brides themselves but blackened the marital prospects of their brothers and cousins.

The Hmong kept less than ten percent of their opium yield for their own use, and sold the rest. It was their only cash crop. One could hardly invent a more perfect commodity for mountain transport: easily portable, immune to spoilage, and possessing a stratospherically high value-to-weight ratio. One kilogram of opium was worth as much as half a ton of rice. The saddlebags of a single modest caravan of ponies, led by a lowland merchant, could carry a village's entire annual output of crude opium bricks. The Hmong accepted no paper currency for their opium, only silver bars or piasters, which they melted down to make jewelry or hoarded for brideprices. Opium production equaled wealth. No wonder that when Christian missionaries first came to Laos, they often found small, meticulously wrapped balls of opium in their offering plates. No wonder that the parents of my interpreter believed that May Ying—Opium Poppy—was the most beautiful name they could give their daughter.

The Hmong grew their opium, as they grew their rice and corn, as a slash-and-burn crop. (The more polite agricultural term is "swidden.") In the dry season the women cut away the forest underbrush with knives, and the men felled the trees with axes. Then the men sprinted down the hillsides, igniting the piles of vegetation with torches. The flames often rose four hundred feet in the air, and the swirling smoke could be seen for miles. When the charred brush had cooled enough to touch, entire families worked together to clear the debris before they planted, leaving only boulders and tree stumps. Swidden farming required no plowing, no irrigation, no terracing, no fertilizing. The topsoil was briefly enriched by the wood ashes, but four or five years of monsoons washed it away, and the remaining soil was so exhausted that twenty years could pass before it was once again productive. In the 1950s, it was estimated that the Hmong of Laos were burning about four hundred square miles of land a year and, by letting the topsoil leach away, causing enough erosion to alter the courses of rivers. Opium was a particularly egregious offender, since instead of eventually reforesting like rice swiddens, old opium swiddens became covered in a coarse grass called imperata, which even animals refused to eat.

The practice of swidden farming is inextricably intertwined with the migrant identity of the Hmong. The residents of a village would farm the contiguous land, abandon it in a few years when the soil became depleted, farm the land within walking distance, abandon that, build overnight shelters in order to farm even more distant land, and then, finally, move the entire village. Like Elizabeth I of England, who scheduled her progresses from castle to castle in the pre-plumbing era by departing whenever the smell became unbearable, the Hmong moved when a village's accumulation of garbage and animal feces grew unpleasant or began to make people sick. If a village got overcrowded, extended family groups sometimes established satellite villages nearby. Hmong houses—split bamboo or wooden planks lashed together with ropes and sinews—were designed to be easily dismantled, portaged, and reassembled. Hmong arts were portable too: no monumental sculpture; highly evolved textiles, jewelry, music, and storytelling. Because they always moved in groups rather than as individuals, their clan structure, their religion, and their cultural identity accompanied them wherever they went, constituting an essential sense of "home" that inoculated them against perpetual homesickness.

The life of the swidden migrant bespoke a certain prodigal faith in the earth's inexhaustible abundance, the confidence that if one field lost its fertility, one village its health, or one region its plenty, no matter: as the Hmong proverb declared, "There's always another mountain." It was not a lazy attitude. Moving is difficult. When the Hmong left China for Indochina, they had committed themselves to migration as a problem-solving strategy on the most arduous scale they could imagine, and in the 1960s and 1970s, when Laos became a battleground for the Vietnam War, they found themselves repeating the process yet again, even more drastically, first within the nation's borders and eventually far beyond them.

In 1961, King Savang Vatthana of Laos, a well-meaning but sinewless intellectual who traced his lineage to the eighth century, quoted Proust, and drove an Edsel, lamented, "Our country is the most peaceful in the world. . . . At no time has there ever arisen in the minds of the Lao people the idea of coveting another's wealth, of quarreling with their neighbors, much less of fighting them. And yet, during the past twenty years, our country has known neither peace nor security. . . . Enemies of all sorts have tried to cross our frontiers, to destroy our people and to destroy our religion and our nation's aura of peace and concord. Foreign countries do not care either about our interests or peace; they are concerned only with their own interests."

The Geneva Accords of 1954, signed after the French lost the battle of Dien Bien Phu, had recognized three independent states in what had formerly been French Indochina: Laos, Cambodia, and Vietnam, which was temporarily partitioned into northern and southern zones that were supposed to be reunited within two years. Laos was to be neutral. But this economically piddling backwater, which in 1960 had one stoplight in its capital and only three million dollars of exports (not counting opium), was cursed by its strategic location. With Thailand and Burma to the west, Vietnam to the east, and Cambodia to the south—all of them stronger and more populous, and none of them walled off by natural barriers—Laos was unlikely to stay neutral for long. Aided by the Vietminh, Ho Chi Minh's North Vietnamese military forces, the communist Pathet Lao became entangled in a protracted struggle with the anticommunist Royal Lao government for control of the country.

At this point the United States, which had provided covert training to the Royal Lao army since 1955, stepped up its involvement. "It may seem incredible in retrospect," wrote Clark Clifford, adviser to presidents Truman, Kennedy, Johnson, and Carter, in his memoirs, "but [President Eisenhower] considered the fate of that tiny, landlocked Southeast Asian kingdom the most important problem facing the U.S." In 1961, on his last day in office, Eisenhower told President-elect Kennedy that if Laos were to fall to communism, it would be only a matter of time before South Vietnam, Cambodia, Thailand, and Burma fell too. Kennedy agreed. There was only one problem. At the Geneva Conference of 1961–62, the United States, the Soviet Union, North and South Vietnam, and ten other nations agreed to a new set of accords in which they reaffirmed the neutrality of Laos and promised not to send in "any foreign troops or military personnel."

This is where the Hmong entered the picture. The United States was anxious to support an anticommunist government in Laos and to cut the military supply line that the North Vietnamese ran to South Vietnam along the Ho Chi Minh Trail, a complex of roads and pathways in southeastern Laos, near the Vietnam border. But how could it intervene while maintaining at least the appearance of legitimacy? Without violating the accords, American troops might be able to go to Vietnam, but not to Laos.* The answer was to fight a war by proxy.

---

* For more than three decades, historians have debated the question of whether the United States broke any international agreements by sending American troops into Vietnam. The 1954 Geneva Accords included a declaration "prohibiting the introduction into Viet-Nam of foreign troops and military personnel as well as of all kinds of arms and munitions." The United States and South Vietnam refused to join in that declaration, but the U.S. stated that it would "refrain from the threat or use of force" to disturb the provisions of the Accords. According to the

Kennedy cut the Gordian knot by dispatching a cadre of CIA advisers—not "foreign troops" themselves, though in retrospect it is clear that they were "military personnel"—who recruited, trained, and armed a secret guerrilla army of Hmong soldiers. Subsequently supported by the Johnson and Nixon administrations, the Hmong Armée Clandestine eventually came to number more than 30,000. Its soldiers fought the ground war, flew combat missions, directed air strikes by Air America pilots, rescued downed American flyers, were dropped by helicopter and parachute to fight behind enemy lines, gathered intelligence on the movements of Pathet Lao and North Vietnamese troops, sabotaged roads and bridges, planted electronic transmitters in enemy units to pinpoint their locations for bombing raids, and intercepted matériel on the Ho Chi Minh Trail.

At its peak, the Armée Clandestine was the biggest CIA operation in the world, but until 1987, when a British investigative journalist named Christopher Robbins published a book called *The Ravens: The Men Who Flew in America's Secret War in Laos*, the American public had heard little about it except rumors and denials. (A typical sample from the *New York Times*, July 4, 1962: "A Defense Department spokesman labelled as 'untrue' today charges that United States planes were dropping arms to Meo [Hmong] tribesmen in Laos.") In 1965, Johnson commented sanctimoniously that "the problem of Laos is the refusal of the Communist forces to honor the Geneva Accords." What he failed to mention was that his own country wasn't honoring them either; it was just doing a better job of keeping its violations secret. According to Robbins, the war was so classified that American Air Force pilots in Vietnam who were recruited to fly planes for Air America, the CIA's proprietary airline in Laos, didn't even know until they arrived in Laos what country they'd volunteered to fight in. It was simply called "the Other Theater."

At first glance, it seems crazy that the CIA recruited the most remote ethnic minority in Laos, one notorious for its lack of national consciousness, instead of the dominant lowland Lao. The explanation

---

historian John Lewis Gaddis, "The [1954] Geneva Accords were so hastily drafted and ambiguously worded that, from the standpoint of international law, it makes little sense to speak of violations of them by either side." The 1962 Accords, however, which dealt only with Laos, were unambiguous.

lay both in the shortcomings of the Lao and in the special assets of the Hmong. A Royal Lao army existed, but its soldiers had never been noted for their bellicosity. A *Life* magazine article of the period observed, "[The Lao] are among the most charming people in Asia— and the most otherworldly and least martial as well. Consequently, Lao troops have sometimes fired over the heads of the enemy rather than hurt anybody, much to the despair of American advisers." It was said that Lao soldiers were likely to lay down their weapons the first time they were attacked, or sell them on the black market. The Hmong, on the other hand—to whom the CIA, like the Lao, referred as "Meo"—had a four-thousand-year-long reputation as scrappy fighters. In Laos, they had already proven their mettle as guerrillas during the Second World War, when they fought on the side of the Lao and the French during the Japanese occupation, and after the war, when, similarly allied, they resisted the Vietminh. The CIA thus conveniently inherited a counterinsurgent network of Hmong guerrillas that the French had organized in northern Laos two decades earlier. Reading American press accounts of the war from the early sixties through the early seventies, I was bemused by their simultaneous condescension toward and admiration for the Hmong, who were portrayed as noble savages with thrillingly ferocious temperaments: "Like many primitive peoples, their word for 'enemy' and 'stranger' is the same, and they are as likely to skewer a visitor on the arrow of a crossbow as to welcome him." "Meo tribesmen [are] tough little primitives skilled in the savage techniques of ambush and night assault." "Sketchy reports trickle down from the hills and tell of heavy damage wreaked on Communist motorcades by Meo tribesmen on the progovernment warpath." "The Meos have never hesitated to kill. Not only are they ready and able to use weapons but they also climb up and down the mountains with the agility of mountain goats, setting ambushes, destroying convoys, spreading terror in the enemy's rear and then fading back into the mountains."

Many Hmong had reasons of their own for defending the Royal Lao government, and thus for collaborating with the United States. Perhaps a fifth of them—mostly members and supporters of the Lo clan, which had a long-standing feud with the anticommunist Ly clan—sided with the Pathet Lao. But the great majority, including those contacted by the CIA, supported the royalist camp, not because communism was ideologically less attractive than capitalism but because it was more apt to threaten their autonomy. It was unlikely that communist agrarian land reformers would look with favor on Hmong swidden agriculture. Moreover, because most Hmong had sided with the French before the collapse of colonial Indochina, they feared reprisals from the North Vietnamese, who had recently inflamed old antagonisms by confiscating Hmong opium crops to trade for weapons. There were also persuasive social reasons for fighting on the royalist side. Traditionally snubbed by the lowland Lao, the Hmong were likely to gain status if they became the heroes of a military victory. Finally, many Hmong had a huge personal stake in the war because they lived in the mountains surrounding its most crucial theater of operation: the Plain of Jars, a plateau in northeastern Laos through which communist troops from the north would have to march in any attempt to occupy the administrative capital of Vientiane, on the Thai border. That the Hmong knew this strategic region like the backs of their hands was not lost on the American military leaders who recruited them. Other hilltribes also supported the royalists, but the Hmong did most of the fighting.

In 1971, while testifying before the Senate Armed Services Committee, an undersecretary of state named U. Alexis Johnson said, "I personally feel that although the way the operation [in Laos] has been run is unorthodox, unprecedented, in many ways I think it is something of which we can be proud as Americans. It has involved virtually no American casualties. What we are getting for our money is, to use the old phrase, very cost-effective." What Johnson was saying, in effect, was that Hmong lives came cheap. The annual cost of financing the Armée Clandestine (via the CIA, the Department of Defense, and the U.S. Agency for International Development) was about $500 million. The annual cost of the Vietnam War was about $20 billion. One of the reasons for this disparity was that in 1971, army privates in Vietnam were paid between $197.50 and $339 a month; Hmong soldiers in Laos were paid an average of 2,000 *kip* ($3) a month. American soldiers in Vietnam ate army field rations (spaghetti, turkey loaf, ham and eggs, frankfurters and beans), with periodic supplements of steak, ice cream, and beer; Hmong soldiers in Laos ate rice. American pilots were sent home after a year or, if they flew over North Vietnam, after their hundredth mission; the most famous Hmong pilot, Lieutenant Ly Lue, flew more than five thousand missions before he was shot down. "There was no tour to complete," wrote Christopher Robbins, "no rest and recreation in Hong Kong or Australia, no end in sight to the war. 'Fly till you die,' the Meo pilots said." Hmong soldiers died at a rate about ten times as high as that of American soldiers in Vietnam.

To call the Hmong American-paid mercenaries, as has often been done, is to forget that mercenaries, whether lured by money or adventure, choose their profession. Not all Hmong became soldiers of their own accord. Some were forced into combat because bombing in northern Laos had obliged them to abandon their fields, and there was no other employment. Some were coerced. General Vang Pao, the CIA-supported Hmong leader of the Armée Clandestine, was said to punish villages that had failed to fill their soldier quotas by cutting off their food supplies or even sending his own troops to attack them. Jonas Vangay, a Hmong leader in Merced, told me soon after I met him, "Vang Pao recruited by force. I was very lucky. My father had money and he pay four other men to serve instead of my three brothers and me. Father sent us to school secretly and those four men fight." Jonas left it at that. It was only when I knew him better, several months later, that I ventured to ask what had happened to the soldiers who had served in their stead. "All four die," he said, and, after a moment of uncomfortable silence, changed the subject.

Vang Pao was both the cornerstone of the war and its most cryptic figure. A natural leader who had begun his military career at thirteen as an interpreter and jungle runner for the French, he rose precipitously through the ranks in the Royal Lao army until, in the early 1950s, he was recommended for officer training school. When the captain overseeing the entrance exam noticed that this promising candidate knew almost no written French, he neatly solved the problem by dictating the answers. (Years later, Vang Pao expressed no embarrassment at having cheated; he emphasized, however, that the captain had merely *told* him the answers, and not, as the story sometimes went, actually guided his hand. "Whorehouse of shit!" he told a Hmong interviewer. "I know how to write!") It is worth noting that this incident, far from tarnishing Vang Pao's reputation—as, for example, Ted Kennedy's fudged Spanish exam at Harvard tarnished his— merely added to his mythology: this was the sort of man who could never be held back by such petty impediments as rules. By 1961, when the CIA tapped him to lead their guerrilla army, Vang Pao was already a colonel—the highest rank a Hmong had ever attained—who had sealed his influence over the Hmong by choosing wives from three major clans. By 1963, he was a major general. He considered himself a modern reformer who supported education, criticized slash-and-burn farming, and urged the Hmong to assimilate into Lao society; yet he once engaged a famous *txiv neeb* to sacrifice two steers in order to coax an influential Hmong neutralist over to the rightist side, and postponed at least one bombing sortie because the leg bones of the chickens he ate for dinner were inauspiciously positioned. He tortured North Vietnamese prisoners with electric shocks and strafed Hmong villages that collaborated with the Pathet Lao; yet he served as a godfather and surrogate provider to hundreds of war widows and orphans. Even his enemies conceded his courage. He often accompanied his soldiers to the front lines, surviving several crash landings as well as bullet wounds in his arm and side.

The CIA considered Vang Pao—according to the narration of a propaganda film of the time—"a charismatic, passionate, and committed man, a patriot without a country." He was twice flown to the United States, invited to the White House, and, as the *New York Times* noted, during a 1969 visit to Disneyland "was given a Zorro suit as a jest [that] he wore recently, according to sources close to him, when he toured the Plaine des Jarres, the vital area his forces recently captured." Realizing that the best way to guarantee Hmong collaboration was to support their opium trade, the CIA used its Air America aircraft to pick up crude opium bricks in remote villages, and gave Vang Pao his own airline, Xieng Khouang Air Transport (nicknamed "Air Opium"), which flew opium from the secret Hmong military base at Long Tieng, in northern Laos, to markets in Vientiane. After it was refined, much of the Hmong opium crop ended up in South Vietnam, where it helped addict an estimated 30,000 American soldiers to heroin. A large portion indirectly subsidized the Armée Clandestine, which is one reason the war was such a bargain. "I knew nothing of this," former CIA director Richard Helms told a reporter for *Frontline*, who obviously didn't believe him, in 1988. "It certainly was not policy."

Some of Vang Pao's recruits were sent to training camps in Thai-

land. Others massed in Long Tieng, an abandoned opium field, surrounded on three sides by a protective barrier of limestone mountains,
which during the war became the largest Hmong settlement in the
world. New recruits drilled on the landing strip built by the CIA to
accommodate cargo planes. Using cardboard targets their wives had
cut from surplus butter boxes, they practiced their marksmanship with
American M-1 rifles and M-2 carbines, as well as with captured Soviet
submachine guns. They also learned how to handle mortars and surplus Air Force rockets, which they fired from homemade launchers.
Since they could not read, trail watchers assigned to spot North Vietnamese convoys were provided with radio transmitters whose buttons
were labeled with pictures of trucks and tanks. Their CIA advisers
marveled at how quickly the Hmong, accustomed to crossbows and
flintlocks, mastered the technology of modern warfare. "You give one
of these little guys an M-1 rifle and fifty rounds of ammunition in the
morning," said an American trainer in 1961, "and when he comes
back that night he'll be able to kill a man at 200 yards." Christopher
Robbins reported the story—perhaps apocryphal, perhaps not—that
in the early days of the war, Hmong villagers peered under the fuse-
lages of airplanes to determine whether they were male or female.
A few years later, some of those villagers were crewing or piloting
propeller-driven T-28 training planes converted to bombers. The
Hmong also impressed the Americans with their adaptability. With
little available timber, soldiers who had transplanted their families to
Long Tieng built houses out of empty rice sacks, knocked-down ammunition crates, and flattened fifty-five-gallon oil drums. They used
grenades to fish, and stuffed them inside chickens as bait for tigers.
They used parachute cord to rope water buffalos.

In the United States the conflict in Laos was called the "Quiet
War"—as opposed to the noisy one in Vietnam, whose escalation had
turned the Laotian civil war into an international free-for-all, with the
Soviet Union and the People's Republic of China throwing their
weight behind the Pathet Lao while the United States continued to
back the Royal Lao. But for the Hmong, the war was anything but
quiet. More than two million tons of bombs were dropped on Laos,
mostly by American planes attacking communist troops in Hmong
areas. There was an average of one bombing sortie every eight minutes
for nine years. Between 1968 and 1972, the tonnage of bombs dropped

on the Plain of Jars alone exceeded the tonnage dropped by American planes in both Europe and the Pacific during World War II. In 1971, an American reporter named T. D. Allman flew over the Plain of Jars and reported that he had counted several hundred bomb craters on a single hundred-foot hill; that most of the plain's vegetation had been stripped by American defoliants; and that napalm fires burned day and night. The Plain of Jars is still pocked with craters and littered with unexploded American-made cluster bombs, ready to detonate at the accidental prodding of a hoe or the curious poke of a child.

During the latter years of the war, as Hmong casualties mounted, younger and younger soldiers were recruited to fight the constant stream of well-trained North Vietnamese, who were rotated annually. In *Tragic Mountains: The Hmong, the Americans, and the Secret Wars for Laos, 1942–1992*, Jane Hamilton-Merritt quoted a former soldier named Vang Xeu who volunteered in 1968, when he was thirteen:

> Everyone knew that Vang Pao had been a soldier at 13, so many young boys volunteered to fight to protect our land. I was a small, weak boy but determined to help my people. . . . In my first fight, I discovered that I couldn't shoot my weapon by hand-holding it; it was too heavy. I had to find a rock or tree to steady it on before firing. That was dangerous. So, I asked Vang Pao if I could be a paratrooper. He agreed and I trained for that. On my first jump, I was so light that I floated and floated and came down far from my unit. To solve my floating problem, the next time I jumped with a B-40 grenade launcher. That brought me down. But once on the ground, I wasn't strong enough to operate the B-40 effectively. I asked Vang Pao if I could be trained in intelligence. He agreed. That was the right place for me.

In 1968, Edgar "Pop" Buell, a retired Indiana farmer who directed the U.S. Agency for International Development relief program in northern Laos, told Robert Shaplen of the *New Yorker*, "A few days ago, I was with [Vang Pao's] officers when they rounded up three hundred fresh [Hmong] recruits. Thirty per cent of the kids were fourteen years old or less, and about a dozen were only ten years old. Another thirty per cent were fifteen or sixteen. The rest were thirty-five or over. Where were the ones in between? I'll tell you—they're all dead."

In 1960, between 300,000 and 400,000 Hmong lived in Laos.

There is wide disagreement over what fraction died during the war and its aftermath, with estimates ranging from a tenth (in a 1975 *Washington Post* report) to half (in a 1970 report to the Senate Judiciary Subcommittee on Refugees and Escapees). Some were soldiers who died in battle; most were civilians killed by cannon and mortar fire, bombs, land mines, grenades, postwar massacres, hunger, and disease. Whether one cause of death was chemical warfare in the form of toxic "yellow rain" has been the subject of abundant controversy—a debate that has diverted attention from the holocaust that the Hmong incontestably suffered from conventional weapons.* Although they suffered far worse losses per capita than the South Vietnamese, whose agonies were featured daily in the American press, the Hmong were almost completely overlooked, partly because all reporters were barred from Long Tieng. (On the one occasion when an American, a British, and a French journalist did manage to sneak into Long Tieng, Vang Pao was so worried about having his secret base exposed that he decided to blow up their jeep, and was dissuaded only with great difficulty by

---

* The yellow rain charges can be summarized as follows: Starting in 1975, after the Pathet Lao victory in Laos, Hmong refugees who had escaped to Thailand reported that while in Laos they had suffered from dizziness, skin rashes, blisters, diarrhea, stomach cramps, nausea, and bleeding from the nose and mouth. Some had died. They said these symptoms had begun after clouds of droplets—usually yellow, but sometimes white, black, blue, or red—fell from the sky, delivered by (according to various and sometimes conflicting reports) jets, prop-driven aircraft, helicopters, artillery shells, grenades, or land mines. The Hmong believed that what came to be called "yellow rain" was a communist reprisal against their continued resistance; anti-Hmong reprisals in other forms had already been well documented. In 1981, Secretary of State Alexander Haig announced that the Soviet Union and its communist allies in Southeast Asia were using chemical weapons in the form of trichothecene mycotoxins, a fungal poison. This was a serious charge, as chemical and biological weapons had been banned by both the 1925 Geneva Protocol and the 1972 Biological and Toxin Weapons Convention. Haig's accusations were called into question in 1983, when Matthew Meselson, a professor of molecular biology at Harvard, noted that every sample of "yellow rain" residue on leaves, twigs, and stones that had been turned in by Hmong refugees contained a high proportion of pollen. When Meselson examined some samples under an electron microscope, he found that the pollen grains were hollow, indicating that they had been digested—that, in fact, these samples were actually bee feces, which fall in yellow clouds when bee colonies take mass defecation flights. One sample even contained a bee hair. Meselson pointed out that most

his CIA advisers.) When the Hmong *were* mentioned, the crucial element of American involvement was usually missing from the account, either because the reporter couldn't confirm it or because the information was embargoed.

In northern Laos, ninety percent of the villages were affected by the war—that is to say, the inhabitants suffered casualties or were displaced, or both. Entire villages fled en masse after their houses were burned and their headmen beaten or killed during nighttime raids by the Pathet Lao or North Vietnamese. Some villages decamped to avoid incidental bombing by American or Royal Lao aircraft. (In 1971, a Hmong leader in Long Pot, a village thirty miles northwest of Long Tieng, was asked which he feared most, attacks by the enemy Pathet Lao or bombs dropped by his own allies. "The bombs!" he replied. "The bombs!") Some were evacuated by Air America, on the theory that in areas where the Pathet Lao were inevitably advancing, the communists' military gains would be diminished if they captured only land and not people. Some villages simply collapsed because all the able-bodied men were dead or fighting, and the remaining women, children, and elderly men were unable to work enough fields to feed themselves. By 1970, forced to adapt their migratory habits to wartime, more than a third of the Hmong in Laos had become refugees within their own country. Yang Dao, a Hmong scholar and government adviser, wrote at the time:

---

of the Hmong-provided yellow rain samples contained no trichothecenes, and that in those that did, the level was too low to be toxic. He postulated that the Hmong were getting sick from natural causes—perhaps moldy food—and misattributing the source of their symptoms. (Many of Meselson's critics misunderstood his theory, mistakenly believing he had claimed that bee feces, which are harmless, had poisoned the Hmong.) Other yellow rain skeptics emphasized the potency of rumor in Hmong culture; some suggested that yellow rain was not mycotoxic poison but a conventional weapon, possibly American-made CS tear gas left by U.S. troops in Vietnam and appropriated by communist Vietnamese. A 1985 federal chemical-warfare team concluded that "information regarding the use of 'yellow rain' against the Hmong in Laos remains too incomplete or implausible" to justify any conclusive claims about its existence. I would agree. It is noteworthy that the extensive press coverage of yellow rain has frequently divided along political lines, with the more conservative *Wall Street Journal* and *Reader's Digest* affirming its existence and the more liberal *New York Times* and *New Yorker* challenging it.

In Houa Phanh and Xieng Khouang provinces, the war has reached into every home and forced every individual, down to the very youngest, to make the agonizing choice of flight or death. . . . [Displaced people] have taken refuge in temporary settlements to the south, where there is little to eat, where schools are nonexistent, where sanitary conditions are deplorable, and where hopelessness and despair are constant companions.

During these troubled times, total disorder prevailed; what government there was intervened only to attend to the most pressing situations. The heat and the rains, compounded by the lack of hygiene among people accustomed to living in relative isolation, quickly led to the spread of disease and epidemics, ravaging the teeming refugee population, particularly the children.

In the space of only a few years the southwest part of the Plain of Jars, once a lush green forest where tigers roamed, has been "urbanized" under the pressure of a continuing exodus that has no relationship whatsoever to the normal sort of economic development linked to industrialization. Today more than 200,000 people live in settlements and military bases ranging from 500 to 30,000 inhabitants, confined to a mountainous strip only 50 by 90 kilometers in area. The rest of the province is total desolation.

In some spheres, the Hmong reacted to these upheavals, as they had to calamities throughout their history, by grasping their traditional culture even more tightly. Yang Dao reported that displaced families who had lost their livestock continued to go through the motions of ritual sacrifice, using stones in place of animals. The dwindling practice of polygyny, which at the beginning of the war was observed mainly by leaders like Vang Pao as a status symbol, became common again as a response to the mismatched wartime survival rates of men and women. The institution of levirate marriage, in which a widow was expected to wed her dead husband's younger brother, was also revived. This practice kept the children and their inheritance in their father's clan but often saddled the new husband, who might well be fifteen years old or have ten children already, with crushing responsibilities.

For the most part, though, the experience of the "internal refugees" was a chaotic and involuntary crash landing into twentieth-century culture. A popularly held notion is that the Hmong refugees who came to the United States after the war were, as one newspaper reporter put it, "transplanted from Stone Age to Space Age." Not only does that view grossly underestimate the complexity of traditional Hmong culture, but it also ignores the immense social, cultural, and economic changes that many Hmong had already gone through during the course of the war itself. The way of life that had survived centuries of persecution in China, as well as the nineteeth-century hegira to Laos, was irreversibly altered, at least in its outward forms, within a few years. I once asked Jonas Vangay to summarize the effects of the war on the Hmong. "My parents used to travel barefoot and on horse," he said. "We lived in a rural and mountainous area where we never saw a car or a bus. Suddenly, in 1960, everything went upside down. The French wars hadn't really influenced us so much. Less than twenty percent of the Hmong were involved in the battle of Dien Bien Phu. But with the U.S. war, it was ninety percent. You couldn't stay in your village. You moved around and around and around. Four years later, when I went to Vientiane, what struck me is that you cannot see a lot of Hmong with their black clothing anymore. All are wearing khaki and green soldier clothing. And where we had lived, before the war it was all covered with forests. After the bombardments . . . *il n'y a plus de forêts, il n'y en a plus, il n'y en a plus, il n'y a rien du tout.*" Jonas tended to lapse into French—his fourth language, after Hmong, Lao, and Thai—when he could not adequately express his emotions in English, his fifth language. ("There are no more forests, there are no more, there are no more, there is nothing at all.")

Although some Hmong had been exposed to lowland life during and after the Second World War, many saw cars, trucks, tractors, bicycles, radios, flashlights, clocks, canned food, and cigarettes for the first time when they were forced to leave their villages for temporary relocation sites. Swidden farming was moribund. A market economy began to rise in its place, encouraged by the soldiers' cash wages and the availability of manufactured goods. Lao *kip* replaced silver as a means of exchange. Long Tieng became a desultory megalopolis, an unpaved, sewerless city of more than 30,000 where Hmong ran noodle stands, cobbled shoes, tailored clothes, repaired radios, ran military-jeep taxi services, and interpreted for American pilots and relief workers. Except for ceremonial occasions, many Hmong women discarded their embroidered black garments and adopted lowland-Lao *lungi* skirts and short blouses of factory-made material. Both men and women wore polyvinyl thongs. Some children attended school; others trailed after the Americans, begging chewing gum and coins, or squatted in the dirt, playing with bullet casings instead of toys made of corncobs and chicken feathers. Even the Hmong language adapted. Many of the traditional onomatopoeic expressions expanded to make room for new associations. *Plij ploj*, the sound of bamboo breaking, gained the additional meaning of "bullet impact." *Vig vwg*, the roar of wind or fire, now meant "small airplane motor" as well. *Plhij plhawj*, the sound of birds making brief flights from roost to roost, also meant "helicopter propellers." A new expression, *ntsij ntsiaj*, meaning "pushing or pulling the bolt on an M-16," came into use.

The most drastic change bred by the war was the loss of the single asset the Hmong prized most highly: their self-sufficiency. With their fields left rotting, their livestock abandoned, and their mountains emptied of game, more than 100,000 Hmong were kept alive by U.S.-sponsored food drops—weather and enemy fire permitting, fifty tons of rice a day, delivered by parachute from Air America cargo planes. As one pilot put it, "There is a whole generation of Meos who are going to be damn surprised when someone tells them that rice doesn't grow in the sky." One consequence of feeding the Hmong was that those who still lived in tillable regions could spend more time growing poppies, to the benefit of the opium trade. Not all Hmong villages and relocation sites were supplied with rice, and in those that were, the daily allotment per person was about a pound, half what the Hmong were used to. The memory of the rice drops still rankles. When I asked Jonas Vangay about them, he said, "Are you accusing the Hmong to be idle or lazy? Do you think they were just waiting for rice from the sky? The Hmong have *always* grown their own rice. Lao used to get rice from Hmong in exchange for salt and material. The Hmong never bought rice from Lao! But in the Plain area, there is not enough rice in the war. *Ils n'ont plus de choix.*" ("They no longer have any choice.")

In January of 1973, the United States signed the Paris Agreement, pledging to withdraw all its forces from Vietnam. Two weeks later, on his way to Hanoi, Henry Kissinger stopped in Vientiane to talk with Prince Souvanna Phouma, the Prime Minister of Laos, who feared the United States would similarly withdraw support from Laos, leaving it to the mercy of North Vietnam. "The very survival of Laos rests on your shoulders," Souvanna Phouma told Kissinger. "But your shoulders are very broad. We are counting on you to make our neighbors understand that all we want is peace. We are a very small country; we do not represent a danger to anybody. We count on you to make them know that the Lao people are pacific by tradition and by religion. We want only to be sovereign and independent. We ask that they let us live in peace on this little piece of ground that is left to us of our ancient kingdom. . . . Therefore we must count on our great friends the Americans to help us survive."

In his 1979 memoirs, Kissinger, whose shoulders turned out to be far less broad than the prince had hoped, wrote, "I cannot, even today, recall Souvanna Phouma's wistful plea without a pang of shame." In February 1973, the Vientiane Agreement was signed, calling for a cease-fire in Laos, a coalition government, and the end of American air support. USAID discontinued its relief program, and in June of 1974, the last Air America plane left Laos. On May 3, 1975, two weeks after the Khmer Rouge took control of Phnom Penh, three days after the North Vietnamese occupied Saigon, and seven months before the communist Lao People's Democratic Republic supplanted the six-hundred-year-old Lao monarchy, the Pathet Lao crossed the cease-fire line into territory held by Vang Pao. On May 9, the *Khao Xane Pathet Lao*, the newspaper of the Lao People's Party, announced: "The Meo [Hmong] must be exterminated down to the root of the tribe." On May 10, surrounded by Pathet Lao and North Vietnamese troops, with few surviving Hmong fighter pilots and no American combat support, Vang Pao reluctantly bowed to the counsel of his CIA case officers and conceded that he could no longer hold Long Tieng. During the next four days, between 1,000 and 3,000 Hmong—mostly high-ranking army officers and their families, including the family of my interpreter, May Ying Xiong—were airlifted by American planes to Thailand. (During the month before the fall of Saigon on April 30, American airlifts and sealifts had evacuated more than 45,000 South Vietnamese.) Hmong fought to board the aircraft. Several times the planes were so overloaded they could not take off, and dozens of people standing near the door had to be pushed out onto the airstrip. On May 14, Vang Pao, in tears, told the assembled crowd, "Farewell, my brothers, I can do nothing more for you, I would only be a torment for you," and boarded an evacuation helicopter. After the last American transport plane disappeared, more than 10,000 Hmong were left on the airfield, fully expecting more aircraft to return. When it became apparent that there would be no more planes, a collective wail rose from the crowd and echoed against the mountains. The shelling of Long Tieng began that afternoon. A long line of Hmong, carrying their children and old people, started to move across the plateau, heading toward Thailand.

11

_____

The Big One

On November 25, 1986, the day before Thanksgiving, the Lees were eating dinner. Lia, who had had a mild runny nose for several days, sat in her usual chair at the round white Formica table in the kitchen, surrounded by her parents, five of her sisters, and her brother. She was normally an avid eater, but tonight she had little appetite, and fed herself only a little rice and water. After she finished eating, her face took on the strange, frightened expression that always preceded an epileptic seizure. She ran to her parents, hugged them, and fell down, her arms and legs first stiffening and then jerking furiously. Nao Kao picked her up and laid her on the blue quilted pad they always kept ready for her on the living room floor.

"When the spirit caught Lia and she fell down," said Nao Kao, "she was usually sick for ten minutes or so. After that, she would be normal again, and if you gave her rice, she ate it. But this time she was really sick for a long time, so we had to call our nephew because he spoke English and he knew how to call an ambulance." On every other occasion when Lia had seized, Nao Kao and Foua had carried Lia to the hospital. I asked Nao Kao why he had decided to summon an ambulance. "If you take her in an ambulance, they would pay more attention to her at the hospital," he said. "If you don't call the ambulance, those *tsov tom* people wouldn't look at her." May Ying hesitated before translating *tsov tom*, which means "tiger bite." Tigers are a symbol of wickedness and duplicity—in Hmong folktales, they steal men's wives and eat their own children—and *tsov tom* is a very serious curse.

It is true that, whether one is Hmong or American, arriving at an emergency room via ambulance generally does stave off the customary two-hour wait. But any patient as catastrophically ill as Lia was that night would have been instantly triaged to the front of the line, no matter how she had gotten there. In fact, if her parents had run the three blocks to MCMC with Lia in their arms, they would have saved nearly twenty minutes that, in retrospect, may have been critical. As it was, it took about five minutes for their nephew to come to their house and dial 911; one minute for the ambulance to respond to the dispatcher's call; two minutes for the ambulance to reach the Lee residence; fourteen minutes (an unusually, and in this case perhaps disastrously, long time) for the ambulance to leave the scene; and one minute to drive to the hospital.

Years later, when Neil Ernst looked over the ambulance report, he sighed and said, "That EMT was in way over his head. *Way* over." According to the report, when the ambulance arrived at 37 East 12th Street at 6:52 p.m., this is what the emergency medical technician found:

Age: 4
Sex: ♀
Illness: Seizure/Convulsions
Airway: Compromised
Respiratory Effort: None
Pulses: Thready
Skin Color: Cyanotic
Pupils: Fixed
Chest: Tense
Pelvis: Incontinent of urine
Eyes Open to Voice or Pain: None
Verbal Response: None

Lia was on the verge of death. The emergency medical technician fitted a plastic airway over her tongue to prevent it from blocking her throat. After suctioning her mucus and saliva, he placed a mask over her nose and mouth and forced oxygen down her trachea by squeezing a hand-held resuscitation bag. He then attempted to insert an intravenous line in one of her antecubital veins, in front of the elbow, in order to administer an anticonvulsant drug. He failed, realized crucial minutes were being lost, and ordered the driver to head at top speed for MCMC with the ambulance on Code III (the most emergent, with lights flashing and sirens blaring). En route, the EMT tried desperately to insert the IV again, and failed two more times. As he later noted, in shaky handwriting, "Pt continued to seize."

The ambulance arrived at MCMC at 7:07. Lia's gurney was rushed into Room B. Of the emergency room's six cubicles, this was the one reserved for the most critical cases, since it contained a crash cart, a defibrillator, and intubation equipment. Lia had been there several times before. Room B is a twenty-by-twenty institutional-beige cell smelling faintly of disinfectant, sheathed from floor to ceiling in synthetic materials from which blood, urine, and vomit can be easily cleaned: a clean, bland backdrop against which hundreds of cataclysmic dramas have been played out and then scrubbed away. Lia was thrashing violently. Her lips and nail beds were blue. There was no time to undress her. A nurse tore off the blanket in which she was wrapped and, using bandage scissors, cut off a black T-shirt, an undershirt, and a pair of underpants. An emergency physician, two family practice residents, and the nurse surrounded Lia, trying to start an intravenous line. They took more than twenty minutes to insert a butterfly needle, attached to a small-bore tube, in the top of her left foot—a stopgap measure, since any movement on Lia's part was likely to cause the needle, which was left in the vein, to poke through the vessel wall and spill the IV solution into her tissues instead of her bloodstream. A large dose of Valium, a sedative that usually halts seizures by depressing the central nervous system, was pushed into the line. It had absolutely no effect. "We gave her Valium, more Valium, and more Valium," recalled Steve Segerstrom, one of the residents. "We did everything, and Lia's seizures only got worse. I went very rapidly from calm to panic." Steve tried repeatedly to start a more reliable IV, and failed. Lia continued to seize in twenty-second bursts. Vomited rice began to pour from her nose and mouth. The aspirated vomit, in combination with the impaired ability of her diaphragm to move air into her lungs, was compromising her ability to breathe. A respiratory therapist was summoned. An arterial blood-gas test showed that over the last hour or so, Lia's blood had probably contained levels of oxygen so low as to be nearly fatal: she was asphyxiating. Despite her seizures and her clenched jaw, one of the residents somehow managed to pass a breathing tube into her trachea, and she was placed on a hand ventilator.

Neil's pager went off at 7:35. He and Peggy were eating dinner with their two sons. They were planning on spending the evening at home, packing for their Thanksgiving vacation at the family cabin in the Sierra foothills, for which they would leave the next morning. Neil called the emergency room. He was told that Lia was in prolonged status epilepticus, that no one could get in a good IV, and that the Valium wasn't working. "As soon as I heard that," he recalled, "I knew that this was it. This was the big one."

Neil had been afraid for months that when this moment came, he would be the one on call, and he was. He told the resident to give Lia more Valium and, if that didn't work, to switch to Ativan, another sedative, which, when administered in large doses, is less likely than Valium to make a patient stop breathing. He jumped in his car, drove to MCMC as fast as he could without breaking the speed limit, and at 7:45 walked briskly—no matter how frantic he felt, he made a point of never running—through the emergency room door.

"It was an incredible scene," Neil said. "It was like something out of *The Exorcist*. Lia was literally jumping off the table. She had restraints on, but her motor activity was so unbelievable that she was just jumping, just hopping off the table, just on and on and on and on. It was different from any seizure I had ever seen before. I remember seeing her parents standing out in the hall, just outside the emergency room. The door was open and people were running in and out. They must have seen everything. I caught their eye a couple of times but I was too busy to talk to them right then. We had to get in a more substantial IV and there were the usual problems—her fat, her sclerosed veins from previous IVs—only much worse this time because of her absolutely tremendous muscular activity. Steve Segerstrom said, Do you think it's worth trying a saphenous cutdown?" (To perform a "cutdown," a physician makes a skin incision, nicks a blood vessel —in this case a large vein above Lia's right ankle—with a scalpel, dilates the hole with forceps, introduces an intravenous catheter, and sutures it into place.) "And I said, Gee, Steve, at this point, anything is worth it, go ahead and try. The atmosphere in the room was just *charged*. People were literally lying on Lia's legs while Steve started the cutdown. And he got it! And then we gave Lia just a ton of medicine, a lot, and a lot, and a lot. And finally, she stopped seizing. She finally stopped. It took a long time, but she finally stopped."

I had never seen Neil so upset as he was when he told me this. Steve Segerstrom sounded upset too when he recalled the incident, but Steve is an excitable man and a fast talker, so the contrast between his normal tone and his tone as he described the scene in Emergency Room B was far less noticeable than it was with Neil, who is usually so calm. When Neil finished talking, I could hear him breathing—not heavily, but audibly, as if he had been interrupted partway through his morning's eight-mile run.

This was Lia's sixteenth admission to MCMC. Everyone at the hospital—the emergency room nurses, the residents, the respiratory therapist, Neil—all assumed that Lia had the same thing wrong with her that she had had on her previous fifteen admissions, only worse. All the standard tests were run: blood counts, blood chemistries, blood pressures, and a chest X ray to confirm the placement of the breathing tube. Of course, Lia's blood was tested to find out if her parents had been giving her the prescribed amount of Depakene. Like every test since Lia's return home from foster care, it showed that they had. No one thought of taking her temperature, which was 101°, until after Neil had returned home. Two other unusual signs—diarrhea and a very low platelet count—were simply noted without comment on Lia's chart, eclipsed into invisibility by the monumental scale of her seizures. No antibiotics were administered because no infection was suspected.

A twenty-minute bout of status epilepticus is considered life-threatening. Lia had seized continuously for nearly two hours. When she stopped, she was unconscious, though breathing. Because MCMC does not have a children's Intensive Care Unit, it was obvious that Lia, like all of Merced's critical pediatric cases, had to be transferred to Valley Children's Hospital in Fresno. During the thick of the crisis, no one had said a word of explanation to Foua and Nao Kao, who had been forbidden to enter Emergency Room B. Steve Segerstrom's

Procedure Note for the saphenous cutdown tersely states, "Consent is implied due to severity of patient's illness." At some point, a nurse handed Foua the ruined clothes that had been cut off her daughter. After Lia's vital signs were stable, Neil walked slowly out into the hall. He had sweat stains running from his armpits to his waist. Using the English-speaking nephew as an interpreter, he explained the situation to Foua. "I told her that this had been the big one," he recalled later. "This was the worst seizure Lia had ever had, and it was very, very difficult to stop it, but we had stopped it. She was still very, very sick. I told the mother about the need to go to Fresno, because Lia would need stuff that Peggy and I couldn't do. I also told her that we were leaving town but we would be back next week. And she understood that." On Lia's Progress Record, Neil scrawled, "Transport arranged for VCH ICU. Parents spoken to and understand critical condition."

In fact, the parents understood an entirely different version of reality from the one Neil intended to convey. When I asked them why they thought Lia had been sent to Fresno, Nao Kao said, "Her doctor was going on vacation, so there wasn't any doctor here, so they sent her away." Foua said, "Lia's doctor was good at taking care of Lia. Sometimes when she was very, very sick, we would take her to him and he would make her better in a couple of days and she would be bouncing around and walking around. But that time he went to play, so they had to send Lia to someone else." In other words, the Lees believed their daughter was transferred not because of her critical condition but because of Neil's vacation plans, and that if she had stayed at MCMC, he would have restored her to health, just as he had on every other occasion.

At 9:30, after he had arranged for an ambulance to take Lia to Fresno, instructed his staff on how to prepare her for transfer, and discussed her case by telephone with the Pediatric Intensive Care Unit at Valley Children's, Neil drove home. He told Peggy, "That was it. She did it this time." The two of them talked until almost midnight, retracing every moment of Lia's crisis and each of Neil's decisions. "I was so fired up," he recalled, "I just couldn't come down. When I'm like that I have trouble sleeping, and I start food-cramming—I just start stuffing stuff in my mouth. And I have to tell Peggy all about what happened." Peggy was accustomed to talking Neil down from hospital emergencies, but she had never seen him this wound up.

"That night my feelings were mixed," said Neil. "It had been just like my nightmares—that Lia would have the most terrible seizure of her life and it was going to be my fault because I couldn't keep her from dying—but she *hadn't* died, and with some real capable people helping, I stopped it and I took care of it and I was able to meet the challenge. So I felt a certain amount of satisfaction. But I also felt terrifically sad because I didn't know what Lia was going to be like when she came out of this. I was pretty sure she wasn't going to be the same."

During the seventy-minute ambulance ride to Fresno, Lia "just crumped," as Neil put it when he looked over her chart later. She arrived at Valley Children's Hospital just before midnight in the throes of yet another grand mal seizure, with all four limbs flailing. Her fingers and toes were blue, her chest was mottled and cold, her blood pressure was precariously low, her white blood-cell count was precariously high, and her temperature was 104.9°. In a report sent to Neil Ernst, a critical care specialist named Maciej Kopacz noted that for an entire hour, it was impossible to start an arterial line "as no pulses could be palpable in any location." Dr. Kopacz also commented that while he was performing a spinal tap (a procedure during which his nose was less than a foot from Lia's buttocks), "the patient had explosive diarrhea showing large amount of water, foul smelling stools, with pus appearance." It is hard to imagine a more difficult or unpleasant case than Lia's must have been during her admission, which, to aggravate matters, took place during the early hours of Thanksgiving Day. Nonetheless, Dr. Kopacz, using the surreally courteous boilerplate of the standard consultation note, concluded his report—three single-spaced pages detailing one calamity after another—with the jolly sign-off, "Thank you very much for referring this patient to Pediatric Intensive Care Unit. Pediatric Critical Care Consultants will be happy to follow this patient."

Happy or not, the team of critical care consultants—supported by an auxiliary force of neurologists, infectious disease specialists, pediatric residents, respiratory therapists, radiologists, technicians, nurses, and nurse's aides—did indeed follow the patient. Their technology was cutting-edge and their clinical skills irreproachable. At first, however, they were too busy trying to save Lia's life to focus on a great deal besides her pathology. Dr. Kopacz, for example, who worked on

Lia for more than twelve hours straight, failed to notice her sex. "His metabolic acidosis was decreased after initial bolus of bicarbonate," he wrote. "His peripheral perfusion improved and pulse oximetry started reading a value that correlated with saturation on the arterial blood samples." Here was American medicine at its worst and its best: the patient was reduced from a girl to an analyzable collection of symptoms, and the physician, thereby able to husband his energies, succeeded in keeping her alive.

As soon as he saw Lia, Dr. Kopacz diagnosed her condition as "profound shock, probably of septic origin." Septic shock, the result of a bacterial invasion of the circulatory system, is a systemic siege that overwhelms the entire body, first causing acute circulatory failure, and then, if the toxins are not disarmed and the blood is unable to deliver sufficient oxygen, triggering the failure of one organ after another. The lungs usually falter first, followed by the liver and the kidneys. The impaired perfusion of the tissues also bollixes up the gastrointestinal tract: Lia's diarrhea was a typical symptom. Eventually the brain starts to die of oxygen deprivation, just as it would if the patient were drowning or being strangled. The mortality rate for septic shock is between forty and sixty percent.

There were so many things going wrong with Lia at once that a standard course of treatment, plotted with orderly deliberation, was out of the question. She required an immediate, unremitting, multipronged assault. First, as at MCMC, her seizures had to be stopped. Valium didn't work. In desperation, Dr. Kopacz loaded her with thiopental—a barbiturate so potent that, in effect, she was put under general anesthesia. Lia quickly went from convulsive agitation to stunned immobility. From that point on, the word "epilepsy" is rarely mentioned in her hospital chart. The doctors had too much else to worry about. To resuscitate her, they placed her on a respirator that delivered one-hundred-percent oxygen, the maximum. To monitor her blood pressure and deliver drugs—her diarrhea made it impossible to give anything by mouth—they inserted two more intravenous catheters, one in her left femoral artery and one in her right femoral vein. To monitor her heart function, they threaded a Swan-Ganz catheter through two chambers of her heart into her pulmonary artery. After each of these highly aggressive interventions, Dr. Kopacz noted, "The patient tolerated the procedure well." By this he did not mean that

Lia didn't complain (though this was true too, since she was unconscious throughout), simply that he encountered no technical problems and didn't kill the patient.

At 11:00 a.m. on Thanksgiving, Lia crashed. As a result of her septic shock, she had developed a disorder called disseminated intravascular coagulation. The ability of her blood to clot had gone haywire, and she began to bleed and ooze both from her IV sites and internally. Her low platelet count at MCMC had been an early, unrecognized sign of this condition. Dr. Kopacz decided to try a desperate measure: a double volume exchange transfusion. Little by little, over a period of fifteen hours, her entire blood supply was removed and replaced twice with fresh blood whose ability to clot was unimpaired. The old blood went out the femoral artery; the new blood came in the femoral vein. Though her blood pressure plunged almost fatally during the first half hour, the transfusion finally worked. For the first time in thirty-eight hours, her lips, fingers, and toes were pink.

Of all the trials to which Lia's body was subjected, the spinal tap —a routine and only moderately invasive attempt to find out if the sepsis had passed from her blood into her central nervous system— was the one that most distressed her father, who heard about it after it was performed. "The doctors put a hole in her back before we got to the hospital," he said. "I don't know why they did it. I wasn't there yet and they didn't give me any paper to sign. They just sucked her backbone like that and it makes me disappointed and sad because that is how Lia was lost." In other words, Nao Kao attributed Lia's deteriorating condition to the spinal tap, a procedure many Hmong believe to be potentially crippling both in this life and in future lives. Foua's explanation was, "They just took her to the hospital and they didn't fix her. She got very sick and I think it is because they gave her too much medicine."

It was true that Lia was given a great deal of medicine. To prevent fluid from seeping out of her blood vessels, she was given Plasmanate. To raise her blood pressure and stimulate her heart, she was given dobutamine, dopamine, and epinephrine. To improve the circulation of her blood, she was given nitroprusside. To fight her infection, she was given a succession of antibiotics: ampicillin, chloramphenicol, gentamicin, nafcillin, ceftriaxone, clindamycin, tobramycin, and ceftazidime. To dry her oral secretions, she was given Robinul. To prevent seizures, she was given Ativan. (Her attending neurologist, Terry Hutchison, would have preferred Depakene, but it cannot be administered intravenously.) To nourish her, she was given Pedialyte and Osmolite through a nasogastric tube.

During Lia's first week at Valley Children's, she also underwent a series of diagnostic tests. To attempt to locate the infection that had precipitated her septic shock, she had an abdominal ultrasound and a Gallium scan, in which radioactive tracing material was injected into her bloodstream. The Gallium scan suggested that the culpable site might be her left leg, though this finding was not conclusive. To identify the infection, her blood was cultured. It tested positive for *Pseudomonas aeruginosa*, a devastating bacterium that favors immunosuppressed patients, often in hospitals.

While all this was going on, Foua and Nao Kao lived in the waiting room of Valley Children's Hospital, sleeping in chairs for nine consecutive nights. Relatives took care of their other children in Merced. The Lees didn't understand why they were not permitted to stay by Lia's bedside, as they always had at MCMC. Here, they were allowed only one ten-minute visit every hour: standard protocol for an Intensive Care Unit at the time. They had no money to pay for a motel room or buy food at the hospital cafeteria. "Our relatives in Merced brought us rice," Nao Kao told me, "but only once a day, so we felt hungry." During their brief periods with their daughter, they saw a plastic breathing tube sticking out of her throat, connected to a respirator; a feeding tube coming out of her nose; lines filled with clear fluids snaking into her arms and legs; plastic boards taped to her limbs to stabilize the intravenous lines; a blood pressure cuff on her arm that automatically inflated and deflated; electrodes on her chest, connected to wires that were in turn connected to a heart monitor next to her bed. The respirator hissed, the IV pump beeped, the blood pressure cuff crackled and sighed. Lia's parents noticed that her buttocks were red and ulcerated from her diarrhea. Her hands and feet were swollen from fluid that had oozed from her capillaries into her tissues. The tip of her tongue was covered with blood clots because she had bitten it while she was seizing.

"I met with father in PICU [Pediatric Intensive Care Unit] waiting room, using VCH interpreter Yee," wrote a hospital social worker early in Lia's stay. "I am not certain how completely father understands the seriousness of his daughter's critical condition because he is equating this hospitalization with past hospitalizations." Valley Children's Hospital was a much larger and richer institution than MCMC, and could afford not only to practice medicine on a grander scale but also to employ interpreters on some shifts. Nonetheless, the Lees remained baffled by most of what was happening. And though Valley Children's was well known for its efforts to reach out to patients' families, Foua and Nao Kao did not realize that their "counseling" sessions, which usually left them confused and angry, were intended to reduce their stress.

On Lia's seventh day in Fresno, her doctors attempted to explain to Foua and Nao Kao that they wanted to perform two more invasive diagnostic tests: a bronchoscopy, to see if the infection had originated in her right lung, and a sinus wash, to see if it had originated in her sinuses. They also wanted to perform a tracheostomy, a hole cut through the neck into the windpipe, just below the larynx, to make it easier to ventilate her. "Parents counseled of Risks/Benefits/Alternatives thru interpreter," noted one of her doctors. "Appear to understand and wish to proceed." In fact, her parents had no idea what any of these procedures, which were scheduled for the following two days, entailed. They also did not understand why Lia was comatose. With a relative interpreting, Foua asked a nurse if the doctors had given Lia "sleeping shots."

Later that same day, Lia's doctors gave her a CT scan and an EEG to see how her brain had weathered its prolonged oxygen shortage. A neurologist had noted earlier that Lia had no gag reflex, no corneal reflexes, and "no response to deeply painful stimulations." Those findings were ominous. The new tests were catastrophic. "CAT scan of the head . . . revealed marked cerebral edema with very poor differentiation between white and gray matter," wrote one of the residents. "An EEG was obtained which revealed essentially no brain activity with very flat brain waves." Lia was effectively brain-dead.

Jeanine Hilt, the Lees' devoted social worker, got a call at 6:00 one evening informing her of Lia's condition. She borrowed a Human Services Agency van and drove half a dozen Lee relatives to Fresno. "I don't know who they were," she recalled. "They just piled in. When we got down there, the doctors were preparing the family for

Lia to die." That night, writing in tiny, crabbed handwriting in her field notebook, she summarized Lia's situation with heartsick concision: "Lia seizured 11/25/86. Transferred Valley Children's. Massive septic blood. Transfusions. Diarrhea. Comatose. Brain Damage. Vegetable."

Dee and Tom Korda, Lia's former foster parents, also drove to Fresno. "It was awful," Dee recalled. "The doctors wouldn't even look at Foua and Nao Kao. They'd only look at us and Jeanine. They saw us as smart and white, and as far as they were concerned the Lees were neither."

Between notations on turning, cleaning, and suctioning Lia, one of her critical care nurses recorded the following:

12/1/86. 1700. EEG was flat.

1800. Dr. Singh [an attending physician] speaking to family with son as interpreter in lounge. Family in to pt. room. Father called by mother. Very tearful.

2000. Family insisting on being @ bedside. Language barrier prohibits verbal communication but TLC given to mom.

2100. Father here with family interpreter asking questions.

2115. Family states "Wants medicine to fix Brain."

The nurse tried to explain that there was no medicine that could fix Lia's brain. The next morning at 3:00 a.m., she wrote, "Mom @ bedside very upset, crying & chanting."

Foua was with Lia when one of Lia's critical care physicians walked in and disconnected the intravenous lines. "The doctor seemed like she was a good doctor," Foua told me, "but she wasn't. She was really mean. She came in and she said that Lia was going to die and then she took out all the rubber stuff and she said that Lia's brain is all rotted and she is going to die. So she wanted to take Lia's medicine away from her and give it to someone else. At that moment I was so scared that it seemed like something was just going up and down my body and I thought I was going to die too."

This doctor was merely following Terry Hutchison's orders—to which he believed the family had agreed—to discontinue all life-sustaining measures so that Lia could die as naturally as possible. Dr. Hutchison also canceled the bronchoscopy, the sinus wash, and the tracheostomy. Finally, he made a decision that is recorded in the most startling sentence in Lia's long, bleak Valley Children's Hospital chart: "The patient was taken off anticonvulsives [following] the abnormal EEG." Because there was no electrical activity in her cerebral cortex, nothing could cause her to seize anymore. The epilepsy that had governed Lia's life since she was three months old was over.

Lia's doctors expected her to die quickly, and they assumed that she would stay at Valley Children's, where she could be made comfortable during her remaining hours or days. One social worker, trying to be helpful, suggested a local mortuary that the Lees might want to contact. Nao Kao was furious. "They wanted to keep her there and they didn't want to send her to Merced and they'd already found a funeral home for her in Fresno," he recalled. "But I refused to listen. I said, No, I want them to send her home. I want them to bring her to Merced so she can die here for the older children to see. So then they wanted me to sign some papers because they said when she gets out of the hospital she is going to die anyway."

The papers were a court order that Jeanine Hilt arranged, with full cooperation from Valley Children's Hospital, as soon as she learned of the Lees' wishes. Although Foua and Nao Kao would have preferred to take Lia back to their apartment, it was decided that she should be transferred to MCMC for supportive care. The Superior Court of the State of California recorded the following declaration, written by Jeanine on behalf of Foua and Nao Kao, "In the Matter of LIA LEE, a Dependent Child of the Juvenile Court":

> Lia Lee is our daughter and has resided back in our home since April 1986 after having been in foster care for ten months. . . . She has since contracted pneumonia [sic] and is now in a coma with irreparable brain damage. Valley Children's Medical Center is unable to provide any further medical care at this point, and we are requesting that Lia be transported by ambulance back to Merced Community Medical Center and then released to us if authorized by Dr. Neil Ernst. We would like to be able to bring Lia home to be with her family before she dies.

We declare under penalty of perjury that the foregoing is true and correct to the best of our knowledge. Executed on December 5, 1986, in Merced, California.

Nao Kao Lee, Father
Foua Yang, Mother

12

Flight

A t the age of three and a half, my family including all the other relatives decided it to move to Thailand," wrote Lia's sister May in an autobiography she was assigned in her eighth-grade Language Arts class at Merced's Hoover Junior High School.

On our way to Thailand was something my parent will never forget. It was one of the scariest time of my life, and maybe my parents. We had to walked by feet. Some of family, however, leave their kids behind, kill, or beat them. For example, one of the relative has tried to kill one of his kid, but luckily he didn't died. And manage to come along with the group. Today, he's in America carrying a scar on his forehead.

My parents had to carried me and two of my younger sisters, True and Yer. My mom could only carried me, and my dad could only my sister, True with many other things which they have to carry such as, rices (food), clothing, and blankets for overnight. My parents pay one of the relative to carry Yer. One of my sister who died in Thailand was so tire of walking saying that she can't go on any longer. But she dragged along and made it to Thailand.

There was gun shot going on and soldier were close to every where. If there was a gun shot, we were to look for a place to hide. On our trip to Thailand, there were many gun shots and instead of looking for a place to hide, my parents would dragged our hands or put us on their back and run for their lifes. When it gets too heavy, my parents would tossed some of their stuff away. Some of the things they had throw away are valuable to them, but our lives were more important to them than the stuffs.

"You have had an exciting life!" wrote her teacher at the end of the essay. "Please watch verbs in the past tense."

The Lees' "trip to Thailand," which took place in 1979, was their second attempt to escape from Laos after the war. On their first attempt, in 1976, they and about forty other families from Houaysouy, with whom they were fleeing, were captured by Vietnamese soldiers on the third day of their journey, while they were hiding in an abandoned rice field. They were herded back to their village at gunpoint. "Even when our children had to go to the bathroom in the forest, they still held a gun at them, and the guns were as big as the children," recalled Nao Kao. Phua, one of the Lee daughters, fell ill and died soon after their return. "At that time a lot of people were decaying and there wasn't medicine, and so we didn't have eight children anymore. We had seven."

The Lees spent three more years in Houaysouy, under intermittent guard. Like most Hmong villages in Sayaboury, Houaysouy had seen no fighting during the war, and none of its men had been recruited by Vang Pao. Sayaboury is the only province in Laos that lies west of the Mekong, and this natural barrier had isolated it from the prolonged warfare that destroyed hundreds of villages on the other side of the river. After the war, however, Houaysouy was tossed into the political melee along with the rest of the country. Because they were Hmong, the village's residents were regarded as traitors and were systematically abused by the occupying forces from the former North Vietnam.

"If you did anything," said Nao Kao, "the Vietnamese would kill you. If you stole a knife or food, they would call the citizens to come and watch and they would just shoot you right there. If you harvested three hundred buckets of rice in a year, the Vietnamese would take two hundred. If you had five chickens, they would take away four and leave you one. The Vietnamese would give you only two yards of material"—here Foua interrupted, saying, "and it wasn't good material!"—"to make clothes for the whole family. I ask you, if it is like this, how do you divide that cloth between ten people?"

In the spring of 1979, the Lees' infant son, Yee, died of starvation. "My little baby was cold and hungry and I was hungry too," said Foua. "I didn't have anything to eat, and the baby just ate my milk, and I didn't have any more milk. I just held him like this and he died in my arms."

One month later, the Lees, along with about four hundred other members of the Lee, Yang, Vang, and Xiong clans, decided to try to escape again. This was the journey May described in her essay.

"The saddest thing was that I had a couple of really beautiful horses," said Nao Kao, "and I had to just take the rope off and let them go in the forest and I never knew whether they were alive or not. Then we just left. We had bought a lot of guns and hidden them, and the young men would walk in the front and the side, and they would hold the guns. The Vietnamese found out that we were running away. They started to burn all around us so we couldn't walk. The flames were as high as our house here in Merced. Some fires were in the front and some fires were in the back, and the children were really scared. But some people were really brave and they just jumped through the flames and somehow we survived. After we crossed the fire, the Vietnamese thought we were taking the usual route where most Hmong go, and they planted some mines in the ground. But we went a different way, and the Vietnamese walked into their own trap and they got hurt. We carried the babies and when we came to steep mountains we tied ropes to the children and the old people and we pulled them up. It was cold and the children were hungry. I was very scared because we had a lot of children and it would be easy for the soldiers to kill them. Some other people who came from our village just before us, two of their little children started running across a rice field, and the Vietnamese shot them, I don't know how many times they shot them, but their heads were all squashed." After twenty-six days on foot, the Lees crossed the border into Thailand, where they spent a year in two refugee camps before being cleared to emigrate to the United States. Their daughter Ge, whom May described in her essay as being "so tire of walking saying that she can't go on any longer," died in the first camp.

The Lees never considered staying in Laos. They and the 150,000 other Hmong who fled to Thailand after the war were exercising the immemorial Hmong preference for flight, resistance, or death over persecution and assimilation. The Hmong rapidly learned that because most of them had either supported the United States or attempted to remain neutral, the Lao People's Democratic Republic viewed them as enemies of the state. (The twenty percent who had supported the communist cause were rewarded with soft treatment and, in some cases, government positions. To teach a lesson on the importance of subordinating ethnicity to party principles, some were selected to execute pro-American Hmong prisoners.) Three weeks after General Vang Pao was airlifted to Thailand, nearly 40,000 Hmong men, women, and children marched toward Vientiane. Some say they hoped to cross the Mekong River and rejoin their leader; others say they planned to ask the Vientiane government for guarantees of security. Outside the town of Hin Heup, Pathet Lao troops opened fire on several hundred of these Hmong while they were crossing a narrow bridge over the Nam Lik River. At least four were killed by gunfire or drowning. Dozens were wounded. When he heard about the Hin Heup Massacre, former Prime Minister Souvanna Phouma, a neutralist who was kept on as an "adviser" to the new government, is said to have remarked to a foreign diplomat, "The Meo [Hmong] have served me well. It is unfortunate that the price of peace in Laos is their liquidation."

One afternoon in Merced, I was invited to tea at the small, spartan apartment of Blia Yao Moua, the Hmong leader who had arranged my first meeting with the Lees. Blia's father was the *chao muong*, or administrative leader, of the city of Xieng Khouang. He was assassinated, presumably by the Pathet Lao, when Blia was nine. Two of Blia's brothers died during the war. I asked Blia what had happened to the Hmong after the war was lost. In polished but idiosyncratic English—like Jonas Vangay, he had learned it after he was fluent in Hmong, Lao, Thai, and French—he replied, "People from the Western sphere cannot understand what it was like. In the new vision of the country of Laos, there is no reason to let the Hmong live. If you don't agree with the Pathet Lao, they can kill you just like a pig or a chicken. They try to force you down to the lowlands. If you don't go, they would kill the animals and burn everything in your village: your house, your rice, your cornstalk. They separate Hmong families and send the kids far away from the parents. They make you change your name so there would be no more clan names. They tell you to stop speaking Hmong. You are not supposed to practice Hmong rituals. When I was a boy, my mother would call in the *txiv neeb* whenever we were sick, even if it was just a headache, but after the war, anybody that would do that, security would hear about it, and a few days later they would come to take you to a kind of meeting, and ask you the reason, and if your explanations are too rightist, they would take you away. They wanted Hmong culture to disappear. But the Hmong cannot be assimilated. The Chinese cannot assimilate the Hmong. The Pathet Lao cannot assimilate the Hmong. After two thousand years we can still say we are Hmong."

The Lees consider themselves fortunate to have been permitted to return to their village after their capture in 1976, even if living conditions were miserable. Many highland Hmong were forcibly relocated to lowland or plateau areas, where they were assigned to state-owned collective farms. The traditional Hmong fear of the lowlands proved justified. Resettled families frequently contracted tropical diseases to which they had not previously been exposed—particularly malaria, which is borne by mosquitoes that cannot survive at high elevations. In highland villages that were left intact, any Hmong who was found practicing slash-and-burn agriculture was arrested. Most villages were infiltrated by Pathet Lao soldiers. "Very politely, one who seemed to be the leader would ask each Hmong family to shelter, by turns, two of their comrades who 'only want to serve you,' " wrote the Hmong scholar Yang Dao.

> But the Hmong soon realized that the two Pathet Lao placed in their family had as their sole mission to watch them day and night. . . . Soon the husband did not dare talk to his wife, nor the parents to their children. The two Pathet Lao were listening to every word and spying on every move. Nobody could trust anybody. From time to time, the people would be awakened in the middle of the night and the houses searched under the pretense that a "reactionary" was hiding there. Then the husband or the son was led away, a gun against his back, to an unknown destination.

The unknown destination was often a "seminar camp" near the Lao-Vietnamese border. Seminar camps, which combined forced labor and political indoctrination, were not reserved for the Hmong, although many Hmong who had held government positions or worked for American agencies were sent there, some for years. More than 10,000 Lao intellectuals, civil servants, teachers, businessmen, military and police officers, and other suspected royalist sympathizers were also interned in camps, as well as the king, the queen, and the crown prince, all three of whom died there. The prisoners cleared land, tilled fields, felled trees, built roads, and were hitched like animals to plows. Some of them were also forced, at gunpoint, to search for and remove unexploded cluster-bombs.

"I know two people who were sent to seminar camps," Blia Yao Moua told me. "One of them my wife and I asked him to lunch here in Merced. He don't want to eat. It is very strange because he was hungry for many years. One day when he's working in the camp he sees a lizard. He picks it up very fast because if a guard sees you do that he would hit you to death. He puts it in his pocket and when no one is watching he gets it out and eats it immediately. He's very happy. That lizard is fresh meat! He told me that story. That man, every day he had to sign a confession accepting you are wrong by collaborating with the Americans. Every day his confession became better. After two years, three years, five years, that speech became part of himself. Before he was in the camp he had a very strong personality. After ten years it changed him. The camp has completely broken his personality."

While two or three thousand Hmong were being "reeducated" in Pathet Lao camps—an exercise in coerced submission that violated the core of the Hmong temper—tens of thousands were able to respond to the new regime in more characteristic Hmong fashion, through armed rebellion. After Vang Pao's departure, former members of the Armée Clandestine organized a resistance movement based in the Phou Bia massif, the highest mountain range in Laos, south of the Plain of Jars. In late 1975, after Pathet Lao forces attacked a group of Hmong, mostly women and children, who were working in a Phou Bia field, Hmong rebels began a campaign of furious retaliation. Using weapons they had concealed in caves, they shot Pathet Lao soldiers, dynamited bridges, blocked roads, blew up food convoys, and—just as Hmong warriors in 1772 had rolled boulders on the heads of the Chinese army in eastern Kweichow—pushed rocks off cliffs while enemy troops were walking below. Although nearly 50,000 Hmong died, Phou Bia did not fall until 1978. Afterwards, Hmong guerrillas continued to live in the jungles along both sides of the Lao-Thai border, crossing back and forth between the two countries, launching irregular raids on the Lao People's Army. Most of the rebels belonged to a messianic group called Chao Fa (Lords of the Sky), led by Pa Kao Her, a former Vang Pao lieutenant who had broken ranks; some belonged to Neo Hom (the United Laotian National Liberation Front), a group founded in the United States and headed by Vang Pao.* Sporadic resistance by both groups—each of which has dwindled from thousands of guerrillas to three or four hundred—continues to this day, more than two decades after the war's official conclusion.

The most widespread Hmong response to the terrors of postwar Laos, however, was migration: the same problem-solving strategy that had moved them around China for more than three millennia and then, starting at the beginning of the nineteenth century, had brought them to Laos. Most feared retribution, though some were motivated

---

* Neo Hom is a controversial organization. It is financed almost entirely by refugees from Laos. (The U.S. Council for World Freedom, a right-wing group chaired by retired Major General John Singlaub, contributed clothing, medicine, and advice during the late 1980s.) At its height, in the early 1980s, an estimated eighty percent of all Hmong in the United States were donating regularly to Neo Hom—typically, a $100 down payment followed by $2 a month for each family member. Vang Pao promised that their donations would be used "to carry out guerrilla activities and the eventual overthrow of the communist government presently controlling Laos." ("He may as well believe in the tooth fairy," Phillip Hawkes, who was then the director of the federal Office of Refugee Resettlement, said in 1984, "but his people want to hear it.") Those who donated $500 received a certificate promising free airfare back to Laos after the liberation. Others have said they were promised important military and government jobs in the "imminent" Lao democracy—as army officers, mayors, police chiefs, and so on—if they contributed large sums. Some Hmong who had recently arrived in California reported that they were told their contributions were a condition of receiving welfare assistance. (Several county welfare offices had contracts with Lao Family Community, a state-financed mutual assistance organization founded by Vang Pao. Most branches of Lao Family Community were not involved in the Neo Hom scheme.) In 1990, when the California Department of Social Services conducted an investigation of the alleged extortion, several Hmong witnesses received death threats from other Hmong, though none were harmed. There have also been charges that not all of the money donated to Neo Hom has actually reached the guerrilla army, but has instead been diverted to the pockets of Hmong resistance leaders in America.

more immediately by famine, the consequence both of nationwide resource scarcity and of the increasing Hmong dependence, toward the
end of the war, on American rice drops, handouts in resettlement sites,
and soldiers' wages. For nearly 10,000 Hmong, there were no crops
to harvest. (Some of the Hmong who left because they were starving
were later stigmatized as undeserving "economic migrants" rather
than legitimate political refugees.) In June of 1975, the Vientiane Domestic Service, the capital's official radio station, broadcast the government's interpretation of the mass Hmong decampment: "With the
collusion of the Thai reactionary clique, the U.S. imperialists have
now forced the Meo tribesmen to flee from Laos into Thailand. The
aim of such an evacuation is not based on the so-called humanitarian
basis, but is to exploit their labor at cheap prices and to foster them
as their henchmen so that they can be sent back to Laos to sabotage
peace in this country in the future."

Every Hmong refugee has an exodus story. In the hierarchy of
good fortune, my interpreter, May Ying Xiong, and her family, along
with the families of other military officers airlifted from Long Tieng,
ranked at the top. All they had to do was leave behind every relative
who did not belong to their immediate family as well as virtually everything they owned, and, overnight, trade the high status they had
enjoyed in Laos for a communal dormitory in a Thai refugee camp,
where one bed was provided for their family of eight, and they stood
in long lines for every meal, holding bowls for their rations of rice.
"You were so lucky!" I heard Nao Kao tell May Ying one night, when
they were comparing their postwar experiences. A notch further
down—an option for only a few privileged families—was escaping
from Vientiane or another urban area by "taxi," which meant forking
over one's life savings to a Lao driver who, along with his passengers,
might or might not be arrested before reaching the Thai border.

Most Hmong walked. Some traveled in small extended-family
bands, others in convoys of up to 8,000 people. I never heard of a
Hmong who fled alone. In the first months after the fall of Long
Tieng, when Pathet Lao efforts to block the Hmong hegira were still
disorganized, it was sometimes possible to drive one's livestock along
major trails. "Those people could just kill their animals along the way,
so they didn't starve," Nao Kao told me. "They took it really easy."
Later groups followed tiger and elephant trails, or steered clear of

established routes altogether, walking the ridgelines whenever they could in order to avoid mines and detection. Most families, like the Lees, took about a month to reach Thailand, though some lived in the forests for two years or more, moving constantly to evade capture, sleeping under bamboo leaves, subsisting on game (though that soon became scarce), fruit, roots, bamboo shoots, the pith of trees, and insects. Desperate to fill their stomachs, some people chopped up their sweat-soaked clothes, mixed them with water and salt, and ate them. They lit fires only at night, so the smoke would not be visible. Sometimes they used fox fire—luminescent rotting wood—to light their way in the dark.

Many people carried children on their backs. The babies presented a potentially fatal problem: they made noise. Silence was so essential that one Hmong woman, now living in Wisconsin, recalled that her son, who was a month old when the family left their home village, didn't know a single word when they arrived in Thailand two years later, because no one had talked during that entire period except in occasional whispers. Nearly every Hmong family I met in Merced had a story to tell about a baby—a relative's child, a neighbor's child, a member of the group they escaped with—who had been drugged with opium. "When the babies would cry," a young mother named Yia Thao Xiong told me, "we would mix the opium in water in a cup and give it to them so they would be quiet and the soldiers would not hear, because if they heard the babies, they would kill all of us. Usually the baby just went to sleep. But if you give too much by mistake, the baby dies. That happened many many times." When I heard these stories, I recalled something I had once read about an Israeli child, hiding from Palestinian terrorists, who, when she began to cry, was accidentally smothered to death by her mother. That death, in 1979, was said to have driven the entire Israeli nation into mourning. The horror of the opium overdoses was not only that such things happened to the Hmong, but that they happened so frequently that, far from driving a nation into mourning, they never made headlines, never caught the world's ear, never reached beyond a community of families that numbly accepted them as a fact of life.

Sometimes worse things happened. When I asked Nao Kao about the boy with the scar on his forehead whom May Lee had mentioned in her eighth-grade essay, he said, "You had to be very quiet. The father of that little baby tried to kill him so he wouldn't cry and everyone would get killed. He had a slash on his head. Somebody saved him and now he is living in Merced."

Able-bodied adults usually took turns carrying the elderly, the sick, and the wounded until they were no longer able to do so. At that point, by a process of agonizing triage, the burdensome relatives were left by the side of the trail, usually with a little food and a little opium. People who died en route were left to rot. It was too dangerous to take time to bury them. To understand what these choices were like, it is important to remember that the Hmong revere their elders, and also that the soul of anyone who is not accorded the proper funerary rites—being washed, dressed in special clothes, honored with animal sacrifices, verbally guided back to the place where one's placenta is buried, lamented with death drum and *qeej*, and laid to rest in a hand-hewn coffin on the shoulder of a sloping mountain—is doomed to an eternity of restless wandering. Jonas Vangay said, "Not to bury the dead is terrible. Not to carry your relatives is terrible. It is the worst thing in the world to have the responsibility to choose between you and them."

On their way to Thailand, Hmong families walked through abandoned villages and untended fields. They passed piles of jewelry, silver bars, and embroidered garments—Foua discarded her entire dowry of *paj ntaub*—which previous refugees had jettisoned. They also passed many decomposing corpses. Dang Moua, a Merced businessman whose family lived during their three-week journey on birds he shot with a homemade crossbow and poison-tipped bamboo arrows, saw dozens of ragged orphaned children in the forest, eating leaves and dirt. He gave them food but walked on past. His wife found a baby, less than a year old, trying to nurse from the breast of its dead mother. They walked past it, too.

Because Houaysouy was west of the Mekong River, the Lees were able to cross the Thai border on foot. Farther south, the Mekong, which is up to a mile wide, forms the Lao-Thai boundary for more than five hundred miles. Most Hmong refugees had to cross it. "The Mekong River is ten times bigger than the Merced River," said Jonas Vangay. "So how do you cross? Most Hmong people do not swim. If you have money maybe you can pay Lao for a boat. You can hold a tree branch. Bamboo floats better than wood, so you can lash it together, but later on all the bamboo is gone because people have already cut it down, and you have to carry it all the way down from the mountains. Crossing this river, everyone here in the United States continue to dream of that nightmare."

Some people attempted to float across the Mekong with bamboo stalks placed under their armpits, on banana-wood rafts, or in inner tubes purchased from Lao traders. The inner tubes were hard to find and very expensive, because the Pathet Lao border patrol killed people who sold them. Many babies and small children who had survived the journey this far drowned while crossing the river strapped to their parents' backs. Their bodies were left in the Mekong. "A few [Hmong refugees] manage to bring empty plastic gallon containers, still others inflate ordinary grocery plastic bags," wrote Dominica Garcia, a doctor working in a Thai refugee camp, in a 1978 letter to the director of the International Rescue Committee. "It is not unusual to find these survivors clinging to their makeshift 'life-savers' even long after they have been in the detention centers. They carry them up to the hospital wards where they finally get proper treatment."

One resident of Merced was sixteen years old when he and his extended family reached the Mekong. They were able to obtain a boat large enough to hold half their party. He and another adult crossed the river first, bringing all the children. The other man paddled the boat back to the Lao side and picked up the rest of the adults. On the return trip, when the boat was halfway across the river, the border patrol sank the boat and fired on the passengers. From the Thai shore, the teenager and the children watched their parents, uncles, and aunts all die from bullets and drowning.

Dang Moua's cousin Moua Kee once unsuccessfully tried to procure federal disability benefits for a mentally disturbed Hmong woman in Merced who, a decade earlier, had attempted to cross the Mekong with a party of 170 people. "They wait for the sun to go down and do a night crossing," he explained, "and then, one group of Pathet Lao open three machine gun. This lady, she saw more than twenty people fall down and die in one place, and one of them was her husband. I think she is sick now because maybe she saw too many trouble."

One afternoon, when Blia Yao Moua and I were chatting, as we had on many previous occasions, I happened to make a casual remark about the cohesiveness of Hmong society. He said, "Yes, if a person outside the community see a Hmong person, they look that way. But inside they have guilt. Many feelings of guilt. You go from the north of Laos and then you go across the Mekong, and when the Pathet Lao soldiers fire, you do not think about your family, just yourself only. When you are on the other side, you will not be like what you were before you get through the Mekong. On the other side you cannot say to your wife, I love you more than my life. She saw! You cannot say that anymore! And when you try to restick this thing together it is like putting glue on a broken glass."

An unknowable fraction of the Hmong who attempted to flee Laos—some survivors estimate it was half, some much less—died en route, from Pathet Lao and Vietnamese bullets and mines, as well as from disease, starvation, exposure, snakebite, tiger maulings, poisoning by toxic plants, and drowning. Most of those who reached Thailand ended up, often after being robbed and occasionally after being raped by Thai bandits, in district police stations. From there, they were sent to refugee camps. When they arrived, eighty percent were found to be suffering from malnutrition, malaria, anemia, and infections, especially of the feet.

At first, the Hmong were placed in a string of makeshift camps near the Lao border. Officially speaking, because Thailand had not signed the 1951 Geneva Convention on the status of refugees, they were illegal immigrants, but the Thai government was willing to grant them temporary residency as long as other nations paid the bills and promised them permanent asylum. Eventually most of the Hmong— who kept streaming across the Lao border until the early 1990s—were consolidated into one large camp in northeast Thailand, fifteen miles south of the Mekong River. At its peak, in 1986, the Ban Vinai camp had 42,858 inhabitants, of which about ninety percent were Hmong. It was the largest Hmong settlement in history, larger even than Long Tieng, General Vang Pao's former military base. Ban Vinai was, in effect, a large-scale charitable institution that continued the job, effectively begun by wartime rice drops, of eroding Hmong self-sufficiency. Depending on how you looked at it, life there was either a catastrophic deracination or a useful dress rehearsal for life in the

American inner cities to which many of its inhabitants would ultimately relocate. Though it lacked electricity, running water, and sew-
age disposal, the camp was so densely populated that it was, in effect,
urban. A 1986 survey by a Catholic relief agency concluded, "Like
other poor urban communities, Ban Vinai has problems of inadequate
health, overcrowding, welfare dependency, unemployment, substance
abuse, prostitution, and anomie (suicide, abandonment, loneliness)."
Jonas Vangay told me, "In Ban Vinai, you don't have the right to do
anything except get a ration of rice and beans, and go to your tent,
and you do that for five or ten years. People were born and grew up
there. The young ones play soccer and volleyball. The elderly person
just sleep day and night, they just wait and see and wait and eat and
wait and die and wait and die."

According to Dwight Conquergood, the enthusiastic ethnographer
from the International Rescue Committee who organized the Ban
Vinai Rabies Parade, the camp officials tended to hold the Hmong
responsible for their own dependence, poor health, and lack of clean-
liness. "Instead of seeing the Hmong as struggling within a constrain-
ing context of historical, political, and economic forces that have
reduced them from proud, independent, mountain people to landless
refugees, the Hmong are blamed for their miserable condition," he
observed. Conquergood was astonished at how violently most of the
other Westerners at the camp disliked the Hmong, whom he liked
very much. He wrote:

> I began to collect the phrases used regularly to describe the Hmong by
> agency officials who worked in Ban Vinai. The word I heard most often
> was "filthy," followed closely by "dirty," and often part of a cluster of
> terms that included "scabies," "abscesses," "feces," and "piles of gar-
> bage." A phrase regularly employed to cover a multitude of perceived
> sanitation sins was the following, "They're one step out of the Stone Age,
> you know." A meaning-packed word heard about the Hmong almost
> every day was "difficult," and its ramified derivatives: "difficult to work
> with," "the most difficult group," "set in their ways," "rigid," "stub-
> born," "you cannot get through to them," "backward." One dedicated
> humanitarian agency employee who had worked with the Hmong for
> several years told me that "the hand of God is on this place," but as for
> the Hmong living here, "they're a fearful lot . . . you cannot work with
> them."

Conquergood believed that this focus on "dirtiness" and "difficulty" was actually "an expression of Western expatriates' uneasiness when confronted with Difference, the Other. A Western aid official's encounter with the Hmong is a confrontation with radical difference—in cosmology, worldview, ethos, texture of life. . . . Unfortunately, as [the French critic] Tzvetan Todorov reminds us, 'The first, spontaneous reaction with regard to the stranger is to imagine him as inferior, since he is different from us.' "

Most of the people who made those disparaging comments about the Hmong came from the United States, to which the majority of the inhabitants of Ban Vinai eventually emigrated. About 10,000 Hmong resettled in France, Canada, Australia, Argentina, French Guiana, and elsewhere; but because of their American military ties and because Vang Pao had already established residence in Montana, they preferred the United States by a huge margin. In 1975, the U.S. was willing to admit fewer than 300 Hmong—mostly army officers and their families—but both the quotas and the eligibility requirements were liberalized over the years, with about 25,000 Hmong admitted in 1980 alone. As with Vietnamese and Cambodian refugees, the best-educated Hmong and Lao came to America in the first wave of immigration and the least-educated in later waves. Because for several years the U.S. refused to accept extended family groups of more than eight people, but did not limit the size of nuclear families, the Hmong, none of whom had birth certificates, grew accustomed to lying when they were interviewed by immigration officials. Second wives became daughters or sisters; nieces and nephews became daughters and sons.

According to the office of the United Nations High Commissioner for Refugees, which supervised Ban Vinai, every refugee problem has three possible "durable solutions": local integration, voluntary repatriation, and resettlement in another country. Thailand, which was buffeted simultaneously by refugees from Laos, Vietnam, and Cambodia, emphatically rejected the first solution. The Hmong emphatically rejected the second solution. In 1981, they also began to reject the third solution, leading Ban Vinai to become a kind of never-ending camp, or, as one U.S. refugee official termed it, "a non-durable non-solution." In 1984, Eric E. Morris, the U.N. deputy refugee representative in Thailand, said in bewilderment, "This is a unique situation historically. The Hmong are the first refugees we know who were

offered resettlement and in large numbers simply turned it down."
Some of them worried that the Hmong resistance movement in Laos,
which was fueled by manpower and leadership in Ban Vinai, as well
as by money funneled through the camp from refugees in the United
States, would collapse if they left Asia. Most of them, however, had
heard rumors about life in America from earlier immigrants, and were
just plain scared: of tenements, of urban violence, of welfare dependence, of never being able to farm again, of being forbidden to sacrifice animals, of being thrown in jail if their grandfathers smoked
opium, of ogres, of dinosaurs, and—as they made clear during the
notorious 1982 meeting on the Ban Vinai soccer field—of doctors who
ate the livers, kidneys, and brains of Hmong patients.

Ban Vinai started to look pretty good. It may have been dirty,
crowded, and disease-ridden, but culturally it was still powerfully
Hmong. Women sewed *paj ntaub* (though some of them forsook the
old motifs of elephant's feet and ram's horns for embroidered soldiers
with bayonets); men made jewelry (though when silver was unavailable
some of them melted down discarded aluminum cans); many families
raised chickens or tended small vegetable plots. Most compellingly,
according to Dwight Conquergood,

> no matter where you go in the camp, at almost any hour of the day or
> night, you can simultaneously hear two or three performances, from sim-
> ple storytelling and folksinging to elaborate collective ritual performances
> for the dead . . . including drumming, stylized lamentation, ritual chant-
> ing, manipulation of funerary artifacts, incense, fire, dancing, and animal
> sacrifice. Nearly every morning I was awakened before dawn by the
> drumming and ecstatic chanting of performing shamans.

The older a Hmong was, the less willing he or she was to leave. "At
the camp, the cultural tradition was still there," Blia Yao Moua told
me. "There was patrilineage. Children still listened to Grandpa. What
is the good to go over there to America if all that change? And a lot
of elderly people, though they never, never say it openly to strangers,
what really haunt them is they are afraid in America they will not have
a good funeral ceremony and a good grave, and that is more important
than any other thing in the world."

Thailand closed Ban Vinai in 1992. Its 11,500 inhabitants were told they absolutely, positively had only two choices: to apply for re-settlement in another country, or to return to Laos. As an interim measure, the resettlers were to move to one camp, and the repatriators to another. Panic ensued. Hmong who for more than a decade had resisted coming to the United States now decided it was the safer of two abhorrent options—and then were rejected. With the support of the United States, where anti-immigrant sentiment was gathering steam, the Thai government and the United Nations High Commissioner for Refugees instituted a new and more stringent set of eligibility requirements under which nearly 2,000 Hmong applicants were denied refugee status. Since 1991, about 7,000 Hmong have uneasily returned to Laos, persuaded that repressive conditions there have slackened: no more forced collectivization, no more seminar camps. Although those who repatriate in groups are assigned to lowland sites, may not return to their home villages, and may not practice slash-and-burn agriculture, at least their families (or so they have been assured) will no longer be in danger. There have been reports, however—all of them denied by the Laotian, Thai, and U.S. governments and by the United Nations High Commissioner for Refugees —that some Hmong have been forced by Thai authorities to return to Laos against their will, and, once there, have been persecuted or killed.*

More than 10,000 Hmong, most of them inhabitants of Ban Vinai, simply said no to both choices and fled—whether temporarily or permanently, no one knows—to the sanctified grounds of Wat Tham Krabok, a Buddhist monastery north of Bangkok. Surrounded by coercive pressures on all sides, they managed to find a way out, as they had done so many times before during their intransigent history, by moving in a direction none of their keepers could have predicted.

Thai authorities were reportedly astonished that 10,000 Hmong

---

* The most celebrated case involved a respected Hmong leader named Vue Mai, who was persuaded to repatriate in 1992 as an example to other Hmong. In 1993 he disappeared from Vientiane and has not been heard from since. According to the U.S. Committee for Refugees, more than 700 members of the Vue clan living in a Thai camp, who had intended to join their leader in Laos, changed their minds after his presumed death and requested admission to the United States. The Thai government and the United Nations High Commissioner for Refugees rejected their request.

had managed to slip through their fingers. They should have known better. For as long as there have been Hmong, there have been ways to get out of tight spots. In the greatest of all Hmong folktales, Shee Yee, a healer and magician who was the forerunner of today's *txiv neebs*, was once ambushed by nine evil *dab* brothers who ate human flesh and drank their blood. In the version collected by Charles Johnson, the brothers lay in wait for Shee Yee at a mountain crossroads where nine paths led to every corner of the earth, and where the rocks looked like tigers and dragons. When the brothers transformed themselves into water buffalos, so did Shee Yee. When they tossed him on their horns, he changed back into a man, and he chopped them into small pieces with his magical saber. When the pieces joined together and came back to life, he turned into a cloud and mounted high in the sky. When the brothers became a strong wind, Shee Yee became a drop of water. When one of the brothers became a leaf that would catch the drop of water, he became a deer, and he ran into the forest. The brothers became wolves, and they chased Shee Yee until the sun was low in the western sky, hanging at the edge of the earth. Eight of the brothers were too tired to go on, but the oldest one kept running. When Shee Yee saw an abandoned rat's burrow, he changed himself into a rat. The oldest brother turned into a cat, and waited at the edge of the burrow. Shee Yee changed into a caterpillar with stinging fuzz, and the cat spat him back into the hole. As he waited in the hole, Shee Yee got angrier and angrier. When the cat fell asleep, Shee Yee turned himself into a very tiny red ant. Quickly and fiercely, he bit the cat on the testicle. Then he went home to his wife.

13

Code X

The night the Lees told me about their postwar experiences, I remember saying, because I did not know what to say, "That must have been terrible." And Foua gave me a brief, opaque look, and said, "Yes, it was very sad. But when we were running from Laos at least we hoped that our lives would be better. It was not as sad as after Lia went to Fresno and got sick."

At first I thought I had misunderstood her. In Laos, Foua and Nao Kao had lost three children in three years. They had dodged bullets, land mines, and walls of fire. They had left their village behind, and then their country, knowing they would never see them again. How could anything, even the catastrophic illness of their favorite child, be worse than that? But I had not misunderstood her. Violence, starvation, destitution, exile, and death were, however horrific, within the sphere of known, or at least conceivable, tragedies. What had happened to Lia was outside that sphere.

After eleven days in the Pediatric Intensive Care Unit at Valley Children's Hospital, Lia was transferred to MCMC by ambulance on December 5, 1986. She was examined by Dave Schneider, a second-year resident with a reputation for being brainy and nervous. In his examination note, Dave described Lia as "a comatose, overweight Laotian girl" whose admitting diagnoses were:

1. Severe hypoxic brain damage.
2. *Pseudomonas* septicemia.
3. Severe seizure disorder.
4. Status post disseminated intravascular coagulation.
5. Status post septic shock.

"I was on Peds rotation," Dave recalled, "and when I heard Lia Lee was coming back from Fresno, basically brain-dead, my heart sank. I didn't know the family very well, but I'd heard that they were noncompliant and difficult. Everyone had. I still have this vision of Lia when she got here, just lying in the bed and not looking anything like she used to. She was very hot and febrile, her eyes were partially rolled back into her head, and she was breathing irregularly and way too fast. She had a lot of mucus and junk in her throat, but it was almost impossible to suction her because her jaw muscles were clamped shut. She wasn't making anything in the way of purposeful movements. Her legs were extended and her arms were alternating between being extended and flexed up to her chest, which is a sign of very weird and ominous stuff going on in the motor strip of the cerebral cortex. She did withdraw from painful stimuli, like when I squeezed tightly on her fingernail beds. Patients usually tell you to get the hell away when you do that. Lia couldn't tell me to go to hell, though on some level I'm sure she wished I would."

Lia was admitted to the pediatric unit. "I remember the first time I went up to see her," said Peggy Philp. "She was awful. Lia had been a real cute little kid—I mean, she had bad seizures, but she was so *alive*—and now, she was just . . . well, there. But not peaceful and asleep-looking, like you might expect with a coma. I mean, it would be one thing if she lay there like Sleeping Beauty, all pretty and comfortable, but she didn't. She seemed to be in pain. She'd stiffen whenever you touched her. She was *struggling*. She made terrible, loud noises when she breathed"—Peggy demonstrated with a torturous rattling wheeze—"and I kept thinking, God, she can't go on like this, this is exhausting her, she is going to wear herself out and die any minute. I remember being real angry at Hutch"—Terry Hutchison, Lia's neurologist in Fresno—"you know, God, you sent me *this*?"

When Peggy finished talking, I turned to Neil to ask what his impressions had been. He shifted uneasily in his chair. "Well, I didn't see her right away. I knew she'd been transferred back to our care to die. There she was, and that was what I had been afraid of, and I was just so—I mean, that episode in the emergency room burnt me out, it emotionally drained me, and facing Lia was real difficult for me at that point."

"So I took care of her," interjected Peggy.

"You did. I mean, you probably took care of her almost exclusively. I probably chose to avoid it a little bit. More than a little bit. I chose to avoid it. I have to admit, I bailed out."

It took Neil three days, walking past Lia's room innumerable times, before he could bring himself to look at the patient who had dominated his professional life and his private thoughts for much of four years. I asked him what he found when he finally saw her.

"She was in a vegetative state. But that was one angry vegetable."

Calling Lia a vegetable was, it seemed to me, just one more form of avoidance. In describing what had happened to her, he and Peggy both used the kinds of terms favored by the doctors in *MASH*, gallows-humor slang wielded in times of extreme stress on the theory that if you laugh at something it can't break your heart. "Lia got gorked." "She crumped." "She fried her brain." "She vegged out." "She crapped out." "She went to hell." "No one's at home, the lights are out."

The first Nurse's Note after Lia's admission read: "Pulse rate fast at 130 & has a temp of 102°. Offers no recognition or acknowledgment. N/G tube in place." Then, without comment: "Family in room and Shaman performing a ceremony."

When I asked Gloria Rodriguez, Lia's nurse during that shift, about that note, she said, "Oh yeah, they had a medicine man come in. He brought some kind of white ointment, and they chanted and rubbed it all over Lia. It smelled like vodka and herbs. I remember her mom wouldn't let us give her a bath because that would take off the white stuff."

In any case, Foua preferred to care for her daughter herself. She sat by Lia's bed around the clock. "Mother encouraged to hold child while linens changed," noted a nurse. "Mother stroking & chanting to child." The nurses showed her how to apply Vaseline to Lia's cracked lips, rub Desitin on her diaper rash, cool her forehead with a moist washcloth, suction her secretions, and feed her formula through a nasogastric tube. Once, Foua and Nao Kao brought in an herbal remedy—"a thick, stringy, gooey, gross, green liquid," as Peggy remembered it—and tried to feed it to Lia. When they realized Lia couldn't swallow, they decided to pour it down the nasogastric tube, and Peggy, certain Lia would die anyway, instructed the nurses to let them do so.

The Hmong New Year, a multi-day holiday that is traditionally celebrated in the twelfth month of the year, starting at first cock crow on the first day of the waxing moon, happened to fall during Lia's stay at MCMC. It is the most important and merriest holiday of the Hmong year, a time to banish harmful *dabs*, ask for the assistance of benevolent household spirits, summon home the souls of dead ancestors, and, in general, secure good fortune for the coming year. It is also a time to dance, sing, play courting games, and dress in embroidered finery, which, even in America, many Hmong women start sewing months in advance. It is thought that anyone who wears old clothes at New Year's will bring poverty on the family. That year, Foua had made new *paj ntaub* for all her daughters, using Thai cloth worked with American thread and decorated with antique Indochinese coins. She showed these garments to me once. Lia's skirt was by far the fanciest, with embroidered stripes of pink, green, and black, and pleats so numerous and fine they looked like the gills of a mushroom. "These are the clothes Lia was going to wear," she told me. "They were the most beautiful clothes because we loved her so much. No one else is allowed to wear them because they are Lia's and only Lia's. I made them because I thought Lia was going to be up and running around our house at New Year's, but she got sick instead, so she didn't wear them, and it was the only time in our lives that we ever missed the New Year's celebration." May Lee said, "We didn't do anything at New Year's, not even the soul-calling ceremony, because the doctors told us Lia was going to die and my family was just crying all the time."

Instead, Foua brought a different set of clothes to the hospital: funeral garments. "It is Hmong culture to do that," explained Nao Kao. "For us Hmong, if you don't dress them up, then after they pass away, you always dream of them being naked. It is not really good to see a person naked, so we dress them in special clothes. Lia's mother sewed them for her." The special clothes were a black hat, a black jacket, and a high-waisted, appliquéd skirt. The nurses told Foua that Lia couldn't actually wear the jacket, since they needed access to her upper body, so at first Foua laid it over her daughter's hospital gown. Later, when the nurses were out of the room, she disobeyed instructions and dressed Lia properly.

Lia's room was always crowded with siblings, cousins, uncles, aunts, and members of the Lee and Yang clans who had traveled from out of town to join what one Nurse's Note called "the vigil." Though some nurses did their best to be sympathetic, most were exasperated by the unremitting commotion. "Those people would all yak and raise their voices and gesticulate at each other," recalled a nurse named Evelyn Marciel. "They were totally fed up with us. They'd ask us what were we doing? Why were we doing it? There wasn't a question asked that hadn't been answered ten times over. Anything we were doing was wrong." Dee Korda also came frequently—Peggy remembers her sitting next to the bed crying—and Jeanine Hilt was there every day. "There was usually no interpreter," Jeanine recalled, "but you know Foua and I communicated more through the soul anyway. We held each other a lot. When someone was there to translate, Foua and Nao Kao always talked about how much they loved Lia and how special she was to them. I told them how special she was to me too. The only thing I was thankful for is that it had not happened at the foster home. That had been my worst fear, that she would have a massive seizure in foster care. God, it could have happened so easily, and if it had they would have blamed me forever. It would have had ramifications throughout the Hmong community: CPS steals children and they die."

On Lia's second day back at MCMC, Nao Kao demanded that Lia's subclavian line—a central intravenous line placed with great difficulty at Valley Children's Hospital—be removed, and all her medications discontinued. Peggy noted in Lia's Progress Record:

I held a long discussion with both parents through aid of an interpreter. CPS worker Jeanine Hilt was present. Parents understand that the antibiotics are fighting a severe infection and that without medication Lia may get her infection back and die sooner. They understand that once we remove IV, a new line will NOT be replaced. They understand and still refuse medication. Therefore, meds & IV will be withdrawn.

"The impression I had," recalled Peggy, "was that they wanted Lia to be peaceful and not be persecuted anymore. Basically, they wanted her to die with dignity." Peggy was mistaken. She thought that Foua and Nao Kao wanted to withdraw the medicines because they were artificially prolonging Lia's life. In fact, though the Lees believed Lia was so sick she *might* die, they wanted to stop treatment because they thought it was the medicines that were killing her.

After the IV line was taken out, Foua and Nao Kao announced that they wanted to take Lia home. Her brain damage had fouled up the homeostatic mechanisms that regulated her body temperature, and she was spiking fevers as high as 107.4°, which is potentially fatal. Peggy therefore informed the Lees that Lia needed to stay at MCMC for a few days of observation. "I was sure she was dying," she recalled, "but that's the quandary of Western medicine, that you can't let people die." Concerned that Lia be kept comfortable during her final days, Jeanine wrote the following memo:

To: Ernst — Philp
From: Hilt
Re: Lia going home

Before we let Lia go home, let's reevaluate the family's desire to do this.
. . . Are they physically, emotionally and financially able to take this on?
Do they have a bed, linen, prescribed food, stethoscope, pampers etc. etc.
on hand? They must have all this, plus Home Health nursing in place
before I'm ready to say ok. Are you convinced that they can feed Lia
properly? Have they accurately demonstrated their understanding and
skill? Will they feed her every four hours?

By December 9, Jeanine and Peggy had arranged for home nursing visits and for all the necessary supplies, including a suction machine to clear Lia's secretions and, as Dave Schneider noted, "a large supply of diapers as child is incontinent and presently having diarrhea." A nurse wrote the following discharge instructions:

1. Glassrock Health Services will be by at 8:00 p.m. tonight. Give them prescription.
2. Make sure to come to Clinic this Thursday Dec. 11 at 8:00 a.m.

3. Keep egg crate mattress pad on at all times.
4. Turn her every 2 hours so she does not get infected bedsores.
5. Suction her as often as necessary.

Diet instructions: Feed [formula] every 4 hours during daytime (5 feed-ings a day)—10 ounces 5 times a day. All foods or medicines go down tube.

Foua didn't understand the instructions, and in any case had no in-tention of giving Lia medicines or anything else through a nasogas-tric tube (which was intended to circumvent Lia's impaired sucking and gag reflexes and keep food from going down her trachea). None-theless, she signed the line that read, "These instructions have been explained to me and I understand them." Her signature—just as it had been when she signed the discharge papers after Lia's birth at MCMC four and a half years earlier—was the single word FOUAYANG.

At some point that day, Nao Kao was also asked to sign something. It is not included in Lia's chart, so no one knows exactly what it was, although it probably had to do with the Lees' decision to withdraw her from MCMC. It is likely that Nao Kao was told that in two hours, after the discharge paperwork was completed, she would be released, and he could take her home to die. His interpretation was somewhat different. He recalled, "One person gives Lia medicine"—this was probably Tylenol for her fever, which the Nurse's Notes indicate that "father refused"—"and then another person comes and has a paper on a clipboard and makes me sign and says that in two hours, Lia is going to die. They weren't fixing her. I thought even if they fix her she is going to die here, and if they don't fix her, she is going to die here, so I might as well just bring her home right now so the older children can see her. I am not satisfied. I am very disappointed at the hospital. I am mad. Is this a hospital that fixes people or makes them die?"

This was not the first time in the last two weeks that the Lees had been told Lia would die, but for some reason—perhaps because Nao Kao believed it contained such a time-specific prediction—it was the most offensive. In the Hmong moral code, foretelling a death is strongly taboo. It is an unpardonable insult to say to one's aged grand-parent, "After you are dead. . . ." Instead, one says, "When your children are 120 years old. . . ." I asked several Hmong people I knew how they would feel if a doctor told them their child was going to die. "A doctor should never never say that!" exclaimed Chong Moua, a mother of three. "It makes the *dab* come closer to the child. It is like saying okay, okay, take her." Koua Her, an interpreter for the health department, said, "In Laos, that means you're going to kill a person. Maybe poison him. Because how do you know for certain he's going to die unless you're going to kill him?"

One night I told Bill Selvidge that the Lees had perceived the doctors' comments not as candid prognoses but as threats. "I'm not surprised," he said. "All those verb tenses! Lia will die, Lia might die, Lia has a ninety-five percent chance of dying. Those nuances would be very confusing through an interpreter. And if the parents thought that people at MCMC were saying Lia *should* die, maybe they were right. I imagine there were a lot of people here who thought that if Lia was comatose and couldn't communicate and the only sensation she could feel was pain, it would be better for her if she did die."

When Nao Kao thought he was being forced to sign a piece of paper that said his daughter was going to die in two hours, he did what any Hmong in an impossible corner, starting with the legendary Shee Yee, might consider doing: he fled. He grabbed Lia, who was dressed in her funeral clothes, from her bed in the third-floor pediatric unit and started running down the stairs. One of the nurses called a Code X. (Every hospital has a set of emergency codes that are blared over the public address system: Code Blue for dying patients in need of resuscitation; Code Red for fire; Code X for security breaches.) Nao Kao recalled, "They were chasing after me. They called two policemen"—hospital security guards—"and they wanted me to go back to the hospital. When they called the police, the lady that told me that Lia was going to die came to scold me and said, What are you doing? At that time I was so angry I pushed that nurse and her head went blah."

Dave Schneider was paged, *stat*—that is, urgently and immediately. It was late Friday afternoon at the end of what had already been a bad week for him, and it was about to get worse. Exhausted by the stresses of being a resident—the thirty-three-hour shifts, the constant hectoring of resentful patients, the fear of making a fatal mistake—

Dave had requested a three-month leave of absence from MCMC, and had only a few days, which he had hoped would be calm, before he left. "I was about as low as I had ever been in my entire life," he told me, "and I was in no state to put up with any bullshit from a father, whether he was a caring, concerned father who had customs that were different from mine or not. I mean, I really was not particularly feeling like having a discussion with him about cultural differences."

When Dave arrived, at a run, on the pediatric floor, the security guards had already escorted Nao Kao and Lia back to her room. "They'd found this Laotian guy carrying out this basically motionless child, and when I got there, they and the nurses were all yelling at him in a language he didn't understand. I didn't yell at him, but I was very angry. What really pissed me off is that he had pulled out her NG tube. He denied it, but it had been thrown onto the stairs. Obviously they wanted to take Lia home and let her die, and we were willing to do that, but it had to be in a medically acceptable manner, not by starving her to death, which is what would happen if she didn't have an NG tube. So we'd instructed them as to how to use it and everything. Then the father rips her off, runs down the stairs, and takes out the tube. I mean, they had *minutes* to go, or at most an hour or two, before we were going to let them take her home anyway, but they *just couldn't fucking wait.*"

In a sharp voice, Dave told Nao Kao over and over again that if he'd been patient, Lia could have left soon, but now she couldn't, because the nasogastric tube had to be reinserted and then X-rayed to confirm its position. In fact, the new tube was inserted incorrectly, and it had to be repositioned and X-rayed a second time. This, plus the paperwork, took nearly four hours. The hospital staff, including the nurse Nao Kao had pushed against the wall—she hadn't been hurt—went about their business as if the incident, which they later referred to as "the abduction," were an everyday event. Though they were all furious, no one considered reporting Nao Kao for assault or preventing him, at what they decided was the appropriate time, from taking his daughter home.

Lia left MCMC at 10:15 p.m., in her mother's arms. At the time of her discharge, her temperature was 104°. Her parents carried her back to their apartment, took off her funeral clothes, and laid her on a shower curtain they had spread on the living room floor. "Lia was going to die if she stayed in the hospital," said Nao Kao, "but we boiled up some herbs and we washed her body. At the hospital she was so sick that when she was sleeping on the bed, she sweated so much her bed got all wet. She had too much medicine and her body just gave way. But then we boiled the herbs and we washed her and her sweat stopped, and she didn't die."

14

The Melting Pot

The Lee family—Nao Kao, Foua, Chong, Zoua, Cheng, May, Yer, and True—arrived in the United States on December 18, 1980. Their luggage consisted of a few clothes, a blue blanket, and a wooden mortar and pestle that Foua had chiseled from a block of wood in Houaysouy. They flew from Bangkok to Honolulu, and then to Portland, Oregon, where they were to spend two years before moving to Merced. Other refugees told me that their airplane flights—a mode of travel that strained the limits of the familiar Hmong concept of migration—had been fraught with anxiety and shame: they got airsick, they didn't know how to use the bathroom but were afraid to soil themselves, they thought they had to pay for their food but had no money, they tried to eat the Wash'n Dris. The Lees, though perplexed, took the novelties of the trip in stride. Nao Kao remembers the airplane as being "just like a big house."

Their first week in Portland, however, was miserably disorienting. Before being placed by a local refugee agency in a small rented house, they spent a week with relatives, sleeping on the floor. "We didn't know anything so our relatives had to show us everything," Foua said. "They knew because they had lived in America for three or four months already. Our relatives told us about electricity and said the children shouldn't touch those plugs in the wall because they could get hurt. They told us that the refrigerator is a cold box where you put meat. They showed us how to open the TV so we could see it. We had never seen a toilet before and we thought maybe the water in it was to drink or cook with. Then our relatives told us what it was, but we didn't know whether we should sit or whether we should stand on it. Our relatives took us to the store but we didn't know that the cans and packages had food in them. We could tell what the meat was, but the chickens and cows and pigs were all cut up in little pieces and had plastic on them. Our relatives told us the stove is for cooking the food, but I was afraid to use it because it might explode. Our relatives said in America the food you don't eat you just throw away. In Laos we always fed it to the animals and it was strange to waste it like that. In this country there were a lot of strange things and even now I don't know a lot of things and my children have to help me, and it still seems like a strange country."

Seventeen years later, Foua and Nao Kao use American appliances, but they still speak only Hmong, celebrate only Hmong holidays, practice only the Hmong religion, cook only Hmong dishes, sing only Hmong songs, play only Hmong musical instruments, tell only Hmong stories, and know far more about current political events in Laos and Thailand than about those in the United States. When I first met them, during their eighth year in this country, only one American adult, Jeanine Hilt, had ever been invited to their home as a guest. It would be hard to imagine anything further from the vaunted American ideal of assimilation, in which immigrants are expected to submerge their cultural differences in order to embrace a shared national identity. *E pluribus unum*: from many, one.

During the late 1910s and early '20s, immigrant workers at the Ford automotive plant in Dearborn, Michigan, were given free, compulsory "Americanization" classes. In addition to English lessons, there were lectures on work habits, personal hygiene, and table manners. The first sentence they memorized was "I am a good American." During their graduation ceremony they gathered next to a gigantic wooden pot, which their teachers stirred with ten-foot ladles. The students walked through a door into the pot, wearing traditional costumes from their countries of origin and singing songs in their native languages. A few minutes later, the door in the pot opened, and the students walked out again, wearing suits and ties, waving American flags, and singing "The Star-Spangled Banner."

The European immigrants who emerged from the Ford Motor Company melting pot came to the United States because they hoped to assimilate into mainstream American society. The Hmong came to the United States for the same reason they had left China in the nineteenth century: because they were trying to *resist* assimilation. As the anthropologist Jacques Lemoine has observed, "they did not come to our countries only to save their lives, they rather came to save their selves, that is, their Hmong ethnicity." If their Hmong ethnicity had been safe in Laos, they would have preferred to remain there, just as their ancestors—for whom migration had always been a problem-solving strategy, not a footloose impulse—would have preferred to remain in China. Unlike the Ford workers who enthusiastically, or at least uncomplainingly, belted out the "The Star-Spangled Banner" (of which Foua and Nao Kao know not a single word), the Hmong are what sociologists call "involuntary migrants." It is well known that involuntary migrants, no matter what pot they are thrown into, tend not to melt.

What the Hmong wanted here was to be left alone to be Hmong: clustered in all-Hmong enclaves, protected from government interference, self-sufficient, and agrarian. Some brought hoes in their luggage. General Vang Pao has said, "For many years, right from the start, I tell the American government that we need a little bit of land where we can grow vegetables and build homes like in Laos. . . . I tell them it does not have to be the best land, just a little land where we can live." This proposal was never seriously considered. "It was just out of the question," said a spokesman for the State Department's refugee program. "It would cost too much, it would be impractical, but most of all it would set off wild protests from [other Americans] and from other refugees who weren't getting land for themselves." (It would be interesting—though to my knowledge no one has ever done it—to compare the hypothetical costs of Vang Pao's land scheme with the real costs of the federal and state funds that have been paid out

over the last twenty years to welfare-dependent Hmong who were
originally settled in urban areas.)*

Just as newly arrived immigrants in earlier eras had been called
"FOBs"—Fresh Off the Boat—some social workers nicknamed the
incoming Hmong, along with the other Southeast Asian refugees who
entered the United States after the Vietnamese War, "JOJs": Just Off
the Jet. Unlike the first waves of Vietnamese and Cambodian refugees,
most of whom received several months of vocational and language
training at regional "reception centers," the Hmong JOJs, who arrived
after the centers had closed, were all sent directly to their new homes.
(Later on, some were given "cultural orientation" training in Thailand
before flying to the United States. Their classes covered such topics
as how to distinguish a one-dollar bill from a ten-dollar bill and how
to use a peephole.) The logistical details of their resettlement were
contracted by the federal government to private nonprofit groups
known as VOLAGs, or national voluntary resettlement agencies,
which found local sponsors. Within their first few weeks in this country, newly arrived families were likely to deal with VOLAG officials,
immigration officials, public health officials, social service officials,
employment officials, and public assistance officials. The Hmong are
not known for holding bureaucrats in high esteem. As one proverb
puts it, "To see a tiger is to die; to see an official is to become des-
titute." In a study of adaptation problems among Indochinese refugees, Hmong respondents rated "Difficulty with American Agencies"
as a more serious problem than either "War Memories" or "Separa-

* The only place where Vang Pao's plan has actually been carried out is French
Guiana, on the northern coast of South America. In 1977, the French government
arranged for about 500 Hmong to emigrate from Thai refugee camps to an un-
inhabited jungle site near the Comté River. Two other colonies were later established to the northwest and east. The original colonists were accompanied by
French missionaries, one of whom, Father Yves Bertrais, had worked with the
Hmong in Laos since 1948 and was one of the inventors of the most widely used
system of Hmong writing. The settlers cleared land, built Lao-style houses, and
within two years were economically self-sufficient. Although some of the original
settlers decamped to France, the three colonies, with a current combined population of 1,400, are still prospering, producing more than seventy percent of all
the vegetables sold in French Guiana. The colony where Father Bertrais serves
as an adviser has also become an internationally known center for the publication
of Hmong-language books.

tion from Family." Because many of the VOLAGs had religious af-
filiations, the JOJs also often found themselves dealing with Christian
ministers, who, not surprisingly, took a dim view of shamanistic animism. A sponsoring pastor in Minnesota told a local newspaper, "It
would be wicked to just bring them over and feed and clothe them
and let them go to hell. The God who made us wants them to be
converted. If anyone thinks that a gospel-preaching church would
bring them over and not tell them about the Lord, they're out of their
mind." The proselytizing backfired. According to a study of Hmong
mental health problems, refugees sponsored by this pastor's religious
organization were significantly more likely, when compared to other
refugees, to require psychiatric treatment.

The Hmong were accustomed to living in the mountains, and most
of them had never seen snow. Almost all their resettlement sites had
flat topography and freezing winters. The majority were sent to cities,
including Minneapolis, Chicago, Milwaukee, Detroit, Hartford, and
Providence, because that was where refugee services—health care, language classes, job training, public housing—were concentrated. To
encourage assimilation, and to avoid burdening any one community
with more than its "fair share" of refugees, the Immigration and Naturalization Service adopted a policy of dispersal rather than clustering.
Newly arrived Hmong were assigned to fifty-three cities in twenty-
five different states: stirred into the melting pot in tiny, manageable
portions, or, as John Finck, who worked with Hmong at the Rhode
Island Office of Refugee Resettlement, put it, "spread like a thin layer
of butter throughout the country so they'd disappear." In some places,
clans were broken up. In others, members of only one clan were resettled, making it impossible for young people, who were forbidden
by cultural taboo from marrying within their own clan, to find local
marriage partners. Group solidarity, the cornerstone of Hmong social
organization for more than two thousand years, was completely ig-
nored.

Although most Hmong were resettled in cities, some nuclear families, unaccompanied by any of their extended relations, were placed
in isolated rural areas. Disconnected from traditional supports, these
families exhibited unusually high levels of anxiety, depression, and
paranoia. In one such case, the distraught and delusional father of the
Yang family—the only Hmong family sponsored by the First Baptist

Church of Fairfield, Iowa—attempted to hang himself in the basement of his wooden bungalow along with his wife and four children. His wife changed her mind at the last minute and cut the family down, but she acted too late to save their only son. An Iowa grand jury declined to indict either parent, on the grounds that the father was suffering from Post-Traumatic Stress Disorder, and the mother, cut off from all sources of information except her husband, had no way to develop an independent version of reality.

Reviewing the initial resettlement of the Hmong with several years' hindsight, Lionel Rosenblatt, the former United States Refugee Coordinator in Thailand, conceded that it had been catastrophically mishandled. "We knew at the start their situation was different, but we just couldn't make any special provisions for them," he said. "I still feel it was no mistake to bring the Hmong here, but you look back now and say, 'How could we have done it so shoddily?'" Eugene Douglas, President Reagan's ambassador-at-large for refugee affairs, stated flatly, "It was a kind of hell they landed into. Really, it couldn't have been done much worse."

The Hmong who sought asylum in the United States were, of course, not a homogeneous lump. A small percentage, mostly the high-ranking military officers who were admitted first, were multilingual and cosmopolitan, and a larger percentage had been exposed in a desultory fashion to some aspects of American culture and technology during the war or while living in Thai refugee camps. But the experience of tens of thousands of Hmong was much like the Lees'. It is possible to get an idea of how monumental the task of adjustment was likely to be by glancing at some of the pamphlets, audiotapes, and videos that refugee agencies produced for Southeast Asian JOJs. For example, "Your New Life in the United States," a handbook published by the Language and Orientation Resource Center in Washington, D.C., included the following tips:

Learn the meaning of "WALK"—"DON'T WALK" signs when crossing the street.

To send mail, you must use stamps.

To use the phone:

1) Pick up the receiver
2) Listen for dial tone
3) Dial each number separately
4) Wait for person to answer after it rings
5) Speak.

The door of the refrigerator must be shut.

Never put your hand in the garbage disposal.

Do not stand or squat on the toilet since it may break.

Never put rocks or other hard objects in the tub or sink since this will damage them.

Always ask before picking your neighbor's flowers, fruit or vegetables.

In colder areas you must wear shoes, socks, and appropriate outerwear. Otherwise, you may become ill.

Always use a handkerchief or a kleenex to blow your nose in public places or inside a public building.

Never urinate in the street. This creates a smell that is offensive to Americans. They also believe that it causes disease.

Spitting in public is considered impolite and unhealthy. Use a kleenex or handkerchief.

Picking your nose or your ears in public is frowned upon in the United States.

The customs they were expected to follow seemed so peculiar, the rules and regulations so numerous, the language so hard to learn, and the emphasis on literacy and the decoding of other unfamiliar symbols so strong, that many Hmong were overwhelmed. Jonas Vangay told me, "In America, we are blind because even though we have eyes, we cannot see. We are deaf because even though we have ears, we cannot hear." Some newcomers wore pajamas as street clothes; poured water on electric stoves to extinguish them; lit charcoal fires in their living rooms; stored blankets in their refrigerators; washed rice in their toilets; washed their clothes in swimming pools; washed their hair with Lestoil; cooked with motor oil and furniture polish; drank Clorox; ate cat food; planted crops in public parks; shot and ate skunks, porcupines, woodpeckers, robins, egrets, sparrows, and a bald eagle; and hunted pigeons with crossbows in the streets of Philadelphia.

If the United States seemed incomprehensible to the Hmong, the Hmong seemed equally incomprehensible to the United States. Journalists seized excitedly on a label that is still trotted out at regular intervals: "the most primitive refugee group in America." (In an angry letter to the *New York Times*, which had used that phrase in a 1990 news article, a Hmong computer specialist observed, "Evidently, we were not too primitive to fight as proxies for United States troops in the war in Laos.") Typical phrases from newspaper and magazine stories in the late seventies and eighties included "low-caste hill tribe," "Stone Age," "emerging from the mists of time," "like Alice falling down a rabbit hole." Inaccuracies were in no short supply. A 1981 article in the *Christian Science Monitor* called the Hmong language "extremely simplistic"; declared that the Hmong, who have been sewing *paj ntaub* with organic motifs for centuries, make "no connection between a picture of a tree and a real tree"; and noted that "the Hmong have no oral tradition of literature. . . . Apparently no folk tales exist." Some journalists seemed to shed all inhibition, and much of their good sense as well, when they were loosed on the Hmong. My favorite passage is a 1981 *New York Times* editorial about the large number of Hmong men who had died unexpectedly in their sleep, killed—or so it was widely believed at the time—by their own nightmares.* After explaining that the Hmong "attributed conscious life to natural objects," the writer asked,

---

* Sudden Unexpected Death Syndrome, which until the early 1980s was the leading cause of death among young Hmong males in the United States, is triggered by cardiac failure, often during or after a bad dream. No one has been able to explain what produces the cardiac irregularity, although theories over the years have included potassium deficiency, thiamine deficiency, sleep apnea, depression, culture shock, and survivor guilt. Many Hmong have attributed the deaths to attacks by an incubuslike *dab* who sits on the victim's chest and presses the breath out of him.

What were these nightmares? Did a palm tree's fronds turn into threatening fingers? Did a forest move and march with the implacability of the tide? Did a rose stretch on its stalk and throttle the sleeper?

Or did a gasoline hose curl and crush like a python? Was one of the dreamers pinned by a perambulating postbox? Or stabbed by scissors run amok?

("Or did the editorial writer drop acid?" I wrote in the newspaper margin when I first read this.)

Timothy Dunnigan, a linguistic anthropologist who has taught a seminar at the University of Minnesota on the media presentation of Hmong and Native Americans, once remarked to me, "The kinds of metaphorical language that we use to describe the Hmong say far more about us, and our attachment to our own frame of reference, than they do about the Hmong." So much for the Perambulating Postbox Theory. Dunnigan's comment resonates with Dwight Conquergood's observation about the uneasiness Westerners feel when confronted with the Other—for who could be more Other than the Hmong? Not only did they squat on toilets and eat skunks, not only did they bang gongs and sacrifice cows, but they also displayed what struck many people as an offensively selective interest in adopting the customs of the majority culture. For example, many Hmong quickly learned how to use telephones and drive cars, because those skills fit their own agenda of communicating with other Hmong, but failed to learn English. In 1987, when Senator Alan Simpson, then the ranking minority member of the Senate Subcommittee on Immigration and Refugee Affairs, called the Hmong "the most indigestible group in society," he sounded much like the authorities in China long ago who were grievously insulted when the Hmong refused to speak Chinese or eat with chopsticks.

It could not be denied that the Hmong were genuinely mysterious—far more so, for instance, than the Vietnamese and Cambodians who were streaming into the United States at the same time. Hardly anyone knew how to pronounce the word "Hmong." Hardly anyone—except the anthropology graduate students who suddenly realized they could write dissertations on patrilineal exogamous clan structures without leaving their hometowns—knew what role the Hmong had played during the war, or even what war it had been,

since our government had succeeded all too well in keeping the Quiet
War quiet. Hardly anyone knew they had a rich history, a complex
culture, an efficient social system, and enviable family values. They
were therefore an ideal blank surface on which to project xenophobic
fantasies.

The most expedient mode of projection has always been the rumor, and the Hmong attracted more than their share. This was to be
expected. After all, the Hmong of China had had wings under their
armpits and small tails. In prevalence and nastiness, American rumors
about the Hmong are at least an even match for the Hmong rumors
about America that circulated in the refugee camps of Thailand. Some
samples: The Hmong run a white slave trade. The Hmong are given
cars by the government. The Hmong force their children to run in
front of cars in order to get big insurance settlements. The Hmong
sell their daughters and buy their wives. Hmong women think speed
bumps are washboards for scrubbing clothes, and they get run over
by eighteen-wheelers. The Hmong eat dogs.* (That one comes complete with its own set of racist jokes. "What's the name of the Hmong
cookbook? *101 Ways to Wok Your Dog.*") The dog-eating rumor has
joined the national pantheon of deathless urban legends, right up there
with alligators in the sewers and worms in the Big Macs. Roger Mitchell, an emeritus professor of anthropology at the University of Wisconsin at Eau Claire, has collected a number of variants:

> [Rumored] methods of [dog] procurement vary. Some are coaxed home
> by Hmong children. Some were adopted from the animal shelter (until

---

* Like most false rumors, these all grew from germs of truth. The white-slavery
rumor originated in press accounts of Vietnamese crimes in California, most of
which were themselves probably unfounded. The car rumor originated in the
Hmong custom of pooling the savings of several families to buy cars and other
items too expensive for one family to afford. The insurance rumor originated in
the $78,000 that a Hmong family in Wisconsin was awarded after their fourteen-
year-old son died after being hit by a car. The daughter-selling rumor originated
in the Hmong custom of brideprice, or "nurturing charge," as it is now sometimes
called in the United States in order to avoid just such misinterpretations. The
speed-bump rumor originated in the many nonlethal domestic faux pas the
Hmong have actually committed. The dog-eating rumor, which, as I've mentioned elsewhere, is current in Merced, originated in Hmong ritual sacrifices.

those in charge noted a high rate of adoption). Others are strays. The most common accusation is theft, often from backyards, sometimes leaving the head and collar as mute testimony to Rover's passing. . . . The dog is usually an expensive one, often owned by a doctor. The theft is observed, the license plate number marked down. When the police check, the dog is already in some Hmong family's pot.

The supposed proof varies. That fixture in the urban legend, the garbage man, reports the presence of canine remains in Hmong garbage cans. Carcasses are seen hanging in the cellar by meter readers, salesmen, or whomever. Elementary school children recognize dog meat in Hmong sandwiches. Freezers are said to be full of frozen dogs. A bizarre touch is that the dogs are supposedly skinned alive to make them more tasty.

Not everyone who wanted to make the Hmong feel unwelcome stopped at slander. In the words of the president of a youth center in Minneapolis, his Hmong neighbors in the mid-eighties were "prime meat for predators." In Laos, Hmong houses had no locks. Sometimes they had no doors. Cultural taboos against theft and intra-community violence were poor preparation for life in the high-crime, inner-city neighborhoods in which most Hmong were placed. Some of the violence directed against them had nothing to do with their ethnicity; they were simply easy marks. But a good deal of it, particularly in urban areas, was motivated by resentment for what was perceived as preferential welfare treatment.*

In Minneapolis, tires were slashed and windows smashed. A high school student getting off a bus was hit in the face and told to "go back to China." A woman was kicked in the thighs, face, and kidneys, and her purse, which contained the family's entire savings of $400, was stolen; afterwards, she forbade her children to play outdoors, and her husband, who had once commanded a fifty-man unit in the Armée Clandestine, stayed home to guard the family's belongings. In Provi-

---

* Like all low-income refugeès, newly arrived Hmong were automatically eligible for Refugee Cash Assistance. The RCA program enabled Hmong who would otherwise have been ineligible for welfare in some states—for instance, because an able-bodied male was present in the home—to receive benefits. But it did not enable Hmong families to receive more money than American families. In a given state, Refugee Cash Assistance payments were always identical to benefits from AFDC (Aid to Families with Dependent Children, the most common form of public assistance before the 1996 welfare reform bill).

dence, children walking home from school were beaten. In Missoula, teenagers were stoned. In Milwaukee, garden plots were vandalized and a car was set on fire. In Eureka, California, two burning crosses were placed on a family's front lawn. In a random act of violence near Springfield, Illinois, a twelve-year-old boy was shot and killed by three men who forced his family's car off Interstate 55 and demanded money. His father told a reporter, "In a war, you know who your enemies are. Here, you don't know if the person walking up to you will hurt you."

In Philadelphia, anti-Hmong muggings, robberies, beatings, stonings, and vandalism were so commonplace during the early eighties that the city's Commission on Human Relations held public hearings to investigate the violence. One source of discord seemed to be a $100,000 federal grant for Hmong employment assistance that had incensed local residents, who were mostly unemployed themselves and believed the money should have been allocated to American citizens, not resident aliens. In one of the most grievous incidents, Seng Vang, a Hmong resident of Quebec who was visiting his mother, brothers, and sisters in west Philadelphia, was beaten with steel rods and a large rock, and left on the street with two broken legs and a brain injury. Later that day, a rifle shot was fired into his mother's apartment, breaking a window near the spot where she stood washing dishes. When Vang was treated at the University of Pennsylvania hospital, he was given a blood transfusion that was probably tainted. He was gravely ill for months with a rare form of hepatitis, and, seized by justifiable paranoia, became convinced that his doctors, too, had tried to kill him.

One thing stands out in all these accounts: the Hmong didn't fight back. I pondered that fact one day as I was thumbing through the index of Charles Johnson's *Dab Neeg Hmoob: Myths, Legends and Folk Tales from the Hmong of Laos*, which contained the following entries:

Fighting
    Enemies fighting . . . 29–46, 52–58, 198, 227, 470–471
Revenge
    Murdered man reincarnated to revenge his death . . . 308–309
    Cruel 9-tongued eagle has tongues cut out . . . 330
    Ngao Njua boils king who sent away her husband . . . 362
    Family kills tiger murderer of daughter, husband & children . . . 403

To quote from the last folktale cited: "Quickly, the rooster came down, seized the cat, threw him into the mortar of the rice mill, and started in immediately pounding him with the heavy pestle: DA DUH NDUH! DA DUH NDUH! He kept pounding until all the wildcat's bones were completely broken. And that's how the wildcat died, and that's how the story ends." It was clear that the Hmong were hardly the docile, passive, mild-mannered Asians of popular stereotype. Why hadn't the Americans who tormented the Hmong ended up like that wildcat?

Charles Johnson's background notes to another tale in *Dab Neeg Hmoob* provide a partial explanation:

> Our interviews indicate that the Hmong do not fight very much. When they do, it is with fists and feet. (In contrast with some neighboring peoples [in Laos] who tend to fight a lot, seem to take it lightly, and can be friends later, if two Hmong fight once, they are likely to take it very seriously, as a big issue which they do not forget, and may remain enemies forever.)
>
> . . . The Hmong do have an ideal of patience and stoical self-control, alluded to in the idiomatic expression often used by the Hmong to admonish someone who is acting impatiently or impulsively, or by parents in teaching good behavior to their children: "Ua siab ntev" (literally, Make, do, or act with a long liver, that is, a spirit or attitude of long-suffering, patient endurance of wrongs or difficulties).

Although on the battlefield the Hmong were known more for their fierceness than for their long livers, in the United States many were too proud to lower themselves to the level of the petty criminals they encountered, or even to admit they had been victims. An anthropologist named George M. Scott, Jr., once asked a group of Hmong in San Diego, all victims of property damage or assault, why they had not defended themselves or taken revenge. Scott wrote, "several

Hmong victims of such abuse, both young and old, answered that to have done so, besides inviting further, retaliatory, abuse, would have made them feel 'embarrassed' or ashamed. . . . In addition, the current president of Lao Family [a Hmong mutual assistance organization], when asked why his people did not 'fight back' when attacked here as they did in Laos, replied simply, 'because nothing here is worth defending to us.' "

There were exceptions, of course. If he was threatened with what he perceived as unbearable *poob ntsej muag* (loss of face), a Hmong sometimes decided that his shame and embarrassment would be even greater if he didn't fight back than if he did. Several Hmong in Fresno, hearing rumors that their welfare grants might be terminated because they owned cars, sent death threats ("You take away my grant and I'm going to blow your head off") to the county Social Services Department. As visual aids, they enclosed bullets and pictures of swords in their envelopes. (The grants were not terminated, and the bullets and swords were never used.) In Chicago, an elderly Hmong man and his son, insulted because an American driver had honked at them loudly and persistently, hit the American over the head with a steering-wheel locking device. The injury required thirteen stitches. When the men, Ching and Bravo Xiong, were brought to trial for aggravated battery, they asked the judge to allow each party to tell his side of the story and then drink a mixture of water and the blood of a sacrificed rooster. According to Hmong tradition, anyone who drinks rooster blood after telling a lie is destined to die within a year, so if a man partakes willingly, he is recognized as a truthteller. The judge denied this request. Instead, he sentenced the younger Xiong to two weekends in jail and six hundred hours of community service. He also ordered both men to learn English and study American culture.

Such incidents were rare. Most Hmong kept an apprehensive distance from the American penal system, which was radically different from their own. There were no prisons in their villages in Laos. The Hmong sense of justice was pragmatic and personal: how would incarceration benefit the victim? Corporal punishment was also unknown. Instead, various forms of public humiliation—a powerful deterrent in a society where loss of face was considered a worse fate than death—were employed. For example, a thief who had stolen four bars of silver might be forced to repay five bars to the victim and then be hauled off to the village chief with his hands tied, while the entire community jeered. The victim ended up enriched, the criminal suffered the shame he deserved, the criminal's innocent family kept its primary provider in the household, and any would-be thieves in the village were discouraged from potential crimes by witnessing the disgraceful spectacle. The Hmong who came to this country had heard that if they hurt someone, for whatever the reason, they would be sent to an American prison, and most of them were willing to do almost anything to avoid such an unimaginable calamity. Chao Wang Vang, a Fresno resident who had been charged with misdemeanor manslaughter after a fatal traffic accident, hanged himself in the county jail before his case came to court, not knowing he had the right to a trial and believing he would be imprisoned for the rest of his life.

In any case, Hmong who were persecuted by their neighbors could exercise a time-honored alternative to violence: flight. (It is worth remembering that when the nine evil *dab* brothers were trying to kill Shee Yee, he attempted only one defensive counterattack before switching his strategy to evasion.) Between 1982 and 1984, three quarters of the Hmong population of Philadelphia simply left town and joined relatives in other cities. During approximately the same period, a third of all the Hmong in the United States moved from one city to another. When they decided to relocate, Hmong families often lit off without notifying their sponsors, who were invariably offended. If they couldn't fit one of their possessions, such as a television set, in a car or bus or U-Haul, they left it behind, seemingly without so much as a backward glance. Some families traveled alone, but more often they moved in groups. When there was an exodus from Portland, Oregon, a long caravan of overloaded cars motored together down Interstate 5, bound for the Central Valley of California. With this "secondary migration," as sociologists termed it, the government's attempt to stir the Hmong evenly into the melting pot was definitively sabotaged.

Although local violence was often the triggering factor, there were also other reasons for migrating. In 1982, when all refugees who had lived in the United States for more than eighteen months stopped receiving Refugee Cash Assistance—the period of eligibility had previously been three years—many Hmong who had no jobs and no prospects moved to states that provided welfare benefits to two-parent families. Their original host states were often glad to get rid of them. For a time, the Oregon Human Resources Department, strapped by a tight state budget, sent refugees letters that pointedly detailed the levels of welfare benefits available in several other states. California's were among the highest. Thousands of Hmong also moved to California because they had heard it was an agricultural state where they might be able to farm. But by far the most important reason for relocating was reunification with other members of one's clan. Hmong clans are sometimes at odds with each other, but within a clan, whose thousands of members are regarded as siblings, one can always count on support and sympathy. A Hmong who tries to gain acceptance to a kin group other than his own is called a *puav*, or bat. He is rejected by the birds because he has fur and by the mice because he has wings. Only when a Hmong lives among his own subspecies can he stop flitting restlessly from group to group, haunted by the shame of not belonging.

The Hmong may have been following their venerable proverb, "There's always another mountain," but in the past, each new mountain had yielded a living. Unfortunately, the most popular areas of secondary resettlement all had high unemployment rates, and they got higher. For example, in the Central Valley—which had no Hmong in 1976 and more than 20,000 seven years later—the economic recession of 1982 shut down dozens of factories and other businesses, driving up local unemployment and forcing the Hmong to compete with out-of-work Americans for even the most unskilled jobs. The dream of farming quickly fizzled for all but a few hundred. Hmong farmers knew a great deal about torching fields for slash-and-burn agriculture, planting mountain rice with dibble sticks, and tapping opium pods, but they had much to learn (to quote from the course plan for a not-very-successful Hmong training program) about

> crop varieties, soil preparation, machinery and equipment, timing and succession of planting, seeds and transplants, fertilizer, pest and weed management, disease control, irrigation, erosion control, record-keeping, harvesting, washing and handling, grading and size selection, packing, conditioning, market selection, product planning, pricing strategies, shipping and receiving, advertising, merchandising, verbal and non-verbal communication skills for dealing with consumers, etc.

By 1985, at least eighty percent of the Hmong in Merced, Fresno, and San Joaquin counties were on welfare.

That didn't halt the migration. Family reunification tends to have a snowball effect. The more Thaos or Xiongs there were in one place, the more mutual assistance they could provide, the more cultural traditions they could practice together, and the more stable their community would be. Americans, however, tended to view secondary migration as an indication of instability and dependence. Dwight Conquergood has described the gulf between the American ideal of rugged individualism and the Hmong ideal of group interdependence:

> In a thousand ways, our separatist, individualistic ethic gets enunciated daily: individual place settings at meals, the importance of "a room of one's own" even for children, advertising appeals and jingles such as "Have it your way" and "We do it all for you." The enactment of Hmong culture, on the other hand, is like a symphony; every part plays the themes of returning, recalling, restoring, reincorporating, binding together, and reuniting separated parts into a collective identity.

A Hmong proverb observes: "One stick cannot cook a meal or build a fence." If a meal needed to be cooked or a fence built, the sticks had no choice but to pick themselves up and bundle together.

Seeing that the Hmong were redistributing themselves as they saw fit, and that they were becoming an economic burden on the places to which they chose to move, the federal Office of Refugee Resettlement tried to slow the migratory tide. The 1983 Highland Lao Initiative, a three-million-dollar "emergency effort" to bolster employment and community stability in Hmong communities outside California, offered vocational training, English classes, and other enticements for the Hmong to stay put. Though the initiative claimed a handful of modest local successes, the California migration was essentially unstoppable. By this time, most Hmong JOJs were being sponsored by relatives in America rather than by voluntary organizations, so the government no longer had geographic control over their placements. The influx therefore came—and, in smaller increments, is still coming—from Thailand as well as from other parts of America. Therefore, in addition to trying to prevent the Hmong from moving to high-welfare states, the Office of Refugee Resettlement started trying to encourage the ones who were already there to leave. Spending an average of $7,000 per family on moving expenses, job placement, and a month or two of rent and food subsidies, the Planned Secondary Resettlement Program, which was phased out in 1994, relocated about 800 unemployed Hmong families from what it called "congested areas" to communities with "favorable employment opportunities"— i.e., unskilled jobs with wages too low to attract a full complement of local American workers.

Within the economic limitations of blue-collar labor, those 800 families have fared well. Ninety-five percent have become self-sufficient. They work in manufacturing plants in Dallas, on electronics assembly lines in Atlanta, in furniture and textile factories in Morganton, North Carolina. More than a quarter of them have saved enough money to buy their own houses, as have three quarters of the Hmong families who live in Lancaster County, Pennsylvania, where the men farm or work in food-processing plants, and the women work for the Amish, sewing quilts that are truthfully advertised as "locally made." Elsewhere, Hmong are employed as grocers, carpenters, poultry processors, machinists, welders, auto mechanics, tool and die makers, teachers, nurses, interpreters, and community liaisons. In a survey of Minnesota employers, the respondents were asked "What do you think of the Hmong as workers?" Eighty-six percent rated them "very good."

> This was particularly true in organizations where the Hmong were employed in assembly, or piecework occupations. . . . In general, employers are impressed by the productivity of the Hmong. Initially, there appears to be a period of some difficulty in training due to English language skills. Once trained, however, Hmong are reported to be better workers than the average American workers.

Some younger Hmong have become lawyers, doctors, dentists, engineers, computer programmers, accountants, and public administrators. Hmong National Development, an association that promotes Hmong self-sufficiency, encourages this small corps of professionals to serve as mentors and sponsors for other Hmong who might thereby be induced to follow suit. The cultural legacy of mutual assistance has been remarkably adaptive. Hundreds of Hmong students converse electronically, trading information and gossip—opinions on the relevance of traditional customs, advice on college admissions, personal ads—via the Hmong Channel on the Internet Relay Chat system. (They include Lia Lee's older sister True, whose parents are baffled by the two hours she spends each day hunched over a computer terminal at her school.) There is also a Hmong Homepage on the World Wide Web (http://www.stolaf.edu/people/cdr/hmong/) and several burgeoning Hmong electronic mailing lists, including Hmongnet, Hmongforum, and Hmong Language Users Group.*

The M.D.s and J.D.s and digital sophisticates constitute a small, though growing, minority. Although younger, English-speaking Hmong who have been educated in the United States have better employment records than their elders, they still lag behind most other Asian-Americans. As for Hmong workers over thirty-five, the majority are immovably wedged at or near entry level. They can't get jobs that require better English, and they can't learn English on their current jobs. The federal *Hmong Resettlement Study* cited, as an example, a Hmong worker in Dallas who after three years on the job was unable to name the machine he operated. He stated that he never expected a promotion or a pay raise other than cost-of-living increases. Other Hmong have been thwarted by placing a higher value on group solidarity than on individual initiative. In San Diego, the manager of an electronics plant was so enthusiastic about one Hmong assembly worker that he tried to promote him to supervisor. The man quit, ashamed to accept a job that would place him above his Hmong coworkers.

For the many Hmong who live in high-unemployment areas, questions of advancement are often moot. They have no jobs at all. This is the reason the Hmong are routinely called this country's "least successful refugees." It is worth noting that the standard American tests of success that they have flunked are almost exclusively economic. If one applied social indices instead—such as rates of crime, child abuse,

* The Hmong Channel is accessed almost exclusively by Hmong users. The Hmong Homepage and the electronic mailing lists also have an audience of Americans with an academic or professional interest in Hmong culture, as well as a number of Mormon elders who have been assigned missionary work in Hmong communities.

illegitimacy, and divorce—the Hmong would probably score better than most refugee groups (and also better than most Americans), but those are not the forms of success to which our culture assigns its highest priority. Instead, we have trained the spotlight on our best-loved index of failure, the welfare rolls. In California, Minnesota, and Wisconsin, where, not coincidentally, benefits tend to be relatively generous and eligibility requirements relatively loose, the percentages of Hmong on welfare are approximately forty-five, forty, and thirty-five (an improvement over five years ago, when they were approximately sixty-five, seventy, and sixty). The cycle of dependence that began with rice drops in Laos and reinforced with daily handouts at Thai refugee camps has been completed here in the United States. The conflicting structures of the Hmong culture and the American welfare system make it almost impossible for the average family to become independent. In California, for example, a man with seven children—a typical Hmong family size—would have to make $10.60 an hour, working forty hours a week, to equal his welfare stipend and food stamp allowance. But with few marketable skills and little English, he would probably be ineligible for most jobs that paid more than the minimum wage of $5.15 an hour, at which he would have to work an improbable eighty-two hours a week in order to equal his welfare allotment. In addition, until the mid-nineties in most states, if he worked more than one hundred hours a month—as a part-time worker trying to acquire job skills, for example, or a farmer in the start-up phase—his family would lose their entire welfare grant, all their food stamps, and their health insurance.*

The 1996 welfare reform bill, which in its present form promises to deny benefits to legal immigrants, has stirred up monumental waves of anxiety among the Hmong. Faced with the possibility of having their assistance cut off, some have applied for citizenship, although many middle-aged Hmong find the English language requirement an

---

* At the request of local public assistance agencies, the infamous "100-Hour Rule," which prevented so many Hmong from becoming economically self-sufficient, was waived in the majority of states, starting with California, between 1994 and 1996. "Basically, it required people not to work," explained John Cullen, who directed Merced's Human Services Agency during the last years of the rule's sway. The 100-Hour Rule was replaced by a formula of gradually decreasing benefits based on earnings.

insuperable obstacle. (The hurdles are lower for older Hmong who came to the United States shortly after the end of the war in Laos. The language rule is waived for "lawful permanent residents" age fifty or older who have been in this country for at least twenty years, and for those age fifty-five or older who have been here at least fifteen years. The Lees, who are considering applying for citizenship, would qualify for this waiver.) Some Hmong have moved, or are planning to move, to states with better job markets. Some will become dependent on their relatives. Because a few states will probably elect to use their own funds to assist legal immigrants, some will simply continue to depend on welfare in altered, reduced, and more precarious forms.

Few things gall the Hmong more than to be criticized for accepting public assistance. For one thing, they feel they deserve the money. Every Hmong has a different version of what is commonly called "The Promise": a written or oral contract, made by CIA personnel in Laos, that if they fought for the Americans, the Americans would aid them if the Pathet Lao won the war. After risking their lives to rescue downed American pilots, seeing their villages flattened by incidental American bombs, and being forced to flee their country because they had supported the "American War," the Hmong expected a hero's welcome here. According to many of them, the first betrayal came when the American airlifts rescued only the officers from Long Tieng, leaving nearly everyone else behind. The second betrayal came in the Thai camps, when the Hmong who wanted to come to the United States were not all automatically admitted. The third betrayal came when they arrived here and found they were ineligible for veterans' benefits. The fourth betrayal came when Americans condemned them for what the Hmong call "eating welfare." The fifth betrayal came when the Americans announced that the welfare would stop.

Aside from some older people who consider welfare a retirement benefit, most Hmong would prefer almost any other option—if other options existed. What right-thinking Hmong would choose to be yoked to one of the most bureaucratic institutions in America? (A tip from "Your New Life in the United States," on applying for cash assistance: "You should have as many of the following documents available as possible: I-94—take the original, if you can; rent bill or lease; Social Security card; any pay stubs; bank account statement or savings passbook; utility bills; medical bills or proof of medical disability; employment registration card.") What Hmong would choose to become addicted to a way of life that some clan leaders have likened to opium? And what Hmong would choose the disgrace of being *dev mus nuam yaj*, a dog waiting for scraps? Dang Moua, the Merced businessman who had kept his family alive en route to Thailand by shooting birds with a homemade crossbow, once told me, "One time when I am first in America, a Korean man tell me that if someone is lazy and doesn't work, the government still pay them. I say, you crazy! That doesn't ring my bell at all! I am not afraid of working! My parents raised me as a man! I work till the last day I leave this earth!" And indeed, Dang held three concurrent nearly full-time jobs, as a grocer, an interpreter, and a pig farmer. He was once a clerk-typist in the American Embassy in Vientiane and speaks five languages, so his success is not one most Hmong could reasonably be expected to emulate. More typical are two middle-aged men who were interviewed in San Diego for a survey on refugee adaptation. The first said:

I used to be a real man like any other man, but not now any longer. . . . We only live day by day, just like the baby birds who are only staying in the nest opening their mouths and waiting for the mother bird to bring the worms.

The second said:

We are not born to earth to have somebody give us feed; we are so ashamed to depend on somebody like this. When we were in our country, we never ask anybody for help like this. . . . I've been trying very hard to learn English and at the same time looking for a job. No matter what kind of job, even the job to clean people's toilets; but still people don't even trust you or offer you such work. I'm looking at me that I'm not even worth as much as a dog's stool. Talking about this, I want to die right here so I won't see my future.

These men were both suffering from a global despair to which their economic dependence was only one of many contributing factors. In the survey for which they were interviewed, part of a longitudinal study of Hmong, Cambodians, Vietnamese, and Chinese-Vietnamese refugees, the Hmong respondents scored lowest in "happiness" and "life satisfaction." In a study of Indochinese refugees in Illinois, the Hmong exhibited the highest degree of "alienation from their environment." According to a Minnesota study, Hmong refugees who had lived in the United States for a year and a half had "very high levels of depression, anxiety, hostility, phobia, paranoid ideation, obsessive compulsiveness and feelings of inadequacy." (Over the next decade, some of these symptoms moderated, but the refugees' levels of anxiety, hostility, and paranoia showed little or no improvement.) The study that I found most disheartening was the 1987 California Southeast Asian Mental Health Needs Assessment, a statewide epidemiological survey funded by the Office of Refugee Resettlement and the National Institute of Mental Health. It was shocking to look at the bar graphs comparing the Hmong with the Vietnamese, the Chinese-Vietnamese, the Cambodians, and the Lao—all of whom, particularly the Cambodians, fared poorly compared to the general population—and see how the Hmong stacked up: Most depressed. Most psychosocially dysfunctional. Most likely to be severely in need of mental health treatment. Least educated. Least literate. Smallest percentage in labor force. Most likely to cite "fear" as a reason for immigration and least likely to cite "a better life."

The same bleak ground was covered from the Hmong point of view by Bruce Thowpaou Bliatout, a public health administrator in Portland, Oregon. Dr. Bliatout, who is Hmong, explained in an article on mental health concepts that such issues as job adjustment and family happiness are regarded by the Hmong as problems of the liver. If patience, as Charles Johnson noted in *Dab Neeg Hmoob*, is attributed to a long—that is, a robust and healthy—liver, what Americans would call mental illness is attributed to a liver that has become diseased or damaged through soul loss. According to Bliatout, who provided case histories for each one, some illnesses common among Hmong in the United States are:

Nyuab Siab
Translation: Difficult liver.
Causes: Loss of family, status, home, country, or any important item that has a high emotional value.
Symptoms: Excessive worry; crying; confusion; disjointed speech; loss of sleep and appetite; delusions.

Tu Siab
Translation: Broken liver.
Causes: Loss of family member; quarrel between family members; break
   of family unity.
Symptoms: Grief; worry; loneliness; guilt; feeling of loss; insecurity.

Lwj Siab
Translation: Rotten liver.
Causes: Stressful family relations; constant unfulfillment of goals.
Symptoms: Loss of memory; short temper; delusions.

Before I came to Merced, Bill Selvidge described to me the first Hmong patient he had ever seen. Bruce Thowpaou Bliatout would have diagnosed this patient as having a difficult liver; Bill thought of it, not so differently, as a broken heart. "Mr. Thao was a man in his fifties," said Bill. "He told me through an interpreter that he had a bad back, but after I listened for a while I realized that he'd really come in because of depression. It turned out he was an agoraphobe. He was afraid to leave his house because he thought if he walked more than a couple of blocks he'd get lost and never find his way home again. What a metaphor! He'd seen his entire immediate family die in Laos, he'd seen his country collapse, and he never *was* going to find his way home again. All I could do was prescribe antidepressants."

Mr. Thao turned out to be the first of a long procession of depressed Hmong patients whom Bill was to treat over the next three years. Bill cut to the nub of the matter when he described the man's profound loss of "home." For the Hmong in America—where not only the social mores but also the sound of every birdsong, the shape of every tree and flower, the smell of the air, and the very texture of the earth are unfamiliar—the ache of homesickness can be incapacitating. In "Lament upon Leaving Our Country," a Hmong poet named Doua Her wrote:

We remember the bird songs at sunrise.
We remember the grasshoppers jumping at dawn.
We remember the sound of heavy raindrops on leaves.
We remember the song of the male gibbon.
We remember the fruit trees . . . the pineapple, banana, and papaya.
We can still hear the owls cry to each other like we cry.

John Finck of the Rhode Island resettlement office once took a party of Hmong from Providence to visit Plimoth Plantation, a reconstructed Pilgrim village with thatched houses and free-running chickens. When it came time to leave, one of the older men in the group asked Finck, "Can we move here and make this our home?"

Dang Moua, the energetic grocer-cum-interpreter-cum-pig-farmer, mentioned once that after thirteen years in the United States, he dreamed of Laos every night and had never once dreamed of America. "I talk to more than one hundred Hmong about this," he said. "I talk to General Vang Pao. Same thing for everyone." In a heroic act of denial, only ten percent of the Hmong refugees polled in a Minnesota survey said they were certain they would spend the rest of their lives in the United States; the rest were either certain or hopeful that they would die in Laos. John Xiong, a Hmong leader in Merced, told me, "All the older people, they say, We want to go back. We born over there, we come here. Very nice country but we don't speak the language, we cannot drive, we just stay home isolated. Over there we can have a little piece of farm, raise chicken, pig, and cow, don't forget to wake up early, harvest on time, make enough this year to another coming year. That's it. Then we feeling like peaceful. Here, we do right and they say wrong. Then we do wrong and they say right. Which way we go? We want to go home."

The home to which the older Hmong dream of returning—which they call *peb lub tebchaws*, "our fields and our lands"—is prewar Laos. Their memories of wartime Laos are almost unrelievedly traumatic: a "bereavement overload" that critically magnifies all their other stresses. Richard Mollica, a psychiatrist who helped found the Indochinese Psychiatry Clinic in Boston, found that during the war and its aftermath, Hmong refugees had experienced an average of fifteen "major trauma events," such as witnessing killings and torture. Mollica has observed of his patients, "Their psychological reality is both full and empty. They are 'full' of the past; they are 'empty' of new ideas and life experiences."

"Full" of both past trauma and past longing, the Hmong have found it especially hard to deal with present threats to their old identities. I once went to a conference on Southeast Asian mental health at which a psychologist named Evelyn Lee, who was born in Macao, invited six members of the audience to come to the front of the auditorium for a role-playing exercise. She cast them as a grandfather, a father, a mother, an eighteen-year-old son, a sixteen-year-old daughter, and a twelve-year-old daughter. "Okay," she told them, "line up according to your status in your old country." Ranking themselves by traditional notions of age and gender, they queued up in the order I've just mentioned, with the grandfather standing proudly at the head of the line. "Now they come to America," said Dr. Lee. "Grandfather has no job. Father can only chop vegetables. Mother didn't work in the old country, but here she gets a job in a garment factory. Oldest daughter works there too. Son drops out of high school because he can't learn English. Youngest daughter learns the best English in the family and ends up at U.C. Berkeley. Now you line up again." As the family reshuffled, I realized that its power structure had turned completely upside down, with the youngest girl now occupying the head of the line and the grandfather standing forlornly at the tail.

Dr. Lee's exercise was an eloquent demonstration of what sociologists call "role loss." Of all the stresses in the Hmong community, role loss—the constellation of apparent incompetencies that convinced Lia's mother she was stupid—may be the most corrosive to the ego. Every Hmong can tell stories about colonels who became janitors, military communications specialists who became chicken processors, flight crewmen who found no work at all. Dang Moua's cousin Moua Kee, a former judge, worked first in a box factory and then on the night shift in a machine shop. "When you have no country, no land, no house, no power, everyone is the same," he said with a shrug. Major Wang Seng Khang, a former battalion commander who served as leader for 10,000 Hmong in his refugee camp, took five years to find a job as a part-time church liaison. Even then, he depended on his wife's wages from a jewelry factory to pay the rent and on his children to translate for him. Of himself and his fellow leaders, he said, "We have become children in this country."

And in this country the real children have assumed some of the power that used to belong to their elders. The status conferred by speaking English and understanding American conventions is a phenomenon familiar to most immigrant groups, but the Hmong, whose identity has always hinged on tradition, have taken it particularly hard. "Animals are responsible to their masters, and children to their parents," advised a Hmong proverb that survived unquestioned for countless generations. In prewar Laos, where families worked in the fields all day and shared a single room at night, it was not uncommon for children and their parents to be together around the clock. Remoteness and altitude insulated their villages from the majority culture. Hmong children here spend six hours in school and often several more at large in their communities, soaking up America. "My sisters don't feel they're Hmong at all," my interpreter, May Ying Xiong, once told me. "One of them has spiked hair. The youngest one speaks mostly English. I don't see the respect I gave elders at that age." Lia's sister May said, "I know how to do *paj ntaub*, but I hate sewing. My mom says, why aren't you doing *paj ntaub*? I say, Mom, this is America."

Although Americanization may bring certain benefits—more job opportunities, more money, less cultural dislocation—Hmong parents are likely to view any earmarks of assimilation as an insult and a threat. "In our families, the kids eat hamburger and bread," said Dang Moua sadly, "whereas the parents prefer hot soup with vegetables, rice, and meat like tripes or liver or kidney that the young ones don't want. The old ones may have no driver's licenses and they ask the young ones to take them some place. Sometimes the kid say I'm too busy. That is a serious situation when the kid will not obey us. The old ones are really upset." Rebellious young Hmong sometimes go beyond refusing to chauffeur their parents, and tangle with drugs or violence. In 1994, Xou Yang, a nineteen-year-old high-school dropout from Banning, California, robbed and murdered a German tourist. His father, a veteran of the war in Laos, told a reporter, "We have lost all control. Our children do not respect us. One of the hardest things for me is when I tell my children things and they say, 'I already know that.' When my wife and I try to tell my son about Hmong culture, he tells me people here are different, and he will not listen to me."

Sukey Waller, Merced's maverick psychologist, once recalled a Hmong community meeting she had attended. "An old man of seventy or eighty stood up in the front row," she said, "and he asked one of the most poignant questions I have ever heard: 'Why, when what we did worked so well for two hundred years, is everything breaking down?'" When Sukey told me this, I understood why the man had asked the question, but I thought he was wrong. Much has broken down, but not everything. Jacques Lemoine's analysis of the postwar hegira—that the Hmong came to the West to save not only their lives but their ethnicity—has been at least partially confirmed in the United States. I can think of no other group of immigrants whose culture, in its most essential aspects, has been so little eroded by assimilation. Virtually all Hmong still marry other Hmong, marry young, obey the taboo against marrying within their own clans, pay brideprices, and have large families. Clan and lineage structures are intact, as is the ethic of group solidarity and mutual assistance. On most weekends in Merced, it is possible to hear a death drum beating at a Hmong funeral or a *txiv neeb*'s gong and rattle sounding at a healing ceremony. Babies wear strings on their wrists to protect their souls from abduction by *dabs*. People divine their fortunes by interpreting their dreams. (If you dream of opium, you will have bad luck; if you dream you are covered with excrement, you will have good luck; if you dream you have a snake on your lap, you will become pregnant.) Animal sacrifices are common, even among Christian converts, a fact I first learned when May Ying Xiong told me that she would be unavailable to interpret one weekend because her family was sacrificing a cow to safeguard her niece during an upcoming open-heart operation. When I said, "I didn't know your family was so religious," she replied, "Oh yes, we're Mormon."

Even more crucially, the essential Hmong temperament—independent, insular, antiauthoritarian, suspicious, stubborn, proud, choleric, energetic, vehement, loquacious, humorous, hospitable, generous—has so far been ineradicable. Indeed, as George M. Scott, Jr., has observed, the Hmong have responded to the hardships of life in the United States "by becoming *more* Hmong, rather than less so." Summing up his impressions of the Hmong in 1924, François Marie Savina, the French missionary, attributed their ethnic durability to six factors: religion; love of liberty; traditional customs; refusal to marry outside their race; life in cold, dry, mountainous areas; and the toughening effects of war. Even though their experience here has been suffused with despair and loss, the 180,000 Hmong who live in the United States are doing passably or better on the first four counts.*

---

* About 150,000 Hmong—some of whom resettled in countries other than the United States, and some of whom are still in Thailand—fled Laos. The Hmong now living in the United States exceed that number because of their high birthrate.

I was able to see the whole cycle of adjustment to American life start all over again during one of my visits to Merced. When I arrived at the Lees' apartment, I was surprised to find it crammed with people I'd never met before. These turned out to be a cousin of Nao Kao's named Joua Chai Lee, his wife, Yeng Lor, and their nine children, who ranged in age from eight months to twenty-five years. They had arrived from Thailand two weeks earlier, carrying one piece of luggage for all eleven of them. In it were packed some clothes, a bag of rice, and, because Joua is a *txiv neeb*'s assistant, a set of rattles, a drum, and a pair of divinatory water-buffalo horns. The cousins were staying with Foua and Nao Kao until they found a place of their own. The two families had not seen each other in more than a decade, and there was a festive atmosphere in the little apartment, with small children dashing around in their new American sneakers and the four barefooted adults frequently throwing back their heads and laughing. Joua said to me, via May Ying's translation, "Even though there are a lot of us, you can spend the night here too." May Ying explained to me later that Joua didn't really expect me to lie down on the floor with twenty of his relatives. It was simply his way, even though he was in a strange country where he owned almost nothing, of extending a face-saving bit of Hmong hospitality.

I asked Joua what he thought of America. "It is really nice but it is different," he said. "It is very flat. You cannot tell one place from another. There are many things I have not seen before, like that"—a light switch—"and that"—a telephone—"and that"—an air conditioner. "Yesterday our relatives took us somewhere in a car and I saw a lady and I thought she was real but she was fake." This turned out to have been a mannequin at the Merced Mall. "I couldn't stop laughing all the way home," he said. And remembering how funny his mistake had been, he started to laugh again.

Then I asked Joua what he hoped for his family's future here. "I will work if I can," he said, "but I think I probably cannot. As old as I am, I think I will not be able to learn one word of English. If my children put a heart to it, they will be able to learn English and get really smart. But as for myself, I have no hope."

15

Gold and Dross

When I met Nao Kao's cousin and his family at the Lees' apartment, there was, of course, one child who was not playing games with her newfound cousins or sitting on the doorstep and watching the cars drive down East 12th Street in the spring twilight, the hour the Lees still called "pig-feeding time." Lia was on her mother's back, swaddled in a bright pink *nyias*, an apron-shaped baby carrier that Foua had embroidered with black, yellow, and green cross-stitching and ornamented with eighteen fuzzy pink pom-poms. It was perhaps the largest *nyias* in Hmong history, since Lia was more than three feet tall and weighed thirty-six pounds. Foua preferred it to the pediatric wheelchair, provided by the Merced County Health Department, that sat in a corner of the living room. A shawl was wrapped around them both, and from a distance, because Lia's body lay stiff and motionless against her mother's, they looked like a single person.

Lia was almost seven. For more than two years, her doctors had been waiting for her to die, and her parents had been confounding them with their ability to keep her alive. Although Lia was not dead, she was quadriplegic, spastic, incontinent, and incapable of purposeful movement. Her condition was termed a "persistent vegetative state."

Most of the time her arms were drawn up tightly against her chest and her fists were clenched, a sign of cerebral motor damage. Sometimes her legs trembled. Sometimes her head nodded, not in jerks but slowly, as if she were assenting to a question underwater. Sometimes she moaned or whimpered. She continued to breathe, swallow, sleep, wake, sneeze, snore, grunt, and cry, because those functions were governed by her unimpaired brain stem, but she had no self-aware mental activity, a function governed by the forebrain. Her most conspicuously aberrant feature was her eyes, which, although clear, sometimes stared blankly and sometimes darted to one side as if she were frightened. Looking at her, I could not help feeling that something was missing beyond the neurotransmissive capabilities of her cerebral cortex, and that her parents' name for it—her *plig*, or soul—was as good a term as any.

I once said to Terry Hutchison, Lia's neurologist at Valley Children's Hospital in Fresno, "But she must have *some* consciousness. She can cry, and when her mother picks her up and rocks her, she stops." Dr. Hutchison replied, "Well, you take a Venus flytrap. Does it decide to snap at a fly that is walking on its pod, or does it just do it? I think it just does it. Lia is like a flytrap. It's all reflex. Nevertheless, I do believe, even though there is no way you can ask people like that how they feel, that it is at least theoretically possible for her to have no thoughts, no memories, no conscious life, and yet respond to her mother's touch." I asked Lia's parents what they thought their daughter could sense. Nao Kao said, "When we hold her, she knows it and is smiling." Foua said, "Sometimes when I call her, it seems that she does recognize me, but I don't really know, because it seems that Lia cannot see me. My baby hasn't done anything bad. She is a good girl, but because she is hurt like this it is just as if she is dead. Every day now, she cannot see me."

On December 9, 1986, Lia had returned home from MCMC with a fever of 104°, an irregular breathing pattern, an inability to cough up or swallow her own secretions, and a prognosis of imminent death. Within days, her temperature was normal, her breathing was regular, and her swallowing and gag reflexes were back. Scratching their heads, her doctors attributed these improvements to reduced swelling in the medulla and hypothalamus. Her parents attributed them to the herbal infusion with which they had bathed their daughter when she first came home, and for many days thereafter. "They'd put a shower curtain on the living room floor and lay Lia on it," recalled Jeanine Hilt. "Foua would drench her in this tea remedy that she had cooked up, just sponging it all over her body and her hair and her head. It was really quite a soothing thing. A loving thing."

During Lia's first days home, Jeanine had visited the Lees every day. It was because of her that Foua and Nao Kao left the hated nasogastric tube—which they had been directed to use for the remainder of Lia's life—in place for an entire week. Under Jeanine's guidance, they poured two ounces of infant formula down the tube every two hours, checking its placement by injecting air through a syringe and listening for the bubbles through a stethoscope. "It was really slow," recalled Nao Kao, "and I didn't really know how to use it. That tube had two plastic things, and if the food gets stuck in there, then you can't feed anymore." Finally they yanked it out of Lia's nose and started squeezing formula into her mouth with a baby bottle. This worked perfectly, even though the doctors had predicted that without the tube Lia would choke to death. The only problem was that because the prescribed tube was no longer being used, Medi-Cal refused to pay for the formula, so Neil and Peggy started giving the family entire cases of Similac with Iron, intended to be dispensed as free samples to new mothers.

Medi-Cal was willing to pay for a wheelchair and a suction machine, but it drew the line at a pediatric hospital bed. This bed, which the Lees had never requested, became the focal point toward which all of Jeanine's grief and rage about Lia's condition converged. "When Medi-Cal said they wouldn't pay for it, it just pissed me off to the max," she said. "Some all-powerful doctor in the regional bureau said the Hmong sleep on the floor anyway so they didn't need it. He was a real racist and I told him so. I just went crazy. Berserk. I started calling a million and one places. Finally I got a medical supply company I found in the Yellow Pages to provide a brand-new bed and deliver it to the Lees' home, completely free." Jeanine never found out that Lia did not sleep in this bed, which stood for years next to her parents' double bed, taking up space in their tiny bedroom. "Lia always sleeps with us," Foua told me. "She is the only child who sleeps in our bed. I hold her during the night and we pat her feet all night long because we love her so much. If you don't pat Lia on her foot or her knee, she cries a lot."

The first time Lia returned to the clinic for a checkup, Neil was on duty. During her last stay at MCMC, he had so successfully distanced himself from her case that although he had seen Lia, he had not seen Foua and Nao Kao since their daughter's return from Fresno. Years later, when he looked through Lia's medical chart, he paused for a long time when he came to the clinic note from that visit. I wondered what he found so emotionally compelling about "Today, Lia is afebrile with a temperature of 98.3° axillary, weight 42 pounds, and hemoglobin is 11." He cleared his throat. "That first visit was a very significant visit for me," he said. "It was very emotional. I remember Jeanine Hilt was in the room too. Also an interpreter. I remember talking to the mother and saying it was very hard for me to see Lia the way she was, to actually be in the same room with her, and that what had happened was something I had always feared, and that I was very sorry. And what absolutely blew me away is that I, well, I was afraid they were going to blame me for what happened, but the mother showed me compassion. She understood—somehow she got the—she, well"—Neil was scrabbling uncomfortably for words, but he was determined to forge ahead—"well, I think part of it was that I was crying. What she did was, she thanked me. And she hugged me. And I hugged her." He cleared his throat again. "So anyway."

When I asked Foua about that encounter, all she said was, "Lia's doctor really hurt for her." Nao Kao scowled and remained silent. He had never stopped being angry at MCMC and everyone who worked there. Foua, temperamentally more accommodating than her husband, had managed to divert all her blame to the doctors in Fresno who had given Lia "too much medicine," thereby partially exonerating Neil and Peggy. In her eyes, "the husband and wife doctors" were guilty not of the mortal sin of destroying her daughter but of the lesser sin —a sin of omission—of going on vacation and leaving Lia in the wrong hands.

As the months passed, Lia became, in some cockeyed sense, a radiantly vital child. Although every page of her chart contained the notation "Hypoxic Ischemic Encephalopathy, Static"—irreparable brain damage—one clinic report also noted:

PROBLEM: Seizure Disorder on Depakene ⇒ Resolved.
PROBLEM: Obesity ⇒ Resolved.

In other words, Lia's brain damage had cured her epilepsy, and, over time, as she grew taller—or rather, longer, since she never stood again—her obligatory soft-food diet cured her obesity. "She was real healthy," said Peggy, with jaunty sarcasm. "She was the healthiest she'd ever been. She was just perfect. A perfect vegetable."

Suddenly, Lia was, as Bill Selvidge once told me dryly, "just the sort of patient nurses like." She had metamorphosed from a hyperactive child with a frightening seizure disorder and inaccessible veins into an inert, uncomplaining body who would probably never need another IV. Simultaneously, in the eyes of the family practice staff, her parents were miraculously transformed from child abusers to model caregivers. Teresa Callahan, a resident who had seen Lia during both phases, told me, "Her mom and dad must have taken wonderful care of her because she grew so much. Most kids that are that severely gorked sort of shrivel up and turn into a bag of bones. I've seen seventeen-year-olds who were the size of four-year-olds." Neil said, "Whenever they brought her into the clinic in that baby carrier, Lia was always well-groomed, well-dressed, and immaculate. Just *immaculate*. It was very impressive." Peggy added, "They did a better job than most white families. Most white families would institutionalize her in a second."

Foua and Nao Kao could never figure out why the clinic staff treated them so much better than the hospital staff ever had. From their point of view, their daughter had changed utterly, but their behavior as parents had not changed in the slightest. The only explanation Nao Kao could come up with was, "Lia doesn't go to the bathroom very often, so she is clean and that is why they like her." (When I heard him ascribe Lia's newfound popularity to her constipation, I was reminded of the comment he had once made when I told him I would like to visit Laos some day. Having taken due note of America's obsession with technology and hygiene, he said, "You wouldn't like it. There are no cars. But you would think Chiang Mai in Thailand is very nice." When I asked why, he said, "Because it has a lot of garbage collectors.")

Now that anticonvulsants were no longer prescribed and compliance was no longer an issue, Merced's doctors, nurses, CPS workers, public health workers, and juvenile court officers—the clamorous army of authority figures who had been telling the Lees for four years that they were not taking good care of their daughter—suddenly fell silent. On March 5, 1987, the Lees' probationary status as Lia's guardians, which had been in effect since their daughter was released from foster care, was lifted. "In the Matter of LIA LEE, a Dependent Child of the Juvenile Court," the Superior Court of the State of California for the County of Merced declared:

> WHEREAS, it now appears to the satisfaction of the Court that it is for the best interests of the above named minor that Juvenile Court Jurisdiction be terminated,
> IT IS HEREBY ORDERED that the order heretofore made . . . by this Court, adjudging LIA LEE to be a Dependent Child of the Juvenile Court be, and the same is hereby vacated and set aside, and the said person is hereby released from the operation thereof.

Foua and Nao Kao never trusted this document, which of course they could not read and which in any case would be almost impossible to render in Hmong. They continued to fear that their daughter might once again be made government property. For several years, Foua, who never let herself forget that she had been visiting relatives on the day Lia had been removed to foster care, stayed with her twenty-four hours a day to make sure she was not snatched by the "police." "If we allow," said Nao Kao, "they probably would take her away again, but we just love Lia too much and we don't want anybody to take her. My wife watches Lia every day, so they cannot take her. My wife would not let them."

The anthropologist George M. Scott, Jr., has written that in Laos,

> Children were generally deeply adored. . . . Even those with physical or mental deformities were showered with affection, indeed with even greater affection than normal children, which resulted in part from the belief that, as with miscarriages and stillbirths, the deformity was the consequence of past transgressions on the part of the parents and thus must be borne with equanimity and treated with kindness as means of expiation.

Foua and Nao Kao were fairly sure, but not certain, that transgressions on the part of American doctors, not on their own part, were responsible for Lia's condition. But no expiatory motivation was needed. They showered Lia with affection because they could not imagine doing otherwise. They had always thought of her as an anointed one, a princess. Now, constantly attended by her parents and siblings, she had assumed a position in the family that was, if anything, even more regal. She was a central stillness around which the life of the family condensed. If she sat in her wheelchair, someone was always at her elbow; if she was strapped into a *nyias*, her bearer, whether it was her mother, her father, or one of her older sisters, did a constant little swaying dance to soothe her. More photographs of her hung on the walls than of any of her eight siblings. For years, the schedule Jeanine had once written for her—"Wake-up," "Meds," "Leave for School," "Playtime"—continued to hang there too, even though she no longer took medicines, went to school, or played. Whether she still woke up in the morning was a question of semantics.

Lia was the only Lee child who had birthday parties. Every July 19, the sidewalk outside the East 12th Street apartment overflowed with relatives and Hmong children. Jeanine Hilt brought Frisbees, beach balls, and water pistols. Foua served Hmong eggrolls stuffed with minced pork and onion; steamed bananas with rice; chickens that had been sacrificed that morning, and their skulls and tongues examined for divinatory signs, before they were stewed; and Doritos. There was always an American birthday cake. Jeanine lit the candles and cut the first piece. The guest of honor, of course, could not blow out her candles or eat her cake. She sat in her wheelchair, immobile and impassive, while the children, who had learned a standard repertoire of American songs in school, sang "Happy Birthday."

Lia was still a beautiful child. She was nothing like the patients in vegetative states whom I had seen in hospitals, pasty-skinned carcasses with slack mouths, hair like straw, bodies that smelled of urine even after they were bathed. Lia's black hair was still shiny, her skin was soft and fine, her lips were still pink and shaped like a Cupid's bow. She smelled delicious. It therefore never seemed strange to me that her family treated her as one would an especially winsome baby: a diapered, bottle-fed, fussing baby who just happened to be three feet tall. Foua cuddled her, stroked her, rocked her, bounced her, sang to her, nuzzled her neck, inhaled her hair, played with her fingers, and made raspberry sounds against her belly. There were also times when Lia seemed more like a pet—a golden retriever, perhaps, with strokable fur and a tractable disposition. Her younger sister Pang liked to give her bear hugs, tug her ears, and then, joined by Mai and True, lie on top of her in a heap: three squirming, giggling children and one silent one.

In Laos, Foua had bathed her children on the dirt floor, using a small bowl to pour the stream water that she had warmed on the fire. Now she bathed Lia in the porcelain tub every day—on hot days, twice. "I usually get in with her," she said, "because by the time I'm done I'm all wet anyway." After the bath, she bent and extended Lia's arms and legs, as a child would flex the limbs of a Barbié doll, in a series of range-of-motion exercises, taught her by the health department, that were intended to forestall permanent contractures. She fed Lia by spoon or from a six-ounce bottle with a broad, flat, easy-to-suck nipple designed for babies with cleft palates. A resident's note from the MCMC clinic stated that "parents feed her formula + rice cereal." In fact, Lia also ate pork and chicken that her mother had ground to a fine consistency with the hand-carved mortar and pestle she had brought from Laos. Sometimes Foua simply pre-chewed the chicken, like a mother bird, and stuffed it into Lia's mouth. Every day Foua boiled quantities of a spinachlike vegetable called *zaub*, which she grew specially for Lia in the parking lot, and fed her the broth. Lia usually straddled Foua's lap, her long legs sticking out on either side, while Foua, after putting her lips to the food to make sure it wasn't too hot, coaxed tiny bites into her mouth. She always wiped Lia's drool with her hand rather than with a napkin or a towel. "It takes a long time to eat," she told me once, as she fed Lia rice. "You have to open Lia's mouth to look inside, because if there is already rice in there and you put some more in, she might vomit it back out. You have to hold your hand in back of her neck all the time or she can't swallow." Then she laughed and kissed Lia's ricey mouth.

Sometimes I thought: this is not so terrible. Lia lived at home, not in a chronic care facility. She was a love object, not a pariah. The Hmong community accepted her without reservation. Her mother was not suicidal, as she had been after Lia was placed in foster care. It was true that Foua and Nao Kao sometimes slighted her siblings, especially

Pang, who had never been allowed to assume her rightful place as the youngest and most coddled member of the family. When Pang was barely out of toddlerhood, she zoomed in and out of the apartment unsupervised, playing with plastic bags and, on occasion, with a large butcher knife. Still, none of the Lees, even the teenagers, ever seemed embarrassed by Lia, as most of the American children I knew might be. Because Lia's continual epileptic crises were over, May, as the eldest daughter living at home, had been largely relieved of the pressures of serving as her parents' medical interpreter. "I had to go with my parent to the hospital to translate," she wrote in her eighth-grade autobiography, speaking of the year after Lia's return from foster care. "I never had my way out cause most of my cousin who my parent needed the most are always busy doing this and that. I was like their translater everywhere they go." Carrying her sister in a *nyias*, feeding her formula, and doing the family's shopping at the Save Mart on J Street were far lighter responsibilities.

But whenever I began to be lulled by this relatively rosy picture, I was drawn up short by an explosion of rage from Nao Kao ("My child is lost because of those doctors!") or, more frequently, by a sudden seepage of grief from Foua. One minute Foua would be laughing, and the next she would be in tears. She would go for weeks without a word of complaint, and then exclaim, "Lia is so heavy! She is so hard to carry! Other people see nice places but I never can." She went for two years without sewing any *paj ntaub* except Lia's giant *nyias*. "Lia is too sick," she said, "and I am too sad. I am so busy with Lia that I don't know anything except being alive." Once I saw her rocking back and forth on her haunches, keening. When I asked her what was the matter, she just said, "I love Lia too much."

A half-finished bottle of Depakene syrup, which was no longer prescribed for Lia and which Neil and Peggy assumed had been thrown out long ago, continued to sit on a kitchen shelf for years. It was not there to be used; it was there because the American doctors had once considered it priceless, and discarding it would have been like tossing out a pile of foreign coins that were no longer negotiable but had not altogether shed their aura of value. Foua and Nao Kao treated Lia with what they called "Hmong medicines." "We can't give her any kind of medicine from the hospital," Nao Kao explained, "because if we do, she gets really tense and her body twists into some kind of tight knot." They fed her teas made from powdered roots, imported from Thailand, which they bought at a Hmong-owned market, and from herbs they grew for her in the parking lot. A stainless-steel mixing bowl, filled with sacred water and covered with two pieces of fringed paper, hung by a length of twine from the ceiling of their bedroom. A *txiv neeb* had placed it there as a lure for Lia's errant soul. About twice a year, or more often if they could afford it, a *txiv neeb* came to their apartment to perform a pig sacrifice. For several weeks afterwards, Lia wore soul-binding strings around her wrists.

Because the detested anticonvulsants were no longer prescribed, and because Foua's feelings for Lia's doctors had become almost fond since the day she and Neil had hugged, they continued to carry Lia about once a year to the MCMC clinic, though not to the hospital next door. Lia's problems—constipation, conjunctivitis, pharyngitis—could now be dealt with on an outpatient basis. When Lia missed an appointment, the clinic's computer, fixed in its imperturbable bureaucratic groove, sent her this reminder:

Dear Lia Lee:

On 2–29–88 you had an appointment with Dr. Philp which you did not keep. Your physician feels that you should be seen. Please call the Merced Family Practice Center at 385-7060 so that we can schedule another appointment for you.

Lia never called.

The Lees' most frequent encounters with Merced's medical establishment were now the checkups—first weekly, then monthly, then two or three times a year—performed by a public health nurse who, like a *txiv neeb*, made house calls. The nurse was named Martin Kilgore. Martin was a large, kind, eccentric man who was undoubtedly the only employee of the Merced County Health Department with an all-over tan from vacationing at a nudist camp. His politics were liberal, his I.Q. (as he once confided with a self-deprecating grin) was 150, and his conversation was peppered with references to classical literature. He referred to Lia's *daimon* and her *Moira* as often as to her hypoxic ischemic encephalopathy. Once he compared the relationship between the Lees and their medical providers to the myth of Sisyphus, the Corinthian king who attempted to cheat Death by placing him in fetters. I mentioned Martin's analogy to Neil. He had never heard of Sisyphus, but when I described how the old reprobate had been condemned to roll a boulder up a hill over and over again, only to have it roll back down just before he reached the summit, Neil said, "That's perfect!" (Later it occurred to me that although Neil instinctively identified with Sisyphus, the Lees would undoubtedly have maintained that *they* were the ones who had done the boulder-pushing.)

Martin had first met Lia and her family in the spring of 1985, before she was placed in foster care. He had been sent to the Lee home to determine whether her parents were giving her the proper amounts of Tegretol and phenobarbital. (They weren't.) Not knowing what he was in for, he wrote a note to MCMC that concluded: "Thank you for this interesting referral." The sheaf of impeccably typed, formally phrased letters that he had since dispatched to Neil and Peggy documented, year by year, his own gallant efforts to roll the boulder up the hill, and the boulder's repeated descents. His main concern was now Lia's constipation, part of a generalized gastrointestinal slowdown caused by her neurological impairment. In February of 1988, when Lia's vegetative state had lasted for about a year, he informed Peggy that "Lia continues to have impacted stools on a weekly basis." His next sentence was a model of reportorial tact: "The mother states she is using Metamucil assiduously but their bottle is full and covered with dust."

Martin once invited me to accompany him on one of his home visits. I was curious to see how he and the Lees dealt with each other, since, unlike most of Merced's medical community, Martin was a vocal Hmong partisan. He had a clearer grasp of the Hmong role in the war in Laos than anyone else I met in Merced, and had written dozens of letters to local newspapers castigating the readers for their intolerance. (One reader had been so angry he had threatened to blow Martin away with a shotgun, causing Martin, for reasons more alphabetical than literary, to change his listing in the Merced telephone directory to Joyce Kilmer.) Martin didn't dislike the Lees, or at least preferred them to some of his Caucasian clients, whose parenting skills he described as inferior to those of chimpanzees. He had so strongly disagreed with Neil's decision to place Lia with a foster family that, jettisoning all professional objectivity, he had once told Nao Kao, "Mr. Lee, in America we get lawyers when people do things like that." I figured that if anyone could communicate with the Lees, it would be Martin.

When Martin and his interpreter Koua Her arrived at the Lees' apartment, Foua was kneeling on the floor, feeding Lia a bottle of water, and Nao Kao was sitting next to her with Pang on his lap.

"HELLO MR. LEE!" Martin boomed. Nao Kao focused on the wall-to-wall carpet and said nothing.

Martin lowered himself to the floor. "Now, Mr. Lee," he said, "what is your daughter eating? Is it mostly liquid?" I realized, with surprise, that the Lees had never told him about the chicken and pork Foua mashed with her mortar and pestle. Koua Her, a small, conscientious, self-effacing man, translated Martin's question in a scarcely audible voice, as he translated—or attempted to translate—all of Martin's subsequent questions from English to Hmong, and the Lees' answers from Hmong to English.

Foua mumbled something. "She says it is very soft food," said Koua.

"Well," said Martin, "empirically Lia is not gaining or losing weight. I can tell that whatever they are doing nutritionally is definitely all right."

Without explaining what he was doing, he started to tickle Lia's feet. He noted her Babinski reflex, an extension of the big toe that signifies damage to the central nervous system. He then put his stethoscope against her abdomen. Lia started to howl like a wolf. Foua put her face next to Lia's and crooned, "Tch, tch, tch."

"I am listening for bowel sounds," said Martin. "I hardly hear any bowel sounds so now I am going to listen to her chest. Her lungs are good. Now, the last time I was here, I talked about why it would be nice if we could take her temperature every day, just so we could find out if there is a problem coming up. Do they remember that?"

Koua said, "She said, yes, they do that, every day."

Martin looked pleased. "And what is her usual temperature?"

"She says 30 or 40."

That stopped Martin momentarily, but he pressed on. "Ah. Well. Let's move to the pulse, then." He burrowed his finger between the soul-binding strings on Lia's wrist. "Now I'm counting her pulse. She has a pulse of 100. It is good if the mama can take her pulse every day."

"She says they don't know how to tell the pulse," said Koua.

"Well, you just put your finger here, and take your watch, and count for a minute." Foua didn't own a watch, nor did she know what a minute was.

At this point, Pang, who was three at the time, ran over to Lia and started banging her on the chest.

"Don't do that, there's a good boy," said Martin, addressing the little girl in English, of which she did not speak a word. "Koua, please tell them they have got to watch these other little children. Lia is not a doll." He coughed. "Now, let us proceed to elimination. Does Lia have a bowel movement by herself or do they have to give her a pill first?" He was referring to the Dulcolax tablets that the Lees sometimes used. Like fast-acting antibiotics, laxatives were acceptable to many Hmong because they worked quickly, unambiguously, and without apparent side effects.

"She says they use the pill for it to come out."

"Well, it is really better not to use those pills on a regular basis. It would be better to give her fiber, in the form of Metamucil, because if you keep using the medicine, then Lia will lose the ability to move her bowels by herself and she will always have to have the medicine, and that is a bad thing." When Koua translated this, Foua and Nao Kao stared at him. For four years, they had been told to give Lia medicine that they didn't want to give her. Now they were being told *not* to give her medicine that they *did* want to give her.

"I want to tell them the story of my grandfather," continued Martin. "For the last twenty years of his life, he had to eat Epsom salts because he started using those laxatives and he couldn't stop. Do they know what Epsom salts are? Terrible-looking stuff. Magnesium sulfate." Koua looked baffled; I'm not sure how he translated "magnesium sulfate." "So if I could send my spirit back in time to talk to my grandfather, I would say, Grandfather, don't start down that road! Take Metamucil! But don't put it in her formula, okay? Formula is milk, and milk constipates people. You might as well feed her glue. They could try putting the Metamucil in a bottle of prune juice, okay?

Prune juice would unplug anything. That would be a real depth bomb. Do they know what prune juice is?"

They obviously didn't, and neither did Koua. When he reached that point in his translation, he simply inserted the English words "prune juice" into the middle of a long Hmong sentence. I preferred not even to imagine how he translated "depth bomb."

"It is made out of plums," explained Martin. "You take a plum and you dry it. Then you make juice out of it. I am going to write it down for them so they can look for it in the store." And on a piece of yellow paper, in huge capital letters, he wrote:

PRUNE JUICE

Nao Kao took the piece of paper and looked at it blankly. Even if he had been able to read the words, he had no idea what a prune was.

"Now, Koua," said Martin, "before we leave, I was just curious. I was noticing Lia has some bands on her wrists, and I was recently reading in a book about Hmong people and the Hmong religion, and I wondered how did they explain what happened to Lia in terms of their religion?"

The Lees' faces closed as abruptly as a slammed door.

"He said they don't know anything about that," said Koua.

I thought: But they just spent an hour the other night talking about how *dabs* steal souls! They would have gone on for another hour if May Ying hadn't had to get home. What had come over them today? It seemed as if my open, animated, garrulous friends, faced with someone they viewed as an authority figure—even though he would probably have quit his job before he ever treated them coercively—had entered a vegetative state themselves. They hadn't said twenty words since Martin arrived. They hadn't laughed, smiled, or looked him in the eye. And then I thought: *these* must be the people Neil and Peggy have been dealing with all these years. *No wonder* everyone but Jeanine thinks they are impenetrable and stupid. Of course, Martin had undergone an equally unseemly metamorphosis himself, from savant to bumbler. It was as if, by a process of reverse alchemy, each party in this doomed relationship had managed to convert the other's gold into dross.

"Well," said Martin, rising with difficulty from the floor, "it looks as if that is the best we can do today. They have my card"—which of course might as well have been written in cuneiform—"and they should remember I am here to help them. If you folks can get the prune juice, I would advise it. Goodbye, Mr. Lee. Goodbye, Mrs. Lee."

As we walked to Martin's car, with Koua trailing silently ten paces behind, Martin frowned. He knew that the visit had gone badly, but he couldn't put his finger on why. Had he not been courteous? Had he not shown his respect for the Hmong culture by expressing an interest in the Lees' spiritual beliefs? Had he not refrained from criticizing them, even when he felt they were wrong?

"I gave them my full shot," he said. "You saw how patiently I explained things to them." He sighed, long and slow. "I do the best I can. On some days I think of Lia as a character in a Greek tragedy. By Euripides, perhaps. On other days—well, I just think about Metamucil."

16

Why Did They Pick Merced?

My first day in Merced, several months before I met the Lees, I drove around and around in my rented car, looking for Hmong, and didn't see a single one. My friend Bill Selvidge had told me one out of every six Merced residents was Hmong, and it was on the strength of that prodigious statistic that I had come. I thought he must have made a mistake. The people who strolled their babies along the sycamore-lined avenues north of Bear Creek and gunned their pickups down the quaintly superannuated main street— I didn't know yet that most of the fancy business had shifted to the Merced Mall uptown—all looked as homegrown as characters from *American Graffiti*, which was set in Modesto, the next big town up Highway 99. When I stopped in the R Street Exxon for gas, I asked Frank, the man who Windexed my windshield, whether he knew where the Hmong lived.

"That part of town across the tracks is just crawling with them," Frank said. "It's so crowded with Hmongs you can't hardly move. I sure know we got a lot of them. What I don't know is why they're here. I mean, why did they pick Merced?" He then volunteered an anecdote about some Hmong who had been caught fishing in a county lake without licenses. "When the police came, they got down on their knees. They thought they were going to be executed!" He threw back his head and laughed.

Martin Kilgore told me later that Dumb Hmong stories were a lamentable staple of Merced's agricultural community, some of whose members had hundred-year-old roots in the Central Valley. "In Fresno, the Aggies make ethnic jokes about the Armenians," he said. "In Stanislaus, it's the Portuguese. Here, it's the Hmong." There was the Hmong mother who heard a policeman say, "If your child misbehaves, you can always chain him to the TV," and took it literally. There were the Hmong farmers who fertilized their crops with human excrement. There were the Hmong tenants who punched holes in their walls to communicate with their relatives next door. There was the large Hmong family who lived in a one-bedroom, second-floor apartment. The American couple who lived below them complained that their roof was leaking. When the landlord checked, he found the Hmong had all moved into the bedroom, covered the floor of the living room with a foot of dirt, planted vegetables, and watered them.

Who knew whether these stories were true? In the climate that had fostered Frank's genial bigotry, did it matter? As a Hmong proverb puts it, "All kinds of vessels can be plugged, but you can't plug people's mouths." Over the last century and a half, the Central Valley had involuntarily swallowed wave after wave of foreign-born settlers: Mexicans, Chinese, Chileans, Irish, Dutch, Basques, Armenians, Portuguese, Swedes, Italians, Greeks, Japanese, Filipinos, Yemenites, East Indians. Each had occasioned its own individually tailored flurry of xenophobia, of which the Dumb Hmong stories were merely the most recent model. In the 1880s, the Anti-Chinese Association of Merced had served a similar defensive purpose, provoked by the Cantonese who had come to pan gold along the Merced River and lay tracks for the Central Pacific Railroad, and stayed to work in the brick factory near Bear Creek and run fan-tan parlors along 14th Street. So had the Merced County Anti-Japanese Association, which had tried to expel Japanese farmers in the 1920s. So had Merced's 200-to-1 vote, just before the end of World War II, against permitting Japanese-Americans interned in relocation camps to return to their old homes.

I followed Frank's directions and crossed the tracks of the Southern Pacific Railroad, a freight line that parallels 16th Street in south

Merced, which used to be Chinatown before it was razed in 1950 to make room for Highway 99. He was right. On the wrong side of the tracks, everyone was Hmong: the first Hmong I had ever seen. In front of the dingy two-story apartment buildings, coveys of children were chasing each other, kicking balls—they had learned soccer at Ban Vinai—and playing *txwv*, a form of jacks in which pebbles are tossed and caught. The parking lots harbored more potted herbs than cars, and there were two community gardens, as dense and green as vest-pocket rain forests, striped with rows of bok choy, bitter melon, and lemongrass. In a local grocery, Soua Her and his wife, Yia Moua, sold fifty-pound bags of rice, quail eggs, shredded squid, audiocassettes by local Hmong bands, sequins for decorating *paj ntaub*, mentholated tape for treating headaches, sticky ointments for treating bruises, camphor balm for drawing out fevers, and aromatic wood chips for making a tea that, as Yia Moua explained to me, "flush out the bad dead blood after lady have baby."

I had no idea at the time, but I had landed in the most intensely Hmong place in the United States. Fresno and Minneapolis-St. Paul have larger Hmong populations, but Merced's Hmong constitute a far greater fraction of the local population. When I first visited Merced, the fraction (just as Bill Selvidge had promised) was one sixth; now it is one fifth. That critical mass, as Blia Yao Moua put it, "lets us keep more Hmong culture here than in Vientiane." Sometimes I felt that the other cities of the Central Valley—Fresno, Visalia, Porterville, Modesto, Stockton, Sacramento, Marysville, Yuba City—were mere suburbs of Merced. Hmong families constantly drove from city to city to visit relatives, and if they moved elsewhere in the valley, they returned to Merced for subclan gatherings, just as residents of satellite settlements in Laos had returned to their home villages. With fourteen Hmong clans—Cheng, Fang, Hang, Her, Kong, Kue, Lee, Lor, Moua, Thao, Vang, Vue, Xiong, and Yang—represented in Merced, young people had no problem finding exogamous marriage partners. It was easy, even on short notice, to find a *txiv neeb* to negotiate with a pathogenic *dab*, an herbalist to concoct a healing tisane, a clan elder to mediate a dispute, or a *qeej* player to guide a dead person's soul back through the twelve heavens with his hauntingly resonant cluster of six steamed bamboo tubes. (In Merced, where bamboo is hard to come by, *qeejs* are sometimes made of PVC plumbing pipe. It is said that if the *qeej* player is good, the soul will have no trouble following directions from the plastic.*)

The anthropologist Eric Crystal once told a reporter for the *Merced Sun-Star* how extraordinary it was to hear the Hmong language spoken in the Kmart on J Street, when fifteen years earlier it had been impossible to hear it anywhere in the Western world. Crystal is a former free-speech activist who overflows with so many ideas and enthusiasms that he effervesces rather than converses. He has studied Merced's Hmong community, and he once curated a local exhibit of Hmong folk objects: bamboo vegetable baskets, opium harvesting knives, shamanic regalia. When I went to see Crystal in his office at U.C. Berkeley and told him I was living in Merced, he became so excited he started bouncing up and down in his chair. "You're so lucky!" he exclaimed. "If I lived down in that place, I'd be running around with the Hmong every minute! I mean, I just *love* Merced. Not that the Hmong aren't a hassle. They are a *huge* hassle. When I first went down there they were kind of hostile. You know, what the hell do you want? Who the hell do you think you are? Fuck off! The Mien

---

* The idea that a *qeej*, whether bamboo or plastic, can "speak" to its audience—for example, by giving travel directions to a dead soul—is not a metaphor. Four of its six pipes represent the tones of the Hmong language, and Hmong who have learned to understand the *qeej* can decode actual words "sung" by the resonating pipes. Just as they do not make the conventional Western distinctions between body and mind or between medicine and religion, the Hmong do not distinguish, as we do, between language and music: their language is musical, and their music is linguistic. All Hmong poetry is sung. Several other musical instruments, called "talking reeds," similarly blur the boundary between words and melody. A *nplooj*, or leaf—usually a small piece of a banana leaf—can be curled and placed in the mouth so that it vibrates when blown, its varying pitch representing the tones of words. The most poetic of all Hmong instruments is the *ncas*, a brass Jew's harp that is placed between the lips and twanged with a finger. It is traditionally reserved for lovers. In Laos, a boy would play his *ncas*, which was no louder than a whisper and could not be overheard by eavesdropping parents, just outside the wall of his lover's house. He might begin to court her by speaking softly, but as soon as he reached the most intimate part of his entreaty, he would, out of a combination of shyness and sentiment, switch to his *ncas*. If the girl loved him, she would answer with her own *ncas*; if she did not respond, the sting of the rejection was lessened by the boy's knowledge that it was not he but his instrument who had wooed her. There are many *qeej* players in Merced today, but the use of the *ncas* as a courting instrument is dying out.

are so delighted when anybody pays attention to them that they practically ask you to move in with them about two minutes after you sit down. The Cambodians are really happy if you show that you are interested in Cambodia. But the Hmong—they just test you every minute. Once you pass the test, though, they are fantastic. The Hmong are one of the best organized, most focused groups you could find any place on earth. They have the best leadership, they're the most able to cooperate among themselves, they're the most committed to preserving their ethnic identity, they're the most conscious of their own place in the world. You can see all that down in Merced. Those Hmong are really into being Hmong."

The longer I spent in Merced, the more often I found myself asking: How in heaven's name could this have happened *here*? How could more than 10,000 villagers from the mountains of Laos possibly be living in a place that hosted the Yosemite Dental Society Smile Contest and the Romp 'n Stompers Square Dance; that sent out Welcome Newcomer kits (which no Hmong had ever requested) containing fliers for the Sweet Adeline Singers and the Senior Citizens Whittling Workshop; and that awarded ribbons at its annual county fair for Best Infant Booties, Best Lemon Pie, and Best Udder?

In other words, as Frank had asked, "Why did they pick Merced?" The answer to that question, as I gradually found out, boiled down to two words: Dang Moua. It is probably a good thing that Frank does not know Dang, the indefatigable grocer, interpreter, and pig farmer who had once been a clerk-typist at the American Embassy in Vientiane. If Frank were to learn that from the Hmong point of view Dang bears the same relation to Merced that Daniel Boone bore to Kentucky or the Pied Piper bore to Koppelberg Hill, he might not be properly grateful. On the other hand, Dang might impress him by his almost unbelievably sedulous pursuit of the American dream. The first time I walked into Dang's office at California Custom Social Services, the interpreting and liaison agency he had founded, he was on the phone. He was talking rapidly in Hmong, but every once in a while, when he collided with a concept for which there was no Hmong equivalent, he threw in an English term: "lack of communication," "deposition," "application," "bank manager," "conflict of interest." Dang was round-faced and sturdy, with a CEO's air of authoritative self-possession. He wore a large Casio watch that beeped and a large gold ring that said "D." His business card was red, white, and blue. Commercial patriotism evidently ran in the family. His cousin, Moua Kee, whose office adjoined Dang's, supported his family largely by teaching Hmong about Christopher Columbus, Betsy Ross, and the advantages of the bicameral system in preparation for their naturalization examinations. Although he raised sacrificial pigs, Dang was selective in his spiritual dogmas, and for reasons of expedience he had excluded *dabs*. "I call myself a multi-religious believer," he explained. "I don't believe in ghost because I like to be the boss of the ghost, and if you are afraid of ghost, the ghost is *your* boss." It was clear that no one would ever be Dang's boss but Dang.

Dang Moua and his family used to live in Richmond, Virginia, where they were the only Hmong. The first time they saw snow there, soon after they arrived from Thailand in early 1976, Dang thought someone had come while they were asleep and sprayed all the trees with salt. He worked eighteen hours a day, 9:00 a.m. to 6:00 p.m. and 9:00 p.m. to 6:00 a.m., folding newspapers, a job that took little advantage of his five languages and made him so "deep sleepy," as he put it, that he feared if he kept it up, "I notice I must be dead in three years." He earned $2.90 an hour. In his spare time—I have always wondered when that was—he went to the Richmond library and read about prevailing climates, soil conditions, and crop yields in other states. His brother, who lived in southern California, mentioned that the Central Valley had good weather and many different ethnic groups. Dang had heard through the Hmong grapevine that General Vang Pao was planning to buy a large fruit ranch near Merced, and that also influenced his decision. "So I go buy a white 1970 stick-shift Hornet for $550," he recalled. "I tell my sponsor from the American church, Tomorrow I will leave to California. He was very surprise! He say, You know, it's a robbery, it's an earthquake out there, but I say my mind is made. So then he say, You return that car and we will give you a V-6 Cherokee. I say, I thank you for that but if I take your car I owe you something. They were so mad! Next morning, I burn some joss stick and pray for my ancestor to lead me for a safe trip. My sponsor say, You don't need to do that, you should pray to the Lord! I say, Your Lord let me have too many problem here in America. So I put a pan of water outside with some rice to pray to the god of the mountains, and my tears come. I never cry in my life, not even going to Thailand, and that was hell, but now I cry. I say, I'm small but I am an adult person. I have to pursue now my plan."

With the back end of his Hornet nearly scraping the ground beneath the trunkful of clothing, pots, pans, dishes, and a television set, and the front end sticking up so high he could barely see over the hood, Dang drove his family west for two days and two nights on Interstate 40, following the sun. He arrived in Merced with $34. It was mid-April 1977. The skies were so clear that he could see the Coast Range to the west and the Sierras to the east. The air was sweet with almond blossoms. In mid-summer Merced is an oven, and in the winter, a chilling fog blows off the reservoir whose resident *dab*, according to Foua, once caught her and followed her home. But in the spring—as Steinbeck's Joads were told as they approached the great green expanse, after making a journey much like the Mouas'—the Central Valley is "the purtiest goddamn country you ever seen." There were miles and miles of ripe peaches and figs, which Dang got a job picking, and jackrabbits and squirrels he could easily trap for dinner. The town itself was clean and quiet, with an orderly grid of streets laid out by the Central Pacific Railroad in 1872. There were no beggars or derelicts. Flat as a bowling green and 167 feet above sea level, Merced was in some ways an outlandish address for a montagnard, but it was better than Richmond, and it was incalculably better than the slums of Hartford and Detroit, where some of Dang's clanspeople lived. Most people drive through Merced en route from one place to another—Sacramento to Bakersfield, San Francisco to Yosemite—but to Dang, worn beyond weariness by the journey from Laos to Thailand to Virginia to California, it was the long-desired terminus. Vang Pao's plan to buy the fruit ranch failed, partly because the County Board of Supervisors had public misgivings about the refugees it might attract and partly because the general had an inauspicious dream the night before he was to sign the contract. Nonetheless, the favorable buzz about Merced and the rest of the Central Valley had already spread to discontented Hmong communities across the United States. A trickle, and then a flood, of dilapidated cars began to stream in from the east.

"It was just wild!" recalled Eric Crystal. "You'd see these Arkansas plates and stuff on the streets, I mean they were just pouring in from all over the place! Merced is incredible now, but it was *particularly* incredible then." It is doubtless easier to wax enthusiastic about the Hmong of Merced if you are a visiting anthropologist than if you are a resident taxpayer. "S'pose a fella got work an' saved, couldn' he get a little land?" Tom Joad had asked, and he was told, "You ain't gonna get no steady work." So it was with the Hmong, who couldn't get the high-end agricultural jobs because they had no English and no experience and couldn't get the low-end ones because Mexican migrants had already filled them. At first the *Merced Sun-Star* treated the newcomers like exotic guests, though it was chary of printing the word "Hmong," which could be found in no atlas or dictionary. (Local reporters called the Hmong "Laotians"; Dang Moua's five languages were "a local dialect, Laotian, Thai, French, and English.") Soon, however, the Hmong—for whom the code word became "refugees" —started to make headlines: "Refugees Drain Limited Services"; "Refugee Students Jam the Schools"; "Supervisors Ired by Meager State Funds Allocated for Area Refugees"; "More $$$ Needed for Refugees."

More $$$ were needed because of an economic catastrophe that began in Merced in the early eighties and continues today. Merced was never rich. During the last three decades it has ranked between number 35 and number 53, of California's fifty-eight counties, in per capita income. It was limping along comfortably enough, however, until the Hmong came—an event that happened to coincide with a nationwide recession as well as deepening cutbacks in both federal and state social programs. Seventy-nine percent of the Hmong in Merced County—as compared with eighteen percent of the county's other residents—receive public assistance. By 1995, Merced had achieved the unwanted distinction of having a greater fraction of its population on welfare than any other county in the state. The federal government picks up half the welfare costs, the state picks up 47½ percent, and the county picks up 2½ percent. That 2½ percent sounds like a pittance, but in recent years, it has amounted to nearly two million dollars annually—two and a half times as much as it was in 1980—to which is added nearly a million dollars in administrative costs. While scrambling to meet its other financial obligations, the county has found those millions by closing three libraries; ceasing to maintain twenty-one of its twenty-four parks; leaving five sheriff posts vacant;

increasing the caseloads of all six of its judges; reducing the staff of its probation department; reducing road maintenance; cutting the budgets for arts and culture, recreation, senior citizens' programs, and veterans' services; and transferring all its fire departments to the state department of forestry. The welfare reform bill, if it is not revised, will only make matters worse by forcing the county, which is unlikely to let its residents starve, to make up for at least some of the evaporated federal funds. I asked a county social worker what would happen if neither the bill nor the demographics of Merced's population were to change. "Bankruptcy," she said.

Of course, the Hmong are not solely—or even primarily—responsible for Merced's fiscal crisis. Merced has plenty of white and Hispanic welfare recipients. They occasion less notice and less resentment than the Hmong because, although their numbers are large, their percentages are small: that is, most of the Hmong are on welfare, and most of the members of Merced's other ethnic groups are not. And although welfare has become the most conspicuous focal point for public rage, Merced County has been simultaneously strained by several other even more expensive problems: the accelerating transfer of agricultural work from people to machines; double-digit unemployment—about three times the national level—almost every month since 1980; the 1995 closing of Castle Air Force base, which had provided more than a thousand jobs to local residents; and a 1992 restructuring of California sales and property taxes that returned more to the state and less to the county.

The crucial distinction is that you cannot see a restructured property tax, but when you drive down almost any street on the South Side, you can certainly see the Hmong. In a county where seven out of ten people voted for Proposition 187, California's 1994 referendum to ban public services to illegal immigrants, even legal immigrants are unlikely to be received with open arms. That is not to say that everyone in Merced grumbles about the Hmong. The local churches have always treated them generously. And a small but fervent corps of well-educated professionals, most of them liberal transplants from other cities, concur with Jeff McMahon, a young reporter at the *Sun-Star* who told me, "The one thing that makes Merced different from every other dusty little town in the Central Valley is that there are so many Southeast Asians here. Their culture is a blessing to this community.

How else would Merced ever earn a place in history?" The *Sun-Star* now features a Cultural Diversity Page, and the tourist brochure distributed by the Merced Chamber of Commerce includes, next to pictures of the county courthouse and the local wildlife museum's stuffed polar bear, a photograph of a smiling Hmong woman (albeit dressed in a Lacoste polo shirt) holding a dazzlingly green armful of lettuce and string beans. Especially during the eighties, when the Hmong were novel and exciting, many of Merced's women rallied to their cause. Volunteers in the Befriend-a-Refugee Program took Hmong families to the Applegate Zoo and invited them to backyard barbecues. Dan Murphy's wife, Cindy, taught Hmong women how to use sewing machines and self-cleaning ovens. Jan Harwood, a 4-H Club youth adviser, organized a course (locally referred to as the tidy-bowl class) to train Hmong women for housekeeping jobs. Jan's interpreter, a man named Pa Vue Thao, was so impressed by the enthusiasm with which she demonstrated the use of Lysol, Comet, and Spic and Span that when Jan broke her leg, he reciprocated by gathering moss from the 4-H Camp's trees and teaching her how to make an herbal compress to reduce the swelling.

The warmest welcome I ever saw the Hmong receive was a Naturalization Ceremony, held in the boardroom of the Merced County Administrative Building, in which eighteen Hmong—as well as two lowland Lao, nine Mexicans, five Portuguese, three Filipinos, two Vietnamese, two Indians, a Thai, a Korean, a Chinese, an Austrian, and a Cuban—became American citizens. Each received a copy of the Constitution, a history of the Pledge of Allegiance, a picture of the Statue of Liberty, a congratulatory letter from the President of the United States, a little American flag, and—courtesy of Lodge No. 1240 of the Benevolent and Protective Order of Elks—unlimited free soft drinks. Standing next to a mounted copy of the Merced county song ("We are known for sweet potatoes / And milk and chickens too / Tomatoes and alfalfa / And almonds great to chew"), Judge Michael Hider told the assembled multitude, many of whom could not understand a word but listened respectfully nonetheless, "We've all come together from many places to form one great country—including myself, for my father was a naturalized citizen who came from Lebanon. In America, you don't have to worry about police breaking down your doors. You can practice any religion you want. There's such complete freedom of the press that our newspapers can even attack our leaders. If the government feels they need your land, they cannot just take it away from you. Most importantly, every one of you has the same opportunity as the person sitting next to you. My father never could have dreamed that his son would be a judge. *Your* children can be doctors. I just get carried away when I talk about how wonderful it is to be a citizen of the United States! Congratulations! You're one of us!"

But while I was listening to Judge Hider, I thought of a conversation I had had not long before with Dr. Robert Small, the unfalteringly opinionated MCMC obstetrician, whose views are shared by a large segment of Merced's population. "I and my friends were outraged when the Hmong started coming here," he told me. "*Outraged.* Our government, without any advice or consent, just brought these nonworking people into our society. Why should we get them over anybody else? I've got a young Irish friend who wants to get a U.S. education and wants to work. *He* can't get in. But these Hmong just kind of fly here in groups and settle like locusts. They know no shame, being on the dole. They're happy here." When I mentioned the high rate of depression among Hmong refugees, Dr. Small said, "What do you mean? This is heaven for them! They have a toilet they can poop in. They can drink water from an open faucet. They get regular checks and they never have to work. It's absolute heaven for these people, poor souls."

I had also spoken with the more temperate John Cullen, director of the Merced Human Services Agency, which administers public assistance. "Merced has been a fairly conservative, WASPy community for many years," he said. "The other nationalities that are part of our community came here over a long period of time, but the Hmong came in one big rush. They were a jolt to the system. That inevitably causes more of a reaction. And they do take more than their share of the county's income. You can't deny that the county has been seriously, seriously impacted. I think Merced's reaction to the Hmong is a matter of water swamping the boat, not a matter of racism."

On occasion, however, it *is* a matter of racism. One day Dang Moua was walking out of his grocery store, the Moua Oriental Food Market, when a man he had never seen before drove by and started yelling at him. "He is maybe forty-year-old person," recalled Dang.

"He is driving '84 Datsun. He say to me, Shit man, why you come to this country? Why didn't you die in Vietnam? Well, my father always say to me, if someone act like a beast to you, you must act like a person to him. So I try to smile and be nice. I say, I'm a citizen just like you are. I say, Give me your phone number, you come to my house and eat Hmong food and we talk two or three hour. But he run away. Maybe he is veteran and he convince I am enemy."

Dang's hypothesis is not as farfetched as it sounds. Many people in Merced have confused the Hmong with the Vietnamese—including the former mayor, Marvin Wells, who once informed a Chamber of Commerce luncheon that the "Vietnam refugees" in California were "a problem." It is not uncommon to hear the Hmong called "boat people," although Laos is landlocked, and the only boat most Hmong are likely to have seen was the bamboo raft on which they floated, under fire, across the Mekong River. At least the real boat people, the former South Vietnamese, were United States allies. A more unsettling assumption was revealed by the MCMC maintenance man who, conflating the Hmong with the Vietcong, told Dave Schneider that the hospital was patronized by "too many fucking gooks."

Over and over again, the Hmong here take pains to explain that they fought for the United States, not against it. Dang Moua is a one-man public-relations outfit, constantly hauling out an old *National Geographic* with a picture of his uncle in a military uniform, or popping a videotape about the Armée Clandestine into his VCR. One man from a nearby Central Valley town made sure that even after his death there could be no mistake about his past. His tombstone in the Tollhouse Cemetery northeast of Fresno—where dozens of Hmong, reminded of Laos by the hilly topography, chose to be buried until local residents started complaining about their loud funerals—reads:

BELOVED FATHER AND GRANDFATHER
CHUA CHA CHA
APRIL 20, 1936
FEBRUARY 27, 1989
HE SERVED FOR THE C.I.A. FROM 1961 TO 1975

In 1994, there was a demonstration in Fresno by Hmong welfare recipients, many of whom were former soldiers, protesting a new requirement that they work sixteen hours a week in public service jobs, which they called "slavery." Like older Hmong across the country who still believed in "The Promise"—the CIA's alleged compensation contract—they assumed that aid with no strings attached was no more than their proper due. They expected the Americans to be grateful for their military service; the Americans expected them to be grateful for their money; and each resented the other for not acting beholden.

In the Director's Conference Room at the Merced Human Services Agency, there hangs a huge *paj ntaub* that tells the story of the end of the war in Laos. In a series of embroidered and appliquéd images, Hmong families try to crowd into four American airplanes at Long Tieng, walk to Thailand carrying huge loads on their backs, attempt to swim across a wide river, settle in Ban Vinai, and, finally, load their belongings onto a bus that will take them to an airplane bound for the United States. Across from the *paj ntaub* there is a computer from which the welfare files of thousands of Hmong can be accessed. The Lees, like many Hmong families whose records have been kept here, are intimately familiar with the grief chronicled by the *paj ntaub* but oblivious to the anger induced by the computer files. When I asked Foua and Nao Kao how they felt about being on welfare, Foua said, "I am afraid the welfare will go away. I am afraid to look for a job because I am afraid I could not do it. I am afraid we would not have food to eat." Nao Kao said, "In Laos we had our own animals and our own farm and our own house, and then we had to come to this country, and we are poor and we have to have welfare, and we have no animals and no farm, and that makes me think a lot about our past." Neither of them said a word about what Americans might think of them for not working. For them, that was not the issue. The issue was why the American War had forced them to leave Laos and, via a reluctant trajectory that would have been unimaginable to their parents or their parents' parents, wind up in, of all places, Merced.

Sometimes I felt that the Hmong of Merced were like one of those visual perception puzzles: if you looked at it one way you saw a vase, if you looked at it another way you saw two faces, and whichever pattern you saw, it was almost impossible, at least at first glance, to see the other. From one angle, the welfare statistics looked appalling. From another, it was possible to make out small but measurable signs of progress: that during the past decade, despite the periodic arrival of new JOJs from Thailand, the public assistance rate had declined by five percent; that more than 300 graduates of government-funded job-training programs were now operating sewing machines, making furniture, assembling electronic components, and working in other local industries; that dozens of local Hmong women had started taking English classes following a 1995 change in federal welfare regulations—a warmup to the 1996 bill—that required both parents in intact families to study or work unless there was a child under three or a disabled family member at home. (The requirement to "work" would be more effective if Merced actually had jobs.)

When you looked at the Merced school system, what you saw again depended on your point of view. From one perspective, the Hmong children—who multiplied at a rate that made Dr. Small just shake his head and keep muttering the word "contraception"—were a disaster. In order to relieve overcrowding and to desegregate schools that would otherwise be almost entirely Asian, Merced has had to bus nearly 2,000 of its elementary and middle-school students; build three new elementary schools, a new middle school, and a new high school; teach classes in more than seventy trailers and, while waiting for them to arrive, in cafeterias, on auditorium stages, and in the exhibition hall of the County Fairgrounds; and switch seven schools to a staggered all-year calendar.

On the other hand, Hmong children rarely caused disciplinary problems and regularly crowded the honor rolls.* Four of the Lee

---

* Merced's Hmong students are typical of their counterparts nationwide. According to one Minnesota study, Hmong high school students spent more than twice as much time on homework and had better academic records than non-Hmong students. In San Diego, Hmong students achieved higher grade-point averages than whites, blacks, Hispanics, Cambodians, Filipinos, and lowland Lao—though they were notably less successful than Vietnamese. (The superior performance of the Vietnamese is hardly surprising, given the difference, particularly during the early waves of immigration, between the educational backgrounds of the students' parents. In 1980, adult Vietnamese refugees had completed an average of 12.4 years of education; Hmong surveyed a few years later had completed an average of 1.6.) Although Hmong students do comparatively well in math, they score lower in reading comprehension than other Southeast Asians, including Cambodians and lowland Lao. In some states, they have relatively high secondary-school dropout rates—girls especially, since, even if they are promising students, they

children received their classes' Student-of-the-Month awards. Rick Uebner, who taught May Lee's eighth-grade Language Arts class, once wrote me a letter that described May as "a leader among her peers and a clear-thinking, confident person." He continued:

> Almost exclusively, the Hmong are hard-working, quick-learning students. Their parents are eager to attend conferences, in spite of language barriers. On many occasions students have acted as interpreters for their parents and me. Typically the parents thank me for teaching their child, ask if he or she is working hard enough, wonder if there is any problem with the child showing proper respect and inquire if there is anything that they can do at home to help.

At a conference I attended on college and career planning for Hmong teenagers, Jonas Vangay, standing under a sign that said EDUCATION: THE KEY TO YOUR FUTURE, told his almost preternaturally quiet audience, "In America, even when the child is in the stomach, the mother thinks about books and pencils. *Your* parents grew with knife or hammer or tool. They cannot help you. Let your book be your best friend. For if you cannot learn in school, whose fault is it? Who is to blame?"

No one said a word.

"Answer me!" thundered Jonas.

Finally, in a small voice, a boy said, "Yourself."

"Right!" said Jonas. "Do not be afraid! If you are a chicken boy or chicken girl, and you keep quiet, the examination will come and

---

often conform to the cultural expectation to marry young and start bearing children. Female dropout rates, however, have improved in recent years. In her book *The Other Side of the Asian American Success Story*, Wendy Walker-Moffat points out that the Hmong students' high grades may be misleading, because so many of them are placed in low academic tracks. She posits that the group ethic militates against individualized competition, and that the oral tradition, while it aids in memorization, can lead to problems in standardized test-taking. Walker-Moffat concludes that by being stereotypically lumped with the Asian American "model minority"—a group perceived as having no academic problems—Hmong children have been deprived of such needed services as bilingual classes and bicultural counselors. Wholesale assimilation appears to hinder rather than help. A recent study of Hmong college students found that those who had a strong sense of ethnic identity performed better than those who did not.

you will fail! Those who cannot learn cannot be successful! We want
you to be successful in the year 2000!"

There was silence in the room. Then the students burst, or crept,
into muted applause.

Although many Hmong teenagers in Merced are as wholesome and
deferential as those in Jonas's audience, a few have joined the Men of
Destruction, the Blood Asian Crips, the Oriental Locs, or one of the
other gangs which, in a perverse distortion of the group ethic, started
spreading through the Central Valley in the mid-eighties. Merced has
black and Hispanic gangs as well, but local police officers agree that
the Hmong gangs are the most likely to carry guns and the most likely
to use them.

I occasionally heard mutterings about Hmong gangs, but local residents who disliked the Hmong seemed to be far more obsessed with
smaller, stranger crimes. I was told countless times that the Hmong
kidnapped underage brides. I also heard that they smuggled drugs.
The local police department confirmed that opium had been found
inside ax handles, picture frames, bamboo chairs, teabags, and packages of noodles. There were also many tales about Fish and Game
violations. The *Merced Sun-Star* ran an article about Hmong who
poached bass from the San Luis Reservoir with 1,550-foot setlines,
drove deer into ambushes by banging on pots and pans, and served
stewed pied-bill grebe for dinner. None of these stories was false, but
they were all partial. Left out of the telling were all the extenuating
circumstances: that Hmong marriage customs had a cultural context
unfamiliar to Americans;* that opium smuggling was uncommon, and

---

* According to an article about a Fresno case in the *Loyola of Los Angeles International and Comparative Law Journal*, *zij poj niam*, or marriage by capture, is

> a legitimate form of matrimony practiced by Hmong tribesmen and be-
> gins with the man engaging in ritualized flirtation. The woman responds
> by giving the man a token signifying acceptance of the courtship. The
> man is then required to take the woman to his family's house in order to
> consummate the union. According to Hmong tradition, the woman is
> required to protest: "No, no, no, I'm not ready." If she doesn't make
> overt protestations, such as weeping and moaning, she is regarded as
> insufficiently virtuous and undesirable. The Hmong man is required to
> ignore her mock objections, and firmly lead her into the bedroom and

most of the contraband was intended for medicinal use by the elderly; that in Laos, all the hilltribes had hunted and fished without rules, seasons, or limits; and that once they reached adulthood, the Hmong here, as in other parts of the country, had a low overall crime rate compared with other people below the poverty line.

The most frequent accusation I heard was that the Hmong were terrible drivers. They seemed fine to me, so I went to the Department of Motor Vehicles and asked John McDoniel, the manager, what he thought. He said, "In many respects I am happy to have these people as neighbors, but as far as driving ability goes—well, that's another matter. Violations of pedestrian right-of-way. Going through stop signs. Not realizing their speed. All errors of judgment. Also, when they come to get their licenses, some of them cheat on the written test."

"How do they cheat?" I asked.

"They sew," said Mr. McDoniel.

"They *sew*?"

Mr. McDoniel, who wore trifocals and looked a little like Ed Wynn, opened the top left drawer of his desk. "Well, the ones who don't know English can't read the questions, and they answer at random and take the corrected answer sheets home and share them with their friends. Some of them just memorize the dots on the page. Five different tests, forty-six questions, three answers—let me see, 46 times 15 is 690 dots. They're very good at memorization, but that's an awful lot of dots, so quite a few of them bring in these little cribs."

He reached in the drawer and took out an eyeglass case. In flawless

---

consummate the marriage. If the suitor is not assertive enough to take the initiative, he is regarded as too weak to be her husband.

As Blia Yao Moua put it, "If you ask people of my generation how they got married, ninety percent would be a qualified kidnapper. Including me." However, among the younger generation of Hmong in this country, there have been cases in which the man believed the woman's protestations were pro forma, but the woman was truly objecting. Some of these misunderstandings have led to charges of rape and kidnapping, especially when the woman was underage. Most cases have been resolved by local clan leaders or in juvenile courts. The case cited above reached the Fresno Superior Court, which took the defendant's "cultural defense" into consideration and allowed him to plead to a lesser charge.

cross-stitch—a different color for each of the test's five versions—a *paj ntaub* artist had sewn microscopic X's to indicate whether, for each question, the correct answer was the first, second, or third option.

Next he took out a checked coat. On each lapel, certain squares had been blocked in with thread.

Next he took out a striped pullover with almost invisible white stitches down the front and along each sleeve.

Next he took out a white shirt with minute blue stitches on the cuffs.

"Real neat work, isn't it?" he said admiringly.

I concurred. Then I asked, "What do you do when you catch someone using one of these?"

"He fails the test, and we confiscate the crib."

It occurred to me that an awful lot of Hmong must exit from the Department of Motor Vehicles wearing fewer clothes than when they walked in.

Late that night, I lay on the floor in Bill Selvidge's study, where I was staying. Next to my sleeping bag I had taped photographs of Hmong: Hmong children from the *National Geographic* wearing *paj ntaub*; Hmong teenagers from the *Merced Sun-Star* wearing jeans; the Lee family, wearing slightly off-kilter American clothes, in pictures I had taken myself. I found them all very beautiful, and I often stared at them for hours when I couldn't sleep. That night, for some reason, the phrase "differently abled"—a substitute for "disabled" that had enjoyed a brief vogue among progressive journalists—kept buzzing around my head. I had always disliked the term, which struck me as euphemistic and patronizing. Suddenly, I realized why it was keeping me awake. I had been trying all day to decide whether I thought the Hmong were ethical or unethical, and now I saw it: they were—in this case, it was a supremely accurate phrase—*differently ethical.*

The Hmong, it seemed to me, were abiding, in spades, by E. M. Forster's famous dictum that it is better to betray one's country than one's friend. Since they had never had a nation of their own, and had been persecuted by every nation they had inhabited, they could hardly be expected to harbor an extravagant respect for national jurisprudence. Rules and regulations were particularly breakable if they conflicted with the group ethic—which, after all, is an *ethic*, not just an excuse to flout someone else's ethic. Hmong folktales are heavily populated with characters, clearly meant to be perceived as virtuous, who lie to kings, dragons, *dabs*, and other authority figures in order to protect their families or friends. I had heard innumerable modern versions in which some synecdochical representative of the U.S. government had played the role of righteously deceived *dab*. In the Thai camps, Hmong had claimed their children were older than they really were, so they could receive larger food allotments; claimed their parents were younger than they really were, because it was rumored that the United States considered old people undesirable; and told immigration officials that collateral relatives were members of their immediate families. In the United States, they had claimed their children were younger than they really were, so they could stay in school longer; lied to doctors in order to get disability benefits; claimed they had separated from a spouse in order to increase the family's welfare allowance; and, among the younger generation, let friends copy their schoolwork. Not all the Hmong I knew had done these things. Most had not. But those who had were unashamed. In fact, the ones who had lied to immigration officials had been amazed, when they reached the United States and discussed their experiences with their American sponsors, to find that their behavior was regarded as unethical. What would have seemed unethical—in fact, unpardonable—to them was leaving their relatives behind.

Nao Kao Lee, who couldn't read a word of English, had passed his driving test, in precisely the manner John McDoniel had described, by memorizing where to place the X's on his answer sheet. He had been asked to make a set of prescribed pencil marks; he had done so. In fact, his success on the test—which seemed to him a purely technical challenge, not an assessment of his ability to drive safely—was a triumph of intelligence over bureaucracy. However, it never would have occurred to him to go to so much trouble if he had been able to pass by conventional methods. (Not long after my conversation with John McDoniel, the California Department of Motor Vehicles instituted oral and written tests in Hmong, and the rate of cheating among Hmong applicants declined to a level comparable with that of Merced's other ethnic groups.) Nao Kao viewed his driver's license as a matter of patent necessity: how else was he to visit his relatives? The family came first, then the clan, then the Hmong people, and everything and everybody else ranked so far below those three that it would have been blasphemy to mention them in the same breath. I believe that Nao Kao, like most Hmong, would rather die than deceive a member of his family or clan.

The group ethic enabled Nao Kao not only to pass his driving test but to make unequivocal decisions in every sphere of his life, to assess people's characters with confidence, and to operate almost entirely within the supportive Hmong community rather than within the larger and harsher world of America. On a larger scale, the exigent pull of ethnic solidarity was what made the Hmong so openhanded, so good at teamwork, and so warm. But it seemed to me that, especially for the community's educated leaders, the obligation to put the group before the self also had some negative consequences: stress, loss of privacy, a punishing sense of responsibility. Nao Kao's age and his lack of English insulated him from the conflicts and ambiguities of having one foot in one culture and one in another. His life, if not joyous, was at least *clear*. This was not the case with the Hmong who shared high status in both the Hmong and the American communities.

Dang Moua was an exception. He had so much forward momentum that stresses and doubts simply flowed off him, like water from a torpedo. Also, although Dang spent many hours doing what nearly all literate, English-speaking Hmong of his generation did—deciphering other people's junk mail, filling out their tax forms, telephoning agencies, translating notes from school—he charged for these tasks. Most Hmong did them for free. I heard about one multilingual woman, once a nursing administrator in Xieng Khouang province, who had worked as a Hmong liaison after settling in Minnesota. She became so exhausted by the incessant demands of the Twin Cities' Hmong community, both during and after work hours, that she moved to Merced without telling her clan and got a job that allowed her to deal only with Americans. "Don't call her," I was told. "She's trying to lie low." Family loyalty—the group ethic concentrated to an even more potent form—also had its downside. Pa Vue Thao, the interpreter who had made an herbal compress to heal Jan Harwood's broken leg, told me he had once been offered a lucrative job at U.C. Davis. He had turned it down, with regret but without hesitation, after his father, angry that Pa Vue would even consider leaving his relatives in Merced, asked him, "Does money mean more or does the family mean more?"

In the early seventies, out of the more than 300,000 Hmong in Laos, there were only thirty-four—all men—who were studying at universities overseas. Two of them had resettled in Merced: Blia Yao Moua and Jonas Vangay. Both had won scholarships to the Lycée Nationale, Vientiane's most elite secondary school, and had obtained bachelor's and master's degrees from French universities. Jonas left a job as a computer analyst in a Paris suburb to immigrate to the United States in 1983, just after the largest wave of Hmong refugees, most of them illiterate farmers like the Lees, had been admitted. Blia came the same year, leaving an executive position at an international packaging company. "I move here to help because it was my moral responsibility," he told me. "If my generation stay in France, we would feel guilty." Blia and Jonas were more intellectually cosmopolitan not only than every Hmong they knew, but also than every American they knew, including myself. Their leadership roles in Merced had earned both of them respect, but little money, and, as far as I could see, little peace of mind.

I knew Blia Yao Moua best. There was a period of a few months when I spent almost every afternoon sitting in his office, a windowless cubicle with fake wood paneling, asking questions about Hmong religion, military history, medical practices, kinship patterns, weddings, funerals, music, clothing, architecture, and gastronomy. It was from Blia that I learned, for example, that if I wronged another person, I might be reborn in my next life as my victim's buffalo and used for farm work; that what American doctors called the Mongolian spot— a bluish birthmark on the buttocks of many Asian babies—was in fact the place where the babies had been spanked, in utero, by a *dab*; and that the shoes Hmong corpses wore for burial had upturned toes. Blia looked like a frayed aristocrat, with a high domed forehead and finely drawn features. Although he was almost exactly my age—in his mid-thirties when we first met—I always felt like a child in his presence, partly because I sat in a chair with a tiny desk attached, the way I had in sixth grade, and partly because he knew so much more than I did and was so patient with my ignorance. I remember countless occasions, after I had asked him to provide a rational explanation for a nonrational custom, when he just shook his head gently and said, "Anne, may I explain to you again. The Hmong culture is *not Cartesian*."

Blia was the executive director of Lao Family Community, a

246 / The Spirit Catches You and You Fall Down

mutual-assistance organization that helped Merced's Hmong community negotiate the public-assistance labyrinth, apply for job training, resolve community conflicts, and keep abreast of news from Laos and Thailand.* It was quartered in an old truck depot near the Kmart. Signs on the wall, next to Hmong-language handouts on fair housing laws and disability insurance, said PLEASE HELP YOURSELF OUT and YOU MAY WANTED NEWS. The Hmong community might not always meet the expectations of the American community, but it certainly knew how to run itself. Blia once drew me a flowchart—which *was* Cartesian—delineating how his organization worked. "At the top is the president and advisory board of eight," he explained. "Then eleven Board of Director. Then seventeen district leaders. Then our 6,000 members. Let us say we need a hundred dollars to help out person who will be evicted. The seventeen district leaders carry the news, and everyone donate five cents or ten cents. Tomorrow we get that money. Or if one person die, tomorrow money will flow back to help that family. If there is change in welfare rules, we get out information the same way. If someone have problem with their child, we can solve problem inside Hmong community before it gets to the police. This way, 6,000 people we can serve with four or five people working in our office. No problem."

No problem, that is, if those four or five people had no private life whatsoever. Blia's eyes were often puffed and bloodshot from lack of sleep. Once he came to work after staying up all night mediating between the Merced police and a Hmong family who, while bringing a sacrificed pig home from Fresno, had had a traffic accident that distributed parts of the pig across the northbound lanes of Highway 99. He spent another night dealing with three teenaged girls who had run away from their homes in Fresno and stolen some money from an uncle in Merced. After persuading the uncle not to report the theft to the police, Blia took the girls home, woke his pregnant wife, and asked her to cook them a meal while they waited for their parents. The parents were not grateful. "They are angry because I should have

---

* I have noted elsewhere that several branches of Lao Family Community were investigated in the early nineties for allegedly extorting donations to General Vang Pao's resistance group, Neo Hom. Merced's branch was among those investigated, but no improprieties were found.

acted more severely," he told me. "I did not know until they arrive, but I am related to all those families by my clan and my wife's clan. That is terrible! In our culture, this means I have same duty as parents to give the children a lesson. I should have spank them. I did not do my right duty."

I saw Blia's face light up only once, the time he described an ambitious housing scheme he had conceived. "I would like to share with you what we are dreaming of for the future," he said. "Some of us hope to establish a Hmongtown, on the other side of Childs and Gerard Avenues. If we can make the financial package to buy this land, we can build two, three hundred houses. The Hmong house in Laos has a cross like an X at the top. We can do that here too. Each family can have a small garden. We can have our own Hmong shopping center. Our Hmongtown will boost morale because people will take good care of it. We will lose face if white person is seeing that Hmongtown is dirty. Having our own town will help Hmong people to become more economically self-sufficient. If this dream can come true, this will be very good for Hmong image!"

But when I came back to Merced a year later, no one had heard of Hmongtown, and Blia had resigned from his job at Lao Family Community and was selling insurance door-to-door. An American who knew him told me, "Blia is the most burned-out Hmong I ever saw." He later moved to St. Paul, Minnesota, where he counsels Asian students and teaches a course on Hmong culture at Metropolitan State University. His telephone number is now unlisted.

Like Blia, Jonas Vangay translated, mediated, counseled, and interceded on twenty-four-hour call. At the end of his speech at the college and career conference I had attended, Jonas had told his teenaged audience, "Call me any time during the day or night," and I knew that he would be taken literally. He had heavy family responsibilities as well. Explaining to me once why his family shared their home with two of his brothers, one of whom had nine children, he said, "I have another older brother who is very American now. He refuse to accept our brothers to live with him. He say, Here in the United States it is everyone for himself. I say, *I am Hmong.* For the Hmong, it is *never* everyone for himself."

Jonas was thin and wiry and handsome, although, like almost every well-educated Hmong I knew, he always looked dog-tired. His real name was Vang Na. He had changed it to Jonas Vangay when he was living in France, because he thought that his résumé would garner more job offers if he did not sound so Asian. He now had two jobs, as a bilingual education specialist for the Merced school system and as a Hmong-language teacher at Merced College. I used to talk to him, using a mixture of English and French, in an elementary school classroom, seated again at a child's desk. I never asked a question about Hmong history or linguistics that he was unable to answer.

Because, like Blia, Jonas was always busy but never turned me away, I decided to find a way to thank him for his help. Should I give him a gift? This seemed hazardous; he might feel he should reciprocate. Also, I didn't trust my gift-selecting instincts. Once, in an attempt to bridge the miles between Laos, Merced, and New York City, I had given Foua and Nao Kao a small plastic globe, only to find that they believed the earth was flat. Should I invite Jonas and his wife to Bill Selvidge's house? This might confuse them; there was no recognized Hmong category for platonic friends who shared living quarters.

"Why don't you invite them to a nice restaurant?" suggested Bill.

So one evening, at 7:00 sharp, I sat waiting for Jonas in the lounge at a local steakhouse called the Cask 'n Cleaver. He had told me his wife could not join us because she had to take care of their children. I suspected he might also be embarrassed because her English was rudimentary.

The restaurant's hostess, who wore a silver lamé top and a miniskirt, asked me whom I was waiting for.

"A Hmong man who has helped me with my work," I said.

The hostess looked surprised. "I just moved to Merced," she said, "and I don't know nothing about the Hmongs. I just saw my first one today. My boyfriend said, That's a Hmong. I said, How can you tell the difference? They look just like Chinamen to me. My boyfriend says they're the worst drivers in the world. When he sees one, he goes clear 'cross town to stay away from them! I guess Hmongs don't come to restaurants like this very often." (*They sure don't*, I thought. *And by the way, you're not fit to polish Jonas's boots.*)

Jonas arrived forty-five minutes late, saying he had been delayed by a student. I never knew if he had known from the start that he couldn't make it at seven, and had agreed to the time because he thought that was what I wanted to hear, or whether (the story of his life) he had once again been pulled in two mutually exclusive directions. The dinner was not a success. Despite his five languages, Jonas had difficulty understanding the waitress, a teenager who spoke rapid Valley-Girl, and had to ask me several times what she was saying. Out of politeness—certainly not from lack of sophistication, since he had eaten at plenty of Parisian restaurants that would make the Cask 'n Cleaver look like McDonald's—he ordered the cheapest entrée on the menu. Our conversation was formal and halting. Jonas was obviously relieved when we left. Afterwards, we stood in the parking lot, talking in the dark.

"You know, Anne," he said quietly, "when I am with a Hmong or a French or an American person, I am always the one who laughs last at a joke. I am the chameleon animal. You can place me anyplace, and I will survive, but I will not *belong*. I must tell you that I do not really belong anywhere."

Then Jonas drove home to his wife, his three children, his brothers, his brothers' wives, his brothers' ten children, and his ringing telephone.

The Eight Questions

Lia did not die, nor did she recover. Foua often dreamed that her daughter could walk and talk, but when she awoke, Lia lay curled next to her in bed, a slight, silent husk who hardly seemed big enough to contain her family's load of memory, anger, confusion, and grief. She lay suspended in time, growing only a few inches, gaining little weight, always looking far younger than her age, while the Lee siblings who still lived at home—six athletic, bilingual children who moved with ease between the Hmong and the American worlds—grew up around her. Cheng joined the Marine Reserves and was called to serve in the Gulf War, but to Foua's nearly hysterical relief, the war ended two days before his scheduled flight to Saudi Arabia. May went to Fresno State University, majoring in health science, a choice influenced by her childhood experiences, both positive and negative, as the ad hoc arbitrator between her parents and the medical establishment. Yer, a volleyball star who had won the award for Best Girl Athlete at Merced High School, joined May at Fresno State two years later, majoring in physical education. True became Merced High's student body treasurer and president of its Youth Culture Club, a Hmong social and service organization with more than 200 members. Mai became a stand-out soccer player and was known as one of the most beautiful teenagers in Merced, a reputation that caused boys to fight over her and girls all too frequently to resent her. Pang grew from a harum-scarum toddler into a self-possessed schoolgirl with a flair for traditional Hmong dance. There were a few tremors as the Lee children passed through adolescence, but never the rifts that American families accept almost as a matter of course. "My parents are the coolest parents in the world," True once wrote me. "We don't have everything in the world, but we do have the closeness of us eight sisters, one brother, and our parents. This is the coolest family ever and I would never trade it for anything else in this world."

Nao Kao gained weight and was troubled by high blood pressure. Foua felt tired much of the time. Seeing that their energies were waning, Jeanine Hilt urged the Lees to let Lia return to the Schelby Center for Special Education each day, not to educate her—that was a thing of the past—but to give her parents a few hours' respite each day. Because of their persistent fear that Lia might be stolen from them again by the government, the Lees were reluctant at first, but because they trusted Jeanine, they eventually agreed.

Dee Korda, one of whose foster children was severely retarded and also attended Schelby, frequently saw Lia there, lying on her back with her hands strapped to blocks in order to prevent her fingers from stiffening into claws. She could hardly bear to look. The Kordas had all taken Lia's neurological catastrophe hard. The entire family had gone through therapy at the Merced County Mental Health Department in order to deal with what Dee called "Lia being dead but alive." At their counselor's suggestion, the children—biological, foster, and adopted—drew pictures on butcher paper. "Wendy drew a mom and a baby, because Lia was with her mom," said Dee. "Julie drew a rainbow with clouds and birds, because Lia didn't have to cry anymore. Maria is real withdrawn, but when we told her about Lia she cried. Lia got through to her! She drew a broken heart with a jagged fence and an eye looking in from the outside. The heart was the sadness. The fence was the wall that Lia had gotten over by touching our lives. The eye was my eye, watching the sadness, with a tear that cried."

In 1993, while she was vacationing at Disneyland, Jeanine Hilt had an acute asthma attack, went into respiratory failure, and suffered oxygen deprivation so severe that she lost all brain function: in other words, she developed hypoxic ischemic encephalopathy, exactly the same fate that had befallen Lia. She died three days later with her partner of eighteen years, Karen Marino, at her side. "When I heard Jenny was dead, my heart broke," Foua told me. "I cried because Jenny had told me she wasn't going to get married and she would never have any children of her own, so she would help me raise my children. But she died, so she couldn't do that, and I felt I had lost my American daughter."

Neil Ernst won the MCMC residency program's first Faculty Teacher of the Year award. Peggy Philp became Merced's County Health Officer, a post her father had held more than forty years earlier. They continued to share their pediatric practice as well as housework and child care, scrupulously negotiating what one of their Christmas letters described as "a blur of laundry, lunches, cleaning, patient care, newborn resuscitation, and resident teaching." Their understanding of the Lees, and the Lees' understanding of them, deepened significantly when they, too, experienced a child's grave illness. During his last month of third grade, their elder son, Toby, was diagnosed with acute lymphocytic leukemia. When Neil tried to tell Dan Murphy about the diagnosis, he cried so hard he couldn't talk. After one of Lia's checkups, Neil wrote me:

> Mrs. Lee had heard that our son had leukemia. It was truly amazing how quickly she heard of this. When Peggy saw Lia in our clinic, Mrs. Lee was very concerned about Toby's health, how he was doing etc. There was very genuine concern expressed by her questions and facial expression. At the end of the visit Mrs. Lee was hugging Peggy and they were both shedding a few tears. Sorrows of motherhood cut through all cultural barriers.

Toby underwent three years of chemotherapy and achieved what seems to be a permanent remission. "Lia's mother continues to occupy a special place in our thoughts," wrote Neil in a later letter. "She always asks about Toby. Our contacts with her are very infrequent because her family provides excellent care for Lia, but they are special nonetheless."

Since Lia's brain death, whatever scant trust Foua and Nao Kao had once had in American medicine had shrunk almost to zero. (I say "almost" because Foua exempted Neil and Peggy.) When their daughter May broke her arm, and the doctors in the MCMC emergency room told them it needed a cast, Nao Kao marched her straight home, bathed her arm in herbs, and wrapped it in a poultice for a week. May's arm regained its full strength. When a pot of boiling oil fell from the electric stove onto Foua's skirt, setting it on fire and burning her right hip and leg, she sacrificed two chickens and a pig. When Foua got pregnant with her sixteenth child, and had an early miscarriage, she did nothing. When she got pregnant with her seventeenth child and had a complicated miscarriage in her fourth month, Nao Kao waited for three days, until she started to hemorrhage and fell unconscious to the living room floor, before he called an ambulance. He consented to her dilation and curettage only after strenuous—in fact, desperate—persuasion by the MCMC resident on obstetric rotation. Nao Kao also sacrificed a pig while Foua was in the hospital and a second pig after she returned home.

Before she was readmitted to Schelby, Lia was routinely vaccinated against diphtheria, pertussis, and tetanus. At about the same time, she started to develop occasional seizurelike twitches. Because they were brief, infrequent, and benign—and also, perhaps, because he had learned from bitter experience—Neil decided not to prescribe anticonvulsants. Foua and Nao Kao were certain that the shots had caused the twitches, and they told Neil that they did not want Lia to be immunized ever again, for anything.

Dan Murphy, who became the director of MCMC's Family Practice Residency Program, once told me that when you fail one Hmong patient, you fail the whole community. I could see that this was true. Who knew how many Hmong families were giving the hospital a wide berth because they didn't want their children to end up like the second-youngest Lee daughter? Everyone in Merced's Lee and Yang clans knew what had happened to Lia (those bad doctors!), just as everyone on the pediatric floor at MCMC knew what had happened to Lia (those bad parents!). Lia's case had confirmed the Hmong community's worst prejudices about the medical profession and the medical community's worst prejudices about the Hmong.

At the family practice clinic, the staff continued to marvel at the quality of care the Lees provided to their clean, sweet-smelling, well-groomed child. But at the hospital next door, where the nurses had had no contact with Lia since 1986, the case metastasized into a mass of complaints that grew angrier with each passing year. Why had the

Lees been so ungrateful for their daughter's free medical care? (Neil —who did not share the nurses' resentment—once calculated that, over the years, Lia had cost the United States government about $250,000, not counting the salaries of her doctors, nurses, and social workers.) Why had the Lees always insisted on doing everything *their* way? Why—this was still the worst sin—had the Lees been noncompliant? As Sharon Yates, a nurse's aide, told me, "If only the parents had given Lia the medicine, she wouldn't be like this. I bet when she came back from that foster home, they just didn't give her any medicine."

But I knew that when she returned from foster care, Foua and Nao Kao *had* given Lia her medicine—4 ccs of Depakene, three times a day—exactly as prescribed. Hoping to clear up some questions about Lia's anticonvulsants, I went to Fresno to talk with Terry Hutchison, the pediatric neurologist who had overseen her care at Valley Children's Hospital. I had noticed that in one of his discharge notes, written nine months before her neurological crisis, he had described Lia as "a very pretty Hmong child" and her parents as "very interested and very good with Lia." I had never seen phrases like that in her MCMC chart.

Bill Selvidge had told me that Dr. Hutchison was "a known eccentric," beloved by his residents for his empathy but dreaded for his insistence on doing rounds at 4:00 a.m. He had an exiguous crewcut and on the day I met him was wearing a necktie decorated with a large bright-yellow giraffe. A sign in the hall outside his office, hung at toddler eye level, read:

KIDS ZONE
ENTER WITH CARE AND LOVE

When I asked him about the relationship between Lia's medications and her final seizure, he said, "Medications probably had nothing to do with it."

"Huh?" I said.

"Lia's brain was destroyed by septic shock, which was caused by the *Pseudomonas aeruginosa* bacillus in her blood. I don't know how Lia got it and I will never know. What I do know is that the septic shock caused the seizures, not the other way around. The fact that she had a preexisting seizure disorder probably made the status epilepticus worse or easier to start or whatever, but the seizures were incidental and not important. If Lia had not had seizures, she would have presented in a coma and shock, and the outcome would probably have been the same, except that her problem might have been more easily recognized. It was too late by the time she got to Valley Children's. It was probably too late by the time she got to MCMC."

"Did her parents' past noncompliance have anything to do with it?"

"Absolutely nothing. The only influence that medications could have had is that the Depakene we prescribed might have compromised her immune system and made her more susceptible to the *Pseudomonas*." (Depakene occasionally causes a drop in white blood cells that can hamper the body's ability to fight infection.) "I still believe Depakene was the drug of choice, and I would prescribe it again. But, in fact, if the family was giving her the Depakene as instructed, it is conceivable that by following our instructions, they set her up for septic shock."

"Lia's parents think that the problem was caused by too much medicine."

"Well," said Dr. Hutchison, "that may not be too far from the truth."

I stared at him.

"Go back to Merced," he said, "and tell all those people at MCMC that the family didn't do this to the kid. We did."

Driving back to Merced, I was in a state of shock myself. I had known about Lia's sepsis, but I had always assumed that her seizure disorder had been the root of the problem. *The Lees were right after all*, I thought. *Lia's medicine did make her sick!*

That night I told Neil and Peggy what Dr. Hutchison had said. As usual, their desire to ferret out the truth outweighed their desire —if indeed they had one—to defend their reputation for infallibility. They immediately asked for my photocopy of Lia's medical chart, and they sat together on Bill Selvidge's sofa, combing Volume 5 for evidence, overlooked during the crisis, that Lia might already have been septic at MCMC. Murmuring to each other in their shared secret language ("calcium 3.2," "platelets 29,000," "hemoglobin 8.4"), they might have been—in fact, were—a pair of lovers exchanging a set of emotionally charged intimacies.

"I always thought Lia got septic down at Children's when they put all those invasive lines in," said Peggy. "But maybe not. There are some signs here."

"I did too," said Neil. "If I'd thought she was septic here at MCMC, I would have done a lumbar puncture. I didn't start her on antibiotics because every single time Lia had come in before that, she was not septic. Every other time, the problem was her seizure disorder, and this was obviously the worst seizure of her life. I stabilized her, I arranged for her transport, and then I went home before all the lab results were back." He didn't sound defensive. He sounded curious.

After Neil and Peggy went home, I asked Bill Selvidge whether he thought Neil had made a mistake in not recognizing and treating Lia's sepsis, even though Dr. Hutchison believed that her fate was probably sealed before she arrived in the MCMC emergency room—and even though the increasing severity of her epilepsy might eventually have led to serious brain damage if sepsis had never entered the picture.

"Neil leaves no stone unturned," said Bill. "If Neil made a mistake, it's because every physician makes mistakes. If it had been a brand-new kid walking off the street, I guarantee you Neil would have done a septic workup and he would have caught it. But this was Lia. *No one* at MCMC would have noticed anything but her seizures. Lia *was* her seizures."

To MCMC's residents, Lia continued to be her seizures—the memory of those terrifying nights in the emergency room that had taught them how to intubate or start IVs or perform venous cutdowns. They always spoke of Lia in the past tense. In fact, Neil and Peggy themselves frequently referred to "Lia's demise," or "what may have killed Lia" or "the reason Lia died." Dr. Hutchison did the same thing. He had asked me, "Was Lia with the foster parents when she died?" And although I reminded him that Lia was alive, five minutes later he said, "Noncompliance had nothing to do with her death." It wasn't just absentmindedness. It was an admission of defeat. Lia was dead to her physicians (in a way, for example, that she was never dead to her social workers) because medicine had once made extravagant claims on her behalf and had had to renounce them.

Once I asked Neil if he wished he had done anything differently. He answered as I expected, focusing not on his relationship with the Lees but on his choice of medication. "I wish we'd used Depakene sooner," he said. "I wish I'd accepted that it would be easier for the family to comply with one medicine instead of three, even if three seemed medically optimal."

Then I asked, "Do you wish you had never met Lia?"

"Oh, no, no, no!" His vehemence surprised me. "Once I might have said yes, but not in retrospect. Lia taught me that when there is a very dense cultural barrier, you do the best you can, and if something happens despite that, you have to be satisfied with little successes instead of total successes. You have to give up total control. That is very hard for me, but I do try. I think Lia made me into a less rigid person."

The next time I saw Foua, I asked her whether she had learned anything from what had happened. "No," she said. "I haven't learned. I just feel confused." She was feeding Lia at the time, making baby noises as she spooned puréed *zaub*, the spinachlike green she grew in the parking lot, into the slack mouth. "I don't understand how the doctors can say she is going to be like this for the rest of her life, and yet they can't fix her. How can they know the future but not know how to change it? I don't understand that."

"Well, what do *you* think Lia's future will hold?" I asked.

"I don't know these things," said Foua. "I am not a doctor. I am not a *txiv neeb*. But maybe Lia will stay hurt like this, and that makes me cry about what will happen. I gave birth to Lia, so I will always take care of her with all my heart. But when her father and I pass away, who will take care of Lia? Lia's sisters do love her, but even though they love her, maybe they will not be able to take care of her. Maybe they will need to study too hard and work too hard. I am crying to think that they are just going to give Lia away to the Americans." Foua wept soundlessly. May Ying embraced her and stroked her hair.

"I know where the Americans put children like Lia," she continued. "I saw a place like that in Fresno where they took Lia once, a long time ago." (Foua was recalling a chronic care facility for retarded and disabled children where Lia had been temporarily placed, before her year in foster care, while her medications were monitored and stabilized.) "It was like a house for the dead. The children were so poor and so sad that they just cried. They cried all over. One child had a big head and a really small body. Other children had legs that were all dried up and they just fell on the floor. I have seen this. If the Americans take Lia there she will want to die, but instead she will suffer."

Foua brushed her tears from her cheeks with the back of her hand, in a quick, brusque gesture. Then she wiped Lia's mouth, far more gently, and slowly started to rock her. "I am very sad," she said, "and I think a lot that if we were still in Laos and not in the United States, maybe Lia would never be like this. The doctors are very very knowledgeable, your high doctors, your best doctors, but maybe they made a mistake by giving her the wrong medicine and they made her hurt like this. If it was a *dab* that made Lia sick like this in Laos, we would know how to go to the forest and get herbs to fix her and maybe she could be able to speak. But this happened here in the United States, and Americans have done this to her, and our medicine cannot fix that."

It was also true that if the Lees were still in Laos, Lia would probably have died before she was out of her infancy, from a prolonged bout of untreated status epilepticus. American medicine had both preserved her life and compromised it. I was unsure which had hurt her family more.

Since that night with Foua, I have replayed the story over and over again, wondering if anything could have made it turn out differently. Despite Dr. Hutchison's revisionist emendation of the final chapter, no one could deny that if the Lees had given Lia her anticonvulsants from the beginning, she might have had—might still be having—something approaching a normal life. What was not clear was who, if anyone, should be held accountable. What if Neil *had* prescribed Depakene earlier? What if, instead of placing Lia in foster care, he had arranged for a visiting nurse to administer her medications? What if he had sought out Blia Yao Moua or Jonas Vangay or another Hmong leader who straddled both cultures, and had asked him to intervene with the Lees, thus transferring the issue of compliance to a less suspect source? What if MCMC had had better interpreters?

When I presented my "what if" list to Dan Murphy one day in the MCMC cafeteria, he was less interested in the Depakene than in the interpreters. However, he believed that the gulf between the Lees and their doctors was unbridgeable, and that nothing could have been done to change the outcome. "Until I met Lia," he said, "I thought if you had a problem you could always settle it if you just sat and talked long enough. But we could have talked to the Lees until we were blue in the face—we could have sent the Lees to *medical school* with the world's greatest translator—and they would still think their way was right and ours was wrong." Dan slowly stirred his lukewarm cocoa; he had been on all-night call. "Lia's case ended my idealistic way of looking at the world."

Was the gulf unbridgeable? I kept returning, obsessively, to the Lees' earliest encounters with MCMC during Lia's infancy, when no interpreters were present and her epilepsy was misdiagnosed as pneumonia. Instead of practicing "veterinary medicine," what if the residents in the emergency room had managed to elicit the Lees' trust at the outset—or at least managed not to crush it—by finding out what *they* believed, feared, and hoped? Jeanine Hilt had asked them for their version of the story, but no doctor ever had. Martin Kilgore had tried, but by then it was years too late.

Of course, the Lees' perspective might have been as unfathomable to the doctors as the doctors' perspective was to the Lees. Hmong culture, as Blia Yao Moua observed to me, is not Cartesian. Nothing could be more Cartesian than Western medicine. Trying to understand Lia and her family by reading her medical chart (something I spent hundreds of hours doing) was like deconstructing a love sonnet by reducing it to a series of syllogisms. Yet to the residents and pediatricians who had cared for her since she was three months old, there was no guide to Lia's world *except* her chart. As each of them struggled to make sense of a set of problems that were not expressible in the language they knew, the chart simply grew longer and longer, until it contained more than 400,000 words. Every one of those words reflected its author's intelligence, training, and good intentions, but not a single one dealt with the Lees' perception of their daughter's illness.

Almost every discussion of cross-cultural medicine that I had ever read quoted a set of eight questions, designed to elicit a patient's "explanatory model," which were developed by Arthur Kleinman, a psychiatrist and medical anthropologist who chairs the department of social medicine at Harvard Medical School. The first few times I read these questions they seemed so obvious I hardly noticed them; around the fiftieth time, I began to think that, like many obvious things, they might actually be a work of genius. I recently decided to call Kleinman to tell him how I thought the Lees might have answered his questions after Lia's earliest seizures, before any medications had been administered, resisted, or blamed, if they had had a good interpreter and had felt sufficiently at ease to tell the truth. To wit:

1. *What do you call the problem?*
Qaug dab peg. That means the spirit catches you and you fall down.

2. *What do you think has caused the problem?*
Soul loss.

3. *Why do you think it started when it did?*
Lia's sister Yer slammed the door and Lia's soul was frightened out of her body.

4. *What do you think the sickness does? How does it work?*
It makes Lia shake and fall down. It works because a spirit called a *dab* is catching her.

5. *How severe is the sickness? Will it have a short or long course?*
Why are you asking us those questions? If you are a good doctor, you should know the answers yourself.

6. *What kind of treatment do you think the patient should receive? What are the most important results you hope she receives from this treatment?*
You should give Lia medicine to take for a week but no longer. After she is well, she should stop taking the medicine. You should not treat her by taking her blood or the fluid from her backbone. Lia should also be treated at home with our Hmong medicines and by sacrificing pigs and chickens. We hope Lia will be healthy, but we are not sure we want her to stop shaking forever because it makes her noble in our culture, and when she grows up she might become a shaman.

7. *What are the chief problems the sickness has caused?*
It has made us sad to see Lia hurt, and it has made us angry at Yer.

8. *What do you fear most about the sickness?*
That Lia's soul will never return.

I thought Kleinman would consider these responses so bizarre that he would be at a loss for words. (When I had presented this same material, more or less, to Neil and Peggy, they had said, "Mr. and Mrs. Lee thought *what*?") But after each answer, he said, with great enthusiasm, "Right!" Nothing surprised him; everything delighted him. From his vantage point, a physician could encounter no more captivating a patient than Lia, no finer a set of parents than the Lees.

Then I told him what had happened later—the Lees' noncompliance with Lia's anticonvulsant regimen, the foster home, the neurological catastrophe—and asked him if he had any retroactive suggestions for her pediatricians.

"I have three," he said briskly. "First, get rid of the term 'compliance.' It's a lousy term. It implies moral hegemony. You don't want a command from a general, you want a colloquy. Second, instead of looking at a model of coercion, look at a model of mediation. Go find a member of the Hmong community, or go find a medical anthropologist, who can help you negotiate. Remember that a stance of mediation, like a divorce proceeding, requires compromise on both sides. Decide what's critical and be willing to compromise on everything else. Third, you need to understand that as powerful an influence as the culture of the Hmong patient and her family is on this case, the culture of biomedicine is equally powerful. If you can't see that your own culture has its own set of interests, emotions, and biases, how can you expect to deal successfully with someone else's culture?"

18

The Life or the Soul

I do not know if Lia would be able to walk and talk today had she been treated by Arthur Kleinman instead of by Neil Ernst and Peggy Philp. However, I have come to believe that her life was ruined not by septic shock or noncompliant parents but by cross-cultural misunderstanding.

Lia's case—or "narrative," as Kleinman would put it, since he believes every illness is not a set of pathologies but a personal story—was one of perhaps a hundred Hmong medical cases I heard about over the years. Most turned out badly. The sample is probably skewed, since doctors and patients remember calamities—their own and others'—more vividly than they remember successes. Still, the imbalance is disquieting.

A child in San Diego was born with a harelip. Her doctors asked the parents' permission to repair it surgically. They cited the ease of the operation, the social ostracism to which the child would otherwise be condemned. Instead, the parents fled the hospital with their baby. Several years earlier, while the family was escaping from Laos to Thailand, the father had killed a bird with a stone, but he had not done so cleanly, and the bird had suffered. The spirit of that bird had caused the harelip. To refuse to accept the punishment would be a grave insult.

A child in Michigan had a retinoblastoma, a malignant tumor of the eye. His doctors asked the parents' permission to remove his eye in order to prevent metastasis. His parents fled the state, certain that if their son had the surgery he would be reincarnated, over and over again, with an incomplete body.

A child in Minnesota had a spinal deformity. His doctors asked his parents for permission to perform corrective surgery. After his birth in a Thai refugee camp, a *txiv neeb* had told the parents that the boy was destined for greatness as a Hmong leader. The *txiv neeb* had also warned that if the boy's body were ever altered, his parents would die. A few days after his parents reluctantly acceded to the operation, but before it was performed, his father died. His mother fled the state with her son.

A woman in Merced, who had delivered five children without complications, arrived at the hospital in the final stage of labor with her sixth child. Observing that the umbilical cord had prolapsed—a potentially fatal problem if the cord is compressed by the baby's head—the nurses attempted to relieve pressure on the cord by forcing the woman to crouch on her hands and knees and pushing the head back inside the birth canal, while screaming at the husband to sign a consent form for a cesarean section. He did so, under duress, but while his wife was being prepared for the surgery, the baby was born vaginally. No interpreter was present. The parents believed that the nurses wished to harm the baby because they thought Hmong refugees had too many children, and that the doctor wished to perform surgery in order to make a larger profit. Accordingly, the mother decided to give birth to all her future children at home.

There were, of course, some good outcomes, mostly not in pediatric cases. Here are three.

A young combat veteran who had just arrived in the United States attempted to hang himself in the shower room of the California transit facility in which he had been temporarily placed. During the next several days, he was isolated in a hospital room, offered American food, and forced to submit to a comprehensive medical workup, including blood tests. He neither ate nor slept. Finally, his doctors discontinued the blood work. They gave him Hmong food, and he ate. They let a Hmong man stay with him overnight, and he slept. Learning that he had feared he would be unable to feed his children, they explained the mechanics of Refugee Cash Assistance and showed him photographs of his future home. He and his family resettled successfully in Iowa.

A middle-aged man in Merced, hospitalized for an infection, was asked by an interpreter who was filling out a routine nursing admission form whether he wished, in case of death, to donate his organs. The man, believing that his doctors planned to let him die and take his heart, became highly agitated and announced that he was leaving the hospital immediately. The interpreter managed to calm him and assured him that the doctors' intentions were honorable. The man stayed until his recovery a few days later, and a sympathetic hospital administrator, anticipating similar misunderstandings with other Hmong patients, fought successfully to have the organ donor box removed from the admission form.

A hospital social worker in San Francisco, accompanied by an interpreter, was sent by the public health department to visit a woman with tuberculosis who had refused to take her isoniazid tablets. The social worker, whose name was Francesca Farr, began to talk to the patient, who was in her eighth month of pregnancy. "No, no," said the interpreter. "You should talk to her *husband*." So Farr asked the husband why he didn't want his wife to take the medicine. "No, no," said the interpreter. "Don't ask him that yet. First, you should wish him some things." Farr told the husband she wished that his children would never be sick, that their rice bowls would never be empty, that his family would always stay together, and that his people would never be in another war. As she spoke, the husband's hands, which had been clenched, relaxed. "Now," said the interpreter, "you can ask him why his wife isn't taking the medicine." Farr did. The husband answered that if she took the medicine, their baby would be born without arms or legs. Farr touched the patient's abdomen, and told the husband that if the baby didn't already have arms and legs, the woman wouldn't be so big, and the baby wouldn't be kicking. The husband nodded, walked into the other room, returned with a giant bottle, dumped the contents into Farr's hands, and said that his wife would take the pills.

This last case warrants particular scrutiny, because Francesca Farr did a number of things that generally weren't done at MCMC, and certainly weren't done with Lia. She made a house call. She took along a capable and assertive interpreter whom she treated as a cultural broker (by definition her equal, and in this case her superior), not a translator (her inferior). She worked within the family's belief system. She did not carry *her* belief system—which included a feminist distaste for being forced to deal with the husband instead of the wife—into the negotiations. She never threatened, criticized, or patronized. She said hardly anything about Western medicine. She flew completely by the seat of her pants.

Also, Francesca Farr *liked* the Hmong. Loved them, I should say. That was something she had in common with everyone I knew who had ever worked successfully with Hmong patients, clients, or research subjects. Dan Murphy once said that of the ten most admirable people he had met in the last decade, seven or eight were Hmong. Jeanine Hilt told me that if her house caught on fire, the first thing she would grab was a framed *paj ntaub* that Foua had stitched for her. (It still hangs in a position of honor over her partner's dining table.) Sukey Waller said that after she spent time with her Hmong clients, Americans, by comparison, seemed dry. The anthropologists Eric Crystal and Dwight Conquergood were so intoxicated by Hmong culture that their ethnographic commentaries, while academically unimpeachable, sometimes sounded like mash notes.

Neil and Peggy liked the Hmong, too, but they did not love them. They could have had a practice full of white middle-class patients who always took their medicine and whose insurance companies always paid on time. Instead, because they were altruists, they had the antithesis. Their choice was morally satisfying, but whenever a patient crossed the compliance line, thus sabotaging their ability to be optimally effective doctors, cultural diversity ceased being a delicious spice and became a disagreeable obstacle. Neil and Peggy were excellent physicians, but by Kleinman's definition—a concern for the psychosocial and cultural facets that give illness context and meaning—they were, at least during their early years with Lia, imperfect healers.

But love, unlike the etiology and diagnosis of pediatric seizures, cannot be taught. It can only be granted. (I believe that Neil and Peggy now love Foua.) In its absence, is there anything else that doctors can do to take better care of their Hmong patients?

Bruce Thowpaou Bliatout, the Hmong medical administrator who wrote about mental health problems as traditional ailments of the liver, has some suggestions. Not surprisingly, almost all of them are cultural, not medical. To improve Hmong health care in general, arrange for female doctors to treat female patients, and male doctors to treat male patients. Involve the patients' families in all decisions. Use interpreters who are both bilingual and bicultural.* To persuade Hmong people to undergo necessary surgery, and to improve the outcomes if they consent, enlist the support of family and community leaders. Minimize blood-drawing. Allow relatives or friends in the hospital room around the clock. Allow shamanic ceremonies in the hospital. To improve mental health, encourage traditional arts such as weaving, music, dance, and silversmithing. Acknowledge Hmong contributions to U.S. military operations in Laos. Promote clan reunification through secondary resettlement. Be careful not to undercut the father's authority in Hmong families. Give refugees more opportunities to help themselves. Fuss over them less.

Most important, says Bliatout (and many others as well), practice conjoint treatment—that is, integrate Western allopathic medicine with traditional healing arts, or, as Nao Kao Lee put it, use "a little medicine and a little *neeb*." Kleinman, who has commented that the doctor cures the disease but the indigenous healer heals the illness, believes that conjoint treatment does more than promote trust between the doctor and the patient; because illness is so profoundly affected by psychosocial factors, it actually improves the outcome. Although the Lees did treat Lia with herbs, dermal therapies, and animal sacrifices, their regimen ran parallel to Lia's medical course

---

* Sensitive bicultural interpreting, while it makes life easier for the doctor and the patient, can be extraordinarily stressful for the interpreter. John Xiong, a Hmong leader in Merced who often did informal medical interpreting, told me, "If the patient do not do like the doctor want, doctor get mad at interpreter. If the doctor do not do like the patient want, patient get mad at interpreter. I am in the middle, and I say, I try to help you both, but you both get mad at me." It is rare for doctors to defer to their interpreters, as Francesca Farr did, or to acknowledge the degree of painful identification the interpreters may feel with patients from their own ethnic groups. Thai Fang, an interpreter at Valley Medical Center in Fresno who compiled *Tuabneeg Lubcev Hab Kev Mobnkeeg Rua Cov Haslug Hmoob: Basic Human Body and Medical Information for Hmong Speaking People*, a Hmong-English glossary of anatomical and medical terms, wrote, "I decided to develop this book in response to my feeling of sympathy. Seeing my fellow Hmongs going through panic and worry so they have no energy left wounds my spirit as if bringing a disease to my soul."

rather than intertwining with it. Neil and Peggy were dimly aware of some of these remedies (for example, when Lia had marks on her chest from coin rubbing), but they never asked about them, and they certainly never recommended them. It would never have occurred to them to emulate Luis Estevez, a pediatrician at Lincoln Hospital in the Bronx, who has referred Puerto Rican and Dominican patients to a Santería high priest as he might refer them to an ophthalmologist, or Yasmin Collazo, a psychiatrist at Elmhurst Hospital Center in Queens, who has allowed a Mexican *curandero*, or folk healer, to perform a cleansing ceremony in the hospital for a schizophrenic patient. Dr. Collazo said that after the visit, the patient was far more compliant in taking her antipsychotic medications, which she believed the *curandero* had sanctified.

Bliatout wrote, "Since Hmong health treatments never hurt anyone, but could possibly help a patient, [they] should be seriously considered as part of a client's course of treatment." Unfortunately, his first premise is not always true. Some Hmong folk remedies contain arsenic, lead, and opium. However, intervention by a *txiv neeb*, whose work is conducted entirely on a metaphysical plane, is always safe, and many people (including Bliatout, Sukey Waller, Dwight Conquergood, and the French anthropologist Jacques Lemoine) believe that because the mind-body dichotomy does not exist in Hmong culture and because so much illness among Hmong refugees has a psychogenic element, the *txiv neeb* is an ideal collaborator in the healing process. Indeed, according to Conquergood, no one is better qualified to span the gap between the medical and the spiritual:

> Shamans are, first and last, quintessential mediators. They are threshold crossers, endowed creatures who can go between the earth and the sky. Grand articulators, shamans' special gift and mission is to bring opposites together—to bring the physical and moral worlds into meaningful conjunction. That is why they are identified with archetypal connectors such as images of ladders, bridges, ropes, and cosmic trees that sink roots into the earth while branching towards the sky. . . .
>
> It is the special responsibility of the shaman to celebrate and actualize the coincidences between these two kingdoms and to amplify their resonances, one into another. Perhaps that is why shamans do not resist prescription medicine and physical treatments. These forms of medicine do not directly compete with the shamans' manipulation of symbols and

management of belief. Indeed, I saw bottles of prescription medicine resting without contradiction on shamans' altars inside thatched huts in
Camp Ban Vinai. . . .

They see the two modes of healing, natural and supernatural, as com-
plementary rather than contradictory.

Conquergood should know, having been a *txiv neeb*'s patient himself
when he had dengue fever. He has described his soul-calling ceremony, which was attended by most of his friends at Ban Vinai—and
which he claims was truly restorative—as a festive and affectionate
drama that was "saturated with care and humankindness."

Lemoine has commented that a *txiv neeb* is far more like a psychiatrist than like a priest. However, there is a crucial distinction:

Comparing his work to psychiatric procedure, I noticed that while the
analyst tries to provoke self-analysis by scratching the wounded part of
the self, a Hmong shaman will provide an explanation which avoids all
self-involvement of the patient. [The patient] is always represented as a
victim of an assault from outside powers or of an accidental separation
from one part of his self. When this situation has been identified and
overcome by the shaman, health is recovered. At no point has there been
a feeling of guilt associated with suffering.

When I read this, I thought of how often the Hmong react to threat
or blame by fighting or fleeing, which in the medical arena translate
to various forms of noncompliance. The *txiv neeb*'s exclusion of guilt
from the transaction dovetails perfectly with the Hmong temperament. The doctor's standard message ("If you don't take these pills/
have this operation/see me again next Tuesday, you'll be sorry!") does
not.*

---

* When Dwight Conquergood was living at Ban Vinai, he intuitively took advantage of the no-fault dynamic when he designed his performance-art program for
improving camp hygiene. Mother Clean, the eight-foot dancing puppet who led
the sanitation campaign, informed the camp inhabitants:

When you lived in the mountains
The wind and the rain cleaned the garbage.
Now with so many people in Ban Vinai
We all must be careful to clean up the garbage.

During the mid-eighties, the Nationalities Service of Central California in Fresno received a short-term federal grant of $100,965 to establish what it termed "an integrated mental health delivery service utilizing Hmong healers and western mental health providers." Eight *txiv neebs* were hired as consultants. They treated 250 patients, most of whom had complaints that transcended the usual boundaries of "mental health." The resulting project report, which contains descriptions of eighteen healing ceremonies, including Ceremony to Dispel Ogre Spirits, Ceremony to Separate This World from That of the Afterlife, and Ceremony to Appease the Spirit Above the Big Stove, is one of the most amazing documents ever financed by American taxpayers. "Sometimes the ceremony by itself was enough," it concluded. "In other cases, once such a ceremony was performed the client was more amenable to recommended medical procedures, such as surgery or medication, administered by licensed health care providers." Here are the report's summaries of two cases that had different, though equally positive, resolutions:

Case No. 3

Complaint/Symptomatology—Gall Bladder Problem (mob tsib): The client suffered from a sharp pain on the right side of the chest extending to the back. He reported inability to engage in any activity other than passive relaxation.

Assessment: A licensed physician diagnosed the condition as a gall bladder problem requiring surgery for correction. The Neng [*txiv neeb*] was consulted following this diagnosis.

Treatment Plan: The Neng performed a ceremony during which healing powers [were] bestowed on water which was then used to wash the painful area in order to release the pain. However, the pain persisted and the client accepted that it was not a spiritual problem. He then returned to the physician and consented to surgery.

Result: The surgery was successful and the client reported that his illness was cured.

As Conquergood pointed out, "She exhorted a change in behavior without degrading the people whom she was trying to persuade, locating responsibility in the environmental circumstances."

Case No. 9

Complaint/Symptomatology: The client's penis had been swollen for about a month. He reported that he'd been treated by licensed physicians, but that the treatment had only given intermittent relief from pain and swelling.

Assessment: The Neng determined that the client had offended the stream spirits.

Treatment Plan: The Neng called upon the Neng spirits to effect a cure and release the pain. The Neng used a bowl of water to spray from the mouth over the infected area. The offended spirits were offered payment of five sticks of incense to release the pain and relieve the swelling.

Result: The client got better after the ceremony.

After fourteen months, the grant for the program expired, and, as far as I know, that was the first and last penile exorcism to be sponsored by the Department of Health and Human Services. However, in many less recondite ways, the medical establishment appears to be waking up to the fact that since 1990, more than half the population growth in the United States has come from immigrants and their children—and that many of these immigrants, even if they can get to the hospital and pay for their treatment, may find mainstream health care culturally inaccessible. The 1992 edition of the *Merck Manual of Diagnosis and Therapy*, the world's most widely used medical text, included, for the first time, a chapter called "Cross-Cultural Issues in Medicine." The chapter was allotted only three pages out of 2,844, and it was not cross-referenced in the chapter on "Patient Compliance," or indeed in any other chapter. However, merely printing such phrases as "spirit attack," "trance state," and "cultural relativism" granted them an ex cathedra legitimacy. Where *Merck* went, others could follow without fear of sounding like cranks.

Ten years ago, hardly any medical-school or residency curricula included cross-cultural training. In 1995, for the first time, the national guidelines for training psychiatry residents stipulated that they learn to assess cultural influences on their patients' problems. In 1996, the American Academy of Family Physicians endorsed a set of "Recommended Core Curriculum Guidelines on Culturally Sensitive and Competent Health Care." Among the resources suggested by the guidelines' authors was BaFá BaFá, a simulation game in which the participants are divided into two mythical cultures, each assigned a different set of manners, conventions, and taboos. Each group inevitably misperceives the other by applying its own cultural standards; each inevitably offends the other; and each, until the groups meet at the end of the game to discuss the pitfalls of ethnocentrism, is inevitably certain that its culture is superior.

Today most medical students at least brush shoulders with cross-cultural issues, and some form more than a glancing acquaintance. The University of Wisconsin recently developed an "integrated multicultural curriculum" that includes panel and group discussions, case conferences, student interviews, role-playing exercises, and home visits. At Harvard, all first-year students are required to take a course called "Patient-Doctor I" (significantly, not "Doctor-Patient I"), in which they learn to work with interpreters, study Kleinman's eight questions, and ponder such conundrums as "Can an American pediatrician truly explain a surgical consent form to newly arrived parents of a Southeast Asian baby?" and "Is it ethical to use psychotherapy when therapist and patient are ethnically unmatched?" Some residency programs are evolving along the same lines. At San Francisco General Hospital, all family practice residents are required to do a rotation at the Refugee Clinic, in which, since 1979, more than 20,000 refugees, speaking dozens of languages, have received health screenings. (Francesca Farr, who persuaded the Hmong man to let his wife take her isoniazid, was a social worker at the Refugee Clinic.) In addition to briefings on hepatitis B, thalassemia, and intestinal parasites, the residents' orientation manual includes an article on assessing symptoms in Southeast Asian survivors of mass violence and torture; a set of guidelines for working with interpreters; and an eight-page chart that compares the social and cultural customs of the Vietnamese, Cambodians, Lao, and Hmong.

Highmindedness in the big leagues is all very well. But how much of this kind of thing was likely to trickle down to a place like Merced? As it turns out, a lot more than I expected. In 1996, the Merced County Health Department invited a Seattle-based cross-cultural education program called "Bridging the Gap" to train its nursing, administrative, and interpreting staffs in advocacy skills and "cultural competence." The health department now produces a segment for the local Hmong cable channel that features a tour of MCMC and answers, in Hmong, some commonly asked questions, including "Why are doctors so rude?" At MCMC, a fifty-five-year-old Hmong man nearly died recently from a perforated bowel after his family took three days to consent to surgery. Because he stayed in the hospital for more than two months, and every resident either cared for him or debated his case in the corridors, he galvanized interest in such questions as: Could *txiv neebs* be certified, like clergy, to visit MCMC patients?* Could Hmong serve as cultural brokers?† If MCMC employed certified interpreters instead of lab assistants and nurse's aides who translated on the side—a plan that had previously been dismissed as too expensive—would hospital stays be shortened and costs thereby *reduced*? (This last question was particularly germane, since managed care had drastically eroded MCMC's referrals and hospitalizations, and the county was so nervous about the resulting deficit that it was planning to lease the hospital to a large health-care corporation.)

But change comes hard, especially in the trenches. It is one thing to read in medical school that the ideal doctor-patient-interpreter "seating configuration" is a right triangle, with the patient and interpreter forming the hypotenuse, and another to recollect the diagram in a roomful of gesticulating Hmong toward the end of a twenty-four-hour shift. When I heard of Merced's latest cross-cultural efforts, I remembered an elderly Hmong woman with stomach cancer whom I had once met at MCMC. Her family, unable to understand either the

---

* *Txiv neebs* had previously visited some of MCMC's Hmong patients, including Lia, but they had never been officially sanctioned. Bill Selvidge, however, had occasionally suggested that his Hmong patients, especially depressed ones, consult *txiv neebs*, and at Merced Community Outreach Services, Sukey Waller had made numerous *txiv neeb* referrals for her mental health clients.

† Since 1995, Marilyn Mochel, the coordinator of the health department's refugee program, has served as a cultural broker whom MCMC can summon to mediate between Hmong patients and the hospital staff. (Mochel was also responsible for the health department's cross-cultural innovations.) While the man with the perforated bowel was hospitalized, she was on call twenty-four hours a day to consult with relatives, clan members, community leaders, doctors, nurses, and dieticians, as well as with security guards who objected to the crowds of visitors, sometimes sixty at a time, who filled MCMC's hallways. Mochel says that her Hmong staff's "strong deference to professionals" disqualifies them from assuming the assertive role of broker themselves, though she hopes that will change.

resident's English or his drawings of the digestive system, had refused to consent to surgery. I had expected the resident to move heaven and earth to bring in a decent interpreter. Instead, I found him in the Preceptor Library, his head bowed over four articles on poorly differentiated gastric adenocarcinoma. I also remembered a Morbidity and Mortality Conference during which Dan Murphy presented the case of a middle-aged Hmong woman rendered comatose by a stroke. Her family had staged an insurrection at her bedside, demanding that her intravenous and nasogastric tubes be removed and that a *txiv neeb* be permitted in the Intensive Care Unit. (MCMC had acceded, and she had died.) Every time Dan tried to steer the discussion toward cultural issues, the residents yanked it back to a debate on the relative merits of labetalol and hydralazine as antihypertensives.

This is the kind of thinking that has begotten the cartoon-version M.D., the all-head-no-heart formalist who, when presented with a problem, would rather medicate it, scan it, suture it, splint it, excise it, anesthetize it, or autopsy it than communicate with it. Fortunately, most real-life doctors, including MCMC's, are not automatons. However, they often seem myopically overreliant on what Kleinman calls "the culture of biomedicine" (which, when he says it, sounds every bit as exotic as the culture of the Ainu or the Waiwai). Their investment in this culture does not make them resist change on general principle; quite the contrary. They eagerly embrace new drugs, technologies, and procedures as soon as clinical trials prove their effectiveness. Yet they may not feel the same way about Kleinman's eight questions ("But diseases *aren't* caused by spirits. Why should I indulge delusions?") or his proposition that ethnographic methods should be part of every doctor's job description ("But I'm not an anthropologist, I'm a gastroenterologist!"). The same doctors who listen to Continuing Medical Education audiocassettes on their car stereos, intent on keeping up with every innovation that might improve their outcome statistics, may regard cross-cultural medicine as a form of political bamboozlement, an assault on their rationality rather than a potentially lifesaving therapy.

On the wall above my desk, flanked by pictures of Lia and her family, are two Xeroxed passages that, in a jaundiced mood, I once captioned THE HMONG WAY and THE AMERICAN WAY. THE HMONG WAY is the page from the Fresno mental health report that summarized the *txiv neeb*'s successful treatment of his patient's swollen penis. THE AMERICAN WAY is a page from the *Journal of the American Medical Association*. It was excerpted from an article called "Doctors Have Feelings Too." Its author, a Harvard Medical School instructor named William M. Zinn, posited that because doctors may be busy "doing multiple other tasks," "maintaining a clinical distance," or harboring guilt about negative reactions to their patients, they run the risk of overlooking their feelings. So, if you're a doctor, how can you recognize that you're having a feeling? Some tips from Dr. Zinn:

> Most emotions have physical counterparts. Anxiety may be associated with a tightness of the abdomen or excessive diaphoresis; anger may be manifested by a generalized muscle tightness or a clenching of the jaw; sexual arousal may be noted by a tingling of the loins or piloerection; and sadness may be felt by conjunctival injection or a heaviness of the chest.

I first read this article at Bill Selvidge's house. Every night, while I waited for Bill to come home from MCMC, I alternated between his old anthropology texts and his piles of medical journals, and pondered which was the more arcane. I remember sitting on the dilapidated sofa, thinking that if any of my Hmong friends heard that American doctors had to read an article in order to learn how to tell if they were angry, they would never, ever return to MCMC. In lurched Bill, nearly ataxic from fatigue after a thirty-three-hour shift. I read him the paragraph that is now on my wall. We both laughed so loud we probably woke his fundamentalist neighbors, the ones who had smashed their TV set and danced a jig around it.

Bill assured me that he was so remarkably in touch with *his* feelings that he could tell if he was anxious or sad without benefit of diaphoresis or conjunctival injection. I believed him. Bill was a G.P. of the old school, the sort of doctor who relieved his stress by going to MCMC's newborn nursery, selecting a crying baby, and walking back and forth with it until it quieted down. Yet I feared that Dr. Zinn had a point. Medicine, as it is taught in the United States, does an excellent job of separating students from their emotions. The desensitization starts on the very first day of medical school, when each student is given a scalpel with which to penetrate his or her cadaver: "the ideal patient," as it is nicknamed, since it can't be killed, never complains, and never sues. The first cut is always difficult. Three months later, the students are chucking pieces of excised human fat into a garbage can as nonchalantly as if they were steak trimmings. The emotional skin-thickening is necessary—or so goes the conventional wisdom—because without it, doctors would be overwhelmed by their chronic exposure to suffering and despair. Dissociation is part of the job. That is why doctors do not treat their own relatives (feelings would handicap their effectiveness); why, beyond routine issues of sterility, the heads of open-heart patients are screened from the surgeon's view (individuality would be a distraction); and why Neil Ernst avoided Lia Lee after she returned from Fresno with irreparable brain damage (he couldn't bear it).

At Stanford Medical School, in an admirable attempt to fight this trend, students are informed during the first semester that their empathy may already have peaked; if they succumb to the norm, it will plunge steadily during their four years of medical school and their first year of residency. "What changes?" an appalled student once asked. His professor answered, "As you get more skilled, you belittle what you had before you started."

Stanford, like several other medical schools, is trying to bring back what has been called the "whole doctor–whole patient" model, in which the doctor brings his or her full humanity (not just the part that aced the MCATs) to the hospital, and the patient is viewed as a complete person (not just the appendix in Room 416). This model is nothing new; in fact, it is what all doctors used to be taught. As William Osler once said—or is said to have said—"Ask not what disease the person has, but rather what person the disease has." Between 1992 and 1995, the percentage of medical-school seniors who chose to become generalists—internists, general pediatricians, and family physicians—nearly doubled: a trend that may help bring Osler's charge back into circulation. Some of these choices have been influenced by economic factors (managed care plans prefer primary to subspecialized care because it's cheaper), but others are surely idealistic. If there were more Osler-type generalists around, the Hmong, among others, would stand to benefit. The anthropologist Elizabeth Kirton has commented that a Hmong patient she knew, referred to a specialist for further treatment, did not ask the referring physician to find someone skilled or famous. He asked, "Do you know someone who would care for me and love me?"

It was probably unfair of me to caption Dr. Zinn's article THE AMERICAN WAY. Once, several years ago, when I romanticized the Hmong more (though admired them less) than I do now, I had a conversation with a Minnesota epidemiologist at a health care conference. Knowing she had worked with the Hmong, I started to lament the insensitivity of Western medicine. The epidemiologist looked at me sharply. *"Western medicine saves lives,"* she said. Oh. Right. I had to keep reminding myself of that. It was all that cold, linear, Cartesian, non-Hmong-like thinking which saved my father from colon cancer, saved my husband and me from infertility, and, if she had swallowed her anticonvulsants from the start, might have saved Lia from brain damage. Dwight Conquergood's philosophy of health care as a form of barter, rather than a one-sided relationship, ignores the fact that, for better or for worse, Western medicine *is* one-sided. Doctors endure medical school and residency in order to acquire knowledge that their patients do not have. Until the culture of medicine changes, it would be asking a lot of them to consider, much less adopt, the notion that, as Francesca Farr put it, "our view of reality is only a view, not reality itself." However, I don't think it would be too much to ask them to *acknowledge* their patients' realities—to avoid the kind of blind spot that made a Merced health department employee once write, about a child from a family that views the entire universe as sacred:

Name: LEE, LIA
Principal Language: HMONG
Ethnic Group: HMONG
Religion: NONE

Dwight Conquergood's *txiv neeb* may have had no trouble crossing the threshold between earth and sky, natural and supernatural, medical and spiritual. Regular mortals find the transit difficult. *How* difficult was borne out to me the night I invited Bill Selvidge and Sukey Waller to dinner at the Red Snapper Seafood Grotto. (Since my experience with Jonas Vangay, I was steering clear of the Cask 'n Cleaver.) Although they knew each other by reputation, Bill and Sukey had never met. I thought that because they were both Peace Corps veterans, and because they both worked with the Hmong—Bill as a doctor, Sukey as a psychotherapist—they would have much in common.

Over our fish, we discussed Hmong shamanism, about which Sukey knew a great deal. She volunteered that she had once told a doctor at MCMC that a *txiv neeb* of her acquaintance had a direct line to God. The doctor had responded, "Well, I have a direct line to biochemistry." Although it was clear where Sukey's sympathies lay, Bill did not appear offended.

By dessert, we had moved on to Lia's case in particular, and cross-cultural pediatrics in general.

"You have to act on behalf of the most vulnerable person in the situation," said Bill, "and that's the child. The child's welfare is more important than the parents' beliefs. You have to do what's best for the child, even if the parents oppose it, because if the child dies, she won't get the chance to decide twenty years down the road if she wants to accept her parents' beliefs or if she wants to reject them. She's going to be dead."

"Well," said Sukey tartly, "that's the job you have taken on in your profession."

"I'd feel the same way if I weren't a doctor," said Bill. "I would feel I am my brother's keeper."

"That's tyranny," said Sukey. "What if you have a family who rejects surgery because they believe an illness has a spiritual cause? What if they see a definite possibility of eternal damnation for their child if she dies from the surgery? Next to that, death might not seem so important. Which is more important, the life or the soul?"

"I make no apology," said Bill. "The life comes first."

"The soul," said Sukey.

19

The Sacrifice

Long before Shee Yee turned into a tiny red ant and bit the evil *dab* on the testicle, he spent three years apprenticed to a sorcerer. He learned how to change himself into anything he wished, to kill *dabs*, to fly like the wind, to heal the sick, and to raise the dead. Shee Yee's services as a healer were sorely needed, because there was much illness in the world.

This is how the illness had come. The wife of a wicked god named Nyong laid an egg as large as a pig house. For three years, the egg did not hatch. Nyong's father chanted to the egg and, in response, heard the jabbering voices of many evil *dabs* inside it. He ordered Nyong to burn the egg, but Nyong refused. So the egg burst, and out swarmed the *dabs*. The first thing they did was to eat Nyong's wife, down to the last bone, hair, and eyelash. Then, still hungry, they came after Nyong. Nyong opened the door that led from the sky, where he lived, to the earth. Through it flew the *dabs*, as big as water buffalos and as red as fire, with showers of sparks in their wake. Nyong was safe, but from that day on, the people of the earth have known illness and death.

Shee Yee spent many years fighting the *dabs* and restoring sick people to health. He was assisted by a winged horse, a bowl of holy water, a set of magical healing tools, and a troupe of familiar spirits.

One day Nyong murdered Shee Yee's infant son and tricked Shee Yee into eating the flesh. When Shee Yee realized what he had done, he was so stricken with grief and horror that he fled the earth and climbed the staircase up through the door in the sky. To avenge his son's death, he pierced both of Nyong's eyes. Nyong, blind and enraged, now lives at the foot of a mountain in the sky, and Shee Yee lives in a cave at its summit, surrounded by his familiar spirits.

Shee Yee never returned to earth, but he did not leave its people entirely at the mercy of illness and death. After he climbed the staircase through the sky, he poured the bowl of holy water into his mouth, and then he spat it, with great force, on his healing tools: a saber, a gong, a rattle, and a pair of finger bells. The tools broke into pieces and fell to earth. Anyone who was sprayed with holy water, or who caught a fragment of one of Shee Yee's tools, was elected to be a *txiv neeb*, a host for a healing spirit. The door in the sky is now closed to everyone but *txiv neebs*. When they pursue the lost soul of a sick person, they summon Shee Yee's familiar spirits and ride Shee Yee's flying horse up the staircase through the sky. In order to deceive any evil *dabs* they may meet en route, they pretend they *are* Shee Yee, and thus they partake of the first healer's cunning, courage, and greatness.

The *txiv neeb* who was to perform a healing ceremony for Lia brought his own tools: saber, gong, rattle, finger bells. He also brought his own flying horse. The horse was a board about ten feet long and ten inches wide which, when attached to a pair of sawhorselike supports that fitted into four slots, became a bench. To the people who filled the Lees' living room, the bench was not a piece of furniture. Nor was it a metaphor. It was truly a flying horse, just as to a devout Roman Catholic, the bread and the wine are not a symbol of Christ's body and blood but the real thing.

The Lees had risen well before dawn. Foua told me, "We must have the *neeb* ceremony early in the morning, when it is cool, because that is when the soul can come back better. Also, if it is hot, the pig will get tired and die." (I thought: But the pig is going to get killed anyway! Then I realized that a dead pig cannot be sacrificed.) The sun was rising when I arrived, sending pale shafts of light through the door that opened onto East 12th Street. Two translucent plastic painter's tarps had been laid over the threadbare brown wall-to-wall carpet to protect it from the blood of the pig—or rather, pigs, since a small pig was to be sacrificed for the whole family and a large pig was to be sacrificed for Lia. The Lees had bought them the previous day at a local farm, paying $225, which came partly from welfare savings and partly from relatives' contributions, for the pair.

On the electric stove, three large aluminum pots, filled with water that would be used to singe the pigs' bristles, had been set to boil. Bags of fresh vegetables and herbs, grown by the Lees and their relatives, rested next to the mortar and pestle Foua had brought from Laos. They would be used in the preparation of the traditional festal dishes: minced pork and vegetables rolled in rice wrappers; pig bones and meat boiled with homegrown greens; chopped intestines, liver, heart, and lungs (the dish May Ying called "doo-doo soup"); raw jellied pig's blood; stewed chicken; two kinds of pepper sauce; and steamed rice. A Hmong proverb says, "With friends, flavorless vegetables are as tasty as meat, and water is as good as wine." However, the combination of friends and good food is better still. The feast, which was to follow the *neeb* ceremony, would continue far into the night.

Early this morning, Nao Kao had used a special paper punch to cut a stack of spirit-money, which would pay the pig for its soul and settle other spiritual accounts. The spirit-money, thick and cream-colored and pinked into scallops, lay on the carpet next to the *txiv neeb*'s altar, which represented the cave of Shee Yee. In Laos, the altar would have been made from one of a pair of identical trees; one would have been left standing, and one would have been felled with an ax in the direction of the setting sun. Here, the altar was a crude wooden table that had been covered with the sports section of the *Merced Sun-Star*. Arrayed on top of a refrigerator ad that said NO DOWN PAYMENT FOR 90 DAYS! were the *txiv neeb*'s sacred tools, the same ones Shee Yee had used: a short saber ornamented with red and white streamers; an ancient iron gong; a monkey bone with a padded end wrapped in black cloth, which was used to beat the gong; a tambourine-sized iron ring strung with rattling metal disks; and two finger bells, which looked like bronze doughnuts and enclosed little tintinnabula made of jingling metal pellets. Next to the tools was a brown plastic bowl containing rice and a single uncooked egg, sustenance for the familiar spirits. Three Styrofoam coffee cups and a white china bowl—a lake into which the *txiv neeb*'s soul could plunge if he were pursued by evil *dabs*—were filled with holy water. A small candle at the front of the altar, not yet lit, would shed light on the unseen realm into which the *txiv neeb* was to travel.

I had read a number of ethnographic commentaries on the power and influence of *txiv neebs*. Somehow, I had never imagined that when I finally met the ultimate metaphysical interlocutor, the great plea-bargainer for the soul, the preeminent champion in the struggle for the demonic—to cite three of the many reverential epithets I had come across—he would be sitting in front of a television set, watching a Winnie-the-Pooh cartoon. The *txiv neeb* who was to perform today's ceremonies was named Cha Koua Lee. He wore blue flip-flops, black pants, and a white T-shirt decorated with dancing pandas. May Ying Xiong had told me all *txiv neebs* were skinny, because they expended so much energy in the shaking trance during which they traveled to the realm of the unseen, and indeed Cha Koua Lee, who looked to be in his late forties, was thin and muscular, with sharp features and a stern expression. It was against his code of honor to charge for his services—especially with the Lees, who were members of his clan—and although some families voluntarily paid him, he was forced to live on public assistance. However, he always received compensation in the form of the heads and right front legs of the pigs over whose sacrifices he presided. After eating the meat, he left the lower jaws to dry outside his apartment, and then added them to a collection he kept on a shelf, to be ritually burned at the end of the Hmong year. At that time the pigs' souls would be released from their duties as proxies for the souls of the people for whom they had given their lives, and allowed to be reborn. In Laos, Cha Koua Lee had burned his pig jaws in a fire pit. In Merced, he burned them in a disposable turkey-roasting pan. Then he placed the charred remains in the branches of a tree outside town, beneath the sky through which they had already journeyed.

After the smaller pig, a tan-and-white female, was carried into the living room and laid on one of the plastic tarps, the *txiv neeb* performed the day's first order of business: a ceremony to safeguard the health and well-being of the family for the coming year. The Lee family stood in a closely packed huddle in the middle of the living room. Wearing a black cloth headdress, the *txiv neeb* tied a cord around the pig's neck. The pig grunted softly. Then he ran the cord from the pig to the Lees, wrapping it tightly around the whole group. The pig's soul was thus bonded to the souls it would protect. The *txiv neeb* regarded each person's soul as a tripartite entity, composed of one part that, after death, would stand guard at the grave; one part that would go to the land of the dead; and one part that would be reincarnated. All three parts would be secured today. Then the pig's throat was slit—by a Lee cousin, not by the *txiv neeb*, who must always maintain good relations with the animals of whom he has requested such a priceless gift.

In Laos, this ceremony would have taken place in the Lees' house, which Nao Kao and Foua had built to shelter not only their family but also a host of kindly domestic spirits: the chief household spirit, who lived in the central pillar, above the place where the placentas of the Lee sons were buried; the spirits of the ancestors, who lived in the four side pillars; the spirits of wealth, who lived near the uphill wall; the spirit who watched over the livestock, who lived in the downhill door; and the spirits of the two fireplaces. The presence of these spirits would have been felt by everyone in the house. It seemed to me that at 37 East 12th Street, Apartment A—where there were no pillars, no fireplaces, and indeed, according to the Lees, no benevolent spirits, because it was rented—the maintenance of a sacred atmosphere was an uphill battle. The television was still on, though without sound. Winnie-the-Pooh had been succeeded by a wrestling match between Hulk Hogan and Randy "Macho Man" Savage, broadcast from Atlantic City. Five feet from the altar, on the other side of the wall, hummed a refrigerator that contained a case of Budweisers, one of which would later be consumed by the *txiv neeb*. To the left of the front door, through which the familiar spirits would pass, there was a king-size carton of Attends youth diapers. The door was open. This worried me. What if an American were to stroll past and see a dead pig on the floor and nine people tied up with twine?

While the *txiv neeb* prepared for the next ceremony, several of the Lees' male relatives carried the slaughtered pig to the parking lot, which, fortunately, was behind the apartment building and could not be seen from the street. First they poured scalding water over the carcass and scraped the hide with knives. Then they expertly gutted the pig, threw the offal in a Rainbow low-suds detergent pail, unfurled and re-coiled the intestines, and rinsed the abdominal cavity with a green garden hose. Rivulets of bloody water, dotted with bits of hair and pig flesh, flowed through the parking lot. Cheng, May, Yer, True, and Mai watched with interest but not surprise. Like children raised on a farm, they were familiar with death, and indeed could probably have done the job themselves. They had all learned how to kill and pluck chickens before they were eight, and the older ones had helped their parents butcher several pigs.

When we walked back inside the apartment, I could tell in an instant that there had been a sea change. By some unaccountable feat of sorcery—I was never able to figure out exactly how it had happened—the bathos had been exorcised from Apartment A. Everyone could feel the difference. The Lee children, who talked and giggled as they walked from the parking lot, fell silent as soon as they crossed the threshold. The television was off. The candle on the altar had been lit. A joss stick was burning, filling the apartment with smoke trails that would guide the familiar spirits. The *txiv neeb* had put on a black silk jacket with indigo cuffs and a red sash. His feet were bare. He had shrugged all the American incongruities off his outer aspect, and his inner aspect—the quality that had singled him out for spiritual election—now shone through, bright and hard. I saw that I had underestimated him.

It was Lia's turn now. Foua and Nao Kao believed that her condition was probably beyond the reach of spiritual healing. Another *txiv neeb* had told them that medicines must have hurt her irreparably, because if the cause were spiritual, the frequency of their *neeb* ceremonies would certainly have restored her ability to talk. However, within her status quo, there were degrees of illness. They hoped this *txiv neeb* would make Lia happier so that she would stop crying at night. And there was still the faintest flicker of a chance, not altogether extinguished even after years of failed sacrifices, that Lia's soul would be found after all, that the *dabs* who were keeping it would accept the pig's soul in its stead, and that she would be restored to health.

Foua sat in the middle of the living room on a red metal folding chair, wearing black pants and a black-and-blue blouse: American clothes, but traditional Hmong colors, the same colors the *txiv neeb* was wearing. A yard of shining black hair fell down her back. Lia sat on her lap, bare-legged, wearing a striped polo shirt and a diaper. Foua nestled Lia's head in the crook of her neck, smoothing her hair and whispering in her ear. Lia fit into the curves of her mother's body as tightly as a newborn infant.

The *txiv neeb* placed a bundle of spirit-money—Lia's expired life-visa, which he would attempt to renew—on the shoulder of her polo shirt. A Lee cousin waved a live brown chicken in the air. It would be sacrificed for Lia's *hu plig*, her soul-calling: a version of the same ceremony that had installed her soul in her body when she was an infant. After it was boiled, the chicken would be examined to find out if Lia's soul had returned. Tight feet, firm eyes, an upcurled tongue, and a translucent cranium would be good auspices. Of these, the most important sign was the feet. A toe which did not match its mates—which, like a Hmong who failed to conform to the group ethic, did not fit gracefully into its community—would signal disharmony and disequilibrium. The cousin chanted to the chicken:

> *I hope your legs are good*
> *I hope your eyes are good*
> *I hope your tongue is good*
> *I hope your beak is good*
> *I hope your head is clear.*

Lia was surrounded by her entire family and by more than twenty of her relatives. Their solicitude converged on her motionless form like sunlight focused by a magnifying glass until it burns. Dee Korda had once said, "Lia knew how to love and how to let people love her." Whatever else she had lost, Lia still knew how to be loved.

Foua kissed Lia's nose and said, "You look very happy!"

One of the cousin's sons took the chicken to the kitchen, quickly sliced its neck, and shook the spurting blood into a plastic garbage bag.

Lia's pig—a bigger, browner one—was carried into the living room, its trotters bound with twine. Because Lia was a girl, her pig was male; their soul-bond would be a kind of marriage. It lay, snorting and struggling, on its plastic tarp. The *txiv neeb* tied a cord around its neck, then wrapped it around the integral unit of Foua and Lia, linking Lia's soul to her mother's as well as to the pig's. He walked the circuit from pig to Foua-and-Lia many times, shaking his rattle loudly so that Lia's soul, wherever it was, would hear it. Then he beat his gong, again and again, to summon his familiar spirits. Finally, he tossed the polished halves of a water-buffalo horn on the floor to divine whether the spirits had heard him. When both horns landed flat side up, the answer was no; when one horn landed flat side up and one horn landed flat side down, the answer was ambiguous; finally, when both horns landed flat side down, he knew that his spirits had all heard their master's call.

The pig had to be paid for the great gift it was about to give Lia. So the *txiv neeb* took a thick sheaf of spirit-money from the floor next to the altar and placed it next to the pig. Squatting low, he spoke quietly to the pig, explaining that it would be well rewarded for its work and that at the end of the year its soul would be set free from its obligations. He threw the divination horns again to see if the pig had accepted. When they told him yes, he thanked the pig, unwound the cord from the pig's neck and from Foua-and-Lia, and brandished his saber to cut Lia's sickness away. Then he took one of the cups from the altar, poured some water in his mouth, and spat it out, as Shee Yee had done, making a trilling noise.

Prrrrrr.

Prrrrrr.

"These are waters of gold and silver," he said. "They will wash the sickness clean."

Prrrrrr.

From the kitchen came the sound of a knife being sharpened.

Two men lifted the pig onto a pair of folding chairs. Three men held it down. A Lee relative stuck it in the neck. It bellowed and thrashed. Another relative held a stainless steel bowl to catch the blood, but a good deal spattered on the plastic tarp, the carpet, and our bare feet. The *txiv neeb* took the pig's spirit-money and held it in the torrent. The blood would indelibly mark the money as belonging to the pig. Calling his familiar spirits, each by name, the *txiv neeb* touched Lia's back with a finger bell he had moistened with the bloody spirit-money. She, too, would now be marked, and any *dabs* who wished her ill would be barred from touching her.

The *txiv neeb* washed away more sickness.

Prrrrrr.

Then he took the spirit-money from Lia's shoulder and placed it on the flank of the sacrificed pig.

With the blood of the pig on her back, Lia could go anywhere in the world—even hundreds of miles away—and still be recognized as the child who needed healing. Since she no longer needed to be within sight of the *txiv neeb*, Foua carried her into the bedroom, laid her tenderly on the double bed, cushioned her legs with the blue blanket the family had brought from Laos, and turned on an electric fan. Lia's gaze, whatever it saw, was focused upward. Her glossy hair floated in the breeze.

Now the *txiv neeb* was ready for the most dangerous part of his mission. Standing in front of the bench, he flipped part of his cloth headdress over his face, completely blocking his sight. When the veil was down, he was blind to this world but able to perceive the realm of the unseen. The veil—along with the incense, the mesmeric iteration of the gong and rattle, and the *txiv neeb*'s own repetitive movements—also helped him enter his ecstatic trance. In Laos he might have used opium, but it was not a necessity. When his familiar spirits were present, he could enter an altered state at will.

The *txiv neeb* sat on Shee Yee's winged horse, crossing and uncrossing his feet on the carpet, doing a rhythmic tap dance as the rattle he held in his right hand and the finger bell he wore on his left hand echoed the sound of his horse's harness bells. Meanwhile, his assistant, a young man who wore black aviator sunglasses, beat the gong to tell the spirits that the journey was beginning. After a little more than half an hour, the assistant placed his hands around the *txiv neeb*'s waist. In a single movement, without missing a beat, the *txiv neeb* rose to his feet and jumped backwards onto the bench. All his familiar spirits were in attendance. Without their aid, his body would have been too heavy for such a leap.

At this point, the *txiv neeb* was risking his life. During his trance, his own soul traveled far from his body, and if he fell before his soul returned, he would die. No one, not even the greatest *txiv neeb* in the world, could help him. Even if he did not fall, he might encounter *dabs* on his journey who wanted him dead, and it would take all his might and guile to fight them off.

The *txiv neeb* started to gallop. Sometimes he was on top of the horse, sometimes on the ground. Sometimes he *was* the horse, neighing and whinnying. He chanted loudly in a minor key, singing ancient incantations that were part Hmong and part Chinese. Even the Lees could not understand him, but they knew he was speaking to his familiar spirits and negotiating with *dabs* for the release of Lia's captive soul.

The front door had been shut for some time, and the room was very hot and close. The air was thick with incense. The gong clanged. The rattle jangled. Someone poured water on the joints of the bench to cool them down. Now the horse was flying up the staircase to the sky. Now the door in the sky was opening. Now the *txiv neeb* was outside Nyong's home. Now he was climbing the mountain to Shee Yee's cave.

While the *txiv neeb* was on his journey, the cousin who had waved the chicken in the air—the soul-caller—opened the front door and stood facing the street. A small table at his feet held the sacrificed chicken, some rice, an egg, and a burning joss stick. In his right hand he held a pair of divination horns, and in his left hand he held a rattle. From time to time he tossed one or the other on the ground, judging the success of his work by the disposition of the horns or the lay of the metal disks.

> *I am calling you*
> *I am calling you*

he chanted to Lia's soul.

> *I have an egg for you*
> *I have rice for you*
> *I have a chicken for you*
> *I have everything waiting for you.*

Inside the apartment, the spirit-money was burned and sent to the realm of the unseen. The gong sounded. The *txiv neeb*'s horse galloped faster and faster. The soul-caller looked out toward East 12th Street and chanted:

> *Where are you?*
> *Where have you gone?*

Are you visiting your brother?
Are you visiting your sister?
Are you visiting your cousin?
Are you looking at a flower?
Are you in Laos?
Are you in Thailand?
Are you in the sky?
Have you gone to the sun?
Have you gone to the moon?
Come home to your house
Come home to your mother
Come home to your father
Come home to your sisters
Come home to your brother
I am calling you!
I am calling you!
Come home through this door
Come home to your family
Come home
Come home
Come home
Come home
Come home
Come home
Come home.

Note on Hmong Orthography, Pronunciation, and Quotations

According to a folktale collected by anthropologist Robert Cooper and his colleagues, the Hmong language once had a written form, and many important things about life and about the journey between death and rebirth were written down in a great book. Unfortunately, the book was eaten by cows and rats. After its disappearance, no text was equal to the task of representing a culture as rich as that of the Hmong, and the Hmong language was therefore spoken but not written.

So matters remained until the end of the nineteenth century. Since then, more than two dozen Hmong writing systems have been devised by missionaries and linguists, based on Chinese characters as well as on Thai, Lao, Vietnamese, and Russian alphabets. There is also a fascinating eighty-one-symbol writing system called Pahawh Hmong—it looks a little like Sanskrit—that was developed in 1959 by Shong Lue Yang, a messianic Hmong leader who was not previously literate in any language. It is used by the Chao Fa, the resistance group that, in reduced numbers, is still waging a guerrilla war against the communist regime in Laos.

To represent the Hmong words in this book, I have used the writing system most generally accepted by both the Hmong people and by linguists: the Romanized Popular Alphabet. RPA, as it is usually called, was devised in 1953 in Laos by three missionary linguists, Linwood Barney, William Smalley, and Yves Bertrais. It represents all the sounds of the Hmong language with Roman letters, using no diacritical marks—a godsend for typists. RPA can be exasperating if you expect it to be phonetic. (For example, *txiv neeb*—a Hmong shaman—is, improbably enough, pronounced "tsi neng." What happened to the *v*? What happened to the *b*? Where did the *ng* come from?) However, if you view it as a kind of code, it is remarkably ingenious and not nearly as difficult as it looks.

The Hmong language is monosyllabic (except for compound words) and, like many Asian languages, tonal. That is, a word's meaning depends not only on its vowel and consonant sounds but on its pitch and on whether the voice rises, falls, or stays on the same level. The most unusual aspect of RPA is that these tones are represented by a word's final consonant. (Words spoken with a mid-tone that neither rises nor falls are the exception: they are spelled without a final consonant.) Most Hmong words end in vowel sounds, so final consonants are always tonal markers and are never pronounced.

For example, *dab*—a spirit—is pronounced "da." (The final *b* indicates the tone, in this case high and level. Because tones are hard to master without hearing them, I am ignoring them in my suggested pronunciations of the other words and phrases here.) *Paj ntaub*—literally, "flower cloth," an intricately worked textile—is pronounced "pa ndow." *Qaug dab peg*—literally, "the spirit catches you and you fall down," the Hmong term for epilepsy—is pronounced "kow da pay."

There are many other aspects of RPA pronunciation, most of them too complex to describe here. I will mention just three. One is that *x* sounds like *s*. Another is that a double vowel represents a nasal sound, like the *ng* in "sing." (These two oddities, along with the fact that the final consonants aren't sounded, explain why *txiv neeb* is pronounced "tsi neng.") A third is that *w* is a vowel, pronounced something like a French *u*. For example, the unlikely-looking word *txwv*—a children's game resembling jacks—is pronounced, roughly, "tsu."

In order to make their own names reasonably easy for Americans to pronounce, the Hmong in the United States do not use RPA for proper nouns. Capitalized words are pronounced more or less the way they are spelled. For example, the word "Hmong," which in RPA would be spelled *Hmoob*, is simply pronounced "Mong," with an almost inaudible aspiration at the beginning of the word. "Lia Lee," which in RPA would be spelled Liab Lis, is pronounced just as you would expect: "Leea Lee."

There are two principal groups of Hmong living in Laos and Thailand, the White Hmong and the Blue Hmong. (White and blue are the colors favored for each group's traditional skirts.) Their dialects are similar but vary slightly in pronunciation. I have used White Hmong spellings in this book.

I have quoted conversations with Hmong people in this book in the forms in which I heard them. That is to say, English-speaking Hmong are quoted verbatim, and non-English-speaking Hmong are quoted in the words my interpreter, May Ying Xiong, used as she translated their comments sentence by sentence. This has the paradoxical effect that highly educated Hmong such as Jonas Vangay and Blia Yao Moua, because of the grammatical idiosyncrasies of their English, seem to speak less "perfectly" than, say, Nao Kao Lee and Foua Yang, whose speech is filtered through an American-educated, and therefore grammatically conventional, interpreter. However, the alternatives—messing up May Ying's translations or cleaning up the speech of English-speaking Hmong—seemed to me far worse. The first was out of the question, and the second would rob the reader of the rich texture of English underlain by Hmong, French, and other languages, as well as removing him or her one further step from my own experience as a listener.

Notes on Sources

In form and intent, this book resembles the Hmong-style Fish Soup described at the beginning of the second chapter. When a Hmong makes Fish Soup, or tells a story, the ingredients tend to come from many different places. My own Fish Soup is similarly eclectic.

The material on Lia Lee is based mostly on interviews. (I relied on these sources for all the chapters about Lia, so I have not repeated their names under the individual chapter headings below.) Family members: Foua Yang, Nao Kao Lee, May Lee, True Lee, Yer Lee. Foster parents: Dee and Tom Korda. Merced Community Medical Center: Teresa Callahan, Benny Douglas, Neil Ernst, Kris Hartwig, Evelyn Marciel, Dan Murphy, Peggy Philp, Gloria Rodriguez, Dave Schneider, Steve Segerstrom, Bill Selvidge, Sharon Yates. Valley Children's Hospital: Terry Hutchison. Merced County Health Department: Effie Bunch, Koua Her, Martin Kilgore, Kia Lee. Child Protective Services: Jeanine Hilt. Schelby Center for Special Education: Zeb Davis, Sunny Lippert. I also drew on Lia's case log at the Merced County Health Department; her file at Child Protective Services, including legal records from the California Superior Court; her medical records at Valley Children's Hospital and Merced Community Medical Center; and her mother's medical records at MCMC. (Since this book was completed, Merced Community Medical Center was leased by a nonprofit corporation called Sutter Health and is now named Sutter Merced Medical Center.)

Conversations with the following people provided insights into various aspects of Hmong culture: Dwight Conquergood, Eric Crystal, Koua Her, Annie Jaisser, Luc Janssens, Kia Lee, Linda Lee, May Lee, Nao Kao Lee, True Lee, Pheng Ly, Blia Yao Moua, Chong Moua, Dang Moua, Moua Kee, Lao Lee Moua, Yia Moua, Court Robinson, Long Thao, Pa Vue Thao, Lee Vang, Peter Vang, Jonas Vangay, Sukey Waller,

John Xiong, Mayko Xiong, May Ying Xiong, Xay Soua Xiong, Yia Thao Xiong, and Foua Yang.

A good deal has been written about the Hmong during the last two decades. The Refugee Studies Center at the University of Minnesota publishes three Hmong bibliographies and a newsletter that reviews recent publications about refugees. These resources helped me navigate the labyrinth of Hmong scholarship.

I would like to single out three books, all of which reappear in more specific contexts below, to which I am especially indebted—and also which I especially enjoyed.

My indispensable historical reference was Keith Quincy's lucid and comprehensive *Hmong: History of a People*.

My understanding of the Hmong character was immeasurably deepened by F. M. Savina's *Histoire des Miao*, an ethnographic and linguistic monograph, unfortunately long out of print, by an empathetic French missionary in Laos and Tonkin. Translations from Savina are mine.

Finally, for inspiration and sheer pleasure, I found myself returning again and again to Charles Johnson's *Dab Neeg Hmoob: Myths, Legends and Folk Tales from the Hmong of Laos*, a bilingual anthology of oral literature, with a splendid introduction and extensive explanatory notes on Hmong culture, collected by a language professor who helped sponsor Minnesota's first Hmong family.

In the notes that follow, I have cited each work's title in full the first time it is mentioned, and used a shortened title on subsequent mentions. The Bibliography on page 313 contains complete references for all cited sources.

1. Birth (pages 3–11)

Foua Yang, Kia Lee, Blia Yao Moua, Chong Moua, Lao Lee Moua, Yia Moua, and John Xiong told me about many of the customs mentioned in this chapter.

Hmong shamanism is described in Jean Mottin, "A Hmong Shaman's Séance"; Dwight Conquergood et al., *I Am a Shaman: A Hmong Life Story with Ethnographic Commentary*; and Charles Johnson, ed., *Dab Neeg Hmoob: Myths, Legends and Folk Tales from the Hmong of Laos*. (I used Johnson's 1983 edition; an edition with an updated introduction was published in 1992.) The latter two works also discuss traditional methods for preventing and curing infertility.

Hmong pregnancy, birth, and postpartum customs are explained in Kou Vang et al., *Hmong Concepts of Illness and Healing with a Hmong/English Glossary*; Gayle S. Potter and Alice Whiren, "Traditional Hmong Birth Customs: A Historical Study"; Ann Bosley, "Of Shamans and Physicians: Hmong and the U.S. Health Care System"; and George M. Scott, Jr., "Migrants Without Mountains: The Politics of Sociocultural Adjustment Among the Lao Hmong Refugees in San Diego." Scott's dissertation contains a wealth of information on many topics; I have used it throughout this book. The description of the placenta as a Hmong's first and finest garment is from Charles

Johnson, *Dab Neeg Hmoob*, and the account of its posthumous journey is from Ruth Hammond, "Tradition Complicates Hmong Choice."

Background on the Hmong clan system is from Tou-Fou Vang, "The Hmong of Laos," and Timothy Dunnigan, "Segmentary Kinship in an Urban Society: The Hmong of St. Paul-Minneapolis."

Five works by Bruce Thowpaou Bliatout, the leading Hmong authority on health issues, examine traditional views on the causes of illness, including soul loss: "Causes and Treatment of Hmong Mental Health Problems"; "Hmong Beliefs About Health and Illness"; "Traditional Hmong Beliefs on the Causes of Illness"; "Guidelines for Mental Health Professionals to Help Hmong Clients Seek Traditional Healing Treatment"; and *Hmong Sudden Unexpected Nocturnal Death Syndrome: A Cultural Study*. Other sources on this topic are Xoua Thao, "Hmong Perception of Illness and Traditional Ways of Healing"; Elizabeth S. Kirton, "The Locked Medicine Cabinet: Hmong Health Care in America"; Nusit Chindarsi, *The Religion of the Hmong Njua*; Ann Bosley, "Of Shamans and Physicians"; Kou Vang et al., *Hmong Concepts of Illness and Healing*; and Charles Johnson, *Dab Neeg Hmoob*. On infant soul loss and soul-retaining clothing, see Eric Crystal, "Buffalo Heads and Sacred Threads: Hmong Culture of the Southeast Asian Highlands"; Jane Hamilton-Merritt, "Hmong and Yao: Mountain Peoples of Southeast Asia"; and Paul and Elaine Lewis, *Peoples of the Golden Triangle*.

The baby-naming ceremony is described in Nusit Chindarsi, *The Religion of the Hmong Njua*, and Gayle S. Potter and Alice Whiren, "Traditional Hmong Birth Customs."

2. Fish Soup (pages 12–19)

Luc Janssens told me the Fish Soup story.

My summary of Hmong history from ancient times until the early twentieth century is deeply indebted to Keith Quincy's *Hmong: History of a People*. (I relied primarily on the 1988 edition; a revised edition was published in 1995.) Were I citing the source of each detail, Quincy's name would attach itself to nearly every sentence in the pages on the Hmong in China.

I drew many ideas from F. M. Savina's *Histoire des Miao*. The story of King Sonom, also retold by Quincy, comes from an extraordinary contemporary document, a 1775 letter by a French missionary in China named Joseph Amiot, which Savina reproduces in full.

Other useful works on Hmong history include Jean Mottin's charming *History of the Hmong*; W. R. Geddes, *Migrants of the Mountains: The Cultural Ecology of the Blue Miao (Hmong Njua) of Thailand*, the standard anthropological study of the Hmong; Hugo Adolf Bernatzik, *Akha and Miao: Problems of Applied Ethnography in Farther India*; Sucheng Chan, *Hmong Means Free: Life in Laos and America*; and Yang See Koumarn and G. Linwood Barney, "The Hmong: Their History and Culture."

Background on the terms "Miao," "Meo," and "Hmong" is from the above sources (Bernatzik is the most detailed), and also from Yang Dao, *Hmong at the Turning*

Point, and Christopher Robbins, *The Ravens: The Men Who Flew in America's Secret War in Laos*.

The passage by anthropologist Robert Cooper is from his *Resource Scarcity and the Hmong Response*.

3. The Spirit Catches You and You Fall Down (pages 20–31)

Delores J. Cabezut-Ortiz, *Merced County: The Golden Harvest*, recounts how Tony Coelho was rejected by the Jesuits because of his epilepsy. Blia Yao Moua told me about the offer to perform a Hmong healing ceremony for Coelho in Merced.

On becoming a *txiv neeb*: Dwight Conquergood, *I Am a Shaman*; Jacques Lemoine, "Shamanism in the Context of Hmong Resettlement"; Bruce Thowpaou Bliatout, "Traditional Hmong Beliefs"; and Kathleen Ann Culhane-Pera, "Description and Interpretation of a Hmong Shaman in St. Paul."

On how Hmong parents treat their children: Hugo Adolf Bernatzik, *Akha and Miao*; Nusit Chindarsi, *The Religion of the Hmong Njua*; Brenda Jean Cumming, "The Development of Attachment in Two Groups of Economically Disadvantaged Infants and Their Mothers: Hmong Refugee and Caucasian-American"; E. M. Newlin-Haus, "A Comparison of Proxemic and Selected Communication Behavior of Anglo-American and Hmong Refugee Mother-Infant Pairs"; Charles N. Oberg et al., "A Cross-Cultural Assessment of Maternal-Child Interaction: Links to Health and Development"; and Wendy Walker-Moffat, *The Other Side of the Asian American Success Story*.

The information on Merced Community Medical Center was provided by Vi Colunga, Arthur DeNio, Doreen Faiello, Ed Hughell, Liz Lorenzi, Betty Maddalena, Marilyn Mochel, Dan Murphy, Theresa Schill, Bill Selvidge, Betty Wetters, and Janice Wilkerson.

The Hmong population of Merced City is an estimate based on projections from the 1990 census. It attempts to take into account new refugees from Thailand, secondary migrants from other parts of the United States, and births (using Hmong, not American, birthrates). The Demographic Research Unit of the California Department of Finance and Rhonda Walton at the Merced Human Services Agency provided assistance.

Much of the information here and elsewhere on the medical aspects of epilepsy is drawn from conversations with neurologist Elizabeth Engle of Boston Children's Hospital and with Neil Ernst and Peggy Philp of Merced Community Medical Center. I also found these works helpful: Owen B. Evans, *Manual of Child Neurology*; Orrin Devinsky, *A Guide to Understanding and Living with Epilepsy*; Robert Berkow, ed., *The Merck Manual of Diagnosis and Therapy*; Alan Newman, "Epilepsy: Light from the Mind's Dark Corner"; and Jane Brody, "Many People Still Do Not Understand Epilepsy." Eve LaPlante discusses the relationship between epilepsy and creativity in *Seized: Temporal Lobe Epilepsy as a Medical, Historical, and Artistic Phenomenon*. Owsei Temkin recounts the history of epilepsy in his fascinating work *The Falling Sickness: A History of Epilepsy from the Greeks to the Beginnings of Modern Neurology*. The Hippocrates quotation is from *On the Sacred Disease*, quoted in Richard Restak, *The Brain*; the Dostoyevsky quotation is from *The Idiot*.

4. Do Doctors Eat Brains? (pages 32-37)

Mao Thao's visit to Ban Vinai is recounted in "Hmong Medical Interpreter Fields Questions from Curious," and in Marshall Hurlich et al., "Attitudes of Hmong Toward a Medical Research Project."

Hmong health care taboos, and the differences between *txiv neebs* and doctors, are discussed in Charles Johnson, *Dab Neeg Hmoob*; Dwight Conquergood et al., *I Am a Shaman*; Ann Bosley, "Of Shamans and Physicians"; Elizabeth S. Kirton, "The Locked Medicine Cabinet"; John Finck, "Southeast Asian Refugees of Rhode Island: Cross-Cultural Issues in Medical Care"; Joseph Westermeyer and Xoua Thao, "Cultural Beliefs and Surgical Procedures"; Marjorie Muecke, "In Search of Healers: Southeast Asian Refugees in the American Health Care System"; Scott Wittet, "Information Needs of Southeast Asian Refugees in Medical Situations"; and two works by Bruce Thowpaou Bliatout, "Hmong Refugees: Some Barriers to Some Western Health Care Services" and "Hmong Attitudes Towards Surgery: How It Affects Patient Prognosis." See also the five Bliatout sources on the causes of illness cited under Chapter 1.

Asian dermal treatments are described in Donna Schreiner, "Southeast Asian Folk Healing"; Lana Montgomery, "Folk Medicine of the Indochinese"; and Anh Nguyen et al., "Folk Medicine, Folk Nutrition, Superstitions." Koua Her, Kia Lee, Chong Moua, and Foua Yang also explained these treatments to me.

Jean-Pierre Willem tells the story of the typhoid epidemic at Nam Yao in *Les naufragés de la liberté: Le dernier exode des Méos*. Catherine Pake presents her research at Phanat Nikhom in "Medicinal Ethnobotany of Hmong Refugees in Thailand." Dwight Conquergood describes his health program at Ban Vinai in my hands-down favorite account of working with the Hmong: "Health Theatre in a Hmong Refugee Camp: Performance, Communication, and Culture."

5. Take as Directed (pages 38–59)

I first met the concept of "angor animi" in *Migraine*, by Oliver Sacks.

The side effects of anticonvulsant drugs are noted in Orrin Devinsky, *A Guide to Understanding and Living with Epilepsy*; Warren Leary, "Valium Found to Reduce Fever Convulsions"; and *Physicians' Desk Reference*. (I used the 1987 edition of the *PDR* here and elsewhere because it is roughly contemporaneous with Lia's case.) In the opinion of pediatric neurologist Elizabeth Engle of Boston Children's Hospital, the studies on phenobarbital's association with lowered I.Q. scores are not conclusive. She believes it is a safe drug.

Blia Yao Moua, Dia Xiong, Vishwa Kapoor, and Vonda Crouse told me about the case of Arnie Vang. It is also described in Pablo Lopez, "Hmong Mother Holds Off Police Because of Fear for Her Children."

6. High-Velocity Transcortical Lead Therapy (pages 60–77)

Most of the works cited under Chapter 4 were also useful here. Two particularly helpful introductions to Hmong health care issues are Ann Bosley, "Of Shamans and Physicians," and Elizabeth S. Kirton, "The Locked Medicine Cabinet."

Rumors about life in America are mentioned in Bruce Thowpaou Bliatout, *Hmong Sudden Unexpected Nocturnal Death Syndrome*, and Marc Kaufman, "Why the Hmong Spurn America." May Ying Xiong and Long Thao also told me about some of these rumors.

Koua Her, Kia Lee, Linda Lee, Nao Kao Lee, Blia Yao Moua, Chong Moua, Dang Moua, Moua Kee, Lao Lee Moua, Long Thao, Pa Vue Thao, Lee Vang, Peter Vang, Jonas Vangay, Sukey Waller, John Xiong, Xay Soua Xiong, Yia Thao Xiong, and Foua Yang helped me understand Hmong attitudes toward doctors. John Aleman, Steve Ames, Raquel Arias, Nancy Brockington, Teresa Callahan, Rick Dehn, Benny Douglas, Donna Earle, Neil Ernst, Doreen Faiello, Roger Fife, Kris Hartwig, Tim Johnston, Martin Kilgore, Phyllis Lee, Mari Mockus, Dan Murphy, Karen Olmos, Peggy Philp, Dave Schneider, Steve Segerstrom, Bill Selvidge, Barbara Showalter, Robert Small, Tom Sult, Richard Welch, and Fern Wickstrom helped me understand health care workers' attitudes toward the Hmong.

Alan M. Kraut has written a cogent historical summary of immigrant health issues, "Healers and Strangers: Immigrant Attitudes Toward the Physician in America—A Relationship in Historical Perspective," and a comprehensive book on the subject, *Silent Travelers: Germs, Genes, and the "Immigrant Menace."*

The challenges of treating Hmong patients in Merced are described in "Salmonellosis Following a Hmong Celebration"; Thomas Neil Ernst et al., "The Effect of Southeast Asian Refugees on Medical Services in a Rural County"; and Doreen Faiello, "Translation Please."

The Hmong-English medical glossary mentioned here is Thai Fang, *Tuabneeg Lubcev Hab Kev Mobnkeeg Rua Cov Haslug Hmoob: Basic Human Body and Medical Information for Hmong Speaking People.*

Other sources on Hmong health care include Scott Wittet, "Information Needs of Southeast Asian Refugees"; Kathleen Ann Culhane-Pera, "Analysis of Cultural Beliefs and Power Dynamics in Disagreements about Health Care of Hmong Children"; Marjorie Muecke, "Caring for Southeast Asian Refugee Patients in the USA"; Amos S. Deinard and Timothy Dunnigan, "Hmong Health Care: Reflections on a Six-Year Experience"; Debra Buchwald et al., "Use of Traditional Health Practices by Southeast Asian Refugees in a Primary Care Clinic"; Roy V. Erickson and Giao Ngoc Hoang, "Health Problems Among Indochinese Refugees"; Agatha Gallo et al., "Little Refugees with Big Needs"; and Rita Bayer Leyn, "The Challenge of Caring for Child Refugees from Southeast Asia."

On somatization: Joseph Westermeyer et al., "Somatization Among Refugees: An Epidemiologic Study."

On pregnancy and childbirth: James M. Nyce and William H. Hollinshead,

"Southeast Asian Refugees of Rhode Island: Reproductive Beliefs and Practices Among the Hmong"; Andrea Hollingsworth et al., "The Refugees and Childbearing: What to Expect"; Linda Todd, "Indochinese Refugees Bring Rich Heritages to Childbearing"; Peter Kunstadter, "Pilot Study of Differential Child Survival Among Various Ethnic Groups in Northern Thailand and California"; Helen Stewart Faller, "Hmong Women: Characteristics and Birth Outcomes, 1990"; Deanne Erickson et al., "Maternal and Infant Outcomes Among Caucasians and Hmong Refugees in Minneapolis, Minnesota"; and Deborah Helsel et al., "Pregnancy Among the Hmong: Birthweight, Age, and Parity."

On the high Hmong birthrate: Rubén Rumbaut and John R. Weeks, "Fertility and Adaptation: Indochinese Refugees in the United States," which provides fertility-rate statistics; Wendy D. Walker, "The Other Side of the Asian Academic Success Myth: The Hmong Story"; George M. Scott, Jr., "Migrants Without Mountains"; "Making Up for the Ravages of Battle: Hmong Birthrate Subject of Merced Study"; and Donald A. Ranard, "The Last Bus."

The fertility rates for white and black Americans are from the Population Branch of the U.S. Census Bureau. Note that "fertility rate" means not the average number of children that a group of women of various ages have at a given time, but the average number of children they have during their entire childbearing lives. The first statistic would be lower, since it would include women who had not yet completed their childbearing.

7. Government Property (pages 78–92)

The information on reporting child abuse is from "Child Abuse Laws: What Are Your Obligations?" and from the National Clearinghouse on Child Abuse and Neglect. The legal conflict between religious freedom and the obligation to provide medical care for one's children is reported in Martin Halstuk, "Religious Freedom Collides with Medical Care"; David Margolick, "In Child Deaths, a Test for Christian Science"; "Court Says Ill Child's Interests Outweigh Religion"; James Feron, "Can Choosing Form of Care Become Neglect?"; and Caroline Fraser, "Suffering Children and the Christian Science Church." Kathleen Ann Culhane-Pera, "Analysis of Cultural Beliefs and Power Dynamics," is a penetrating study of the problem from the Hmong perspective.

Justice Robert Jackson's statement about parents making martyrs of their children is from *Prince v. Massachusetts*, 321 U.S. 158, 170 (1943).

Linda Greenhouse, "Christian Scientists Rebuffed in Ruling by Supreme Court," and Stephen L. Carter, "The Power of Prayer, Denied," discuss the case of *McKown v. Lundman*.

Useful background information was provided by CHILD (Children's Healthcare Is a Legal Duty), an organization founded by Rita Swan, a former Christian Scientist whose sixteen-month-old son died of meningitis.

8. Foua and Nao Kao (pages 93–105)

My sources on Hmong etiquette included Charles Johnson, *Dab Neeg Hmoob*; Don Willcox, *Hmong Folklife*; and "Social/Cultural Customs: Similarities and Differences Between Vietnamese—Cambodians—H'Mong—Lao."

The tale of the Hmong princess who mistook her rescuer for a hungry eagle is from Charles Johnson, *Dab Neeg Hmoob*. The tale of the arrogant official who was turned into a mouse is from W. R. Geddes, *Migrants of the Mountains*. Keith Quincy, *Hmong*, notes that Hmong were forced to crawl when they approached Lao officials.

The traditional Hmong divisions of the year and the day are described in W. R. Geddes, *Migrants of the Mountains*; Yang See Koumarn and G. Linwood Barney, "The Hmong"; Charles Johnson, *Dab Neeg Hmoob*; and Ernest E. Heimbach, *White Hmong-English Dictionary*.

For more on *paj ntaub*, see Paul and Elaine Lewis, *Peoples of the Golden Triangle*; George M. Scott, Jr., "Migrants Without Mountains"; Egle Victoria Žygas, "Flower Cloth"; and Michele B. Gazzolo, "Spirit Paths and Roads of Sickness: A Symbolic Analysis of Hmong Textile Design."

9. A Little Medicine and a Little *Neeb* (pages 106–118)

Jacques Lemoine, "Shamanism," and Dwight Conquergood et al., *I Am a Shaman*, contain sympathetic interpretations of Hmong animal sacrifice. The following describe the sacrificial practices of other sects, chiefly Santería: Jeffrey Schmalz, "Animal Sacrifices: Faith or Cruelty?"; Richard N. Ostling, "Shedding Blood in Sacred Bowls"; Larry Rohter, "Court to Weigh Law Forbidding Ritual Sacrifice"; Russell Miller, "A Leap of Faith"; and Lizette Alvarez, "A Once-Hidden Faith Leaps into the Open."

Merced's ban on animal slaughter is reported in Ken Carlson, "Hmong Leaders Seek Exemption" and "Sacrifice Ban Remains," and Mike De La Cruz, "Animal Slaughtering Not All Ritualistic" and "Charges Filed After Animal Slaughtering Probe."

Bruce Thowpaou Bliatout, *Hmong Sudden Unexpected Nocturnal Death Syndrome*, explains the ploy of changing a sick person's name in order to fool the soul-stealing *dab*.

Thomas Neil Ernst and Margaret Philp, "Bacterial Tracheitis Caused by *Branhamella catarrhalis*," discusses Lia Lee's tracheal infection.

10. War (pages 119–139)

Here, as elsewhere, all the stories and quotations from F. M. Savina are from his *Histoire des Miao*. Jonas Vangay told me about the Hmong language's rich stock of mountain vocabulary. Jean Mottin, *History of the Hmong*, classifies the ethnic groups of Laos by altitude. George M. Scott, Jr., "Migrants Without Mountains," contains a nuanced discussion of Hmong attitudes toward the lowland Lao. The intimate relation between the Hmong of Laos and their natural environment is explored in Eric Crystal,

"Buffalo Heads and Sacred Threads"; Keith Quincy, *Hmong*; Paul and Elaine Lewis, *Peoples of the Golden Triangle*; Don Willcox, *Hmong Folklife*; Charles Johnson, *Dab Neeg Hmoob*; and Charles Johnson and Ava Dale Johnson, *Six Hmong Folk Tales Retold in English*. Christine Sutton, ed., "The Hmong of Laos," and Yang See Koumarn and G. Linwood Barney, "The Hmong," also provide good basic background on traditional village life.

The onomatopoeic phrases are from Martha Ratcliff's fascinating linguistic study, "Two-Word Expressives in White Hmong." Ratcliff notes that her translations of these expressions are not definitions but associations; many of the expressions have multiple associations.

Two works by William Smalley, *Phonemes and Orthography* and "Adaptive Language Strategies of the Hmong: From Asian Mountains to American Ghettos," make interesting distinctions between illiteracy, the inability to read within a literate culture, and preliteracy, the inability to read within an oral culture. W. J. Ong, *Orality and Literacy: The Technologizing of the Word*, notes the magical potency of the word in oral cultures.

Sources on opium include Sucheng Chan, *Hmong Means Free*; Alfred W. McCoy, *The Politics of Heroin: CIA Complicity in the Global Drug Trade*; Yang Dao, "Why Did the Hmong Leave Laos?"; Ken Hoffman, "Background on the Hmong of Laos"; W. R. Geddes, *Migrants of the Mountains*; Robert Cooper, *Resource Scarcity*; Christopher Robbins, *The Ravens*; Yang See Koumarn and G. Linwood Barney, "The Hmong"; Paul and Elaine Lewis, *Peoples of the Golden Triangle*; and Keith Quincy, *Hmong*. It is Quincy who tells the legend of the opium poppy that grew from the grave of the promiscuous Hmong girl.

Many of the above works also touch on the Hmong migrant identity, as does Nusit Chindarsi, *The Religion of the Hmong Njua*. The most detailed source is Cheu Thao, "Hmong Migration and Leadership in Laos and in the United States." For a thought-provoking rebuttal of the idea that Hmong migration is a cultural phenomenon, see Ray Hutchison, *Acculturation in the Hmong Community*.

My account of the war in Laos was enriched by Jonas Vangay; Vincent Demma, of the Center for Military History; Yvonne Kincaid, of the Air Force Research division; writer Gayle Morrison; and historian Gary Stone.

Within the extensive corpus of work on the war, three nonacademic accounts deserve special mention. The first is Jane Hamilton-Merritt's *Tragic Mountains: The Hmong, the Americans, and the Secret Wars for Laos, 1942–1992*. This ambitious book is essential reading for anyone interested in the Hmong. It has caused some controversy in scholarly circles because of the author's partisan support of Vang Pao and her convictions about yellow rain. However, Hamilton-Merritt's wealth of eyewitness reporting and her passionate commitment to the Hmong people are unmatched. The second is Christopher Robbins's *The Ravens*, a swashbuckling but well-researched account of the U.S. Air Force pilots recruited by the CIA to fly in the Laos war. I have drawn many details from it. The third is Roger Warner, *Back Fire: The CIA's Secret War in Laos and Its Link to the War in Vietnam*, which tells the story of the war by focusing on a few principal players. Most are American, but there is much on Vang

Pao that I have read nowhere else. Warner's book has since been republished in somewhat different form as *Shooting at the Moon: The Story of America's Clandestine War in Laos*.

My understanding of the war also depended on many previously mentioned works, especially Keith Quincy, *Hmong*; Yang Dao, *Hmong at the Turning Point*; Jean Mottin, *History of the Hmong*; and Elizabeth S. Kirton, "The Locked Medicine Cabinet." One of the least confusing summaries of the conflict can be found in Joan Strouse, "Continuing Themes in U.S. Educational Policy for Immigrants and Refugees: The Hmong Experience." I also drew on Victor Marchetti and John D. Marks, *The CIA and the Cult of Intelligence*; Stan Sesser, "Forgotten Country"; Tom Hamburger and Eric Black, "Uprooted People in Search of a Home"; Donald A. Ranard, "The Hmong: No Strangers to Change"; W. E. Garrett, "No Place to Run"; Clark Clifford, *Counsel to the President*; William E. Colby, testimony to the House Subcommittee on Asia and the Pacific, April 26, 1994; Toby Alice Volkman, "Unexpected Bombs Take Toll in Laos, Too"; and Henry Kamm, "Decades-Old U.S. Bombs Still Killing Laotians."

American Foreign Policy, 1950–1955: Basic Documents; *American Foreign Policy: Current Documents, 1962*; "Text of Cease-Fire Agreement Signed by Laotian Government and the Pathet Lao"; and *Dictionary of American History* helped me decipher the international agreements involving Laos and Vietnam.

I have quoted from the following pieces of contemporary reporting: Hugh Greenway, "The Pendulum of War Swings Wider in Laos"; Don Schanche, "The Yankee 'King' of Laos"; "Laos: The Silent Sideshow"; Michael T. Malloy, "Anti-Communists Also Win Battles in War-Torn Laos"; "'Reds' Advance in Laos Menaces Hill Strongholds of Meo Tribe"; Henry Kamm, "Meo General Leads Tribesmen in War with Communists in Laos"; Robert Shaplen, "Letter from Laos"; Nancy Shulins, "Transplanted Hmong Struggle to Adjust in U.S."; and "Rice in the Sky."

The CIA film that praised Vang Pao was "Journey from Pha Dong." The transcript was by Vang Yang.

Roger Warner, *Back Fire*; Victor Marchetti and John D. Marks, *The CIA*; and Alfred W. McCoy, *The Politics of Heroin*, examine the role opium played in the Laos war, as does the PBS broadcast "Frontline: Guns, Drugs and the CIA." Frontline and McCoy report an intimate connection between the CIA and the opium trade; Warner believes some of their allegations are exaggerated.

Jane Hamilton-Merritt, *Tragic Mountains*, and Sterling Seagrave, *Yellow Rain: Chemical Warfare—The Deadliest Arms Race*, present the case for the existence of mycotoxic yellow rain. The opposing view is presented most exhaustively in Lois Ember, "Yellow Rain"; and also in Thomas Whiteside, "The Yellow-Rain Complex," and Thomas Seeley et al., "Yellow Rain."

11. The Big One (pages 140–153)

As they did throughout the book, Neil Ernst and Peggy Philp helped me fathom the medical material in this chapter. Elizabeth Engle, Robert Kaye, and especially Fred Holley also cleared up many points of confusion. Sherwin B. Nuland, *How We Die:*

Reflections on Life's Final Chapter, helped me understand septic shock; Robert Berkow, *The Merck Manual*, explained disseminated intravascular coagulation.

12. Flight (pages 154–170)

May Lee sent me her autobiographical essay.

George Dalley, Randall Flynn, Bob Hearn, Tony Kaye, Blia Yao Moua, Jonas Vangay, and Jennifer Veech all joined in the hunt for the precise location and spelling of the Lees' village, Houaysouy. True Lee definitively pinned it down. Good sources on the geography of Laos include the 1:100,000-scale map published by the Service Géographique d'Etat of the République Democratique Populaire Lao and *Laos: Official Standard Names Approved by the United States Board on Geographic Names*.

Yang Dao, Paul DeLay, Dennis Grace, Bob Hearn, Marc Kaufman, Blia Yao Moua, Dang Moua, Moua Kee, Court Robinson, Hiram Ruiz, Vang Pobzeb, Jonas Vangay, May Ying Xiong, Xay Soua Xiong, and Yia Thao Xiong clarified many aspects of the postwar period in Laos and Thailand.

Many of the sources cited under Chapter 10—most instructively, Stan Sesser, "Forgotten Country," and Yang Dao, *Hmong at the Turning Point* and "Why Did the Hmong Leave Laos?"—recount the fate of the Hmong in postwar Laos. Souvanna Phouma's comment on the liquidation of the Hmong is quoted, in varying translations, in Yang Dao, *Hmong at the Turning Point*; Keith Quincy, *Hmong*; and Roger Warner, *Back Fire*. Jane Hamilton-Merritt, *Tragic Mountains*, quotes the Vientiane Domestic Service radio broadcast on the Hmong decampment. The background on Neo Hom is from Marc Kaufman, "As Keeper of the Hmong Dream, He Draws Support and Skepticism"; Ruth Hammond, "Sad Suspicions of a Refugee Ripoff"; and Seth Mydans, "California Says Laos Refugee Group Has Been Extorted by Its Leadership."

The following helped me reconstruct the experience of fleeing on foot to Thailand: Henry Kamm, "Meo, Hill People Who Fought for U.S., Are Fleeing from Laos"; May Xiong and Nancy D. Donnelly, "My Life in Laos"; David L. Moore, *Dark Sky, Dark Land: Stories of the Hmong Boy Scouts of Troop 100*; Arlene Bartholome, "Escape from Laos Told"; Dominica P. Garcia, "In Thailand, Refugees' 'Horror and Misery,' "; and Matt Franjola, "Meo Tribesmen from Laos Facing Death in Thailand." Hmong funeral customs are detailed in Kou Vang, *Hmong Concepts of Illness and Healing*. The story of the Israeli child who was accidentally smothered by her mother is from Roger Rosenblatt, *Children of War*.

On Thai refugee camps and refugee politics, I consulted David Feith, *Stalemate: Refugees in Asia*; Lynellen Long, "Refugee Camps as a Way of Life" and *Ban Vinai: The Refugee Camp*; Court Robinson, "Laotian Refugees in Thailand: The Thai and U.S. Response, 1975 to 1988"; Jean-Pierre Willem, *Les naufragés de la liberté*; Henry Kamm, "Thailand Finds Indochinese Refugees a Growing Problem"; Donald A. Ranard, "The Last Bus"; Marc Kaufman, "Why the Hmong Spurn America"; Joseph Cerquone, *Refugees from Laos: In Harm's Way*; and Jim Mann and Nick B. Williams, Jr., "Shultz Cool to New Indochina Refugee Effort." The Dwight Conquergood passages are from "Health Theatre."

Two even-handed discussions of repatriation to Laos, voluntary and otherwise, are Marc Kaufman, "Casualties of Peace," and Lionel Rosenblatt, testimony to the House Subcommittee on Asia and the Pacific, April 26, 1994.

The most reliable source of information on refugee issues worldwide is the *World Refugee Survey*, published annually by the U.S. Committee for Refugees in Washington, D.C. I have drawn many facts and figures from it.

The story of Shee Yee is from Charles Johnson, *Dab Neeg Hmoob*. It is greatly condensed, but my phrasing hews as closely as possible to that of Johnson's informant, Pa Chou Yang.

13. Code X (pages 171–180)

The Hmong New Year is described in Kou Vang, *Hmong Concepts of Illness and Healing*; Keith Quincy, *Hmong*; and W. R. Geddes, *Migrants of the Mountains*. Kathleen Ann Culhane-Pera, "Analysis of Cultural Beliefs and Power Dynamics," helped me understand the Hmong taboo against foretelling a death, as did conversations with Koua Her, Kia Lee, Chong Moua, and Long Thao.

14. The Melting Pot (pages 181–209)

Several previously cited works provide particularly accessible or interesting entrées into the Hmong experience in the United States. "Migrants Without Mountains," George Scott's dissertation on the Hmong of San Diego, is the most intelligent study of Hmong acculturation I have read. *Hmong Means Free*, a collection of interviews with a long historical introduction by Sucheng Chan, contains absorbing oral histories of five Hmong families in California, though her sample is heavily skewed toward Christian converts. *Acculturation in the Hmong Community*, Ray Hutchison's study of Hmong in northern Wisconsin, thoughtfully challenges many stereotypes. Two useful brief overviews are Timothy Dunnigan et al., "Hmong," and the Hmong chapter in Sanford J. Ungar, *Fresh Blood: The New American Immigrants*. *The Hmong Resettlement Study*, a comprehensive government report, is a trove of information, interviews, and recommendations on how refugee programs might be improved.

Father Edward Avery, Toyo Biddle, Loren Bussert, Yee Chang, Eric Crystal, Paul DeLay, Timothy Dunnigan, Francesca Farr, Tim Gordon, Glenn Hendricks, Marc Kaufman, Sue Levy, Blia Yao Moua, Dang Moua, Ron Munger, George Schreider, Peter Vang, Jonas Vangay, Doug Vincent, John Xiong, and May Ying Xiong provided helpful background information.

The Ford Motor Company Americanization classes are described in Stephen Meyer, *The Five Dollar Day*; Stephan Thernstrom, "Ethnic Groups in American History"; and Joan Strouse, "Continuing Themes in U.S. Educational Policy." Jacques Lemoine, "Shamanism," comments on the Hmong resistance to assimilation. Marc Kaufman, "Why the Hmong Are Fleeing America's Helping Hand," reports Vang Pao's request for land, as well as other details of acculturation that I have mined throughout this chapter. Eric Martin, "Hmong in French Guyana: An Improbable

Gamble," discusses the South American settlements, about which Bruce Downing, Father Daniel Taillez, and Yang Dao provided further details.

The resettlement bureaucracy is described in Richard Lee Yamasaki, "Resettlement Status of the Hmong Refugees in Long Beach," and Robert E. Marsh, "Socio-economic Status of Indochinese Refugees in the United States: Progress and Problems." The adaptation study in which Hmong complained about American agencies is Woodrow Jones, Jr., and Paul Strand, "Adaptation and Adjustment Problems Among Indochinese Refugees." Ruth Hammond, "Tradition Complicates Hmong Choice," and Joseph Westermeyer, "Prevention of Mental Disorder Among Hmong Refugees in the U.S.: Lessons from the Period 1976–1986," describe efforts to convert Hmong to Christianity. The Westermeyer article also takes a critical look at the policy of dispersing Hmong refugees, as do Stephen P. Morin, "Many Hmong, Puzzled by Life in U.S., Yearn for Old Days in Laos"; Simon M. Fass, "Through a Glass Darkly: Cause and Effect in Refugee Resettlement Policies"; and Frank Viviano, "Strangers in the Promised Land."

The ordeal of the Yang family in Fairfield, Iowa, is chronicled by Calvin Trillin, "Resettling the Yangs," and Wayne King, "New Life's Cultural Demons Torture Laotian Refugee."

The helpful hints for newly arrived Southeast Asian refugees are from "Your New Life in the United States." Journalistic characterizations of the Hmong are from Seth Mydans, "California Says Laos Refugee Group Has Been Extorted"; Frank W. Martin, "A CIA-Backed Guerrilla Who Waged a Secret War in Laos Puts Down Roots in Montana"; Nancy Shulins, "Transplanted Hmong Struggle to Adjust"; Stephen P. Morin, "Many Hmong"; and Susan Vreeland, "Through the Looking Glass with the Hmong of Laos." The angry letter to the editor about the "primitive" epithet is Paul Pao Herr, "Don't Call Hmong Refugees 'Primitive.' "

"Bangungut" is the deliciously hysterical editorial on Sudden Unexpected Death Syndrome. For background on this syndrome, which was called Sudden Unexpected Nocturnal Death Syndrome until several daytime deaths were reported, see Jacques Lemoine and Christine Mougne, "Why Has Death Stalked the Refugees?"; Bruce Thowpaou Bliatout, *Hmong Sudden Unexpected Nocturnal Death Syndrome*; Ronald Munger, "Sudden Death in Sleep of Asian Adults" and "Sudden Death in Sleep of Laotian-Hmong Refugees in Thailand: A Case-Control Study"; and Ronald Munger and Elizabeth Booton, "Thiamine and Sudden Death in Sleep of South-East Asian Refugees."

Senator Alan Simpson's characterization of the Hmong as "indigestible" is from Dwight Conquergood, "Health Theatre." Rumors about the Hmong are reported in Charles Johnson, "Hmong Myths, Legends and Folk Tales," and Roger Mitchell, "The Will to Believe and Anti-Refugee Rumors."

Examples of anti-Hmong vandalism and violence come from Tom Hamburger and Eric Black, "Uprooted People"; Eddie A. Calderon, "The Impact of Indochinese Resettlement on the Phillips and Elliot Park Neighborhoods in South Minneapolis"; David L. Moore, *Dark Sky, Dark Land*; Stephen P. Morin, "Many Hmong"; Margot Hornblower, " 'Hmongtana' "; Dennis R. Getto, "Hmong Families Build New Lives";

Richard Abrams, "Cross Burnings Terrify, Bewilder Hmong"; "Slaying of Boy Stuns Refugee Family"; Jane Eisner, "Hearings on Attacks on Asians"; William Robbins, "Violence Forces Hmong to Leave Philadelphia"; and Marc Kaufman, "Clash of Cultures: Ill Hmong Rejects Hospital" and "At the Mercy of America."

George M. Scott, Jr., "Migrants Without Mountains," explains why some Hmong refugees choose not to defend themselves. Amy Pyle, "Refugees Allegedly Threaten Welfare Workers," reports death threats by angry Hmong in Fresno. "Hmong Sentenced to Study America," and Jack Hayes, "Ching and Bravo Xiong, Laotian Hmong in Chicago," report the case of the Hmong men who attacked an American driver. The Hmong justice system is described in Charles Johnson, *Dab Neeg Hmoob*. The suicide of Chao Wang Vang is reported in Shirley Armbruster, "Hmong Take Root in Fresno."

The Hmong Resettlement Study and Cheu Thao, "Hmong Migration and Leadership," provide useful background on secondary migration. Timothy Dunnigan, quoted in Don Willcox, *Hmong Folklife*, observes that Hmong who try to gain membership in other kin groups are called "bats." Among my sources on Hmong in the Central Valley of California are John Finck, "Secondary Migration to California's Central Valley"; Mike Conway, "The Bill Stops Here in Refugee Policy"; David Abramson, "The Hmong: A Mountain Tribe Regroups in the Valley"; and Kevin Roderick, "Hmong Select San Joaquin to Sink Roots." The intimidating agricultural course plan, from a 1982 training program in Homer, Minnesota, is quoted in *The Hmong Resettlement Study*. Dwight Conquergood's passage about the Hmong group ethic is from "Establishing the World: Hmong Shamans."

United States government programs for encouraging economic independence by Hmong and other refugee groups are documented in the following publications by the Office of Refugee Resettlement: Teng Yang et al., *An Evaluation of the Highland Lao Initiative: Final Report*; *Evaluation of the Key States Initiative*; and annual *Reports to the Congress* on the Refugee Resettlement Program. Simon M. Fass, "Economic Development and Employment Projects," is a good source on Hmong employment in the 1980s. Ruth Hammond, "Strangers in a Strange Land," takes an unsentimental look at welfare. George M. Scott, Jr., "Migrants Without Mountains," mentions the man who refused to accept a job that would place him above his coworkers. Charlie Chue Chang and Nouzong Lynaolu provided information on Hmong National Development; the Yang Wang Meng Association, on Hmong in the professions; and Robin Vue-Benson, on electronic resources. Vue-Benson edits the electronic *Hmong Studies Journal*, which can be found on the World Wide Web at http://www.como.stpaul.k12.mn.us/Vue-Benson/HSJ.html.

The welfare statistics are based on information provided by the Minnesota Department of Human Services, the Wisconsin Department of Health and Social Services, and the California Department of Social Services. They are estimates.

The Hmong Resettlement Study and Christopher Robbins, *The Ravens*, describe "The Promise" made by the CIA in Laos. Lue Vang and Judy Lewis, "Grandfather's Path, Grandfather's Way," likens dependent people to dogs waiting for scraps.

I consulted the following mental health studies: Rubén Rumbaut, "Mental Health and the Refugee Experience: A Comparative Study of Southeast Asian Refugees"; Perry M. Nicassio, "Psychosocial Correlates of Alienation: Study of a Sample of Indochinese Refugees"; Joseph Westermeyer, "Acculturation and Mental Health: A Study of Hmong Refugees at 1.5 and 3.5 Years Postmigration"; and Westermeyer et al., "Psychosocial Adjustment of Hmong Refugees During Their First Decade in the United States." I also drew on Elizabeth Gong-Guy, *California Southeast Asian Mental Health Needs Assessment*, and Bruce Thowpaou Bliatout, "Understanding the Differences Between Asian and Western Concepts of Mental Health and Illness."

Doua Her's poem, "Lament upon Leaving Our Country," comes from Don Willcox, *Hmong Folklife*, as does the observation that to Hmong refugees in America, even the birds, trees, and flowers are unfamiliar. The stories about Plimoth Plantation and about former battalion commander Major Wang Seng Khang are both from Stephen P. Morin, "Many Hmong." The Hmong Community Survey, done by the University of Minnesota in 1982 and quoted in Tom Hamburger and Eric Black, "Uprooted People," contains the fraction of Hmong who were certain they would live out their lives in America. Although I am not aware of any later surveys, I would expect that the fraction has markedly increased, especially among younger Hmong.

Richard F. Mollica poignantly describes his psychiatric work with Indochinese refugees in "The Trauma Story: The Psychiatric Care of Refugee Survivors of Violence and Torture," and, with James Lavelle, in "Southeast Asian Refugees." Bruce Thowpaou Bliatout et al., "Mental Health and Prevention Activities Targeted to Southeast Asian Refugees," contains a good basic discussion of role loss.

The murder of a German tourist by a Hmong teenager is reported in Seth Mydans, "Laotians' Arrest in Killing Bares a Generation Gap." George M. Scott, Jr., "The Hmong Refugee Community in San Diego: Theoretical and Practical Implications of Its Continuing Ethnic Solidarity," observes that hardship has strengthened the Hmong identity.

15. Gold and Dross (pages 210–224)

Robert Berkow, *The Merck Manual*, and Lawrence K. Altman, "Quinlan Case Is Revisited and Yields New Finding," helped me understand persistent vegetative states. George M. Scott, Jr., "Migrants Without Mountains," notes that Hmong parents treat deformed children with special affection.

16. Why Did They Pick Merced? (pages 225–249)

The following furnished valuable background on the history, ethnic composition, and economy of Merced: *Merced Sun-Star Centennial Edition*; "A Chronicle in Time"; Gerald Haslam, "The Great Central Valley: Voices of a Place"; Delores J. Cabezut-Ortiz, *Merced County*; Kevin Roderick, "Hmong Select San Joaquin"; and literature and information from the Merced County Chamber of Commerce, the Merced County Economic Development Corporation, and Lao Family Community of Merced. Dan Campbell, Burt Fogleburg, Jan Harwood, Luc Janssens, Jeff McMahon, Kai Moua,

Cindy Murphy, Robert Small, and Debbie Vrana also provided useful general background. Rosie Rocha located several articles from the *Merced Sun-Star*.

Hmong music and musical instruments are described in Amy Catlin, "Speech Surrogate Systems of the Hmong: From Singing Voices to Talking Reeds"; Don Willcox, *Hmong Folklife*; Charles Johnson, *Dab Neeg Hmoob*; Megan McNamer, "Musical Change and Change in Music"; Rick Rubin, "Little Bua and Tall John"; Mike Conway, "Recording the Ways of the Past for the Children of the Future"; and "New People/Shared Dreams: An Examination of Music in the Lives of the Hmong in Merced County."

Some of the details of Dang Moua's story come from Frank Viviano, "Strangers in the Promised Land," and Arlene Bartholome, "Future Is Uncertain for Area Refugees." Dang Moua and Jonas Vangay told me about Vang Pao's plan to buy a local fruit ranch. Jeff McMahon provided minutes from the June 7, 1977, and June 21, 1977, meetings of the Merced County Board of Supervisors on the proposed purchase, which was also reported in "Laotians Drop Ranching Plan." The *Merced Sun-Star* headlines about the Hmong influx are from January 21, 1983; October 20, 1982; and May 11, 1983. The John Steinbeck quotations are from *The Grapes of Wrath*.

A great deal of helpful information on Merced's economic and welfare situation was provided by Andrea Baker and Rhonda Walton; also by Jim Brown, John Cullen, Michael Hider, Bev Morse, George Rodriguez, Van Vanderside, Houa Vang, and Charles Wimbley. The California State Department of Finance and the California State Census Data Center also assisted. Ron Dangaran, Jean Moua, and Terry Silva supplied background on Merced schools; Joe Brucia, Randy Carrothers, Charlie Lucas, Pat Lunney, and Rick Oules, on crime; and John McDoniel and Margaret Ogden on driver's license examinations. "Gang Pak" contains information on Merced's youth gangs. Pat McNally and Daniel Silva, "Asians, Game Laws in Conflict," reports on Hmong hunting and fishing. Mark Arax, "A Final Turf War," describes the Tollhouse Cemetery where "CIA veteran" Chua Cha Cha is buried.

The most authoritative source on Hmong education is Wendy Walker-Moffat, *The Other Side of the Asian American Success Story*. See also "The Other Side of the Asian Academic Success Myth" by Wendy D. Walker (Walker-Moffat's former name); Rubén Rumbaut and Kenji Ima, *The Adaptation of Southeast Asian Youth: A Comparative Study*; Donald A. Ranard, "The Hmong Can Make It in America"; Chia Vang, "Why Are Few Hmong Women in Higher Education?"; George M. Scott, Jr., "Migrants Without Mountains"; Miles McNall and Timothy Dunnigan, "Hmong Youth in St. Paul's Public Schools"; and Susan Dandridge Bosher, "Acculturation, Ethnicity, and Second Language Acquisition: A Study of Hmong Students at the Post-secondary Level."

Malek-Mithra Sheybani, "Cultural Defense: One Person's Culture Is Another's Crime," discusses marriage by capture. For more on Hmong marriage, see T. Christopher Thao, "Hmong Customs on Marriage, Divorce and the Rights of Married Women," and William H. Meredith and George P. Rowe, "Changes in Lao Hmong Marital Attitudes After Immigrating to the United States."

Paul DeLay, Karen Olmos, Court Robinson, and Jonas Vangay told me some of the examples of "different ethics." (They all mentioned these examples to illustrate how Hmong and American ethical systems differ, not to disparage the Hmong system.) Charles Johnson, *Dab Neeg Hmoob*, and Ruth Hammond, "Strangers in a Strange Land," also explore Hmong ethics.

For a provocative, though to my eye lopsidedly anti-Hmong, view of a Wisconsin city's response to a Hmong influx similar to Merced's, see Roy Beck, "The Ordeal of Immigration in Wausau."

17. The Eight Questions (pages 250–261)

Arthur Kleinman's "Eight Questions" have been published often, in slightly differing versions. The original version appeared in Kleinman et al., "Culture, Illness, and Care: Clinical Lessons from Anthropologic and Cross-Cultural Research." I consulted Dr. Kleinman on the phrasing that appears here.

18. The Life or the Soul (pages 262–277)

The literature of social and cross-cultural medicine is rich, and rapidly getting richer. I suggest that interested readers start with the unfailingly perceptive Arthur Kleinman, who wrote the seminal article cited under the previous chapter as well as *Patients and Healers in the Context of Culture*; *The Illness Narratives: Suffering, Healing, and the Human Condition*; and other works on related subjects.

Recommended brief introductions to cross-cultural health issues include Shotsy C. Faust, "Providing Inclusive Healthcare Across Cultures"; Debra Buchwald et al., "The Medical Interview Across Cultures"; Karen Olness, "Cultural Issues in Primary Pediatric Care"; and Daniel Goleman, "Making Room on the Couch for Culture." Those who wish to pursue this subject further are directed to the excellent cross-cultural bibliography in Robert C. Like et al., "Recommended Core Curriculum Guidelines on Culturally Sensitive and Competent Health Care."

Among those who provided ideas and details for this chapter are Daniel Goodenough and Arthur Kleinman, Harvard Medical School; Ronald Garcia and Gary Lapid, Stanford Medical School; Shotsy Faust and Chloë Wurr, Refugee Medical Clinic, San Francisco General Hospital; Gerald Hejduk, American Academy of Family Physicians; Robert Berkow and William R. Harrison, *Merck Manual*; Garry Shirts, Simulation Training Systems; Ira SenGupta, Cross-Cultural Health Care Program, Pacific Medical Center; Dan Murphy, Merced Community Medical Center; and Marilyn Mochel, Merced Refugee Health Program, Merced County Health Department. Many themes I have developed here were sparked when I audited a course on the Psychosocial Aspects of Illness at Stanford Medical School and spent time in Stanford's anatomy laboratory.

I learned of the Hmong medical cases summarized at the beginning of the chapter from lectures by or conversations with Tuan Nguyen, Long Thao, Blia Yao Moua, Roger Fife, Yia Thao Xiong, Thomas Bornemann, Doreen Faiello, and Francesca Farr. Bruce Thowpaou Bliatout's suggestions for improving Hmong health care are from "Hmong Refugees," "Hmong Attitudes Toward Surgery," "Mental Health and Prevention Activities," "Guidelines for Mental Health Professionals," "Prevention of Mental Health Problems," and *Hmong Sudden Unexpected Nocturnal Death Syndrome*. The Hmong-English medical glossary mentioned here is Thai Fang, *Tuabneeg Lubcev Hab Kev Mobnkeeg*.

Pam Belluck, "Mingling Two Worlds of Medicine," reports on New York City doctors who work with folk healers. The observations on shamanism are from Dwight Conquergood et al., *I Am a Shaman*, and Jacques Lemoine, "Shamanism." Mother Clean's sanitation poem is from Dwight Conquergood, "Health Theatre." The mental health program in which *txiv neebs* were consulted on ailing gall bladders and penises, among other maladies, is described in Kou Vang, *Hmong Concepts of Illness and Healing*. Sukey Waller recounts her collaborative work with *txiv neebs* in "Hmong Shamans in a County Mental Health Setting: A Bicultural Model for Healing Laotian Mountain People."

The 1996 Course Guide for Community-Based Patient-Doctor I, a division of the Patient-Doctor I course at Harvard Medical School, contained reprints of several helpful articles. San Francisco General Hospital's "Refugee Clinic Orientation Manual" was similarly fertile.

The article instructing doctors on how to recognize their emotions is William M. Zinn, "Doctors Have Feelings Too." Esther B. Fein, "Specialty or General Practice: Young Doctors Change Paths," includes statistics on how many medical students are choosing to become generalists.

19. The Sacrifice (pages 278–288)

Descriptions and interpretations of Hmong healing ceremonies can be found in Dwight Conquergood, "Establishing the World," and Conquergood et al., *I Am a Shaman*; Eric Crystal, "Buffalo Heads and Sacred Threads"; Kathleen Ann Culhane-Pera, "Description and Interpretation of a Hmong Shaman"; Jacques Lemoine, "Shamanism"; Jean Mottin, "A Hmong Shaman's Séance"; Kou Vang, *Hmong Concepts of Illness and Healing*; Don Willcox, *Hmong Folklife*; and Sukey Waller, "Hmong Shamanism." The most exhaustive study is Guy Moréchand, *Le chamanisme des Hmong*. A *txiv neeb*'s ritual work can be seen in "Between Two Worlds: The Hmong Shaman in America," a short documentary film produced by Taggart Siegel and Dwight Conquergood.

Dwight Conquergood, Say Hang, Blia Yao Moua, Chong Moua, Sukey Waller, May Ying Xiong, and Mayko Xiong also provided helpful background information.

There are innumerable, and often inconsistent, versions of the Shee Yee myth. In telling the early parts of his story, I have closely followed the phrasing in Charles Johnson, *Dab Neeg Hmoob*. For Shee Yee's later exploits, I have drawn on retellings in Kathleen Ann Culhane-Pera, "Description and Interpretation of a Hmong Shaman"; Bruce Thowpaou Bliatout, *Hmong Sudden Unexpected Nocturnal Death Syndrome*; Kou Vang, *Hmong Concepts of Illness and Healing*; Keith Quincy, *Hmong*; and Jean Mottin, "A Hmong Shaman's Séance."

Note on Hmong Orthography, Pronunciation, and Quotations
(pages 291–292)

The folktale about the great Hmong book that was eaten by cows and rats is from Robert Cooper et al., *The Hmong.*

Shong Lue Yang's writing system is summarized in William A. Smalley, "The Hmong 'Mother of Writing': A Messianic Figure," and Gary Yia Lee and William A. Smalley, "Perspectives on Pahawh Hmong Writing." For greater detail, see Smalley et al., *Mother of Writing: The Origin and Development of a Hmong Messianic Script,* and Chia Koua Vang et al., *The Life of Shong Lue Yang: Hmong "Mother of Writing."*

The Romanized Popular Alphabet is described in "A Note on Hmong Orthography" in Glenn L. Hendricks, *The Hmong in Transition.* I also relied on unpublished resource materials written by Jonas Vangay for his Hmong language course at Merced College.

For readers interested in learning or teaching the Hmong language, I highly recommend Annie Jaisser's textbook and audiotape, *Hmong for Beginners.* (It can be obtained through the CSSEAS Publications Office, 2223 Fulton Street, Room 338, University of California, Berkeley, California 94720.) There are also two useful dictionaries, Ernest E. Heimbach's comprehensive *White Hmong-English Dictionary* and Brian McKibben's basic *English-White Hmong Dictionary.*

If you wish to speak to a Hmong by phone and need an interpreter, AT&T Language Line Services (800-628-8486) can provide one for a fee.

Bibliography

Abrams, Richard. "Cross Burnings Terrify, Bewilder Hmong." *Sacramento Bee*, March 3, 1988.

Abramson, David. "The Hmong: A Mountain Tribe Regroups in the Valley." *California Living Magazine, San Francisco Examiner*, January 29, 1984.

Altman, Lawrence K. "Quinlan Case Is Revisited and Yields New Finding." *New York Times*, May 26, 1994.

Alvarez, Lizette. "A Once-Hidden Faith Leaps into the Open." *New York Times*, January 27, 1997.

American Foreign Policy, 1950–1955: Basic Documents. Washington, D.C.: Department of State, 1957.

American Foreign Policy: Current Documents, 1962. Washington, D.C.: Department of State, 1966.

Arax, Mark. "A Final Turf War." *Los Angeles Times*, June 14, 1992.

Armbruster, Shirley. "Hmong Take Root in Fresno." In "The Hmong: A Struggle in the Sun," *Fresno Bee*, October 9–12, 1984.

"Bangungut." *New York Times*, June 7, 1981.

Bartholome, Arlene. "Escape from Laos Told." *Merced Sun-Star*, December 8, 1978.

———. "Future Is Uncertain for Area Refugees." *Merced Sun-Star*, October 19, 1977.

Beck, Roy. "The Ordeal of Immigration in Wausau." *Atlantic*, April 1994.

Belluck, Pam. "Mingling Two Worlds of Medicine." *New York Times*, May 9, 1996.

Berkow, Robert, ed. *The Merck Manual of Diagnosis and Therapy*, 16th ed. Rahway, N.J.: Merck & Co., 1993.

Bernatzik, Hugo Adolf. *Akha and Miao: Problems of Applied Ethnography in Farther India*. New Haven: Human Relations Area Files, 1970.

"Between Two Worlds: The Hmong Shaman in America." Taggart Siegel and Dwight Conquergood, producers. Filmmakers Library, New York.

Bliatout, Bruce Thowpaou. "Causes and Treatment of Hmong Mental Health Problems." Unpublished lecture, 1980.

———. "Guidelines for Mental Health Professionals to Help Hmong Clients Seek Traditional Healing Treatment." In Hendricks et al., *The Hmong in Transition*.

———. "Hmong Attitudes Towards Surgery: How It Affects Patient Prognosis." *Migration World*, vol. 16, no. 1, 1988.

———. "Hmong Beliefs About Health and Illness." Unpublished paper, 1982.

———. "Hmong Refugees: Some Barriers to Some Western Health Care Services." Lecture, Arizona State University, 1988.

———. *Hmong Sudden Unexpected Nocturnal Death Syndrome: A Cultural Study*. Portland, Oreg.: Sparkle Publishing Enterprises, 1982.

———. "Prevention of Mental Health Problems." Unpublished paper.

———. "Traditional Hmong Beliefs on the Causes of Illness." Unpublished paper.

———. "Understanding the Differences Between Asian and Western Concepts of Mental Health and Illness." Lecture, Region VII Conference on Refugee Mental Health, Kansas City, 1982.

Bliatout, Bruce Thowpaou, et al. "Mental Health and Prevention Activities Targeted to Southeast Asian Refugees." In Owan, *Southeast Asian Mental Health*.

Bosher, Susan Dandridge. "Acculturation, Ethnicity, and Second Language Acquisition: A Study of Hmong Students at the Post-secondary Level." Ph.D. dissertation, University of Minnesota, 1995.

Bosley, Ann. "Of Shamans and Physicians: Hmong and the U.S. Health Care System." Undergraduate thesis, Division III, Hampshire College, 1986.

Brody, Jane. "Many People Still Do Not Understand Epilepsy." *New York Times*, November 4, 1992.

Buchwald, Debra, et al. "The Medical Interview Across Cultures." *Patient Care*, April 15, 1993.

———. "Use of Traditional Health Practices by Southeast Asian Refugees in a Primary Care Clinic." *Western Journal of Medicine*, May 1992.

Cabezut-Ortiz, Delores J. *Merced County: The Golden Harvest*. Northridge, Calif.: Windsor Publications, 1987.

Calderon, Eddie A. "The Impact of Indochinese Resettlement on the Phillips and Elliot Park Neighborhoods in South Minneapolis." In Downing and Olney, *The Hmong in the West*.

Carlson, Ken. "Hmong Leaders Seek Exemption." *Merced Sun-Star*, September 28, 1995.

———. "Sacrifice Ban Remains." *Merced Sun-Star*, December 2, 1995.

Carter, Stephen L. "The Power of Prayer, Denied." *New York Times*, January 31, 1996.

Catlin, Amy. "Speech Surrogate Systems of the Hmong: From Singing Voices to Talking Reeds." In Downing and Olney, *The Hmong in the West*.

Cerquone, Joseph. *Refugees from Laos: In Harm's Way*. Washington, D.C.: American Council for Nationalities Service, 1986.

Chan, Sucheng. *Hmong Means Free: Life in Laos and America*. Philadelphia: Temple University Press, 1994.

"Child Abuse Laws: What Are Your Obligations?" *Patient Care*, April 15, 1988.

Chindarsi, Nusit. *The Religion of the Hmong Njua*. Bangkok: The Siam Society, 1976.

"A Chronicle in Time." Merced, Calif.: Merced Downtown Association, 1995.

Clifford, Clark. *Counsel to the President*. New York: Random House, 1991.

Conquergood, Dwight. "Establishing the World: Hmong Shamans." *CURA Reporter*, University of Minnesota, April 1989.

———. "Health Theatre in a Hmong Refugee Camp: Performance, Communication, and Culture." *The Drama Review*, vol. 32, no. 3, 1988.

Conquergood, Dwight, et al. *I Am a Shaman: A Hmong Life Story with Ethnographic Commentary*. Minneapolis: Center for Urban and Regional Affairs, University of Minnesota, 1989.

Conway, Mike. "The Bill Stops Here in Refugee Policy." *Merced Sun-Star*, January 21, 1983.

———. "Recording the Ways of the Past for the Children of the Future." *Merced Sun-Star*, November 11, 1988.

Cooper, Robert. *Resource Scarcity and the Hmong Response*. Singapore: Singapore University Press, 1984.

Cooper, Robert, et al. *The Hmong*. Bangkok: Art Asia Press, 1991.

"Court Says Ill Child's Interests Outweigh Religion." *New York Times*, January 16, 1991.

Crystal, Eric. "Buffalo Heads and Sacred Threads: Hmong Culture of the Southeast Asian Highlands." In *Textiles as Texts: Arts of Hmong Women from Laos*, edited by Amy Catlin and Dixie Swift. Los Angeles: The Women's Building, 1987.

Culhane-Pera, Kathleen Ann. "Analysis of Cultural Beliefs and Power Dynamics in Disagreements About Health Care of Hmong Children." M.A. thesis, University of Minnesota, 1989.

———. "Description and Interpretation of a Hmong Shaman in St. Paul." Unpublished paper, Department of Anthropology, University of Minnesota, 1987.

Cumming, Brenda Jean. "The Development of Attachment in Two Groups of Economically Disadvantaged Infants and Their Mothers: Hmong Refugee and Caucasian-American." Ph.D. dissertation, Department of Educational Psychology, University of Minnesota, 1988.

Dao, Yang. *See* Yang Dao.*

Deinard, Amos S., and Timothy Dunnigan. "Hmong Health Care: Reflections on a Six-Year Experience." *International Migration Review*, vol. 21, no. 3, fall 1987.

De La Cruz, Mike. "Animal Slaughtering Not All Ritualistic." *Merced Sun-Star*, February 2, 1996.

---

* Unlike most Hmong in this country, Yang Dao, the leading Hmong scholar, has retained his name's traditional form by placing his clan name before his given name. Yang is his surname.

———. "Charges Filed After Animal Slaughtering Probe." *Merced Sun-Star*, March 21, 1996.

Devinsky, Orrin. *A Guide to Understanding and Living with Epilepsy*. Philadelphia: F. A. Davis, 1994.

Dictionary of American History. New York: Charles Scribner's Sons, 1976.

Downing, Bruce T., and Douglas P. Olney, eds. *The Hmong in the West: Observations and Reports*. Minneapolis: Center for Urban and Regional Affairs, University of Minnesota, 1982.

Dunnigan, Timothy. "Segmentary Kinship in an Urban Society: The Hmong of St. Paul-Minneapolis." *Anthropological Quarterly*, vol. 55, 1982.

Dunnigan, Timothy, et al. "Hmong." In *Refugees in America in the 1990s: A Reference Handbook*, edited by David W. Haines. Westport, Conn.: Greenwood Press, 1996.

Eisner, Jane. "Hearings on Attacks on Asians." *Philadelphia Inquirer*, October 4, 1984.

Ember, Lois. "Yellow Rain." *Chemical and Engineering News*, January 9, 1984.

Erickson, Deanne, et al. "Maternal and Infant Outcomes Among Caucasians and Hmong Refugees in Minneapolis, Minnesota." *Human Biology*, vol. 59, no. 5, October 1987.

Erickson, Roy V., and Giao Ngoc Hoang. "Health Problems Among Indochinese Refugees." *American Journal of Public Health*, vol. 70, September 1980.

Ernst, Thomas Neil, and Margaret Philp. "Bacterial Tracheitis Caused by *Branhamella catarrhalis*." *Pediatric Infectious Disease Journal*, vol. 6, no. 6, 1987.

Ernst, Thomas Neil, et al. "The Effect of Southeast Asian Refugees on Medical Services in a Rural County." *Family Medicine*, vol. 20, no. 2, March/April 1988.

Evaluation of the Key States Initiative. Washington, D.C.: Office of Refugee Resettlement, U.S. Department of Health and Human Services, 1995.

Evans, Owen B. *Manual of Child Neurology*. New York: Churchill Livingstone, 1987.

Faiello, Doreen. "Translation Please." Unpublished paper, 1992.

Faller, Helen Stewart. "Hmong Women: Characteristics and Birth Outcomes, 1990." *Birth*, vol. 19, September 1992.

Fang, Thai. *Tuabneeg Lubcev Hab Kev Mobnkeeg Rua Cov Haslug Hmoob: Basic Human Body and Medical Information for Hmong Speaking People*. Pinedale, Calif.: Chersousons, 1995.

Fass, Simon M. "Economic Development and Employment Projects." In Hendricks et al., *The Hmong in Transition*.

———. "Through a Glass Darkly: Cause and Effect in Refugee Resettlement Policies." *Journal of Policy Analysis and Management*, vol. 5, no. 1, 1985.

Faust, Shotsy C. "Providing Inclusive Healthcare Across Cultures." In *Advanced Practice Nursing: Changing Roles and Clinical Applications*, edited by Joanne V. Hickey et al. Philadelphia: Lippincott-Raven, 1996.

Fein, Esther B. "Specialty or General Practice: Young Doctors Change Paths." *New York Times*, October 16, 1995.

Feith, David. *Stalemate: Refugees in Asia*. Victoria, Australia: Asian Bureau Australia, 1988.

Feron, James. "Can Choosing Form of Care Become Neglect?" *New York Times*, September 29, 1990.

Finck, John. "Secondary Migration to California's Central Valley." In Hendricks et al., *The Hmong in Transition*.

———. "Southeast Asian Refugees of Rhode Island: Cross-Cultural Issues in Medical Care." *Rhode Island Medical Journal*, vol. 67, July 1984.

Franjola, Matt. "Meo Tribesmen from Laos Facing Death in Thailand." *New York Times*, August 15, 1975.

Fraser, Caroline. "Suffering Children and the Christian Science Church." *Atlantic*, April 1995.

"Frontline: Guns, Drugs and the CIA." PBS broadcast, May 17, 1988.

Gallo, Agatha, et al. "Little Refugees with Big Needs." *RN*, December 1980.

"Gang Pak." Merced, Calif.: Merced Union High School District, Child Welfare and Attendance Office, 1993.

Garcia, Dominica P. "In Thailand, Refugees' 'Horror and Misery.'" *New York Times*, November 14, 1978.

Garrett, W. E. "No Place to Run." *National Geographic*, January 1974.

Gazzolo, Michele B. "Spirit Paths and Roads of Sickness: A Symbolic Analysis of Hmong Textile Design." M.A. thesis, University of Chicago, 1986.

Geddes, W. R. *Migrants of the Mountains: The Cultural Ecology of the Blue Miao (Hmong Njua) of Thailand*. Oxford: Clarendon Press, 1976.

Getto, Dennis R. "Hmong Families Build New Lives." *Milwaukee Journal*, August 18, 1985.

Goleman, Daniel. "Making Room on the Couch for Culture." *New York Times*, December 5, 1995.

Gong-Guy, Elizabeth. *California Southeast Asian Mental Health Needs Assessment*. Oakland, Calif.: Asian Community Mental Health Services, 1987.

Greenhouse, Linda. "Christian Scientists Rebuffed in Ruling by Supreme Court." *New York Times*, January 23, 1996.

Greenway, Hugh. "The Pendulum of War Swings Wider in Laos." *Life*, April 3, 1970.

Halstuk, Martin. "Religious Freedom Collides with Medical Care." *San Francisco Chronicle*, April 25, 1988.

Hamburger, Tom, and Eric Black. "Uprooted People in Search of a Home." *Minneapolis Star and Tribune*, April 21, 1985.

Hamilton-Merritt, Jane. "Hmong and Yao: Mountain Peoples of Southeast Asia." Redding, Conn.: SURVIVE, 1982.

———. *Tragic Mountains: The Hmong, the Americans, and the Secret Wars for Laos, 1942–1992*. Bloomington: Indiana University Press, 1993.

Hammond, Ruth. "Sad Suspicions of a Refugee Ripoff." *Washington Post*, April 16, 1989.

———. "Strangers in a Strange Land." *Twin Cities Reader*, June 1–7, 1988.

———. "Tradition Complicates Hmong Choice." *St. Paul Pioneer Press*, September 16, 1984.

Haslam, Gerald. "The Great Central Valley: Voices of a Place." Exhibition catalog, California Academy of Sciences, 1986.

Hayes, Jack. "Ching and Bravo Xiong, Laotian Hmong in Chicago." Unpublished editorial memorandum, *Life*, July 7, 1988.

Heimbach, Ernest E. *White Hmong-English Dictionary*. Ithaca: Cornell University, Southeast Asia Program Data Paper No. 75, 1969.

Helsel, Deborah, et al. "Pregnancy Among the Hmong: Birthweight, Age, and Parity." *American Journal of Public Health*, vol. 82, October 1992.

Hendricks, Glenn L., et al., eds. *The Hmong in Transition*. New York and Minneapolis: Center for Migration Studies and Southeast Asian Refugee Studies Project, University of Minnesota, 1986.

Herr, Paul Pao. "Don't Call Hmong Refugees 'Primitive.' " Letter to the editor, *New York Times*, November 29, 1990.

"Hmong Medical Interpreter Fields Questions from Curious." *St. Paul Sunday Pioneer Press*, March 20, 1983.

The Hmong Resettlement Study, vols. 1 and 2. Washington, D.C.: Office of Refugee Resettlement, U.S. Department of Health and Human Services, 1984 and 1985.

"Hmong Sentenced to Study America." *Modesto Bee*, July 1, 1988.

Hoffman, Ken. "Background on the Hmong of Laos." Unpublished memorandum, 1979.

Hollingsworth, Andrea, et al. "The Refugees and Childbearing: What to Expect." *RN*, November 1980.

Hornblower, Margot. " 'Hmongtana.' " *Washington Post*, July 5, 1980.

Hurlich, Marshall, et al. "Attitudes of Hmong Toward a Medical Research Project." In Hendricks et al., *The Hmong in Transition*.

Hutchison, Ray. "Acculturation in the Hmong Community." Green Bay: University of Wisconsin Center for Public Affairs, and Milwaukee: University of Wisconsin Institute on Race and Ethnicity, 1992.

Jaisser, Annie. *Hmong for Beginners*. Berkeley: Centers for South and Southeast Asia Studies, 1995.

Johns, Brenda, and David Strecker, eds. *The Hmong World*. New Haven: Yale Southeast Asia Studies, 1986.

Johnson, Charles. "Hmong Myths, Legends and Folk Tales." In Downing and Olney, *The Hmong in the West*.

———, ed. *Dab Neeg Hmoob: Myths, Legends and Folk Tales from the Hmong of Laos*. St. Paul: Macalester College, 1983.

Johnson, Charles, and Ava Dale Johnson. *Six Hmong Folk Tales Retold in English*. St. Paul: Macalester College, 1981.

Jones, Woodrow, Jr., and Paul Strand. "Adaptation and Adjustment Problems Among Indochinese Refugees." *Sociology and Social Research*, vol. 71, no. 1, October 1986.

"Journey from Pha Dong." Vang Yang, transcriber. Minneapolis: Southeast Asian Refugee Studies Project, University of Minnesota, 1988.

Kamm, Henry. "Decades-Old U.S. Bombs Still Killing Laotians." *New York Times*, August 10, 1995.

———. "Meo General Leads Tribesmen in War with Communists in Laos." *New York Times*, October 27, 1969.

———. "Meo, Hill People Who Fought for U.S., Are Fleeing from Laos." *New York Times*, March 28, 1978.

———. "Thailand Finds Indochinese Refugees a Growing Problem." *New York Times*, July 1, 1977.

Kaufman, Marc. "As Keeper of the Hmong Dream, He Draws Support and Skepticism." *Philadelphia Inquirer*, July 1, 1984.

———. "At the Mercy of America." *Philadelphia Inquirer*, October 21, 1984.

———. "Casualties of Peace." *Philadelphia Inquirer*, February 27, 1994.

———. "Clash of Cultures: Ill Hmong Rejects Hospital." *Philadelphia Inquirer*, October 5, 1984.

———. "Why the Hmong Are Fleeing America's Helping Hand." *Philadelphia Inquirer*, July 1, 1984.

———. "Why the Hmong Spurn America." *Philadelphia Inquirer*, December 31, 1984.

King, Wayne. "New Life's Cultural Demons Torture Laotian Refugee." *New York Times*, May 3, 1981.

Kirton, Elizabeth S. "The Locked Medicine Cabinet: Hmong Health Care in America." Ph.D. dissertation, Department of Anthropology, University of California at Santa Barbara, 1985.

Kleinman, Arthur. *The Illness Narratives: Suffering, Healing, and the Human Condition.* New York: Basic Books, 1988.

———. *Patients and Healers in the Context of Culture.* Berkeley: University of California Press, 1980.

Kleinman, Arthur, et al. "Culture, Illness, and Care: Clinical Lessons from Anthropologic and Cross-Cultural Research." *Annals of Internal Medicine*, vol. 88, 1978.

Koumarn, Yang See, and G. Linwood Barney. "The Hmong: Their History and Culture." New York: Lutheran Immigration and Refugee Service, 1986.

Kraut, Alan M. "Healers and Strangers: Immigrant Attitudes Toward the Physician in America—A Relationship in Historical Perspective." *Journal of the American Medical Association*, vol. 263, no. 13, April 4, 1990.

———. *Silent Travelers: Germs, Genes, and the "Immigrant Menace".* New York: Basic Books, 1994.

Kunstadter, Peter. "Pilot Study of Differential Child Survival Among Various Ethnic Groups in Northern Thailand and California." Study proposal, University of California at San Francisco, 1987.

Laos: Official Standard Names Approved by the United States Board on Geographic Names. Washington, D.C.: Defense Mapping Agency, 1973.

"Laos: The Silent Sideshow." *Time*, June 11, 1965.

"Laotians Drop Ranching Plan." *Merced Sun-Star*, July 22, 1977.

LaPlante, Eve. *Seized: Temporal Lobe Epilepsy as a Medical, Historical, and Artistic Phenomenon.* New York: HarperCollins, 1993.

Leary, Warren. "Valium Found to Reduce Fever Convulsions." *New York Times*, July 8, 1993.

Lee, Gary Yia, and William A. Smalley. "Perspectives on Pahawh Hmong Writing." *Southeast Asian Refugee Studies Newsletter*, spring 1991.

Lemoine, Jacques. "Shamanism in the Context of Hmong Resettlement." In Hendricks et al., *The Hmong in Transition*.

Lemoine, Jacques, and Christine Mougne. "Why Has Death Stalked the Refugees?" *Natural History*, November 1983.

Lewis, Paul and Elaine. *Peoples of the Golden Triangle*. London: Thames and Hudson, 1984.

Leyn, Rita Bayer. "The Challenge of Caring for Child Refugees from Southeast Asia." *American Journal of Maternal Child Nursing*, May/June 1978.

Like, Robert C., et al. "Recommended Core Curriculum Guidelines on Culturally Sensitive and Competent Health Care." *Family Medicine*, vol. 28, no. 4, April 1996.

Long, Lynellen. *Ban Vinai: The Refugee Camp*. New York: Columbia University Press, 1993.

——. "Refugee Camps as a Way of Life." Lecture, American Anthropological Association, Chicago, 1987.

Lopez, Pablo. "Hmong Mother Holds Off Police Because of Fear for Her Children." *Merced Sun-Star*, January 12, 1988.

"Making Up for the Ravages of Battle: Hmong Birthrate Subject of Merced Study." *Merced Sun-Star*, November 16, 1987.

Malloy, Michael T. "Anti-Communists Also Win Battles in War-Torn Laos." *New York World-Telegram and Sun*, April 1, 1961.

Mann, Jim, and Nick B. Williams, Jr. "Shultz Cool to New Indochina Refugee Effort." *Los Angeles Times*, July 8, 1988.

Marchetti, Victor, and John D. Marks. *The CIA and the Cult of Intelligence*. New York: Alfred A. Knopf, 1974.

Margolick, David. "In Child Deaths, a Test for Christian Science." *New York Times*, August 6, 1990.

Marsh, Robert E. "Socioeconomic Status of Indochinese Refugees in the United States: Progress and Problems." *Social Security Bulletin*, October 1980.

Martin, Eric. "Hmong in French Guyana: An Improbable Gamble." *Refugees*, July 1992.

Martin, Frank W. "A CIA-Backed Guerrilla Who Waged a Secret War in Laos Puts Down Roots in Montana." *People*, August 29, 1977.

McCoy, Alfred W. *The Politics of Heroin: CIA Complicity in the Global Drug Trade*. Brooklyn, N.Y.: Lawrence Hill Books, 1991.

McKibben, Brian. *English-White Hmong Dictionary*. Provo, Utah: 1992.

McNall, Miles, and Timothy Dunnigan, "Hmong Youth in St. Paul's Public Schools." *CURA Reporter*, University of Minnesota, 1993.

McNally, Pat, and Daniel Silva. "Asians, Game Laws in Conflict." *Merced Sun-Star*, December 6, 1983.

McNamer, Megan. "Musical Change and Change in Music." In Johns and Strecker, *The Hmong World*.

Merced Sun-Star Centennial Edition. April 1, 1989.

Meredith, William H., and George P. Rowe. "Changes in Lao Hmong Marital Attitudes After Immigrating to the United States." *Journal of Comparative Family Studies*, vol. 17, no. 1, spring 1986.

Meyer, Stephen. *The Five Dollar Day.* Albany: State University of New York Press, 1981.

Miller, Russell. "A Leap of Faith." *New York Times*, January 30, 1994.

Mitchell, Roger. "The Will to Believe and Anti-Refugee Rumors." *Midwestern Folklore*, vol. 13, no. 1, spring 1987.

Mollica, Richard F. "The Trauma Story: The Psychiatric Care of Refugee Survivors of Violence and Torture." In *Post-traumatic Therapy and Victims of Violence*, edited by Frank M. Ochberg. New York: Brunner/Mazel, 1988.

Mollica, Richard F., and James Lavelle. "Southeast Asian Refugees." In *Clinical Guidelines in Cross-Cultural Mental Health*, edited by Lillian Comas-Diaz and Ezra E.H. Griffith. New York: John Wiley & Sons, 1988.

Montgomery, Lana. "Folk Medicine of the Indochinese." San Diego: Refugee Women's Task Force.

Moore, David L. *Dark Sky, Dark Land: Stories of the Hmong Boy Scouts of Troop 100.* Eden Prairie, Minn.: Tessera Publishing, 1989.

Moréchand, Guy. *Le chamanisme des Hmong.* Paris: Bulletin de l'Ecole Française d'Extrême-Orient, vol. 54, 1968.

Morin, Stephen P. "Many Hmong, Puzzled by Life in U.S., Yearn for Old Days in Laos." *Wall Street Journal*, February 16, 1983.

Mottin, Jean. *History of the Hmong.* Bangkok: Odeon Store, 1980.

———. "A Hmong Shaman's Séance." *Asian Folklore Studies*, vol. 43, 1984.

Muecke, Marjorie. "Caring for Southeast Asian Refugee Patients in the USA." *American Journal of Public Health*, vol. 73, April 1983.

———. "In Search of Healers: Southeast Asian Refugees in the American Health Care System." *Western Journal of Medicine*, December 1983.

Munger, Ronald. "Sudden Death in Sleep of Asian Adults." Ph.D. dissertation, Department of Anthropology, University of Washington, 1985.

———. "Sudden Death in Sleep of Laotian-Hmong Refugees in Thailand: A Case-Control Study." *American Journal of Public Health*, vol. 77, no. 9, September 1987.

Munger, Ronald, and Elizabeth Booton. "Thiamine and Sudden Death in Sleep of South-East Asian Refugees." Letter to the editor, *The Lancet*, May 12, 1990.

Mydans, Seth. "California Says Laos Refugee Group Has Been Extorted by Its Leadership." *New York Times*, November 7, 1990.

———. "Laotians' Arrest in Killing Bares a Generation Gap." *New York Times*, June 21, 1994.

Newlin-Haus, E.M. "A Comparison of Proxemic and Selected Communication Behavior of Anglo-American and Hmong Refugee Mother-Infant Pairs." Ph.D. dissertation, Indiana University, 1982.

Newman, Alan. "Epilepsy: Light from the Mind's Dark Corner." *Johns Hopkins Magazine*, October 1988.

"New People/Shared Dreams: An Examination of Music in the Lives of the Hmong in Merced County." Exhibition brochure, Merced County Library, 1988.

Nguyen, Anh, et al. "Folk Medicine, Folk Nutrition, Superstitions." Washington, D.C.: TEAM Associates, 1980.

Nicassio, Perry M. "Psychosocial Correlates of Alienation: Study of a Sample of Indochinese Refugees." *Journal of Cross-Cultural Psychology*, vol. 14, no. 3, September 1983.

Nuland, Sherwin B. *How We Die: Reflections on Life's Final Chapter*. New York: Vintage, 1995.

Nyce, James M., and William H. Hollinshead. "Southeast Asian Refugees of Rhode Island: Reproductive Beliefs and Practices Among the Hmong." *Rhode Island Medical Journal*, vol. 67, August 1984.

Oberg, Charles N., et al., "A Cross-Cultural Assessment of Maternal-Child Interaction: Links to Health and Development." In Hendricks et al., *The Hmong in Transition*.

Olness, Karen. "Cultural Issues in Primary Pediatric Care." In *Primary Pediatric Care*, edited by R. A. Hoeckelman. St. Louis: Mosby Year Book, 1992.

Ong, W. J. *Orality and Literacy: The Technologizing of the Word*. London: Methuen and Co., 1982.

Ostling, Richard N. "Shedding Blood in Sacred Bowls." *Time*, October 19, 1992.

Owan, Tom Choken, ed. *Southeast Asian Mental Health: Treatment, Prevention, Services, Training, and Research*. Washington, D.C.: National Institute of Mental Health, 1985.

Pake, Catherine. "Medicinal Ethnobotany of Hmong Refugees in Thailand." *Journal of Ethnobiology*, vol. 7, no. 1, summer 1987.

Physicians' Desk Reference, 41st edition. Oradell, N.J.: Medical Economics Company, 1987.

Potter, Gayle S., and Alice Whiren. "Traditional Hmong Birth Customs: A Historical Study." In Downing and Olney, *The Hmong in the West*.

Pyle, Amy. "Refugees Allegedly Threaten Welfare Workers." *Fresno Bee*, March 27, 1986.

Quincy, Keith. *Hmong: History of a People*. Cheney, Wash.: Eastern Washington University Press, 1988.

Ranard, Donald A. "The Hmong Can Make It in America." *Washington Post*, January 9, 1988.

———. "The Hmong: No Strangers to Change." *In America: Perspectives on Refugee Resettlement*, November 1988.

———. "The Last Bus." *Atlantic*, October 1987.

"Reds' Advance in Laos Menaces Hill Strongholds of Meo Tribe." *New York Times*, April 3, 1961.

Report to the Congress. Washington, D.C.: Office of Refugee Resettlement, U.S. Department of Health and Human Services.

Restak, Richard. *The Brain*. New York: Bantam, 1984.

"Rice in the Sky." *Time*, June 3, 1966.

Robbins, Christopher. *The Ravens: The Men Who Flew in America's Secret War in Laos*. New York: Crown, 1987.

Robbins, William. "Violence Forces Hmong to Leave Philadelphia." *New York Times*, September 17, 1984.

Robinson, Court. "Laotian Refugees in Thailand: The Thai and U.S. Response, 1975 to 1988." Unpublished paper.

Roderick, Kevin. "Hmong Select San Joaquin to Sink Roots." *Los Angeles Times*, March 18, 1991.

Rohter, Larry. "Court to Weigh Law Forbidding Ritual Sacrifice." *New York Times*, November 3, 1992.

Rosenblatt, Lionel. Testimony to the House Subcommittee on Asia and the Pacific, April 26, 1994.

Rosenblatt, Roger. *Children of War*. New York: Anchor Press, 1983.

Rubin, Rick. "Little Bua and Tall John." *Portland Oregonian*, July 22, 1984.

Rumbaut, Rubén. "Mental Health and the Refugee Experience: A Comparative Study of Southeast Asian Refugees." In Owan, *Southeast Asian Mental Health*.

Rumbaut, Rubén, and John R. Weeks. "Fertility and Adaptation: Indochinese Refugees in the United States." *International Migration Review*, vol. 20, no. 2, summer 1986.

Rumbaut, Rubén, and Kenji Ima. *The Adaptation of Southeast Asian Youth: A Comparative Study*, vols. 1 and 2. San Diego, Calif.: Southeast Asian Refugee Youth Study, Department of Sociology, San Diego State University, 1987.

Sacks, Oliver. *Migraine*. Berkeley: University of California Press, 1985.

"Salmonellosis Following a Hmong Celebration." *California Morbidity*, September 19, 1986.

Savina, F. M. *Histoire des Miao*, 2nd ed. Hong Kong: Imprimerie de la Société des Missions-Etrangères de Paris, 1930.

Schanche, Don. "The Yankee 'King' of Laos." *New York Daily News*, April 5, 1970.

Schmalz, Jeffrey. "Animal Sacrifices: Faith or Cruelty?" *New York Times*, August 17, 1989.

Schreiner, Donna. "Southeast Asian Folk Healing." Portland, Oreg.: Multnomah Community Health Services, 1981.

Scott, George M., Jr. "The Hmong Refugee Community in San Diego: Theoretical and Practical Implications of Its Continuing Ethnic Solidarity." *Anthropological Quarterly*, vol. 55, 1982.

——. "Migrants Without Mountains: The Politics of Sociocultural Adjustment Among the Lao Hmong Refugees in San Diego." Ph.D. dissertation, Department of Anthropology, University of California at San Diego, 1986.

Seagrave, Sterling. *Yellow Rain: Chemical Warfare—The Deadliest Arms Race*. New York: Evans, 1981.

Seeley, Thomas, et al. "Yellow Rain." *Scientific American*, September 1985.

Sesser, Stan. "Forgotten Country." *New Yorker*, August 20, 1990.

Shaplen, Robert. "Letter from Laos." *New Yorker*, May 4, 1968.

Sheybani, Malek-Mithra. "Cultural Defense: One Person's Culture Is Another's Crime." *Loyola of Los Angeles International and Comparative Law Journal*, vol. 9, 1987.

Shulins, Nancy. "Transplanted Hmong Struggle to Adjust in U.S." *State Journal*, Lansing, Mich., July 15, 1984.

"Slaying of Boy Stuns Refugee Family." *New York Times*, January 2, 1984.

Smalley, William A. "Adaptive Language Strategies of the Hmong: From Asian Mountains to American Ghettos." *Language Sciences*, vol. 7, no. 2, 1985.

———. "The Hmong 'Mother of Writing': A Messianic Figure." *Southeast Asian Refugee Studies Newsletter*, spring 1990.

———. *Phonemes and Orthography*. Canberra: Linguistic Circle of Canberra, 1976.

Smalley, William A., et al. *Mother of Writing: The Origin and Development of a Hmong Messianic Script*. Chicago: University of Chicago Press, 1990.

"Social/Cultural Customs: Similarities and Differences Between Vietnamese—Cambodians—H'Mong—Lao." Washington, D.C.: TEAM Associates, 1980.

Strouse, Joan. "Continuing Themes in U.S. Educational Policy for Immigrants and Refugees: The Hmong Experience." Ph.D. dissertation, Educational Policy Studies, University of Wisconsin, 1985.

Sutton, Christine, ed. "The Hmong of Laos." Georgetown University Bilingual Education Service Center, 1984.

Temkin, Owsei. *The Falling Sickness: A History of Epilepsy from the Greeks to the Beginnings of Modern Neurology*. Baltimore: Johns Hopkins University Press, 1971.

"Text of Cease-Fire Agreement Signed by Laotian Government and the Pathet Lao." *New York Times*, February 22, 1973.

Thao, Cheu. "Hmong Migration and Leadership in Laos and in the United States." In Downing and Olney, *The Hmong in the West*.

Thao, T. Christopher. "Hmong Customs on Marriage, Divorce and the Rights of Married Women." In Johns and Strecker, *The Hmong World*.

Thao, Xoua. "Hmong Perception of Illness and Traditional Ways of Healing." In Hendricks et al., *The Hmong in Transition*.

Thernstrom, Stephan. "Ethnic Groups in American History." In *Ethnic Relations in America*, edited by Lance Leibman. Englewood Cliffs, N.J.: Prentice-Hall, 1982.

Todd, Linda. "Indochinese Refugees Bring Rich Heritages to Childbearing." *ICEA News*, vol. 21, no. 1, 1982.

Trillin, Calvin. "Resettling the Yangs." In *Killings*. New York: Ticknor & Fields, 1984.

Ungar, Sanford J. *Fresh Blood: The New American Immigrants*. New York: Simon & Schuster, 1995.

Vang, Chia. "Why Are Few Hmong Women in Higher Education?" *Hmong Women Pursuing Higher Education*, University of Wisconsin-Stout, December 1991.

Vang, Chia Koua, et al. *The Life of Shong Lue Yang: Hmong "Mother of Writing."* Minneapolis: CURA, University of Minnesota, 1990.

Vang, Kou, et al. *Hmong Concepts of Illness and Healing with a Hmong/English Glossary*. Fresno: Nationalities Service of Central California, 1985.

Vang, Lue, and Judy Lewis. "Grandfather's Path, Grandfather's Way." In Johns and Strecker, *The Hmong World*.

Vang, Tou-Fou. "The Hmong of Laos." In *Bridging Cultures: Southeast Asian Refugees in America*. Los Angeles: Asian American Community Mental Health Training Center, 1981.

Viviano, Frank. "Strangers in the Promised Land." *San Francisco Examiner Image*, August 31, 1986.

Volkman, Toby Alice. "Unexpected Bombs Take Toll in Laos, Too." Letter to the editor, *New York Times*, May 23, 1994.

Vreeland, Susan. "Through the Looking Glass with the Hmong of Laos." *Christian Science Monitor*, March 30, 1981.

Walker, Wendy D. "The Other Side of the Asian Academic Success Myth: The Hmong Story." Ph.D. qualifying paper, Harvard Graduate School of Education, 1988.

Walker-Moffat, Wendy. *The Other Side of the Asian American Success Story*. San Francisco: Jossey-Bass, 1995.

Waller, Sukey. "Hmong Shamanism." Unpublished lecture, 1988.

———. "Hmong Shamans in a County Mental Health Setting: A Bicultural Model for Healing Laotian Mountain People." In *Proceedings of the Fifth International Conference on the Study of Shamanism and Alternate Modes of Healing*, edited by Ruth-Inge Heinze. Berkeley: Independent Scholars of Asia, 1988.

Warner, Roger. *Back Fire: The CIA's Secret War in Laos and Its Link to the War in Vietnam*. New York: Simon & Schuster, 1995.

———. *Shooting at the Moon: The Story of America's Clandestine War in Laos*. South Royalton, Vt.: Steerforth Press, 1996.

Westermeyer, Joseph. "Acculturation and Mental Health: A Study of Hmong Refugees at 1.5 and 3.5 Years Postmigration." *Social Science and Medicine*, vol. 18, no. 1, 1984.

———. "Prevention of Mental Disorder Among Hmong Refugees in the U.S.: Lessons from the Period 1976–1986." *Social Science and Medicine*, vol. 25, no. 8, 1987.

Westermeyer, Joseph, and Xoua Thao. "Cultural Beliefs and Surgical Procedures," *Journal of the American Medical Association*, vol. 255, no. 23, June 20, 1988.

Westermeyer, Joseph, et al. "Psychosocial Adjustment of Hmong Refugees During Their First Decade in the United States." *Journal of Nervous and Mental Disease*, vol. 177, no. 3, 1989.

———. "Somatization Among Refugees: An Epidemiologic Study." *Psychosomatics*, vol. 30, no. 1, 1989.

Whiteside, Thomas. "The Yellow-Rain Complex." *New Yorker*, February 11 and 18, 1991.

Willcox, Don. *Hmong Folklife*. Penland, N.C.: Hmong Natural Association of North Carolina, 1986.

Willem, Jean-Pierre. *Les naufragés de la liberté: Le dernier exode des Méos*. Paris: Editions S.O.S., 1980.

Wittet, Scott. "Information Needs of Southeast Asian Refugees in Medical Situations." M.A. thesis, Department of Communications, University of Washington, 1983.

World Refugee Survey. Washington, D.C.: U.S. Committee for Refugees.

Xiong, May, and Nancy D. Donnelly. "My Life in Laos." In Johns and Strecker, *The Hmong World.*

Yamasaki, Richard Lee. "Resettlement Status of the Hmong Refugees in Long Beach." M.A. thesis, Department of Psychology, California State University, Long Beach, 1977.

Yang Dao. *Hmong at the Turning Point.* Minneapolis: WorldBridge Associates, 1993.

———. "Why Did the Hmong Leave Laos?" In Downing and Olney, *The Hmong in the West.*

Yang, Teng, et al. *An Evaluation of the Highland Lao Initiative: Final Report.* Washington, D.C.: Office of Refugee Resettlement, U.S. Department of Health and Human Services, 1985.

"Your New Life in the United States." In *A Guide for Helping Refugees Adjust to Their New Life in the United States.* Washington, D.C.: Language and Orientation Resource Center, Center for Applied Linguistics, 1981.

Zinn, William M. "Doctors Have Feelings Too." *Journal of the American Medical Association*, vol. 259, no. 22, June 10, 1988.

Žygas, Egle Victoria. "Flower Cloth." *American Craft*, February/March 1986.

Acknowledgments

Ib tug pas ua tsis tau ib pluag mov los yog ua tsis tau ib tug laj kab.
One stick cannot cook a meal or build a fence.

I would like to thank some of the people who enabled me to write this book:

Bill Selvidge, who started it all by telling me stories about his Hmong patients, and who became my host, intermediary, teacher, and sounding board.

Robert Gottlieb, who assigned the germinal story. Robert Lescher, my literary agent, who always knew I had a book in me somewhere. Jonathan Galassi and Elisheva Urbas, extraordinary editors who at every stage were able to see both the forest and the trees.

The John S. Knight Fellowship program at Stanford University, which, among many other boons, allowed me to study at Stanford Medical School. The classes I audited deepened both my medical knowledge and my understanding of what it means to be a doctor.

Michele Salcedo, who helped gather written sources during the embryonic phases. Michael Cassell, Nancy Cohen, Jennifer Pitts, and Jennifer Veech, who checked facts with skill and enterprise. Tony

Kaye, researcher nonpareil, who tracked down answers to hundreds of questions that had stumped me for years.

The dozens of people, cited under individual chapter headings in my Notes on Sources, who were willing to pass on their knowledge.

The doctors and nurses at Merced Community Medical Center who helped and educated me, with especial thanks to Dan Murphy.

Sukey Waller, who introduced me to Merced's Hmong leaders. They trusted me because they trusted her.

The Hmong community of Merced, whose members were willing to share their sophisticated culture with me and who earned my passionate respect.

Jeanine Hilt, whose death was a terrible loss.

Raquel Arias, Andrea Baker, John Bethell, Dwight Conquergood, Jim Fadiman, Abby Kagan, Martin Kilgore, Pheng Ly, Susan Mitchell, Chong Moua, Dang Moua, Karla Reganold, Dave Schneider, Steve Smith, Rhonda Walton, Carol Whitmore, Natasha Wimmer, and Mayko Xiong, for help of many kinds.

Bill Abrams, Jon Blackman, Lisa Colt, Sandy Colt, Byron Dobell, Adam Goodheart, Peter Gradjansky, Julie Holding, Kathy Holub, Charlie Monheim, Julie Salamon, Kathy Schuler, and Al Silverman, who read part or all of the manuscript and offered criticism and enthusiasm, both equally useful. Jane Condon, Maud Gleason, and Lou Ann Walker, priceless friends who not only read the book but let me talk about it incessantly for years.

Harry Colt, Elizabeth Engle, and Fred Holley, who meticulously vetted the manuscript for medical accuracy. Annie Jaisser, who clarified many aspects of the Hmong language and corrected my Hmong spelling. Gary Stone, who set me straight on some important details of the wars in Laos and Vietnam. Any errors that remain are my fault, not theirs.

May Ying Xiong Ly, my interpreter, cultural broker, and friend, who built a bridge over waters that would otherwise have been uncrossable.

Blia Yao Moua and Jonas Vangay, two wise and generous men who taught me what it means to be Hmong. Nearly a decade after we first met, they were still answering my questions. Would that everyone could have such teachers.

My brother, Kim Fadiman, who in dozens of late-night telephone calls responded to faxed chapters and weighed nuances of phrasing so minute that only another Fadiman could possibly appreciate them. Kim also read aloud the entire manuscript into a tape recorder so our father, who lost his sight four years ago, could listen to it.

My mother, Annalee Jacoby Fadiman, and my father, Clifton Fadiman, who through love and example taught me most of what I know about good reporting and good writing.

My children, Susannah and Henry, for the joy they have brought.

Monica Gregory, Dianna Guevara, and Brigitta Kohli, who allowed me to write by caring for my children with imagination and tenderness.

There are three debts that are unpayable.

I owe the first to Neil Ernst and Peggy Philp, physicians and human beings of rare quality, who spent hours beyond count helping me understand a case that most doctors might prefer to forget. Their courage and honesty have been an inspiration.

I owe the second to the Lee family, who changed my whole way of looking at the world when they welcomed me into their home, their daily lives, and their rich culture. Nao Kao Lee was a patient and eloquent educator. Foua Yang was a loving guide and at times a surrogate parent. I thank all the Lee children, but especially True, who helped me immeasurably during the final stages of my research and also became my friend. And to Lia, the gravitational center around which this book revolves, I can only say that of the many sadnesses in the world that I wish could be righted, your life is the one I think of most often in the small hours of the night.

I owe the greatest debt to my husband, George Howe Colt, to whom this book is dedicated. In both a metaphorical sense and a literal one, George has been everything to me. Over the years, he has made fact-checking calls, helped me file thousands of particles of research, taken care of our children while I worked, and talked over every twist and turn of character, style, structure, and emphasis. He read every word—except these—at least twice, and his editing was brilliant. When I got discouraged, knowing that George cared about Lia Lee made me believe others would as well. Were it not for him, my book would never have been written, and my life would be unimaginably dimmer.

Index

acupuncture, 34
Air America, 126, 130, 134, 137, 138
Air Force, U.S., 126, 131
Aleman, John, 51
Allman, T. D., 132
American Academy of Family Physicians, 270
Americanization, 182–83, 207
animal sacrifice, 96, 100, 106–9, 190n, 208, 219, 253, 266, 279–88
antibiotics, 34, 46, 49, 53, 69, 144, 148–49
Anti-Chinese Association of Merced, 226
anticonvulsants, *see specific drugs*
Apgar score, 7
Arias, Raquel, 9, 73n, 75
Armée Clandestine, 126, 128–30, 159, 191, 236
Ativan, 143, 149

BaFá BaFá (simulation game), 271
Ban Vinai refugee camp, 32–33, 35–37, 60, 61, 72, 165–69, 227, 268
Befriend-a-Refugee Program, 234
Bernatzik, Hugo Adolf, 21
Bertrais, Yves, 184n
Biological and Toxin Weapons Convention (1972), 133n
Bliatout, Bruce Thowpaou, 203–4, 265–67
breech birth, 71–72
British East India Company, 122
Buell, Edgar "Pop," 132
Bunch, Effie, 48, 55
Burma, 125

California, University of: at Berkeley, 41, 107, 228; at Davis, 24, 244
California Custom Social Services, 229
California Department of Human Resources, 87

Ritalin, 88
Robbins, Christopher, 126, 129,
  131
Robinul, 149
Rodriguez, Gloria, 45, 173
role loss, 206
Romans, ancient, 30n
Rosenblatt, Lionel, 186
Royal Lao Army, 96, 125, 127, 129,
  134

sacrifice, ritual, *see* animal sacrifice
San Francisco General Hospital, 66,
  271
Santería, 107, 267
Savang Vatthana, King of Laos,
  124
Savina, François Marie, 13–15, 17–
  18, 119–20, 208
Schelby Center for Special Education,
  114, 116, 251, 253
Schneider, Dave, 68–69, 71, 74, 171–
  72, 176, 178–79, 236
Scott, George M., Jr., 193–94, 208,
  215
Segerstrom, Steve, 142–44
Selvidge, Bill, 63–64, 93–94, 101,
  112, 214, 225, 227, 242, 248, 255,
  274; depressed Hmong treated by,
  66, 70, 204, 272n; Hutchison and,
  254, 256; Lia admitted to MCMC
  by, 99; on Lia's prognosis after
  brain damage, 178; Waller and,
  276–77
Senate, U.S.: Armed Services Committee, 128; Judiciary Subcommittee
  on Refugees and Escapees, 133;
  Subcommittee on Immigration and
  Refugee Affairs, 189
septic shock, 147–49, 254–56, 262

shamanism, 20, 34–37, 81, 90, 173,
  185; *see also txiv neebs*
Shapler, Robert, 132
Shee Yee, tale of, 170, 178, 195, 278–
  80, 285–87
Singlaub, John, 160n
slash-and-burn agriculture, *see* swidden
  agriculture
Small, Robert, 9, 73, 235, 238
somatization, 69
Sonom, 16
soul-calling ceremonies, 9–11, 174,
  268, 284, 287–88
soul loss, 10, 100, 260
Souvanna Phouma, Prince, 137–38,
  157
Soviet Union, 125, 131, 133n
spinal deformity, 263
Ssu-ma Ch'ien, 14
Stanford Medical School, 275
State Department, U.S., 183
status epilepticus, 39, 54, 116, 143,
  144, 255, 258
Sudden Unexpected Death Syndrome,
  188n
Sult, Tom, 64
Superior Court of the State of California, 59, 152, 215
Supplemental Security Income (SSI),
  87, 109, 112
Supreme Court, U.S., 80, 107
swidden (slash-and-burn) agriculture,
  123–24, 128, 136, 158, 169,
  196

taboos, Hmong, 61, 71, 177–78, 191,
  208
Tegretol, 46, 56, 58, 88, 220; side effects of, 50
Temkin, Owsei, 30n

Xeu, Vang, 132
Xieng Khouang Air Transport, 130
Xiong, Bravo, 194
Xiong, Chaly, 27, 95–96
Xiong, Ching, 194
Xiong, John, 205, 266n
Xiong, May Ying, 95–102, 109–10,
113, 123, 138, 141, 161, 207–9,
223, 257, 280, 281
Xiong, Sue, 82, 91–92
Xiong, Yia Thao, 162
Xiong clan, 156, 227

Yale University, 80n
Yang, Foua, 96–105, 206, 237, 248;
arrival in U.S. of, 181–83; brings
Lia home, 179–80; cares for Lia in
persistent vegetative state, 210–19,
221–24, 250, 251, 257–58; and catastrophic seizure, 140–41, 144, 145;
court order obtained by, 152–53;
doctors' relationship with, 56, 213;
escapes from Laos, 155–56, 163,
171; and foster care placement, 78–
82, 84–85, 87–92; gives birth to
Lia, 3, 6–9; gulf between Western
medicine and beliefs of, 252–53,
259–61; Hilt's relationship with,

112–15, 252, 265; during hospitalizations, 30–31, 43–44, 55, 116,
148–53, 173–79; in Laos, 3–4, 74,
103–5, 121; Lia as favorite child of,
22–23; Lia returned to, 92, 106–7;
at MCMC emergency room, 25–
26; and medication regimen, 45–
50, 53, 56, 58, 144, 254; Murphy
and, 28, 30; during *neeb* ceremony,
279–87; pregnancies of, 4, 57–58;
in refugee camp, 6, 23, 34; and
soul-calling ceremony, 9–11; and
traditional medicine for Lia, 110–
12
Yang, Xou, 207
Yang clan, 227
Yang Dao, 15n, 134–35, 158
Yang family, 185–86
Yanomamo, 112
Yates, Sharon, 44, 254
yellow rain, 133
Yosemite National Park, 27,
96
Youth Conservation Corps, 96

zij poj niam (marriage by capture),
240–41n
Zinn, William M., 274, 276

Reader's Guide

The Spirit Catches You

and You Fall Down

A Hmong Child,

Her American Doctors

and the Collision of Two Cultures

Anne Fadiman

About This Guide

This guide is intended to enrich your experience of reading *The Spirit Catches You and You Fall Down*, winner of the National Book Critics Circle Award. This moving chronicle of a very sick girl, her refugee parents, and the doctors who struggled desperately to treat her becomes, in Anne Fadiman's deft narrative, at once a cautionary study of the limits of Western medicine and a parable for the modern immigrant experience.

Lia Lee was born in the San Joaquin valley in California to Hmong refugees. At the age of three months, she first showed signs of having what the Hmong know as *qaug dab peg* (the spirit catches you and you fall down), the condition known in the West as epilepsy. While her highly competent doctors saw the best treatment in a dizzying array of pills, her parents preferred a combination of Western medicine and folk remedies designed to coax her wandering soul back to her body. Over the next four years, profound cultural differences and linguistic miscommunication would exacerbate the rift between Lia's loving parents and her caring and well-intentioned doctors, eventually resulting in the loss of all her higher brain functions. Fadiman weaves this personal tragedy, a probing medical investigation, and a fascinating look at Hmong history and culture into a stunningly insightful, richly rewarding piece of modern reportage.

Questions and Subjects for Discussion

1. What do you think of traditional Hmong birth practices (pp. 3–5)? Compare them to the techniques used when Lia was born (p. 7). How do Hmong and American birth practices differ?

2. Over many centuries the Hmong fought against a number of different peoples who claimed sovereignty over their lands; they were also forced to emigrate from China. How do you think these upheavals have affected their culture? What role has history played in the formation of Hmong culture?

3. Dr. Dan Murphy said, "The language barrier was the most obvious problem, but not the most important. The biggest problem was the cultural barrier. There is a tremendous difference between dealing with the Hmong and dealing with anyone else. An *infinite* difference" (p. 91). What does he mean by this?

4. The author says, "I was struck . . . by the staggering toll of stress that the Hmong exacted from the people who took care of them, particularly the ones who were young, idealistic, and meticulous" (p. 75). Why do you think the doctors felt such great stress?

5. Dr. Neil Ernst said, "I felt it was important for these Hmongs to understand that there were certain elements of medicine that we understood better than they did and that there were certain rules they had to follow with their kids' lives. I wanted the word to get out in the community that if they deviated from that, it was not

acceptable behavior" (p. 79). Do you think the Hmong understood this message? Why or why not? What do you think of Neil and Peggy?

6. Dr. Roger Fife is liked by the Hmong because, in their words, he "doesn't cut" (p. 76). He is not highly regarded by some of the other doctors, however. One resident went so far as to say, "He's a little thick." What do you think of Dr. Fife? What are his strengths and weaknesses? The author also speaks of other doctors who were able to communicate with the Hmong. How were they able to do so? What might be learned from this?

7. How did you feel about the Lees' refusal to give Lia her medicine? Can you understand their motivation? Do you sympathize with it?

8. How did you feel when Child Protective Services took Lia away from her parents? Do you believe it was the right decision? Was any other solution possible in the situation?

9. Were you surprised at the quality of care and the love and affection given to Lia by her foster parents? How did Lia's foster parents feel about Lia's biological parents? Was foster care ultimately to Lia's benefit or detriment?

10. How did the EMT's and the doctors respond to what Neil referred to as Lia's "big one"? Do you think they performed as well as they could have under the circumstances?

11. How does the greatest of all Hmong folktales, the story of how Shee Yee fought with nine evil *dab* brothers (p. 170), reflect the life and culture of the Hmong?

12. Discuss the Lees' life in Laos. How was it different from their life in the United States? Foua says, "When we were running from Laos at least we hoped that our lives would be better. It was not as sad as after Lia went to Fresno and got sick" (p. 171). What were the Lees running from? What were they hoping to find in the United States?

13. When polled, Hmong refugees in America stated that "difficulty with American agencies" was a more serious problem than either "war memories" or "separation from family." Why do you think they felt this way? Could this have been prevented? If so, how? What does the author believe?

14. The Hmong are often referred to as a "Stone Age" people or "low-caste hill tribe." Why is this? Do you agree with this assessment of Hmong culture? Does the author?

15. What was the "role loss" many adult Hmong faced when they came to the United States? What is the underlying root cause? How does this loss affect their adjustment to America?

16. What are the most important aspects of Hmong culture? What do the Hmong consider their most important duties and obligations? How did they affect the Hmong's transition to the United States?

17. What does Dan Murphy mean by, "When you fail one Hmong patient, you fail the whole community" (p. 253)?

18. The author gives you some insight into the way she organized her notes (p. 60). What does it say about the process of writing this book? She chooses to alternate between chapters of Lia's story and its larger background—the history of the Lee family and of the Hmong. What effect does this create in the book?

19. The concept of "fish soup" is central to the author's understanding of the Hmong. What does it mean, and how is it reflected in the structure of the book?

20. It is clear that many of Lia's doctors, most notably Neil Ernst and Peggy Philp, were heroic in their efforts to help Lia, and that her parents cared for her deeply, yet this arguably preventable tragedy still occurred. Can you think of anything that might have prevented it?

21. What did you learn from this book? Would you assign blame for

Lia's tragedy? If so, to whom? What do you think Anne Fadiman
feels about this question?

Other Books of Related Interest

Virginia Barnes Lee, *Aman: Story of a Somali Girl*; Michael Bérubé, *Life
as We Know It*; Robert Olen Butler, *The Deep Green Sea*; Lan Cao,
Monkey Bridge; Temple Grandin, *Thinking in Pictures: And Other Reports
from My Life with Autism*; Jamaica Kincaid, *My Brother*; Maxine Hong
Kingston, *Woman Warrior*; Oliver Sacks, *The Man Who Mistook His
Wife for a Hat: And Other Clinical Tales*; Esmeralda Santiago, *When I
Was Puerto Rican*; Susan Sheehan, *Is There No Place on Earth for Me?*;
Abraham Verghese, *My Own Country: A Doctor's Story*.

the message

A GUIDE TO BEING HUMAN · LD THOMPSON

Soul: \\'sōl\\

noun: the immaterial essence,
animating principle, or actuating
cause of an individual life.

*"I have come to guide you, not to
coddle you. The first and greatest
lesson that you are learning is
that you are free. You are free to
choose. You can choose to live a
life that is prescribed by society,
or you can choose to break the
form and know more of yourself
than is ordinarily known."*
—*Solano*

"In *The Message: A Guide to Being Human*, LD Thompson has given us one of the most relevant books for these times; a must-have guide. In concise, clear, and inspired language, he speaks to the heart of our real human challenges and gives a gift of wisdom . . . soothing our fears, dispelling confusion, and making clear the profoundly simple way forward for us individually and collectively. This book is never far from my desk or bedside. I love it."
—Lenedra J. Carroll, Author of *The Architecture of All Abundance*

"*The Message: A Guide to Being Human* is a master class for personal and global transformation. It is filled with powerful lessons to navigate the changes we are all experiencing inside our minds, our hearts... and our world. I was deeply moved by the skill and patience that led me to a shift in awareness that literally changed my perception of reality. This is a jewel of a book that you will open time and time again for reference and solace during this era of great uncertainty and discord on the planet."
—Robin Mastro, Co-author of *Altars of Power & Grace, The Way of Vastu,* and *Making Room for Mr. Right*

"What LD offers in this beautifully written book is a simple, yet profound, path to peace. In a world that is spiraling out of control, LD's words bring comfort to the heart and a wisdom that inspires us to embrace the God within."
—Rob Spears & Brenda Michaels, Hosts of "Conscious Talk" Radio Show

"Simple, profound, and moving! The author has been given a gift... a beautiful way to distill the essence of life into an easy-to-read set of truths, with wonderful examples along the way. Listen... for that's how it all starts."
—Lee Carroll, Author, *Kryon* series; co-author, *The Indigo Children*

"LD Thompson's book *The Message: A Guide to Being Human* is a remarkable achievement. It is more than a guide to being human — it is a deeply felt and wise journey into the inner-most reaches of the soul. The voice of the sage Solano, as told through the author, resonates with simple good sense and quiet authority. I was truly moved by this book. As a manual for lifemanship in the 21st century, *The Message* cannot be bettered."

 —Judy Corbett, Author of *Castles in the Air* and *Envy*

"Just sitting with my soul is one of the many enlightening instructions in *The Message: A Guide to Being Human*. This well laid-out soul master plan comes with a student, LD. His stories reveal his reverence and humility as the pupil and vessel of the messages."

 —Joan Ranquet, Author of *The Communication With All Life*

"*The Message: A Guide to Being Human* is relevant, hopeful, smart, and inarguable."

 —Nancy Lee Grahn, Actress - *General Hospital*

"This is a wonderful book with a clear and beautiful message on how to be authentic and truly live from a place of inner peace and grace. A treasure, especially for these times."

 —Dr. Ellen Tart-Jensen, Author of *Health Is Your Birthright*